Early Muggletonian Polemics

Edited by Mike Pettit

Early Muggletonian Polemics
Edited by Mike Pettit

Visit us online at www.muggletonianpress.com and view our entire range of Muggletonian Literature

Muggletonian Press Publications:

The Collected Works of John Reeve
Print Edition-   978-1-907466-00-7
Ebook Edition-   978-1-907466-10-6

The Collected Works of James Birch
Print Edition-   978-1-907466-01-4
Ebook Edition-   978-1-907466-11-3

The Collected Works of Laurence Clarkson
Print Edition-   978-1-907466-02-1
Ebook Edition-   978-1-907466-12-0

Muggletonian Celestial Harmonies and Divine Songs
Print Edition-   978-1-907466-03-8
Ebook Edition-   978-1-907466-13-7

The Collected Works of Lodowick Muggleton: Works on the Book of Revelation
Print Edition-   978-1-907466-04-5
Ebook Edition-   978-1-907466-14-4

Later Muggletonian Interest: Academic, Literary and Scientific
Print Edition-   978-1-907466-05-2
Ebook Edition-   978-1-907466-15-1

The Collected Works of Lodowick Muggleton: Quakers, Witches and Acts
Print Edition-   978-1-907466-06-9
Ebook Edition-   978-1-907466-16-8

Early Muggletonian Polemics
Print Edition-   978-1-907466-07-6
Ebook Edition-   978-1-907466-17-5

The Collected Works of Thomas Tomkinson & John Saddington: The Muggletonian Disciples
Print Edition-   978-1-907466-08-3
Ebook Edition-   978-1-907466-18-2

The Collected Works of Lodowick Muggleton: Letters and Epistles
Print Edition-   978-1-907466-09-0
Ebook Edition-   978-1-907466-19-9

A Muggletonian Press Book
Copyright © Mike Pettit 2011

All rights reserved. No portion of this publication may be reproduced, stored in a retrieval system, or transmitted in any form or by any means, electronic, mechanical, photocopy, recording or otherwise, without prior written permission of the copyright owner. While many of the original texts which form the basis of this publication are to be found in the public domain the texts found herein have been typographically modernised and reformatted at great expense. Please respect the resulting copyright that such work has created.

ISBN 978-1-907466-07-6

Cover Image: A miniature portrait of Lodowick Muggleton reproduced in George Williamson's 1919 "A Paper Read"

Published by:
Muggletonian Press
129 Hebdon Road
London SW17 7NL
England

I would like to make it clear that in editing and publishing this volume I am not seeking to advocate any element of Muggletonian theology. I fully subscribe to historic orthodox Christianity as expressed in the Reformed Confessions of Faith and would plead with all the readers of this work to consider those sacred claims.

From the Heidelberg Catechism

Question 1. What is thy only comfort in life and death?
Answer: That I with body and soul, both in life and death, am not my own, but belong unto my faithful Saviour Jesus Christ; who, with his precious blood, has fully satisfied for all my sins, and delivered me from all the power of the devil; and so preserves me that without the will of my heavenly Father, not a hair can fall from my head; yea, that all things must be subservient to my salvation, and therefore, by his Holy Spirit, He also assures me of eternal life, and makes me sincerely willing and ready, henceforth, to live unto him.

Contents

Contents.. 5
Introduction 9

The Lying Prophet Discovered and Reproved; 15

Truth Ascended, Or, The Annointed And Sealed Of God Defended. In An Answer Written By Richard Farnsworth As A Testimony Against A Conterfeit Commission And All Injustice And False Judgement Done And Pronounced Under Pretence Of The Same. 33

Something In Answer To Lodowick Muggleton's Book, Which He Calls, The Quakers Neck Broken. 59
    Something in Answer to Thomas Fuller, in his Church-History, to that which he writes to Baron Brook, wherein he Rayles against the Quakers. 86
    Somthing in Answer to Samuel Clarke, who calls himself a Pastor, in his Book called, A Looking Glass for Saints and Sinners. 88

The New Witnesses proved Old Hereticks: 91
    John Reeve and Lodowick Muggleton, Contradicting Themselves, and One Another. 116
    A few Additional Observations upon some Passages, of John Reeve and Lodowick Muggleton, in the before-cited Books. 124
    Ten Queries Propounded. 126
    Postscript. 128
    A Brief Examen Of Reeve His Commission. 128

Observations On Some Passages Of Lodowick Muggleton, In His Interpretation Of The 11th Chapter Of The Revelations........... 131
    The Preface to the Reader.. 131
    Observations on some passages of Lodowick Muggleton, in his Interpretation of the 11th Chapter of the Revelations. 132
    Observations on some Passages in his Letter to Thomas Taylor.. 144

A True Account of the Trial and Sufferings of Lodowick Muggleton, ... 153

The Blasphemer Tryed And Cast: 167

News From The Sessions House In The Old – Bayly, ... 171

A Modest Account Of The Wicked Life Of That Grand Impostor, Lodowick Muggleton: 175

The Proceedings of the Old Bailey - Court Records 179

Muggleton Reviv'd Or, New News Of That Grand Impostor. 181

Muggleton's Last Will & Testament, ... 185

A True Representation Of The Absurd And Mischievous Principles Of The Sect, Commonly Known By The Name Of Mugletonians. 191
- The Preface. 191
- Chap. I. 193
- Chap. II. 210

An Ellegy On Lodowick Muggleton 215

A New-Year's Gift For The Ratcliff Convert to Muggletonianism; 219

Observations On Some Articles Of The Muggletonians Creed: .. 249

The Principles Of The Muggletonians Asserted, ... 265
- ARTICLE I. On The Eternity Of Matter. 266
- ARTICLE II. On the Existence of two eternal Beings, on the Angel's Fall, and the Fall of Man. 268
- ARTICLE III. On God's eternal Existence in the Form of a Man... 275
- ARTICLE IV. That God became a Son, and manifested himself in the Flesh: and the Scripture Doctrine of the Trinity considered. 277
- ARTICLE V. That JESUS CHRIST was God the Creator of the World. 278
- ARTICLE VI. When CHRIST dyed GOD dyed: ENOCH, MOSES, and ELIAS, were taken up into Heaven, and left with deputed Power there, while God was performing the Work of Redemption here on Earth. 280
- ARTICLE VII. Concerning JOHN REEVE'S and LODOWICK MUGGLETON'S Commission, with the Words which God spoke to the former on the 3d, 4th, and 5th, of February 1651, with some Observations on them. 281
- Postscript 286

TRUTH and REASON defended 289
- To the Lord Bishop of London. 290
- The Preface. 291
- Part I. 292
- Part II. 308
- Some Remarks on the Muggletonian Principles, from a Book published by John Reeve and Lodowick Muggleton, ... 334

A Conference Betwixt A Muggletonian And A Baptist, On These Propositions: 339

The Amorous Humours and Audacious Adventures of One Wh*******D. 345

Introduction

The declaration of the Third Commission by the Muggletonian prophets and their followers generated a great deal of opposition, and in the style of the times this opposition often took the form of polemical pamphlets, often scurrilous in nature. The Muggletonians responded in kind with the flow of argument only subsiding as the Muggletonians withdrew from the public arena following the persecution and finally the death of their prophet.

This volume contains the texts of this literature, the prophet Muggleton's polemical works have been republished by the Muggletonian Press in the volume "The Collected Works of Lodowick Muggleton: Quakers, Witches and Acts", this volume containing the anti-Muggletonian works and the responses of lesser Muggletonians.

These works are often very rare and are only available with some difficulty, with the originals often being in very poor condition. These problems have resulted in some difficulty in accurately transcribing the original texts, however these problems only magnify the advantages of accessing these newly typeset works.

This volume includes the full texts of:

The Lying Prophet Discovered and Reproved: In An Answer To Several Particulars in a Book Called The Quakers Downfall Said To Be Written By Lawrence Claxton

This book by John Harwood was written in 1659, responding to Laurence Clarkson's "The Quakers Downfal", published earlier the same year, which has been republished by the Muggletonian Press in the volume "The Muggletonian Works of Laurence Clarkson: The Onely True Bishop"

Truth ascended, or, The annointed and sealed of God defended: in an answer written by Richard Farnsworth as a testimony against a conterfeit commission and all injustice and false judgement done and pronounced under pretence of the same

This 1663 work by the Quaker Richard Farnworth caught the attention of Lodowick Muggleton, who responded with his work "The Neck of the Quakers Broken" later in the same year.

Something in Answer to Lodowick Muggleton's Book which he calls, The Quakers Neck Broken.

George Fox, the lauded founder of Quakerism, responded to Muggleton's "The Neck of the Quakers Broken" with this 1667 work.

The New Witnesses prov'd Old Hereticks

The influential Quaker William Penn wrote this 1667 work, which consists of a theological assault on Muggletonianism as well as a record of a meeting with Muggleton, who responded to this work with his excellent 1673 "An Answer to William Penn, Quaker,"

Observations On Some Passages Of Lodowick Muggleton, In His Interpretation Of The 11th Chapter Of The Revelations as also on some Passages in that Book of his, stiled, The Neck of the Quakers Broken, and in his Letter to Thomas Taylor.

The Quaker Isaac Pennington wrote this 1668 response to Muggleton's 1662 work on the 11th Chapter of the Book of Revelation, Muggleton replied in his 1669 "An Answer to Isaac Pennington", which was not successfully published until 1719.

A True Account of the Trial and Sufferings of Lodowick Muggleton

This contemporaneous 1676 account of Muggleton's trial and punishment written by "Our Friend Powell" (Nathanial Powell) was published by the Muggletonians in 1808.

The blasphemer tried and cast: or, a more full narrative of the tryal of Lodowick Muggleton

This aggressively anti-Muggletonian work was published in 1676 and was written by J.B. (believed to be James Bedloe).

News from the sessions house in the Old-Bayly, being a true account of the notorious principles and wicked practices of that Grand Impostor Lodowick Muggleton

This further instance of an aggressively anti-Muggletonian record of Muggleton's trial is credited to B.H. and was also published in 1676.

A Modest account of the Wicked Life of the Grand Imposter Lodowick Muggleton

Also published in 1676 and credited to B.H. is this anti-Muggletonian tract that erroneously locates Muggleton birthplace as Chippeham and records his life and works up until his 1676 trial.

The proceedings of the Old Bailey 17th January 1676

This text comprises the official record of Muggleton's 1676 trial. While not a polemic as such this record is reproduced due to the importance of the recorded event in the polemical record.

Muggleton Reviv'd or, New News of That Grand Impostor

Published in 1677 this document credited to "D.M." purports to detail his (i.e. Muggleton's) late Behavior since his Sentence and standing in the Pillory the previous year.

Muggleton's last will & testament (who died Novemb. 30, 1679): being an absolute and real recantation of his former notorious blasphemous doctrine.

This 1679 publication credited to J.B. (believed to be "James Bedloe") records Muggleton's purported 1679 deathbed recantation, a polemical fantasy given that Muggleton lived a further nineteen years.

A true representation of the absurd and mischievous principles of the sect, commonly known by the name of Muggletonians

This scholarly 1694 theological refutation of Muggletonianism was written by the Bishop of Chichester, John Williams.

An Ellegy on Lodowick Muggleton who lies bury'd alive in the colledge of Newgate, expecting dayly his happy resurrection

This single page anti-Muggletonian polemical whimsy was written following the death of Muggleton in 1698 by E.O.

A new-year's gift for the Ratcliff convert to Muggletonianism

Published in 1717 by J Sharpe this text seeks to convince a recent convert to Muggletonianism that he should really revert to the Church of England and then addresses John Saddington's The Articles of True Faith on an article by article basis.

Observations on some articles of the Muggletonians creed: ... Proposed more immediately to the consideration of the principal of the modern Muggletonians

This 1735 anti-Muggletonian work by Caleb Fleming was answered by Arden Bonell's "The principles of the Muggletonians asserted"

The principles of the Muggletonians asserted, under the following heads. I. On the eternity of matter. II. On the existence of two eternal beings. III. On God's eternal existence in the form of a man. IV. That God became a son. V. That Jesus Christ was God. VI. When Christ dyed God dyed. VII. Concerning John Reeve's and Lodowick Muggleton's commission

Written in 1735 by the head of the Muggletonian church (following the death of Thomas Tomkinson) Arden Bonell in response to Caleb Fleming's "Observations on some articles of the Muggletonians creed" of the same year.

Truth and Reason Defended against Error and Burning Envy

This work records a well organised public dispute held in 1728 between a Muggletonian and a Quaker, recorded by William Henderson (the Quaker) to which he appends some further observations on the works of Reeve and Muggleton.

A conference betwixt a Muggletonian and a Baptist, On these Propositions: I. There was no God in Heaven when Christ Jesus was on this Earth. II. God became as a Creature, Sin excepted. III. God dyed

This anonymous 1739 Muggletonian work records a public theological debate, I do wonder whether some of the theology that is being advanced represents orthodox Muggletonianism but nevertheless this text gives a fascinating insight into a little known period of Muggletonian history.

The Amorous Humours and Audacious Adventures Of One WHD

This little known gem is a satirical attack, in verse, on the great Evangelist George Whitefield by an anonymous but highly mischievous Muggletonian, it is thought to date from around 1760.

The Lying Prophet Discovered and Reproved;

In an Answer to several particulars in a book called The Quakers Downfal, said to be written by Lawrence Claxton, who blasphemously stiles himself the alone true and faithful Messenger of Christ Jesus; but his spirit being tried by the fruits it hath brought forth, he is found to be a messenger of Satan, and an enemy to Christ and his people, who hath confessed he hath nought of God in him.

With several of his damnable doctrines (seldom the like ever read or heard of) which he hath published in his Book, returned back for him to prove by plain Scripture or to confesse his errour and blasphemy.

Also Twelve Particulars which he and his companion Lodowick Muggleton uttered at Richard Whitpans house in Eastecheap, in a discourse with me and some others, he calls Quakers.

Given forth for the clearing the Truth and the Witnesses of it from his lying aspersions, and the manifesting deceit and deceivers, that simple hearted ignorant people through their policy may not be deceived nor deluded, By a Friend to Truth, John Harwood.

The False Prophet is made manifest by his fruits, according to the Doctrine of Christ, Mat. 7.

LONDON, Printed for *Thomas Simmons* at the *Bull and Mouth* near *Aldersgate 1659.*

To the honest understanding *Reader*, who readeth without Prejudice, or Malice

Reader,

A book coming to my hands, tituled the Quakers downfall, *said to be written by* Laurence Claxton, *(having his name at it) who blasphemously styles himself, the alone, true and faithfull messenger of Christ Jesus, the Lord of Glory; and hath the last Revelation and Commission that ever shall be, as he saith, but his doctrine and Spirit, being truly weighed and tried in the just and equall balance, by the Eternall Spirit of Light and Life; manifest in the Royall seed of God, called Quakers) he is found to be a lying Prophet, a Mesenger of Satan, an enemy to truth, and the witnesses of it, as his fruits will make it plainly appeare; who goes about through his subtilty to pervert Truth and Innocency, and hath in a high manner blasphemed against God and his people: so that in pure love to the Eternal Truth, for the clearing of it from lying Aspersions cast upon it, and the faithfull witnesses of it, by this unreasonable man; I am moved to write something in Answer to severall particulars in his book; that his deceitfull lying spirit in some measure may be made manifest, that the simple hearted, ignorant people, may not be deluded through his subtlety, or by them who are of the same minde, which he calls the last Commissioners the third Writers of the Scriptures, in page marked for the twelfth in his book; And in the fifteenth page he blasphemously says, they are the last Commissioners that ever shall apeare in this unbelieving world: (that is to say,* John Reeve, *and* Lodowick Muggleton; *so would limit the holy One, the unlimited God: (which he knowes not as his fruits of darknesse makes appear) who gives gifts and Commission unto many of his dear servants and children, (in this the day of his glorious and bright appearance, in and amongst the sonnes and daughters of men) who are his true and faithful Messengers, who have manifested the truth of their message (the Lords gift) thorow many tryals and cruel sufferings, whom he sends forth into many Nations and Islands, freely to preach glad tidings, the Gospel of peace, the power of God unto salvation; which is a mysterie hid from that spirit and power of darknesse in L.C. and the other he calls the last Commissioners, who said he had nought of God in him, and also he denies the light of Christ within people; (Gods pure witness) which the Apostles bore testimony unto, and* John *the Baptist; as all the faithful messengers of God doth, (which in scorne he calls Quakers) which true Light, (with which Christ enlighteneth every man) is the only way of Life, Peace and everlasting salvation, which he and all such high Ranting Spirits are shut out of, and into the true knowledge of it cannot enter, with all their Serpents policy; which L.C. would cover with the name of divine knowledge: but with the eternal light, (which he despises) he is discerned, his Covers are too narrow to hide him from the pure eye, which the eternal God by his power hath opened in his innocent babes and children, he calls in derision quaking Ranters; but by them he is seen and comprehended; and by the Life of God, who is a Spirit of Glory, Light, Life, Power and Infinite wisdom, is judged to be an instrument of Satan, an enemy of God, (the Spirit of all flesh) and an unreasonable man, according to his own confession, who saith there is no pure reason in man nor in God, which is high blasphemy; For pure wisdoms and pure reason is one in nature and substance, and neither God, the infinite being of Wisdom, Glory and Life is without it; nor man in the Image of God, unto whom, the light Christ is made Wisdom, Righteousnesse, Santification and Redemption; but the understanding Reader may easily perceive, by what spirit this man is acted, who would have all men to be like him, without pure reason, and also the Livving God, the Eternal Spirit of Glory, (which he denies to be a Spirit) he would have to be without Reason (and so have him unreasonable) who is the Eternal Fountain of*

Wisdome, Kowledge, and pure Reason; for from his pure presence, all the pure streams of divine Wisdom, Knowledge and Reason hath ever flowed, and doth ever flow; which clearly evidenceth, that this man is possessed with, and acted by the same lying spirit and power of darknesse which hath acted all the false Prophets, and deceivers, in all ages as in this age, (so not to be believed, but denied) whose mindes hath been and are blinded, and hearts hardened against the truth of God, acting to the utmost of their strength against it; but with it, L. C. and his Companions, and all the deceivers in all Nations, under what Name or Title soever are comprehended, condemned, and shut out of the knowledge of the mystery of Life, out of the Light and knowledge of God, out of his kingdome, in the it of grosse darknesse and there are to remain untill the Judgement of the great day, and then shall receive the reward of their doings; Oh how he rages against us in his book and scoffes and reviles us because we wilt not deny the Light Christ Jesus in us, as he doth, who saith he is in no creature, but only in heaven above the Stars as a man or person; what cursed doctrine and blasphemy is this which this wicked man hath published, who would limit and confine the Lord of Glory, the unlimited God unto a certain place, (and exclude him from his people) which the Heaven of Heavens cannot contain, who fills Heaven and Earth with his Glory; yet this unreasonable man pretends to won Scripture, though he publish such things as these, which are quite contrary to it ; for the Saints in Light that gave froth the Scriptures, denied not (as he doth) but witnessed as we do, Christ Jesus in them the hope of glory, as in the first Chapter of the Colossians, *verse 27, as also in the second of the* Corinthians, *13.5. Christ in you, except you be Reprobates, and likewise in Galathians 2.20 saith* Paul, *I live, yet not I, but Christ liveth in me, &c. and many other Scriptures might be brought to prove the true Light Christ to be in his people, which this wicked deceiver denies; but the wise in heart may see by this, that the life of the Scripture judges his doctrine to be contrary to the doctrine of the Apostles; and his faith to be contrary to the faith of Gods elect, so out of the doctrine and faith of Gods Elect, in the state of Reprobacy, not to be owned nor credited, but to be denied and sharply reproved by all that fear the Lord. Now I know none of Gods people, that love, and fear him, will believe the Lies, slanders and false aspersions which this unreasonable man in his book hath cast upon us he calls Quakers, but will discern it to be written from an envious wicked hear and Spirit, (because his will hath been crossed by us) and will judge his lying malicious spirit, and not entertain any herd thoughts against us, through his Lies and false accusations; but the ignorant, and such as have an enmity against the truth, and the witnesses of it, who are given up to believe lies may be ready to believe his blasphemous Lying Aspersions, which he hath cast upon God and his people, but however, we are clear in the sight of the Lord and his people; and the truth is over him, and all the world, and whosoever stand up to oppose it, or in any manner appears against it, must bow before it, and come under it, and the witnesses of it: for all*

Nations must bow before the power of Truth manifest in Gods Elect; The Royall sect called Quakers.

J.H.

The Lying Prophet Discovered and Reproved.

Lawrence Claxton

Boasteth and saith, *If I had not the spirit of Inspiration, or Revelation in my own Soul, not any part or portion of the Scripture would belong unto me,* pag. 1.

Answ. It is the Spirit of God with which the Saints were inspired, which unto them revealed the Mysteries and secrets of God, who as they were moved spoke, and writ forth the Scriptures, which thou dost not rightly understand, who wants the same Spirit and Life, for thy lying and boasting manifesteth thy spirit to be none of the true Spirit with which the Saints were and are Inspired; so ignorant of the Mystery and Life of them; but that part or portion of Scripture belongs unto thee, which is against blasphemers, lyars, boasters and ungodly deceivers, and to be applied to thy present condition, but the blessings and promises which appertaineth to the Elect Seed thou hast nothing to do with; And what hast thou to do to speak of the Spirit of Inspiration or Revelation in thy Soul, who said, thou hast nought of God in thee?

L.C. *Also boasteth of the Spirit, To be more fully manifested in him then it was in the Saints that gave forth the Scriptures,* pag.1.

Answ. The lying spirit which was cast out of the Saints, by the power of the Spirit of truth, in a large manner is manifest in thee, as thy fruits makes it appear; and thou may be ashamed to boast thus of thy spirit, who said in the hearing of several honest people, Thou had nought of God in thee; it is the lying imagination of thy corrupt fleshly wisdom, which thou calls the inspiration of the Spirit, by which thou art deceived and deluded, and seeks to deceive and delude others, but the Elect are out of thy reach, and fathomes thee.

L.C. Saith, Moses, *the Prophets and Apostles never rightly understood, neither was required of them to know Christ in their Commission any other but God the Father,* P.4.

Answ. That is false, *Moses* knew a Prophet should arise like unto him, which the people should hear, which was Christ the Son of God; & the Prophet knew a Virgin should conceive and bear a Son, and call his Name Immanuel; and said, Unto us a Son is given, &c. and the Apostles knew the Father, Word and Spirit to be one, and there was them (*Acts 3.15*) that were witnesses of his birth, sufferings and Resurrection, which thou knows nothing of but by tradition, the

Apostles were eye-witnesses of him who was born of the Virgin, and knew him in the flesh a single person, and after his death and Resurrection were to know him no more, 2 *Cor.5*. Let him that readeth understand, for here hast thou manifested thy lyes and confusion, thou hast lyed of *Moses*, the Prophets and Apostles, and of the Scriptures their writings, as the Scripture will make plainly appear; read *Deut. 18. 18. Isa.9.6.Isa. 7. 14.*

L.C. Athrmeth, *That the wisdom of* Solomon *was not natural, p.5. and at the 6.p. faith,* Solomons, *writings was not Scripture, nor the writings of* Job, p.7.

Answ. The wisdom God gave unto *Solomon* was pure and spiritual, it is contrary to the disposition and nature of (*1 Kings 3.12*) God to give gifts unto his people, contrary to himself, that is natural in thee, which wrongs the Lord and calls (*1 Kings 3.28*) *Solomons* wisdom (Gods gift) natural, it is manifest thou sees not with the eye of Faith as thou conceives, but art deceived by the prince of darkness the old serpent, who goes about through thy policy to turn the truth into a lye, but the serpent with all his subtilty cannot prove the writings of *Solomon* to be no Scripture, nor persuade such as fear the Lord to any such thing; none but such as are given up to believe lyes will credit thee, for his writings are truth, and the other Scripture is no more; And as for the writings of Righteous *Job* (whom thou confesses Righteous) who saw the Lord of Glory; they are also to be (*Job 42.5.)*believed (and not scrupled) to be truth given forth from the Spirit of truth; and to be as true as the writings of the Prophets and Apostles; and thou art Judged out of the truth, in the lye, by the Righteous Spirit which was manifest in *Job*; who Judges with thy lying spirit all the translaters and composers of the Scriptures, who put *Job & Solomons* writings amongst the Prophets and Apostles.

L.C. Likewise affirmeth, *That the Scriptures were written for our learning to know God &c.* p.11.

Answ. The Jews and Pharisees which Christ reproved had the Scriptures, the writings of *Moses* and the Prophets, yet knew not Christ, nor God the Father; and thou and many other have the Scriptures, and yet wants the knowledge of God, none knows God the Father but such as the light Christ reveals him unto; here thou contradicts the Doctrine of Christ, and seeking (with the unbelieving Jews) for the knowledge of God, the Life, in the Scriptures, read *Luke* 10. 22. *John* 8. 19. Here thou hast shewen thou knows not the right use of the Scriptures, which are serviceable in their places.

L.C. Boasteth and says, *We write not of other mens labours, but as our Faith within us reveals unto us,* P.13.

The Lying Prophet

Answ. All that reads his book may see him to be an impudent lyar, for he hath written of the works of the Prophets and Apostles, which are none f his; this is the false faith, which reveals such horrible lyes, and none of the Faith of Gods Elect thou boasts of to be in thee; for the true Faith is of God, his own pure gift, but thou hast said there is nought of God in thee, and the fruits of the true faith doth not appear in thee, but the contrary.

L.C. He saith, *The Sun at his presence (viz. Christ Jesus in the form of man) will be put forth as the snuffe of a candle, &c.* pag 15.

Answ. The sun, Moon and Stars receives their glory and clearness from Christ the Word, the Eternal (*John 1.1.*) Son of God; who was before man had a form, and the Son is not put out at the presence of him that made it, whose presence fills Heaven & earth; this is one of thy own foolish imaginations which thou calls the Revelation of Faith, for when the Sun shines in the fullness of the strength and glory, the most of the presence and power of God is seen in it.

L.C. Likewise saith, *The nature of our Revelation, leads us forth to no manner nor form of worship.* P. 8.

Answ. Then thy revelation is contrary to the Revelation of Christ and the Saints, and here thou hast shut thy self out of their Doctrine and Practice; Christ preached and prayed, and taught to pray and to worship (*Luke 11. Matth 6. 1 Thes. 5. 11.*) God who is a Spirit, in the Spirit and in the Truth; and the Saints that lived in the power of Christ, met together, and in love edified one another, Preached, prayed & prophesied as they were moved in the power of the Holy Spirit; so had a form of godliness or worship, though in the power of God, as the chosen of the Lord, who bears his glorious image have now, who are acted in the power of the same Eternal Spirit, who judgeth thy revelations to be foolish and vain imaginations, and out of both form and power of godliness

L.C.Saith, *That one of them (viz the Quakers) declared, that his God was an inifinite spirit, all light, life, power, that filled Heaven and earth with his glory, &c.* and a little before faith, *Neither was this any God at all* p.20.

Answ. I do bear Testimony in the strength of the Eternal (*2 Cor. 3.17. John 4.24*) Spirit of Life, unto the God that I the declared of, which is as I then affirmed, a Spirit of Light, Life, Glory, Power and infinite Wisdom, who is not to be confined or limited to time or place, and his glorious presence doth fill Heaven and earth (though thou would limit him, and have him in Heaven above the stars and in no Creature) but according to the Scripture, Heaven is his Throne, and the earth is his foot-stool (*Isa. 66*), the Heaven of Heavens cannot contain him, who was from all Eternity, and is to all eternity before any thing was formed (*1 kings 8. 27.*), by his own Power and Wisdom gave to man and every Creature his form, the nature of man and Angels (*2 Chron. 6.18.*), gave them not their form, as thou falsly and blasphemously affirmeth, against thee and thy imagined god I do bear witness, in the Spirit and Power of Christ, and all thy lying imaginations, who denies God to be a spirit (*2. Cor. 6. 19.*) and to dwell in his people, contrary to the holy Scriptures and denies the Words of Christ, who saith in *John 4.* God is a Spirit, and a spirit hath neither flesh nor bones, and the (*Luke 24.39.*) flesh profiteth nothing, it is the Spirit that giveth life, and the Spirit is the true God, which thou says is no God, whose dreadful Judgements thou must one day know to thy pain and torment, for thy blasphemy against him and his Tabernacle which is with men, who dwells and (*Rev. 21. 3)* walks in his people, though thou would exclude him from thee and all other; who said, there was naught of God in thee nor in any man, which words proceeded from thee, as several can and will witness that heard thee, which makes it appear thou denies the Scripture, which saith, I in them and they in me, and I will dwell in them and walk with them, saith the Lord; yet thou brings scriptures in a pretence (*2 Cor. 6. 16.*) to prove thy Imaginations, but all thy covers are too narrow to hid thee, thy slights, errours, lyes and blasphemies are seen, and thy wicked unclean spirit which vents all these abhominations is eternally Judged, and condemned by the Spirit and the Power of the eternal unchangeable God; and for all thy craft and subtilty thou shalt be bruised and crushed, the rod is over thee, it is not saying as thou said unto me, Thou art damned to all Eternity (or words to the same effect) that will save thee from the wrath of the Almighty (*Jehovah* our God) which without mixture will be poured forth upon thy head, and all likeminded with thee shall partake of the same; and this was one of thy subtil Evations, when any hard question was asked thee, which thou couldst not or durst not for shame answer, thou art damned already I will not answer thee, and so put things by which came near thee, though several times thou was taken in horrible lyes, and spoke divers times unto us after thou hadst denied it, which manifested the true God thou puts far from thee that should have guided thee, to have spoken the truth, unto which thou appears a strong enemy; Therefore L.C. thou may expect the just judgements which is pronounced against thee, to come speedily upon thee and the unreasonableness is in thy self and in thy Companion, and the rage and wickedness; though thou would falsly charge us with such like stuffe as you trade with, but by us it is denied and returned into your own bosoms, into its proper center; And as for thy saying, a Spirit is nothing without a body, herein also thou manifests thy ignorance, concerning the devine eternal unchangeable substance, the Spirit which give every thing its being, body or form, and the body without the Spirit is dead (*Jam. 2. 26.*), according to Scripture, though thou would have the form, the body, to be the substance of the Spirit; what a mist of thick darkness is over thee, that thou vents such cursed doctrine; where dost thou read in the Scripture that the Spirit is nothing without a body, or who ever dust be so impudent as to broach such a blaspemous doctrine? I never read that the Papists for all their blindness ever held forth such a doctrine, here the Idolaters may Judge thee, and thy cursed opinion; yet the Spirit hath a body, but according to thy own confession thou art none of the Members of it; but such as are baptized with it know his body, nature, vertue and life, who was before man was formed; Learn what that means, the bodies of the Saints are the Temple of the living God (*2. Cor.6.16.*), and prove thy God (which thou sayes is a man above the stars, no where else in no Creature, nor in this world) by plain Scripture, or confess thy gross ignorance and darkness, for I utterl deny thy meanings and corrupt imaginations; and if thy God be so far from tee, thou hast a great way to go for Counsel; but *Moses* said, the Word was nigh in the hearts of *Israels* Children; and likewise *Paul* to the *Romans*; and the Word was God saith *John*; so that thy doctrine and the Saints that gave forth the Scripture accord not, which clearly evidenceth a contrary spirit in thee, if thou hadst not confessed there were nought of God in thee; so that thy commission, the voice of words, which thou pretendest is also judged and denied, being seen by the light of devine glory in us, to be deceit and hypocrisie, and the delusion of Satan which thou professest, who hast uttered such abhominable filthy blasphemies, and railing speeches against the Lord and his onely people, which will hasten thy downfall and destruction, but our foundation stands sure, not to be shaken or moved, mark that, and the sentence of eternal Condemnation, which thou sayes five of us came under, we stand clear from, and under it thou thy self and thy Companion art, and the great darkness you are in (who deny and oppose the light of Jesus Christ within us) in the reprobate state, who know no the light Christ Jesus within you, whom we confess in us (as the Saints did) the hope of our eternal glory, and witness him against you, the world, and all men upon the earth who stand up against him, who is our life, rock, refuge, and the horn of our Salvation, and the Condemnation of all that deny and oppose his light within.

L.C. Thou sayes in the 20 and 21 page, *Both Angel and men hath forms sutable to their natures, and that it was their natures that gave them their form; and after thou sayest towards the latter end of the 21 p. God created man in his own Image; and likewise sayes, God hath the same form that man hath, and yet one is spiritual and the other natural, &c.*

Answ. Mark, The heap of confusion he has compacted by his confused sensual wisdom, which he calls the Seed of Faith; if God created man, then his nature gave him not his form, but God (*Gen. 2:7, John 1.*); and if by the word speaking, came forth both Angel and man, as thou sayes, the their nature gave them not their form, but God that spoke the word; and if God hath the same form as man hath, then not another as thou falsly affirmeth; Is there no difference betwixt a spritiual and a natural form? Herein thou hast contradicted thy self, that all who have a true understanding may see thy darkness and confusion.

L.C. Thou also sayes, *When thou believest him onely an infinite Eternal Spirit, then thy faith is wavering like unto thy God, for a spirit without a body cannot be known, &c.* p.22.

Answ. The Faith God hath given me, by which I see and know him to be an Eternal Sprit, a devine substance is not wavering, but found and stedfast; neither is God the infinite Eternal Spirit wavering as thou falsly affirmeth, but stands and remains in his own being nature and life for ever; and the Saints knew God to be a Spirit, as also Jesus Christ (*John 4.*) hath declared and confessed him, and unto their Testimony I do bear witness against thy lyes and confusion; and God who causeth light to shine forth of darkness, hath shined in our hearts, to give us the knowledge of his glory in the face of Jesus Christ (*2. Cor.4.6.*); so that we know God to be a Spirit of infinite power by his light in us, as the Saints did that gave forth the Scriptures, which knowledge thou and all the world wants who contemns and opposeth his light within; And is not this the blaspemy against the holy Spirit, to deny God to be a Spirit, hast not thou here brought thy self under Eternal Condemnation, is not this the unpardonable sin? But we do not deny that God was in Christ, and that in his body the fullness of the Godhead dwells (*Joh. 16. 23.*), Christ is the same for ever; now in his Saints, and god in him, the Father and Son we do not deny, but confess to be one, and he that hath the Son hath (the life) the Father also, but thou hast excluded him from thee, who sayes, there is nought of God in thee, and Christ hath but one Body, one Church, one Temple and yet there are many Member; but thy corrupt sensual wisdom cannot see into this divine Mystery, though the Scripture in plain words declare it; So that for ever thou may stop thy mouth, for boasting of thy knowledge in the Scriptures.

L.C. Who sayes, *Because we witness Christ manifest in us, that he is but in one of us, unless we can make it appear, that Christ hath so many bodies as there is Quakers, &c* p.2.

Answ. We do say and testifie in the fear of the Lord, with a true and perfect understanding, (notwithstanding thy reviling) that the true light Christ the spiritual body, or Divine substance, is manifest in us; and also do bear witness of his descending, and ascending far above all heavens, and it was the same which ascended, that descended according to the Scripture; and do thou prove the descending of a body of flesh, blood and bones; flesh and blood enters not into the

Kingdom of heaven (*Colos. 1. 2 Cor. 13.5. Eph. 4.10. 1 Cor. 15.50 John 1 .14. Eph.4 .10*), learn what this meaneth, the word was made flesh, and the flesh suffered without the gate at *Jerusalem,* but the life God died not, which was in the body of flesh, but entered into glory, into the same glory it was in before the world was made (Eph. 4. 10.), whose glory and presence filleth all things, and is manifest in us, his beauty, his presence and power is seen know, and rightly understood; and his spiritual body, his pure Divine presence is but one, yet in thousands it is manifest, glory to his eternal name (*Jehovah*) for ever; but this is beyond the reach of thy devilish sensual wisdom, this secret is hid from the Magicians of *Egypt,* the worlds wise men, who want the pure wisdom and reason (*1 Cor 1. 21.*); And this I affirm, who knows not the true light Christ manifest in him, he hath no true ground for his faith, so out of the true faith; but what hast thou to do to boast of thy faith or speak of it, who denies the true light Christ to be in thee; and sayes there is nought of God in thee, is not he true light Christ the Authour of faith? So he that hath not Christ the power of God (*Heb 12.2.*), the ground of faith, which faith stands in, his belief or faith stands in the wrong ground, in the wisdom of mens words, and this is the false faith, the faith of the whorish woman the false Church, the worlds faith, and the faith which L.C. is acted in, which all along in his book he boasts of, who denies the true light Christ within, the ground and Author of our faith.

L.C. In the 17.p.It is said: *Look into thy own body, there thou shalt see the Kingdom of heaven, &c. and in pag. 25.* He saith *Christ is in heaven and in no creature.*

Answ. The Kingdom of heaven being in man, if Christ be in heaven he must needs be in man, would thou eclude Christ from his Kingdom, or can it be properly or truely said to be a Kingdom without a King? But there thou hast manifested thy ignorance of the Reign, Government, Kingdom and power of Christ which is in the Saints, and that another King (the Prince of Darkness) hath the Government thee.

L.C. *He also goes about, through his subtilty, to strengthen the bonds of the wicked persecuters, the enemies of God and his people in New England and other Nations, saying that the suffering of the Quakers in New England or in any other Nation is not for righteousness, &c. p.44.*

Answ. Here thou joyns with *Cains* generation, the persecuters of the innocent, and manifesteth the linage and stock thou art of; where or when did any of the seed of faith persecute any for conscience sake, were not the righteous seed sufferers in all ages? blush and be ashamed of thy wickedness; what unrighteous action canst lay to the charge of any one of these thou calls *Quakers* in New England, that to cruelly suffered by that bloody generation; their innocent sufferings and the patient suffering of those called Quakers in other Nations, shall stand a witness against all Gods enemies there and else where, to the honour of the righteous God, & to their eternal shame and confusion, and Gods judgements is nigh to come upon that bloody generation in New England and else where, who have drunk the blood of the innocent; and all that joyn with them against the Elect seed called Quakers, shall partake of the wrath and indignation of the Lord God, which upon them will speedily be poured forth except they repent, and they and thou, shall know one day that ye have wronged the righteous seed, to your sorrow and torment, who for the innocent truth, and for righteousness have suffered long and cruel imprisonments, stockings, stoning and cruel scourging, the spoiling of their goods, and the losse of some of their members which *Cains* generations must answer for, every drop of innocent blood they must give an account for; the Lord of hosts will avenge the blood of his people, who will render to every one a just recompence of reward according to their works, wo, wo to the merciless, for they shall have no mercy.

L.C. Rages against us and sayes, *You* Quakers *are not Commissionate so counterfeits, yea guilty of spiritual treason; and would have us deny the Lord Jesus within us, &c. pag. 45.*

Ans. Our Authority and Commission stands in the power of Christ Jesus manifest in within us, unto whom we do bear witness (*2. Pet. 1. 21.*) in the power of his own spirit and life, as therein we are moved (as the Saints in all ages did) and his voice we know and hear, (*John 10.*) (which thou art a stranger unto) and his Counsels and commands, through the vertue of his power we are and have been subject unto, thorow the which many times, by *Cains* generation, we have suffered much; but it is thy self and thy generation (*Col. 1.*) which are guilty of high spiritual treason, that denies Christ within, and would have us to do so too; but we deny thy cursed Counsel and Doctrine and know one day that thou shalt answer for all these things at the Bar of Divine Justice, and thy Commission, the voice of words thou speaks of, is seen with the eternal light, and judged to be delusion, and thou proved thy self to be the counterfeit.

L.C. He affirmeth in p.26. *that God or Christ is not in this world, neither in Prophet nor righteous; And also that the seed of nature of God is in all true believers.*

Answ. Here thou would devide God from his seed or nature, which is inseparable, and would exclude God from the world, believers and righteous; what confusion is this, who begets the Seed or nature of God in man, and how is it generated or begotten, or how comes the seed or nature into man, if God be not in man, by his own power to generate it; and what makes a man righteous if the righteousness of

The Lying Prophet

God be not in him? Here thou hast written thou knows no what, uttered words without understanding.

L.C. Also saith, *The seed of the woman is faith, and the seed of the Serpentine Angel is Reason &c. and this Serpents seed Reason put to death Jesus and his Apostles, and that reason hath power to put to death the seed of faith.*

Answ. The seed of the woman is Christ, and the seed of the Serpent is sin and iniquity, they were unreasonable men that murdered the just and innocent, such as thou art, but the seed of faith shall never die; he that believes in me shall never die, never perish, never be confounded (*Joh. 6.47. Joh. 3. 15.*), but shall live for ever, have everlasting life, it is the Serpents seed, the ungodly, the unrighteous, the blasphemers and lyars, that dies and eternally perishes, and the seed of faith is not out of the pure reason, but in it; Reason, doth not destroy but preserveth; the persecutor, the devourer is out of reason, unreasonable.

L.C. *Prove or acknowledge thy folly and blasphemy.*

Several particulars which *L.C.* in his Book hath asserted, desired to be proved, by plain Scripture, or otherwise they will stand upon record, as lying forged imaginations and no true Revelations.

1. That Faith shall die in the heel, and reason in the head
2. That the Angel did descend into the womb of *Eve*.
3. That a spirit cannot live without a body, *p.28*.
4. That we and our God are cursed to all eternity *pag. 28*.
5. That Christ or God is above the Stars with a body of flesh and bones.
6. That God that Christ said was a spirit, the meaning of his Revelation was, that his invisible soul was that God of spirit abiding only in his person *p.29*
7. That Reason is the seed of the Serpent.
8. That by faith, reason shall be kept in Eternal death.
9. That God gave faith, Reason, and sence but once.
10. And that faith reason and sence have in all generated, in its kind form and nature as in *p.40.*
11. That the Devils Kingdom, and reasons Kingdom are one
12. That God doth damn as well as save, and that not for any evil thing done, as he hath asserted in *p.58.*
13. That we acknowledge no other God but what is within us.
14. And that we conceive this God was an infinite nothing, and so made all things of nothing.
15. That the light in us is darkness.
16. That an infinite spirit without a body is nothing
17. That we say God hath no form.

18. That all the time *Paul* was clothed with a corrupt persecuting spirit he was a vessel of honour in the account of God.
19. That God is all Faith and no Reason; and that Reason is of the nature of the Devil. *p. 31.*
20. That it was the wisdom of the flesh that made a chief Magistrate, as in *p. 36.*

This and much more of the like nature hath proceeded from the imagination of thy sensual wisdom, which thou calls the Revelation of thy generated faith, and many railing & reviling expressions against us wch thou calls Quakers, wch I shall pass by, as not being worth mentioning, but for all these things thou must give an account, and terrible and dreadful will be the day of account be unto thee, who hath uttered so many horrible blasphemies, lies and false accusations against the God of life, (who is a spirit) and against his people, and also goes about in thy sensual wisdom, to make a difference amongst believers, as if God answered some and not others.

L.C. pag. 41. *Thou sayes that thou canst not find that ever God did hear or give an answer to any private believer?*

Answ. Which is false: for God hears and answers all believers, it is the lyar and unbeliever that God neither hears nor answers; The whole houshold of faith, who are the family of heaven, of one heart, one soul and one spirit, in and thorow faith have all accesse to him and acceptance with him, all heard and answered by the Lord God who is near unto them (even in their hearts) to hear their requests and to answer their demands, and also to relieve their necessities, and there is no difference in true believers, the devisions and differences are amongst the unbelievers and the wicked: it were in vain for such as thou calls private believers to pray or believe, if God shall neither hear nor answer them, in this all the whole houshold of faith will deny thee & witness against thee, who have all been heard and answered of God; in this also hast thou discovered thy folly.

L.C. Likewise sayes in the *42 p. I shall reveal unto you the difference of a Commissionate faith from a generated faith, and how the one is ceased, the other not,* &c.

Answ. Where dost thou read of a commissionate or a generated Faith in the holy Scriptures? Here thou art not guided by the Scripture, nor the Spirit that gave it forth; Faith is but one, the gift of God (*Eph. 4. 5.*), not to be devided, the Mystery held in a pure Conscience, by which all Gods children had and have victory over the world (*John 5.4.*), its nature and life, and in it reigned over the prince and power of darkness, as all who be in the Faith will witness, one Faith, one Lord, on Baptism, and that is not ceased, nor never ceaseth, but remaineth

The Lying Prophet 29

and endureth in the Church of God, the Assembly of the first-born, his Elect in which they have all access to and acceptance with God; but this Faith and charity thou art of, which is manifested in the Saints, by which they live please God.

L.C. He siath, *The nature of Reason is to cheat, injure and persecute his neighbour, &c.* P. 47.

Answ. That is false, It is the nature of Reason to do the thing which is reasonable, it is contrary to Reason to cheat, lye and persecute, such are out of pure Reason that do such things, unreasonable men like thy self.

L.C. Likewise saith, *For as the Law was made for the lawless, viz. The Seed of reason, &c.* p.49.

Answ. This is also false, The law is not made for the Seed of Reason, which is added because of transgression, and made for the lawless, the Law is grounded upon pure Reason, and the lawless and transgressors are out of the Reason, in the unreasonableness; So the Law hath power over them to condemn them; pure Reason is Law, and what is contrary is no Law, and in this also hast thou opened thy folly.

L.C. Also saith, *Blasphemy is matter of Conscience (as you call it) so in Christs Kingdom, &c.* p.50, 51.

Answ. This is another of thy horrible lyes; blaspemy, errour, deceit, lyes and iniquity is in the Devils Kingdom, in which thou art, and not in the peaceable Kingdom of Christ into which no unclean thing can enter, blaspemers are shut out of it, and hath no part in it.

L.C. Doth likewise say, *The blind Quakers are labouring through the fire of their own Righteousness, intending to find rest but cannot, &c.* p.53.

Answ. The fire which they have laboured in, is a mystery to thee, if ever thou come to know it, and feel the heat of it, it will be a dreadful time unto thee, and our own righteousness, and unrighteousness, in the Lords fiery furnace is consumed (and consuming) and the righteousness of the Lord is our covering, which can stand in the everlasting burnings, and in it many of us can witness true peace, rest and sweet comfort, which is satisfactory to our Souls, notwithstanding the lyes and false accusations, which cannot touch us to hurt us, glory to our God for ever; but they will one day come heavy upon thee and be thy burthen.

L.C. Blasphemously sayes, *This I know God could die, &c.* p. 58.

Answ. This is horrible blasphemy, to say that the everliving God could die, who is eternal life, remains the same in substance, nature, life and being to all eternity (*Gen. 21. 33*), who was before death was, before any thing had a form, gives every thing its form (*Deut. 33. 27*), life to every thing that liveth, and is the Spirit and life of all flesh, never slumbers nor sleeps, immortal, eternal, unchangeable; if he dyes, he changes, and lives not ever; Thou sottish man, how doth thy sensual wisdom blind and deceive thee, can the unchangeable God dye, who can change all things in a moment, in the twinkling of an eye (Mal. 3. 6.), which is changeable? But in this as well as before he hath largely manifested his ignorance concerning the immortal unchangeable God, in whom there is no (*Jam. 1. 17.*) variableness nor shadow of turning; but the death and suffering of Christ in the flesh we believe, own and bear witness unto, according to the Scripture of Truth?

And likewise at *Richard Whitpans* house in *East-cheap* in *London*, in a discourse with some of us, this ensuing confusion proceeded from the mouth of this lying prophet (and his companion) who stiles himself the alone true and faithful messenger of Christ; but the understanding Reader may easily discern whose messenger he is, by his Message, unto which I shall refer thee, which is as followeth; taken from their own mouths, as it was uttered by them at the same time.

1. L.C. Said *he would prove God to be a man, flesh and bones as we are.*
2. *Lodowick Mugleton his companion, that he had more knowledge in the Scriptures, then they that gave them forth.*
3. L.C. Said *he had nothing of God in him.*
4. L.C. Said *he would prove nothing, and before said, he would prove what their God was.*
5. L.C, Said, *The Devil was the Author of this light in the world,* (and Christ saith I am the light of the world, &c).
6. He Said *he would never eat nor drink with* George Fox *Ju. For he was damned to all Eternity, but shortly after said he would drink with him tomorrow.*
7. He also said *he was the judge of the Scriptures, and all must believe the meanings he gives unto them, yet would shew no reason for it.*
8. L.C. Likewise said *he had damned the Lord Mayor seven or eight years ago and 1000 more within this eight years, and that he had justified forty or fifty.*
9. *He pronounced damnation to* George Fox *Ju. And to* John Harwood, *and said several times he would speak no more to them, yet after did, and said also he would answer no question, but after did.*

10. He said *his God was in heaven above the Stars and no where else a man or person.*
11. He said *the words in the Scriptures, in the 1. Chap. of* John *doth not prove God to be a Spirit, where Christ said God is a spirit, yet he pretended to own the Scriptures.*
12. One of them said *that a spirit hath flesh blood and bones contrary to Christs words.*

We whose names are here subscribed were present in the Chamber when these last twelve Particular passages were spoken by *Lawrance Claxton* and *Lodowick Mugleton*, and much more of the like nature, not worth the mentioning, and this is published for no other end but the manifesting of deceit and deceivers, and the clearing of the innocent truth and witnesses of it,

Richard Whitpain
Alice Whitpain
William Sympson
George Fox Jun
John Harwood

THE END.

Truth Ascended, Or, The Annointed And Sealed Of God Defended. In An Answer Written By Richard Farnsworth As A Testimony Against A Conterfeit Commission And All Injustice And False Judgement Done And Pronounced Under Pretence Of The Same.

LONDON, Printed in the Year, 1663

Truth ascended, or the Annointed and sealed of God defended, &c.

Lodowick Muggleton

Though thou pretend to be the chosen Witness of the Spirit, and the last that ever shall speak by Commission from God; and to be the chief Judge in the World ordained of God to give sentence upon men and women spiritual and eternal, and what shall become of them after death; and saist, *that in obedience to thy Commission thou hast already cursed and damn'd many hundreds of people both body and soul from the presence of God; elect men and Angels to Eternity;* and pretend'st *to go by as certain Rule (in so doing) as the Judges of the Land do when they give Judgement according to Law;* and faith, *That no infinite Spirit of Christ, nor any God can, or shall be able to deliver from: thy sentence and curse, &c.* as appears in a Sheet of paper, dated *Aug. 10 1662*, written by thee in answer to *Edward Bourns* to *Dorothy Carter;* and also four sheets dated *November 3 1662*, written by thee, and directed to *Thomas Highfield* in *Nottingham*, for *Samuel Hooston* and W.S.

I am bold (on behalf of the Lord) once again to bear my Testimony against thee, and against thy pretended Commission, and the Doctrine thereof, and shall make it appear, that it ought not to be entertained by any man or woman upon earth, because it is contrary to truth, and that thy judgment ought be all to be reversed, undone, and made void, because it is contrary to truth; and that thy judgement ought by all to be reversed, undone and made void, because it is erroneous and false; for thou art no chosen Witnesse of the Spirit of Truth, neither hast thou received any Commission from Christ, to whom all the Prophets gave witnesse, as hereafter appears.

That there were chosen Witnesses of Christ to whom all the Prophets gave witnesse, is certainly true, *Acts* 10. 38, 39, 40, 41. *Acts 5. 31 32, Acts* 1. 8.

That they had a Commission from Christ, to whom all the Prophets gave witness; or, that he Commanded them to preach to the people, is as true, *Acts* 10 42. But that thou either art, or dost so, I do deny.

The who were chosen Witnesses of Christ (whom God the Father anointed, sealed and sent) and had a Commission from the Spirit and Power of Christ, to whom all the Prophets gave witness, in testifying on the behalf of Christ; their Testimony stands as an evidence against thy pretended Commission, and the Doctrine thereof (because they say (on the behalf of Christ) that he commanded them to preach to the people, and to testifie to them, that it is he which was ordained of God to be the judge of quick and dead, Acts 10. 42. *To him give all the Prophets witness, that through his Name whosoever believes in him shall receive remission of sins,* Acts 10.43. But thou dost not so by thy pretend Commission, and the Doctrine thereof, who instead of preaching to the people, and testifying to them, that Christ is chief judge ordained of God to judge the quick and the dead, thou wouldst dis-throne him to set up thy self in his stead; whereby it appears, That thou art not a chosen Witness of the Spirit of Truth, and that thy pretended Commission is a counterfeit thing, by which thou presumes to give judgement contrary to Truth, which makes it evident, That thy doctrine and judgement is false, and being so, it ought not to be entertained or received by any, but to be denied, and against testified by all that love the Lord Jesus.

By their Commission they were to preach to the people, and by the same Commission, and the Doctrine thereof, they were to testifie to them, that Christ was ordained of God to be the Judge both of quick and dead; but thou art not Christ to whom all the Prophets gave witness; therefore it is evident, that thou art not chief Judge ordained of God to judge the quick and the dead; althou thou presume to say, that the dead after death shall never see any other God or Judge, but the remembrance of that sentence which you the pretended Witnesses of the Spirit did pass upon them in this life, which is a false Doctrine, and contrary to the Doctrine of Truth left upon record in Scripture, where it is said, *That the Father hath given authority to the Son to execute judgement, and all that are in the grave shall hear his voice, and shall come forth, they that have done good unto the resurrection of Life, and they that have done evil unto the resurrection of damnation;* as it is written *john* 5. 26, 27, 28, 29. and Christ shall give judgement upon them Matth. 25. 31, 32, 33, 34, 41, 46.

And as thou wouldst exclude Christ from that great office and work, and assume it to thy self; so thou wouldst exclude his Officers, and deny him of them, to set up thy self alone in their places and stead, because thou falsly faith. No man knows the Scriptures but thy self; and that none ought to officiate the Office of a Minister, Messenger or Ambassador of Christ, but such as are appointed by *John Reeves* and thy self; which assertions or doctrines of thine are false, and not true; for this I say, That the only knowledge and right of interpreting Scriptures, belongs not to thy self, but to the Lord Jesus and his blessed Spirit, who is the true Judge, and hath power to open mens understandings and can give them the true knowledge, and right understanding of Scriptures, *Luke* 24 32. & 24.45.

And the Gospel is preached with the Holy Ghost sent down from Heaven, as it is written I *Pet* 1, 11, 12 and the holy Ghost hath a true power and right Authority (without *John Reeves* and thy self) to make overseers over the Flock of God, to feed the Church of God which he hath purchased with his own blood, *Acts* 20. 58. And to appoint Ministers, Messengers or Ambassadors of Christ; and to call to the work of the Ministry, *Acts* 13.24. and they who by the Holy Ghost are called to the work of the Ministry, may with the Holy Ghost sent down from Heaven, preach the Gospel without the appointment of *John Reeves* and thy self. Take notice of that; for *as every man hath received the gift, even so minister the same one to another, as good stewards of the manifold grace of God; if any man speak, let him speak as the Oracles of God; if any minister, let him do it as of the ability which God giveth, that God in all things may be glorified through Jesus Christ*, as it is written and left upon Record in Scripture, I *Pet.* 4 10, 11.

The chosen Witnesses of Christ who had a Commission from his blessed Spirit, they were anointed, 2 *Cor. 1, 21.* and sealed of God, 2 *Cor* 1 22. but so art not thou; therefore thou art nothing like unto them; and they who are anointed and seal'd of God as such were they may be Ministers, Messengers and Ambassadors of Christ now, without the appointment of *John Reeves* and thy self; neither art thou at all owned by the Doctrine of their commission, (to do as thou dost, and pretendest to do under pretence of thy pretended commission) it takes no notice of thee, and such as thou art, to appoint to so great and glorious a Work, though thou presume in they imaginations to be greater than either Prophets of God, or Apostles of Christ, yet thou never approved thy self to be a Messenger, Minister or Ambassador of Christ, as they do and did, who are and were anointed, sealed and sent of God as aforesaid.

For the Ambassadors who had a commission to preach, and were anointed and sealed of God, 2 *Cor* 1, 21, 22.and had the Ministration of reconciliation given unto them, 2 *Cor.* 5, 8, 19, 20.a glorious Ministration, 2 *Cor* 3. 8, 9, 1, 11, which is the Ministration of the Spirit, 2 (or. 3. 5 6. Their sufficiency was not of any, like *John Reeves* and thy self, but) of God, who made them (ad hath the same power now, without *John Reeves* and thyself, to make) able Ministers of the New Testament, they approved themselves as the Ministers of God (not by reviling, cursing and damning, but on the contrary) in much patience, in a afflictions, in necessities, in distresses, in stripes, in imprisonments, in labours, in watchings, in fastings, by pureness, by knowledge, by long suffering, by kindness, by the holy Ghost, by love unfeigned, by the Word of truth, and by the power of God; see 2. *Cor.* 6. 4, 5, 6, 7, 8, 9, 10. And the Messengers of Christ, whose sufficiency is (not of *John Reeves* and thy self, but) of God, who (by virtue of his blessed power and spirit) are made able Ministers of the New Testament, and are spiritually anointed and sealed of God, they stand approved to God, as the Ministers of God, according to Gospel order, and the dispensation of the Gospel, which is the Ministration of the Spirit; but thou hast not so approved thy self, who fled from *Chesterfield* to *Bakwell* for fear of a few stripes, or a whipping, when the same was but threatened against thee for thy false Judgement and Doctrine in reviling, cursing and damning; whereby it is evident, that thou art nothing like an Ambassador of Christ, and very unfit to appoint to that work, and that thy pretended Commission, and the greatnesse of thy pretended power is nothing worth: Take notice of that.

The Ambassadors of Christ who were anointed and sealed of God, and had the Ministration of Reconciliation given unto them, that glorious Ministration of the Spirit, wherein they approved themselves as the Ministers of God (which thou hast not done) they were so far from reviling, cursing and damning, and rejoicing therein, as thou dost, that they forgave in the person of Christ, 2 *Cor,* 2,10.and by manifestation of the Truth, commended themselves to every man's conscience in the sight of God, 2 *Cor,* 4. 1, 2. but thou dost not so, who art so full of reviling, cursing and damning; whereby it's apparent, that thy pretended Commission, Power and Doctrine thereof is nothing like unto their; though thou falsly saist, it's as true and of a more higher nature then theirs was in their time, thou hast lyed therein, and hast born a false Testimony, which makes it evident, that thou art no chosen Witnesse of the Spirit of Truth.

The Ambassadors of Christ who were anointed an sealed of God, and had the glorious Ministration of the Spirit given unto them, by virtue of their commission of the Spirit, and the doctrine thereof, they commanded for to prove all thing, and hold fast that which is good; and to try the Spirits whether they be of God, because many false Prophets are gone out into the World, 1 *Thess.* 3. 21. 1 *John* 4. I, so the end that they might not entertain the Doctrine of any false Prophet, nor bid such God speed as abide not in the doctrine of Christ, lest they become partakers of their evil deed, 2 *John* 9. 10, 11. but by the Doctrine of thy pretended commission thou denies that, *viz* proving of doctrines, and trying of Spirits, saying *That neither the light of Christ within, nor no man upon earth can, or ought to judge of thy Doctrine, because (*thou saist) *that neither the Light within, nor no man upon Earth can, or ought to judge of the Doctrine of a Prophet, who hath a Commission from God;* and saist, *That there neither is, nor ever shall be any such Prophet but thyself whist the World doth endure,* which is a false assertion or doctrine of thine, but hereby it is manifest, that thou art against trying of spirits, and proving of Doctrines, and so art against the reception thereof, because Judgement in point of Doctrine, is in order to the reception of Doctrine. And for want of judgement in that respect, they may be deceived, who take doctrines upon truth without judging & trying thereof, & how should spirits by tryed, and doctrines be proved? Or how should the Doctrine of Truth be performed, which commands to try and prove them, if none can or ought (as thou falsly saist) to judge of the same: Whereby it appears that thou art not the chosen Witnesse of the Spirit of Truth, and that thy doctrine is contrary to the doctrine of truth, and ought not to be received by any man upon earth; and it is evident thereby, that thy pretended commission is a counterfeit thing, invented to beguile and deceive withal, and not at all owned by the commission and doctrine of the Ambassadors of the Lord Jesus, who were and are anointed and sealed of God.

The Ambassadors of Christ, and chosen Witnesses of the spirit, who were anointed and sealed of God, they were workers together with God, 2 *Cor.* 6.I. and did pray in Christ's stead, 2 *Cor.* 5.20. but thou dost not so, who instead thereof, goes about reviling, cursing and damning the beloved people of God, who preach from the Scriptures and Light within, and by virtue of the power which they have received of God, Devils are cast out, and (as thou saist) much good is done by then, who ought not to be reviled and cursed by thee as they are; whereby it appears that thou art no chosen Witnesse of the Spirit of Truth, nor an Ambassador of Christ, neither art thou anointed and sealed, or sent of God to go about reviling, cursing and damning the beloved people of God, as thou dost; for they who were the chosen Witnesses of the Spirit, and Ambassadors of Christ, did not so; but thou hast exceeded *Balaam* in that who refused to curse those whom God had blessed. And the Ambassadors of Christ, anointed, sealed and sent of God, they approved themselves as the chosen Witnesses of the Spirit, anointed and sealed of God, who being defamed, did entreat; and being persecuted, did suffer it, and not flee, as thou didst, for fear of a whipping threatened against thee for thy misbehaviour in reviling, cursing and damning; the chosen Witnesses of the Spirit anointed and sealed of God, did not so, but being reviled, did blesse, and by the Doctrine of their Commission, said, *Bless, and curse not,* I Cor. 4. 12. Rom. 12 .14. whereby it is evident, that thou art not a chosen Witnesse of the Spirit of Truth, neither art thou anointed and sealed, or sent by the God of Truth; thy pretended

Commission, and the doctrine thereof, and Judgement performed thereby, is erroneous and false, which is Antichristian; and it is no railing to tell thee the same, and reprove thee and thy deceit.

The true Witnesses of the Spirit, and Ambassadors of Christ, by the Father of mercies and God of all comfort, they were comforted themselves in all their tribulations, that they might be able to comfort them that were in any trouble, by the comfort wherewith they themselves were comforted of God, 2 Cor. I 3, 4. but so art not thou by thy reviling, cursing and damning them who are blessed, beloved and justified of God, wherein thou hast exceeded *Balaam* as aforesaid, whereby it appears, that thou art nothing like an Ambassador of Christ, or the chosen Witnesses of the Spirit who were anointed and seald of God; neither is there the like Truth, Power, Virtue and Consolation in the doctrine of thy pretended commission that were in theirs. Thou hast grievously lyed in saying, *That the Doctrine of thy Commission is as true, and of a more higher nature than the Prophets and Apostles was in their time;* but hast made no such proof of thy sayings of Doctrine as they did of theirs; But thou art reprehended, and the truth and power of the Commission and Doctrine of the anointed and sealed of God is defended; and the truth of the Gospel is over and above all thy errors, lyes and false judgement ascended.

By all which hath been said, it remains true, 1. That thou art no chosen Witnesse of the Spirit of Truth. 2. That thou art not the chief Judge in the World ordained of God to judge the quick and the dead. 3. That God may (without *John Reeves* and thy self) make able Ministers of the New Testament. 4. That they who are made able Ministers of the New Testament, whose sufficiency is not of self, but of God, they may officiate the Offices of Ministers, Messengers, or Ambassadors of Christ, without the appointment of *John Reeves* and thy self, who hath nothing to do to appoint to so great and glorious Work. 5. That thou art not anointed, sealed and sent of God to revile, curse and damn the beloved people of God. 6. That thou art no Ambassador of Christ to whom all the Prophets gave witness. 7. That thou hast received no Commission from the God of Truth to pass the sentence of eternal death and damnation upon the souls and bodies of men. 8. That the only knowledge and right of interpreting Scripture, belongs not to thee. 9. That thy Judgement and doctrine is erroneous and false. And 10*thly*, That thy Judgement and Doctrine ought not to be entertained by any, but to be reversed and denied by all that love the Lord Jesus.

And whereas thou saist, *Thou art the chief Judge in the World, and in passing the Sentence of eternal death and damnation upon the souls and bodies of men,* saist, *Thou goes by as certain a Rule as the Judges of the Land do when they give Judgement according to Law;* I say,

Truth Ascended

Thou hast lyed therein, and hast born a false testimony in that respect as well as the rest, as hereafter is evident.

First, Because thou art both Judge, Accuser and Witness thy self,, and dost condemn and give Judgement at thy will and pleasure, contrary to Truth, having no certain known Laws either of God or the Land, as a rule of direction to guide and lead thee in the wayes of right Justice, to give Judgement upon the bodies of men and women, nor cannot manifest a commission to put any known Laws in execution upon them; thou goes not by so certain a Rule (in so doing) as the Judges of the Land do when they give judgement according to Law; for they neither are, nor pretend to be both Judges, Accusers and Witnesses; neither do they go without certain outward known Laws as a rule of direction to guide and lead them to give Judgement accordingly; and they can produce a commission whereby they are impowered to put the same in executions but so canst not thou: Whereby it is evident, that thou hast not cognizance or lawful authority to pass the sentence of death upon the bodies of men and women: Therefore thou art no true and competent Judge in that matter; take notice of that.

2. Thou goes not by so certain a Rule when thou presumes to pass the sentence of death and damnation upon the souls and bodies of men, as the judges of the Land do when they give judgement according to Law; for *Cook* upon the confirmation of the Charters of the Liberties of *England*, Faith, *This Clause is worthy to be written in Letters of Gold,* viz.

That our Justices, Sheriffs, Mayors and other Ministers which under us have the Laws of the Land to guide them, shall allow the said Charters in all their points which shall come before them in Judgement; and here it is to be observed, That the Laws are the Judges Guides and Leaders, according to that old Rule, Lex est exercitus Judicura; *viz. The Law is the Judges Army.* Tutissimus Doctor. *Viz. The safest Teacher, Or,* Lex est optimus Judicis Synagogus; *viz. Their best synagogue. And,* Lex est tutissimus Cassis; *viz. Their safest fortress.*

*There is an old Legal word (*saith he) *called* Guidagium, *viz Guidage, which signifieth an Office of guiding Travellers through dangerous and unknown ways: Here it appeareth, that the Laws of the Realm hath this office to guide the Judges in all causes that come before them in the ways of right Justice, who never yet misguided any man that certainly knew them, and truly followed them.* Cook part 2. Inst. Fol. 566.

Whereby it is apparent, That the Judges of the Land have certain outward known Laws as a Rule of direction to guide and lead them to Judgement, when they give it according to Law; but thou (*Lodowick*) hast no certain outward known Laws either of God or the Land, as a

Rule of direction to guide thee in the ways of right Justice, and to lead thee to give judgment upon the bodies of men accordingly; whereby it is evident, thou hast nothing to do withal, neither dost thou go by so certain a Rule to give judgement upon the bodies of men, as the Judges of the Land do when they give judgement according to Law. Mind how thou art confuted and taken with a lye in thy mouth. Behold how thy pretended most knowing and wisest of men is taken in his own craftiness! Let no man deceive himself, for the wisdom of this World is foolishness with God; for it is written, *He taketh the wise in their own craftiness;* and again *The Lord knoweth the thoughts of the wise, that they are vain* I Cor. 3 18, 19, 20 Thou art snared with the words of thy mouth; thou art taken with the words of thy mouth, Prov. 6, 2. *The wicked is snared by the transgression of his lips,* Prov. 12, 13. and so art thou; take notice of that.

3. Thou goes not by so certain a Rule to give judgment and sentence of death and damnation upon the souls and bodies of men, as the Judges of the Land do when they give judgement according to Law; for by the Law (which is a Rule of direction to them) it is enacted, *That no man from thenceforth shall be attached by any accusation, nor fore-adjudged of Life nor Limb, &c against the form of the great Charter, and the Law of the Land,* 5 Edw.3. 25 Edw. 3. Cook, part 2 Inst, fol. 48.

But thou *Lodowick* fore judges the souls and bodies of men from the presence of God, elect men and Angels to Eternity, contrary to the Law of God, and the Law of the Land; whereby it appears that thou goes by no Legal Rule, neither according to the Law of the Land, nor the Law of God; for thou saist, That the sentence and curse which thou pronounces upon the souls and bodies of men, is not from the Scriptures, or Light within, then not according to the Law of God, and as before is proved, it is quite contrary to the Law of the Land.

What then is thy Rule of direction to give judgement upon the souls and bodies of me, seeing thou pretends to be the chief Judge in the World, and gives not thy judgement and sentence according to the Law of God? Produce us thy Law and commission if thou canst, now thou art put to it, for thou neither goes by the Law of God either without or within, nor by so certain a Rule as the Judges of the Land do when they give judgement according to Law; therefore thou goes not according to the Law of the Land, and it is evident, That thou goes not according to the Law of God as aforesaid.

Seeing then, that the Judges of the Land have certain outward known Laws, as a rule of direction to guide and lead them to give judgement upon the bodies of men, and an outward commission to impower them to put the same in execution; and thou pretends to be a Judge to pass the sentence of death upon men and women, and pretends (in so doing) to go by as certain a Rule as the Judges of the Land do when they give judgment according to Law, and hast no certain known Laws either of God or the Land, as thy rule of direction to guide and lead thee in the ways of right justice, to give judgement upon them, nor can manifest no true commission to put any known Law in execution.

It remains certainly true, That thou art no competent Judg to pass the sentence of death upon men and women; thy pretended Authority is but an usurped thing, whereby thou wouldst destroy and oppresse them; and it's said, That every oppression against Law by colour of any usurped Authority, is a kind of destruction; and it is the worst oppression that is done by colour of office, *Cook* 2. Par. *Inst. Fol.* 48. And thy proceedings are no better then oppression against Law both of God and the Land, and is done by colour of Office under pretence of chief Judge, and in obedience to thy pretended Commission: Therefore the acts of injustice done by thee in condemning the souls and bodies of men as aforesaid, is oppression against Law, and the worst kind of destruction.

And if injustice be so hateful a thing in the eye of the Law, that it deserves to have judgement (in a high measure) turned backward upon it, especially when it is done by colour of office, to make the parties offending, examples to others, that Justice may also turn back into its course; how much more hateful a thing is injustice then in the eye of the Lord, especially when it is done by colour of Office? Doth it not deserve to have his just and righteous judgement (in high measure) turned backward upon it, to make the parties offending, examples to others; that they may fear to do the like, and that his Justice may stand and remain in its course; but we are sure that the judgement of God is according to truth against them which commit such things, *Rom,* 2. 1, 2. And by the Law of God it is declared, *That if a false witness do but rise up against a man to tesifie against him that which is wrong, then both the men between whom the controversie is, shall stand before the Lord and before the Judge that shall be in those days, and the Judge (as his duty is) shall make diligent inquisition (to find out the truth or falsehood of the evidence) and behold, if the Witness be (found out to be) a false Witness, and hath testified falsly against his brother, then shall ye do unto him as he had thought to have done unto his brother, so shall thou put away the evil from among you; and those which remain, shall hear, and fear, and shall henceforth commit no more any such evil among you; thine eye shall not pity, but life shall go for life, eye for eye, tooth for tooth, hand for hand, Deut.* 19. 15, 16, 17, 18, 19, 20, 21. or the like Judgment was to be executed on a false Witness, that had been due to the nature of the offence of him that he was an evidence against, if his Testimony given in evidence against him had been tryed; whereby God hath signified his high displeasure against injustice done by colour of office, for if a false evidence had been taken for truth, and the judgement grounded upon the evidence, it had been false judgment, as thin is; and false judgement is not owned by the Law of God, who commands *to execute true judgement, and to shew mercy and compassion every man to his brother,* Zech. 7. 9. Mic. 6.8. *and forbids to wrest judgment,* Exed. 23. 6. Saying also by way of command, *Thou shalt not raise a false report, put not thine hand with the wicked to be an unrighteous Witnesse,* Exo. 23. I. *Thou shalt not follow a multitude to do evil, neither shalt thou speak in a cause to decline after many, to wrest judgement,* Exo.23.2. *keep thee far from a false matter, the innocent and the righteous slay thou not, for I will not justifie the wicked,* Exo, 23. 7. Likewise see Moses charge to the Judges, *Deut.* 1. 16, 17. *They were commanded to judge the people with just judgement,* Deut. 16.18.*they were forbidden to wrest judgment, and were not to pervert the words of the righteous,* Deut 16. 19. *And that which is altogether just, they were commanded to follow,* Deut, 16. 20. But thou dost not so.

Consider then, that thou hast not only done injustice both in the eye of the Law, and of the Lord, but also thou hast done the same by colour of office: First, in the eye of the Law thou hast done it, because thou presumes to pass the sentence of Death upon the bodies of men and women, as a pretended Judge, and hast no certain outward known Laws as a rule of Direction to guide thee in the ways of right Justice to give judgment upon them, nor can produce no commission to put any known Law in execution or impower thee so to do; and art therefore no competent Judge in that matter. And secondly, injustice in the eye of the Lord thou hast done, and also by colour of office under pretence of chief Judge in the world, and by a pretended commission of the Spirit, pretended to be received from a God *without thee, that spake* (thou saist) *by voice of words to hearing of the ear.*

Consider, that thy injustice done by colour of office, deserves to have a punishment proportionable to the offence, and can the offence in the eye of the Lord be any less then sin against the Holy Ghost, because thou hast pretended to do it in the Name of the Holy Ghost, and so wouldst make the holy Ghost the Author of thy offence, which it is not?

And seeing thou art guilty of sin against the *holy Ghost*, there is a punishment already proportioned for such a n offence; and also thou art punishable by the Law of the Land for presuming under pretence of a commission, and as a Judge, to pass the sentence of death upon the bodies of men and women, and pretends *to go by as certain a rule in so doing, as the Judges of the Land do when thy give Judgement according to Law;* which thou hast no cognizance or right unto, neither hast thou done so, as before I have proved; and I had not medled with the outward Laws of the Land, but that I have such a pretended chief Judge to deal with, to shew him his folly and injustice done by colour of office, as I have done thee, which thou *Lodowick* maist for ever be ashamed of for presumptuously doing as thou hast done, who hast also erred in thy judgement, and hast given it contrary to truth, and against the Law of the Land: And it's said, *That if any Judgement be given contrary to the points of the great Character, it shalt be undone, and holden for nought,* 25 Ed. 1,2. and by a Statute made *Anno* 25, *Ed. 3.* it is declared, *That if any thing be done against the Law, is shall be redressed and holden for none,* as thine is, and is therefore reversed, undone and holden for nought. Take notice of that.

And whereas thou saist, *That in obedience to thy Commission thou hast already cursed and damned many hundreds of people both soul and body to eternity:* I say, the greater is thy presumption and sin, who hast no Right nor Authority to do the same; thy judgement is contrary to truth, and is against the Law of God, and the Law of the Land, and is therefore reversed and holden for none, as aforesaid.

Whereas thou saist, *that no infinite spirit of Christ, nor any God can, or shall be able to deliver from thy sentence and curse:* I say, That is false, or no less than blasphemy, and there is a punishment due to the nature of the offence: Thou hast hereby denied Christ as he is the Advocate with the Father, and the propitiation for the sins of the whole World, *I John* 2. 1,2. What a miserable condition art thou in! And how great is thy sin of presumption and folly!

Wouldst thou have the great King of Heaven, the Lord who is a great God, and a King above all Gods, *psal.* 95.3. and Christ Jesus, who is the Prince of the Kings of the Earth, *Rev.* I.5. to commit their whole power solely to thee, who may abuse it, as thou hast done, under pretence of a Commission, and reserve no power in the Eternal God-head to pardon offences committed against them, and preserve and save poor penitent offenders by shewing mercy unto them, and forgiving of them? And wouldst thou have no power reserved in the Eternal God-head to correct and punish thee, and such as thou art, for abusing the Power and People of God, as thou hast done? Wouldst thou make the Eternal Power and Godhead inferior to the Kings of the Earth? Do not they reserve a pardoning and punishing power in themselves, besides what they give to their Judges by their commission?

But not withstanding thy pretended commission, false judgement and doctrine, This I affirm on the behalf of the Lord and the eternal God-head, That there is a pardoning and a punishing power in them reserved, beyond thy pretended commission.

First, as to the pardoning power, it is declared by them that were sent of the Lord God and his Spirit, saying *Let the wicked forsake his ways, and the unrighteous his thoughts, and let him return to the Lord, and he will have mercy upon him; and to our God, and he will abundantly pardon.* Seeing it is so, it remains certainly true, that there is a pardoning power reserved, and remains in the Eternal Godhead; and is also remains true, That the unrighteous and wicked upon the forsaking of their evil thoughts and wicked ways, and returning to the Lord according to his requiring, are objects of mercy, and pardonable as aforesaid, which is contrary to thy false doctrine and judgement.

Secondly, As to the pardoning power, that remains in the Godhead, is manifested in Christ, whom God the Father hath exalted with his right hand to be a Prince and a Saviour, for to give repentance unto *Israel,* and forgiveness of sins; and we are his Witnesses of these things, and so is the Holy Ghost whom God hath given to them that obey him *Acts* 5.31,32.

Thirdly, Christ Jesus who is the chief Judge ordained of God to judge the quick and the dead, *Acts* 10. 40, 41, 42.he hath manifested the pardoning power that remains with the God-head, by shewing of mercy, and forgiving offences. The Scribes and the Pharisees fought an occasion against him (because he was merciful and forgave sins) *and they took a woman sinner, and brought her to Christ, and ser her in the midst;* First, They brought her before Christ, and set her as an offender before the Judge. Secondly, They accused her unto him of the act of Adultery, *John* 8. 1, 2, 3, 4. Thirdly, They pleaded both Law and Fact to make their case good, and to have shut up Christ's mercy and compassion against her, to have moved him to give judgement upon her, who it's like thought he could not otherwise have done, if he owned *Moses* Law; and if he had denied it, then they would had an occasion against him, which they fought for: They pleaded Fact, saying, *Master, This woman was taken in Adultery, in the very act,* Joh.8. 4. Then they pleaded Law, saying, *Now Moses in the Law commanded that such should be stoned,* Joh 8.5. *but what saist thou? This they said, tempting of him, that they might have to accuse him,* John 8.6. *And they continued asking of him,* John 8.7. *shewing how earnest they were to have had an accusation against him;* they tempted him for that very end, and to see if he would deny putting *Moses* Law in execution upon that woman which they had taken in Adultery, and brought before him to accuse unto him.

But Jesus himself, who was chief Judge ordained of God, and had power or authority given him to execute judgement, *John* 5. 22, 27. He did neither accuse the offender, nor countenance those bloody accusers that brought her before him, thou they pleaded both Law and Fact unto him, as aforesaid, who teacheth by his example in that case, That it is not the duty of a Court to accuse any, though a known offender, nor to countenance bloody accusers, but rather to mollifie their rigour, as Christ did in the same case, who in great wisdom answered their question and said unto them, *He that is without sin among you, let him first cast a stone at her,* Joh. 8. 7. (or put *Moses* Law in execution upon her) but those accusers were none of them without sin, because they sinned in tempting of Christ, and the Witness of God in their own conscience testified the same unto them, whereby they were convicted, and thereupon *went out one by one, beginning at the eldest, even unto the last; and Jesus was left alone, and the women standing in the midst, John 8 ver. 9*

First, By which wise answer of his, he put a stop to their cruelty against the offender, and thereby he delivered her from their cruelty, and took her into his mercy, who knew better how to deal with her, then they would have had him.

Secondly, He by that gracious wise answer unto them, put a stop to their subtiley, and crost their intent which they had in their minds in their temptation against him.

Thirdly, He hath shewed by that wise answer unto them, That criminal persons are no competent Judges to condemn others for that which themselves are guilty of.

4. He also by that wise answer unto them, preserved himself out of their snare, for he thereby owned *Moses* Law in its time and place, which if he had then denyed, they thought to have had an occasion against him, or whereof to have accused him, and hiving preserved himself out of their snare, and taken the woman sinner out of the cruelty, into his mercy, as aforesaid, He then as a gracious and merciful Judge looked upon her with an eye of compassion, saying *Woman, where are all those thine accusers? Hath no man condemned thee,* Joh 8. 10, *she answered and said, No man, Lord.* And Jesus to manifest his mercy, and the pardoning power which remained with the God-head, he said, *Neither do I condemn thee, go, and sin no more,* Joh, 8, 10,11.

And as a merciful Judge he forgave her that offence, and set her free, and gave her commend to abstain from sin for the time to come, saying, *Go, and sin no more*; as much as to say, let mercy held forth in forgiving thy offence that is past, engage thy heart against sin, and unto God for the time to come.

But though thou *Lodowick* pretend to be the chief Judge in the World, thy example, doctrine and practice teacheth quite contrary to the doctrine and example of Christ, whereby it appears, and is plainly made manifest, That thou art not ordained chief Judge in his stead.

First, Thy Example, Doctrine and Practise teacheth to be both Judge, Accuser and Witness, contrary to the Law of God, and the Law of the Land.

Secondly, To condemn at a distance without any due course of Law, or orderly proceedings, before thou have the parties and their Accusers face to face before thee, to hear what they can say.

Thirdly, To condemn as will and pleasure, contrary to any known Law either of God or the Land.

4. It teacheth not the preservation of any known Law, but rather the destruction of all known Laws both of God and the land.

5. Thy example, doctrine and practice teacheth to condemn the bodies of men and women without any known law either of God or the Land, as a rule of direction to guide and lead in the ways of right Justice, to give judgement upon them accordingly.

Lastly, Thou teachest thereby, That if judgement or sentence be given, pronounced, or past, though never so contrary to truth, it out not to be redressed or reversed, undone and holden for nothing; which is quite contrary to the law of the land: And we are sure that the judgement of God is according to truth, *Rom* 2,2. but thine is not so; whereby it is evident, that it is not the judgement of God.

It appears and is evident first, That thou art an unlawful Judge, because thou presumes to pass the sentence of death upon the bodies of men and women without cognizance or lawful Authority so to do.

2. That thou art a foolish unwise Judge, because thou passest the sentence of death upon the bodies of men and women at a distance from thee, without having them and their answers face to face before thee.

Thirdly, That thou art an unjust Judge, because thou passest the sentence of death upon the bodies of men and women contrary to truth, without any known laws either of God or the Land, as a Rule of direction to guide and lead thee in the ways of right justice, to give judgement upon them accordingly.

4. That thou art a cruel unmerciful Judge, because if thy sentence be once pronounced and past (though it be never so erroneous and false) thou wouldst have it impossible for any God to reverse and undo the same, or to deliver therefore.

Seeing that it is so; it remains certainly true, That thou art no true and competent Judge, neither ordained of God nor man to pass the sentence of death upon the bodies of men and women; and it remains as true, That the souls in the Father's hand thou hast nothing to do withal.

First, Because Christ giveth to them eternal life; and they shall never perish, *John 10 28.*

Secondly, Because no man is able to pluck them out of the Father's hand, as it is written *John 10. 29.*

And thirdly, Because the Gates of Hell shall nor prevail against them.

Likewise it remains true, That thou art not the chosen Witness of the Spirit of Truth, and that thou hast not received thy pretended Commission from the God of Truth, to do as thou hast done, and pretendest to do by colour thereof.

First, Because thou denies Almighty God himself.

Secondly, Because thou denies Christ Jesus of his Offices.

Thirdly, Because thou denies him of his Officers, as Messengers, Ministers or Ambassadors.

Fourthly, Because thou denies the holy Scriptures

Fifthly, Because thou hast lyed against God and Christ, and hast born a false Testimony of them, and of the true Prophets of God, and Apostles of Christ.

1   As to the first, That thou denies Almighty God himself, is evident by thy own Doctrine, because thou saist, *That the dead after death shall never see any other God or Judge but the remembrance of that Sentence which you the pretended Witnesses of the Spirit did pass upon them in this life,* which is quite contrary to the doctrine of Christ, and the Scriptures of truth, *John 5 26, 27, 28, 29 Mat 25, 31, 32, 33, 34, 41. 2 Pet 2, 9.*

2   And as to the second, that thou denist Christ of his offices, is evident against thee by thy own doctrine in three particular. First, Thou deniest Christ as chief Judge ordained of God to set up thyself in his stead; because thou saist, *Thou art ordained chief Judge in the world to give sentence upon men and women spiritual and eternal, and what shall become of them after death,* contrary to the Doctrine of Christ, and the Scriptures of truth, *Mat. 25 31, 32 &c, Joh 5 26, 27, 28, 29, 30. Acts 10 42 & 17 31, 2. Tim 4 1 1 Pet 4, 5* and as before is proved. Secondly, Thou denist Christ as he is the Saviour of men, and the Author of eternal salvation to all that obey him; in whom eternal

life is to be had, because thou accounts that there is no eternal life to be had but in the faith of thy doctrine, saying, *There is no eternal life to be had but in the faith of the doctrine or declaration of a Prophet who hath a Commission from God;* & saith, *There neither is, nor ever shall be any such Prophet but thyself whilst the world endureth.* In answer to the which I say, That the holy Scriptures which were spoken and declared from the moving of the Holy Ghost in the holy men of God, 2 *Pet*, I. 20, 21 were better doctrine & declaration of Prophets of God then thine, who had a better commission or authority from God then ever thou hadst. And concerning their declaration, Christ said to the Jews, *Search the Scriptures, for in them ye think ye have eternal life, & they are they which testifie of me, and ye will not come to me that ye might have life, John 5. 39, 40.* And Christ said to his Disciples, *I am the way, and the truth, and the life, no man cometh unto the father but by me, Ioh 14, 6.* And the Ambassador of Christ hath declared and said, *That the wages of sin is death, but the gift of God is eternal life through Jesus Christ our Lord,* as it is written *Rom.* 6, 22 23. (Then not in the faith of thy doctrine.) And Christ doth give unto his sheep eternal life, and they shall never perish, neither shall any man pluck them out of his hand, *Joh 10. 27, 28.* And the Messengers of Christ have declared and said, *This is the record that God hath given to us eternal life, and this life is in his Son,* 1 *Joh. 5. 11* (then not in the faith of thy doctrine). *He that hath the Son, hath life eternal,* though he deny thy doctrine; *and he that hath no the Son, hath no life eternal,* though he may have faith in thy doctrine.

By what hath been said, it is evident, and remains certainly true:

That Christ Jesus is the Saviour of men, and the Author of eternal Salvation to all that obey him, *Acts 5. 31, 32 Heb. 7 25 Heb. 5. 9. and is able to save to the uttermost all that come unto God by him.*

That *he is the way to the Father, without which no man can come unto him, john 14 6*

That *the gift of God is eternal life, which Christ doth give unto his sheep that they may never perish, Rom. 6. 23. John 10. 27, 28.*

That eternal life is not in the faith of thy doctrine or declaration, but in Christ the Son, according to the Record that God hath given, *For he that hath the Son, hath life, and he that hath not the Son, hath not life,* as it is written I *John 5. 11, 12.*

Thirdly, Thou deniest Christ as he is the Advocate with the Father, and the propitiation for the sins of the whole World, because thou saist, *That no infinite Spirit of Christ, nor any God can, or shall be able to deliver from thy sentence and curse;* which is contrary to truth, and the hold Scripture, where it is said, *My little children, these things write I unto you, that ye sin not; and if any man sin, we have a Advocate with the Father, Jesus Christ the righteous, and he is the propitiation for our sins, and not for ours only, but also for the sins of the whole world,* 1 Joh, 2. 1, 2. *Wherefore he is able also to save them to the uttermost that come unto God by him, seeing he ever liveth to make intercession for them,* as it is written, *Heb.* 7. 25.

3. And as to the third, that thou denist Christ of his officers is evident by thy own doctrine, because thou falsly saist, *That no man ought to officiate the Office of a Minister, Messenger or Ambassador of Christ, but such as are appointed by* John Reeves *and thy self;* contrary to the Scriptures *I Pet.* 4 10, 11 *I Pet I.* 10, 11, 12 *Acts* 13. 2. 4. *Acts* 20 28. *Acts* 10, 19, 20, 21. *Acts* 10. 42, 43 2 *Cor.* 3. 1, 2, 3, 4, 5, 6, 2 *Cor.* 4 1, 2, 3, 4, 5, 6, 7. And as before I have proved.

4. And as to the fourth, That thou deniest the holy Scriptures, I prove against thee by thy own doctrine; first, because thou saist, *That the words which Christ said to his disciples, Bleß, and curse not, concerns no thee nor any man upon earth at this day,* contrary to the Doctrine of Christ, where it is said, *whosoever therefor shall break one of these least commandments, and teach men so, he shall be called the least in the Kingdom of Heaven; but whosoever shall do and teach them, he shall be called great in the Kingdom of Heaven,* Matt. 5. 17, 18, 19. *and one jot tittle shall in no wise paß till all be fulfilled.*

Secondly, Thou deniest the holy Scriptures, because thou saist, *The dead after death shall never see any other God or Judge but the remembrance of that sentence which you the pretended Witnesses of the Spirit did passe upon them in this life,* contrary to the Scriptures, as before I have proved.

Thirdly, Thou denist the holy Scriptures, because thou saist, *Thou art chief Judge ordained of God to give sentence upon men and women spiritual and eternal, and what shall become of them after death;* contrary to the Scriptures, and as before I have proved.

Fourthly, Thou deniest the Scriptures, because thou saist, *That no man ought to officiate the Office of a Minister, Messenger or Ambassador of Christ, but such as are appointed by* John Reeves *and thy self;* contrary to the Scriptures, and as before I have proved.

Lastly, Thou deniest the Scriptures, because thou accounts them but *the dead Letter of other mens words, whose Light thou judgest to be but dark in comparison of that Light which comes by they pretended Commission;* contrary to the Scriptures, 2 *Pet.*1.20, 21, *I John* 1. 5. 7 2 *Cor.* 4 6, 7. *I Pet.* 1. 10, 11, 12.

And as to the Fifth, That thou hast lyed against God, and against Christ, and born a false Testimony of them, and of the holy Prophets of God, and Apostles of Christ, is evident by what hath already been said, and also further appears that it is so; because it is certainly true, That the holy Scriptures were spoken forth from God himself, and also from Christ Jesus our Lord; and likewise according to the moving of the holy Ghost in the holy men of God, both Prophets and Apostles: And it is true, that their Light who spoke forth the Scriptures, were not dark in comparison of that light which comes by thy pretended Commission: Therefore it is evident and certainly true, That thou hast lyed against them, and born a false Testimony of them, as aforesaid.

For God is Light, and in him is no darkness at all, I Joh.1. 5. How then can thy pretended Light of thy pretended Commission, be greater then God the Fountain of Light? I say, it is not. Therefor it is evident, That thou hast lyed against God, accounting that he who is the Fountain of Light, is but dark in comparison of the Light which comes by thy pretended Commission.

Christ hath declared himself to be the Light of the World, *John 8, 12.* And *he is the true Light which lighteth every man that cometh into the world, Joh.*1, 9, but thou art not that Light, neither art thou like unto it: And in accounting Christ who is the true Light, as aforesaid, to be but dark in comparison of thin, thou hast lyed against him.

And *David* declared and said, the Lord was his Light; *Ps.* 27. 1 & he spoke forth Scriptures: And to them that spoke forth Scriptures as the words & true sayings of God from the mouth of the Lord, he was, and is an everlasting Light and glory, according to his promise, *Isa.* 60. 19, 20 but so art nor thou; therefore thou hast lyed and born a false Testimony, saying, *That their Light who spoke forth the Scriptures, was but dark in comparison of thine,* behold what a false Witnesse thou art; take notice how thou art confuted.

And whereas thou saist, *That after thy sentence is past upon the Speakers, they shall never grow more to any great experience, neither shall they have those Visions & Revelations and Revelations from that Light within them, as they had before, but shall rather wither and decline.* It seems thou accounts that they have great experience, and both Visions and Revelations from the Light within, until thy (false) sentence be past upon them; and seeing it so, I say, they sentence cannot hinder the same, nor their growth into great experience of truth, neither at all cause them to wither or decline there from; thy testimony is false in that respect, as well as it is against God and Christ, and as aforesaid.

And whereas in thy imagination thou hast accused the *Quakers* to be of the nature and seed of the Serpent, and by thy presumption hast given judgement accordingly; yet notwithstanding to signifie that lyars and false Witnesses stand in need of a good memory lest they contradict themselves, and confute their evidence; for want of which tho hast contradicted thy self, and by thy self-confutation hast cleared the *Quakers* from thy false accusation and judgement grounded thereupon, by saying the *Quakers* do preach from the Scriptures and Light within, and that Devils are cast out, and much good is done by them; and I say, such are not of the nature and seed of the Serpent; thou hast by thy own confutation cleared them therefrom, as before in a former Writing I have proved.

And to conclude, I do affirm, That there is a punishing power reserved in the Eternal Godhead, and doth therewith remain to punish the rebellious, obstinate and presumptuous, such as thou art or as may be read *Heb. 10, 26, 27, 28, 29, 30, 31. 2. Pet. 2. 4, 5, 6, 7, 8, 9. Jude 5, 6.* For we know him that hath said, *Vengence belongeth unto me, I will recompence, saith the Lord,* Heb, 10, 30. *For God will ease himself of his Enemies* (such as thou art) *and he will be avenged of his Adversaries,* as it is written. And seeing vengeance is the Lords, I leave it to him to repay thee accordingly to the nature of thy offences, or as his in justice he is pleased to do.

Concerning the two Witnesses, &c.

Lodowick

IF *John Reeves* and thy self were joint Commissioners, and had your pretended Commission (not severally asunder, but) jointly together, hath not the death of *John Reeves* made void thy pretended Commission to all intents, constructions & purposes whatsoever? Or, if *John Reeves* and thy self did pretend to be the two Witnesses spoken of *Rev. 11. 3* and to have the power given to them; hath not the death of *John Reeves* made it evident against you, to be none of them, because it is said concerning those two Witnesses *Rev. 1.2. That until they had finished their testimony, if any man would hurt them, fire should proceed out of their mouth, and devour their Enemies: And when they should have finished their testimony, the Beast that ascendeth out of the bottomless pit should make war against them, and should overcome them and kill them,* Rev. 11. 7. And it is said concerning them that *their dead bodies should lye in the street of the great City, and they of the people, and kindred, and nations should see their dead bodies three days and a half, and should not suffer their dead bodies to be put in graves,* Rev 11. 8 9 but it was not so with *John Reeves*; whereby it is evident, That he was not one of them Winess's.

Likewise it is said concerning those two Witnesses, That *after three days and a half the Spirit of Life from God entered into them, and they stood upon their feet, and great fear fell upon them which saw them,*

Rev. 11. 11. But it was not so with *John Reeves*, that the Spirit of Life entered into him, to cause him to stand upon his feet after he had been dead three days and a half, neither did any see him so, after he was dead, to case great fear to fall upon them; whereby it is manifest, That *John Reeves* was not one of those Winesses.

Moreover it is said of those two Witnesses, That they ascended up to Heaven in a Cloud (but so did not *John Reeves*) and their Enemies beheld them, *Rev. 11, 12 and the same hour there was a great Earthquake, and the tenth part of the City fell; and in the Earthquake were slain of men seven thousand and the remains were affrighted, and gave glory to the God of Heaven,* Rev. 11. 13.

And as it is evident, That *John Reeves* was not one of those Witnesses spoken of *Rev. 11 3* by what hath been said, & as aforementioned, meant and intended; so likewise it is evident, That thou *Lodowick* art not the other of them two Witnesses, because it is said of them, (that in order to the finishing of their Testimony) *They should prophesie a thousand two hundred and three score days clothed in sack cloth, Rev. 11. 3.* But when dist thou so? And it is said concerning them, *That if any man will hurt them, fire proceedeth out of their mouth and devoureth their enemies, and if any man will hurt them, he must in that manner be killed,* Rev. 11.9. *These have power to shut heaven, that it rain not in the days of their Prophesies and have power over waters to turn them into blood,* Rev 11.6. but when didst thou prophesie a thousand two hundred and three score days in sack cloth? And when did fire proceed out of thy mouth to kill any? And when did thou shut up the heavens that it did not rain during the time of thy pretended prophesie? Or when didst thou turn the waters into blood, whereby it might have been made manifest, that thou hadst been one of them who couldst manifest no such thing by thy pretended Commission, and the greatness of thy pretended power? Whereby it is manifest that thou art not one of those Witnesses.

And seeing thou pretends a new Commission which is not owned by the Scriptures, or by the Doctrine of Christ and his Apostles, & saist, *Thou hast received power since to the contrary*; (to vindicate thy cursing and damning:) When was the new Covenant and Ministry of the Gospel changed? Or how canst thou make it appear by the Scriptures, that it is not so, seeing thou pretends a contrary Commission to what the Scriptures or the Doctrine of Christ & his Apostles do own. And it is said concerning Christ and the new Covenant that he hath obtained a more excellent Ministry (then that of the old Covenant) by how much also he is the Mediator of a better Covenant, which was established upon better promises, *Heb, 8, 6, 7, 8, 9, 10, 11, 12. And because he continueth for ever, he hath an unchangeable Priesthood* (or Ministry) *wherefore he is able to save*

Truth Ascended 53

them to the uttermost that come unto God by him, because he ever liveth to make intercession for them, as it is written *Heb 7. 24, 25.*

And if none ought to officiate the office of a Minister, Messenger or Ambassador of Christ but such as are appointed by *John Reeves* and thy self (as thou saist) wouldst not thou have the Ministry changed now during thy life? And wouldst not thou have the Ministry of the Gospel to cease and dye at thy death, because thou saist, *Thou art the last that ever shall speak by Commission from God; and that the Lord will never chuse any more after thee whilst the world doth endure.*

And it is evident, That thou wouldst have such a Ministry as the scriptures no where own, and quite contrary to the Doctrine of Christ and his Apostles, and not at all owned by the New Covenant and Ministry of the Gospel.

Because those who are appointed by *John Reeves* and thy self to officiate the office of a Minister, Messenger, or Ambassador of Christ, are such as are not chosen of God to that Work.

Those that are appointed by *John Reeves* and thy self to the Work of the Ministry are such as have commission from God to impower them to officiate the office of a Minister, Messenger or Ambassador of Christ, and are therefore very unfit for so great and glorious a Work.

They are such as are never like to have any Commission from God to impower them to the Work of the Ministry, whilst the World doth endure, and that according to they own doctrine.

They are such as know not the Scriptures, neither can they truly interpret the Scriptures, and that according to thy own sayings:

Because (for proof thereof) thou saist, *That thou art the chosen Witness of the Spirit, and the last that ever shall speak by Commission from God:* Then not those that are appointed by *John Reeves* and thy self, they neither have, nor are not like to have any commission from God to impower them to the work of the Ministry thou hast excluded them from that by thy pretended commission, and the Doctrine thereof. Take notice of that.

And thou saist, *That God will never chuse any more after thee whilst the world doth endure:* If so, then God will never chuse those that are appointed by *John Reeves* and thy self: Therefore they are not fit Ministers, Messengers or Ambassadors of Christ that are appointed by *John Reeves* and they self: First, Because they are not chosen of God to that Work, nor ever like to be whilst the World doth endure. Secondly, Because they have no commission from God to impower them to so great and glorious a Work. And thirdly, Because (according to thy doctrine) they are never like to have any commission from God to impower them (whilst the World doth endure) to officiate the office of Ministers, Messengers or Ambassadors of Christ; and there is no need for them to officiate the office aforesaid, after the end of the world. Mind how thou art confuted.

And thou saist, *No man knows the Scriptures but thyself, nor no man can truly interpret the Scriptures by thy self,* if so, then no those that are appointed by *John Reeves* and thee to the Work of the Ministry, if none ought to officiate the office of a Minister, Messenger or Ambassador of Christ, but such as are appointed by *John Reeves* and thy self: And seeing that those whom you appoint, are not fit for that Work, thou hast as much as in thee lieth, excluded all the Ministers, Messengers and Ambassadors of Christ from the work of the Ministry; take notice of that, And all may behold thy presumption & folly, and how thou art confuted, ensnared, and taken in thy own craftiness; at which thou maist blush, & for evermore be ashamed of. Silence deceit and Deceiver, let truth stop thy mouth, and all such, *Tit* 1, 11.

By what hath been said, it is evident, and remains certainly true; 1. That *John Reeves* and *Lodowick Muggleton* are not the two Witnesses spoken of *Rev 11.3* neither are they in any thing like unto them. 2. That the New Covenant which Christ Jesus is the Mediator of is establish'd upon better promises then the old Covenant was. 3. That the Ministry of the Gospel is more excellent Ministry. 4. That the Priesthood of Christ, or the Ministry of the Gospel is an unchangeable Priesthood or Ministry. 5. That Christ the Saints High Priest, & Mediator of the New-covenant, is able to save them to the uttermost that come unto God by him, because he ever liveth to make intercession for them. 6.That none who are appointed by *John Reeves* and *Lodowick Muggleton*, ought to officiate the office of a Minister, Messenger or Ambassador of Christ, because all who are appointed by *John Reeves* and *Lodowick Muggleton*, to the Work of the Ministery, are very unfit for so great & glorious work. 7. That the deceit ought to be silent; or, that the Deceiver & thou *Lodowick* ought to let Truth stop thy mouth, like a false Prophet as thou art, whose mouths must be stopped, according to *Tit 1, 21.*

Postscript: Or, Concerning Error &c.

If none know the Scriptures but they self; then not those that are appointed by John Reeves *and thee to the work of the Ministry. And as Christ said to the* Sadduces *when they came to ask him whose wife she might be in the resurrection which seven brethren had had to wife, because they all had her; in answer thereunto he said,* Ye err, not knowing the Scriptures nor the power of God, *Matth, 22, 23, 24, 25, 26, 27, 28, 29.*

So say I to thee, That those who are appointed by John Reeves *and thee to the work of the Ministry, the err not knowing the Scriptures nor the power of God, because thou saist, No man knows the Scriptures but thy self: Therefore inasmuch as they err not knowing the Scriptures, they must needs err in their expositions, meanings, pretended preachings and interpretation of Scriptures; so that their pretended preaching of Scriptures is error. 2. Their meanings and conceiving of the Scriptures is error. 3. Their expositions and pretended interpretations of Scriptures is error. And inasmuch as they err, not knowing the Scriptures, they also err not knowing the power of God from whence the holy Scripture is given by inspiration of God, 2* Tim. 3, 16. *And so their whole work about your pretended Ministry, is no better then error, and must needs therefore be very unprofitable, and not fit to be owned.*

Lodowick

IN thy pretended Answer (bearing date May 8 1663) to a Letter of mine to thee entitled, *False judgement reversed, and against testified,* thou saist, *Thou shalt first commend me for setting my name to it. And secondly, For setting down thy words so truly and punctually, that it makes thy Commission and Authority to shine the more bright and clear.*

In answer thereunto I say, It may appear unto all that hears of the same, That I have not perverted or wronged thy words or writings: and also, That thou owns thy saying, and hast not repented of thy errors and blasphemies, but still persist therein, and rejoiceth in the same; and therefore all to whom this may come to be heard, seen and read, may take notice what thou art, and be aware of thee and thy deceit.

Thou saist, *That thou art as true an Ambassador of God, and Judge of mens spiritual estate, as any ever was since the Creation of the world,* & thou only saist it, be leaves it as proofless as the rest; but I do deny it, therefore prove it if thou canst. And whereas thou saist, *If you Quakers and others can satisfie your selves that never was any man commissionated of God to bless and curse, then you shall all escape that curst that I have pronounced apon so many hundreds, and I only shall suffer for cursing others without a Commission from God.* I say in answer unto thee, What is all this to the purpose? Admit that we grant that God did commissionare under the Law to bless & to curst, what is that to thee? Must it necessarily follow, that thou art so commissionated? We are satisfied by the Lord, and assured to the contrary; and we know that we shall escape that curse which thou hast pronounced, and are satisfied, That thou shall suffer for cursing so many hundreds without a Commission from God, as thou hast done.

And whereas thou saist, That *thy Commission is no pretended thing, but as true as Moses, the Prophets and Apostles Commission was*: I do deny it, prove that if thou canst; or else let it be granted for true, That thou hast taken upon thee to lye in the Name of the Lord & that thy pretended Commission is but a counterfeit thing, as doubtless it is and therefore thou maist expect a punishment proportionable to thy offence.

And whereas thou saist, *That no man can come to the assurance of the favour of God now in these days, but in believing that God gave this power unto* John Reeves *and thy self:* As first, That *thou hast power given over all other Gods and infinite Spirits whatsoever. 2. That thou hast the pardoning power and the damning power. 3. That thou hast the keys of Heaven and of Hell, and that none can get into Heaven except thou open the gates. 4. That thou hast power to remit their sins who receive thy doctrine, and to retain and bind their sins more close upon their consciences for their despising or not receiving of thy doctrine. 5. That thou hast power to bless and curse men and women to eternity. 6. That it is not the Light of Christ within, nor the Scriptures, no nor God without, that shall deliver from under thy sentence and curse. 7. That thou art single in doctrine, knowledge, judgement and power, above all men either Prophets or Apostles since the beginning of the world, or that shall ever be hereafter whilst the world doth endure. 8. That thou art the only Judge of the two seeds now in these last dayes. 9. That there is no true Minister, Messenger nor Ambassador of God in the World at this day but thy self; neither shall there be any sent of God after thee to the worlds end. 10. That God will have men and women justified and condemned no other way but by man like themselves. And 11. This power* (saist thou) *hath God given unto me, and in this regard I am the only and alone Judge what shall become of men and women after death; neither shall those that are damned by me, see any other God or judge but me,* I say, if these be not errors, lyes and blasphemy, what it? Let God and his people by the Spirit of his Son sent into their hearts, judge in this case, whereby it may appear what spirit thou art of, and what thy pretended Commission is made up of, even of pride, presumption, lyes, errors, false judgement, delusion and blasphemy, as is apparent.

And through the assistance of God the Father of our Lord Jesus Christ, I hope I shall ever be ready to testifie for the Lord & against thy deceit whilst I have breath, as thereunto moved & directed by the Lord. And though thou say, *That a God without thee spoke to thee by voice of words to the hearing of the ear, when he gave thy pretended Commission unto thee;* yet thou saist, That *no person condemned by thee can make his appeal unto God neither by himself, nor by annoy other;* and why? Thy reason is, *because* (thou saist) *god is not in this world at all.*

I say, if it be true, That none can make their appeal to God, neither by themselves, nor by the Lord Jesus, that are condemned by thee, because thou saist, God is not in this World at all; where was he then when thou received thy pretended Commission, seeing thou saist thou received it from a God without thee, that spake by voice of words to the hearing of the ear? Or, is it not a fiction of imagination of thy brain that thou hast received, and art so confident in? And therefore a strong delusion. And whereas thou saist, That *because I am not under the sentence of thy Commission by verbal words or writing, thou shalt give answer unto my Letter; for* (saist thou) *I never give answer in writing to any one that is under the sentence of my Commission.* I say, That's a ready way to shuffle off a sound answer, or passé by with a lame Reply, or passing false judgement at a distance, instead of vindicating & making good what thou art charged withal; and it seems to the end that thou maist slip off, and leave thy master as proofless as before, thou sends me a Bill of Excommunication or Execration, and passeth sentence to exclude thy self from writing any more in answer unto me: A shuffling trick of deceit indeed. But this I am bold in the Lord to testifie unto thee, That thy judgement is false and erroneous, both as to matter and manner, and is a sign and token of a false Judge that never was sent of the Lord; *for who shall lay anything to the charge of Gods Elect, seeing it is God that justifies?* And it is apparent that thou art a false Judge, because thou condemns God's Elect under pretence of judging the Serpents Seed. Thou art a Deceiver indeed, and I am bold to tell thee of it, and do testifie against thee; and thy judgement I value not, it is but like ashes under the soles of my feet, and will never trouble, because it proceeds from an Antichristian spirit, and will never be laid to my charge by the Lord. Therefore silence Deceiver, and give over thy deceit; for what I have said in vindication of the Truth, and in opposition to thy deceit, shall stand over thee in the sight of God and his people that are guided by the Spirit of his Son sent into their hearts. And truly I admire that *Dorothy Carter*, or any that are sober and conscientious people, should not abhor thy delusion and wicked abomination; for assuredly it is not of God, but of the Devil; and this is my faithful Testimony concerning the same, and I am not ashamed to won it under my Name.

R. Farnsworth

THE END

Something In Answer To Lodowick Muggleton's Book, Which He Calls, The Quakers Neck Broken.

Wherein, in Judging others he hath Judged himself; and wherein he hath Cursed others and Called them, *The Seed of the Serpent,* he hath Cursed himself, and proved himself to be the same; and manifested himself to be of the Spirit of Error, and a false Prophet, and a false Witness and a Satans Messenger, having his commission from him, as by his lies which comes from him doth clearly make manifest out of his own mouth, and he to have Satans Sword, and not Christ's, with which he smites the Righteous, and so hath *Broke* and cut off his own *Neck* with it.

ALSO

Something in Answer to *Thomas Fuller,* in his *Church-History,* to the which he writes to Barron *Brook,* wherein he Rayles against the *Quakers.*

AND,

Something in Answer to *Samuel Clarke,* who calls himself a Pastor, in his Book, called, *A Looking Glass for Saints and Sinners.*

By *G.F.*

London, Printed in the Year, 1667.

Muggleton,

Thou saist, *That* Quakers *will not bestow a penny in any Writing but their own (in the 82 page of thy Book) let it cost them never so much pains in Writing, and charge in Printing.*

Answ. This is a Lye known to the Printers and Stationers, and that thou hast manifested a lying Spirit, for the Stationers and Booksellers at *London* in this know thy Spirit to be a Lying Spirit; for there are few *Quakers* in *England,* but they have bought Bookes that were not of their own Printing; and therefore what fruits can be lookt for from a lying Spirit, but Cursings and a lying Commission; for he that will lye in one thing will lye in another: But doth not *Muggleton* grumble because he hath not Money for his Lyes and Curses of the *Quakers?*

Muggleton saith, *It is a vain thing to talk of heavenly Secrets to the* Quakers, *for they will not bestow a penny of them, &c.*

Answ. This is another Lye; for heavenly things are esteemed of, by us, which thou (that art one of the Scorners) callest *Quakers;* but, it seems *Muggletons* heavenly Secrets (as thou callest them) are Money-worth, and may be bought with a price, and he is troubled because he cannot get a price for them, it seems; and this shews an earthly Spirit, wherewith he Blasphemes and Curses so much: And the *Quakers* (as thou callest them) they are free with their Books to give them to any one to Read, but it is a hard thing to get any of thy Books, for several of Friends have gone to thy Disciples to have gotten one of them, and thy Disciples kept them so close and so secret, that they would not let them be brought forth to Light and be seen, lest thy Deeds, Curses and Lyes (which thou callest, *heavenly secrets)* should be made manifest: for the *Quakers* in the divine Light, Power and Spirit of Christ Jesus, have and do comprehend and savour thy spirit, and thy Scoffes at the divine Light of Christ Jesus within.

Mugl. Thou saist, *Thou hast a Commission without thee to Preach, &c.*

Answ. Here thou hast manifested Darkness. Is there any Commission from God, but the understanding of it is given to man by the divine Light within: For, as the Apostle saith, *When it pleased the Father to reveal his Son in me,* he preached him.

Mugl. Thou saist, *That the right Devil became flesh?* and, *The Soul is Mortal; and though speaketh of the knowledge of the Lord, and the Scriptures.*

Answ. Where do the Scriptures say, That the right Devil became flesh? And,The Soul is Mortal? For, God breathed into man the breath of Life, through which he became a Living Soul: And this breath of Life by which man became a Living Soul, Is this *Mortal?* Is this thy Knowledge? *Make* this good by Scripture.--- *Muggleton,* Is this thy Divine Heavenly Mystery?

Mugl. *Thou hast given thy Sentence upon the People called* Quakers, *upon some Information, because some have informed thee, that they have spoken against thy Commission, and yet thou art not certain whether it be true or not.*

Answ. This is very like thy spirit, who judgest by Reports, and yet thou wilt pass Sentence, whether thy Witness speak true or no, in this thou hast manifested thy undiscerning, that thou hast not the savour to judge the Spirits; for thou saist, *If thy Judgement afterward doth not prove true, then it is of no value.* — So thou hast manifested what

Something in Answer

Spirit thou dost judge withal, not to be the Spirit of Truth. So thy spirit is manifested clear enough to be a rash, erring, lying, deceitful spirit; and the People, called *Quakers,* do comprehend thee, (who are of the Faith of *Abraham)* and by thy condemning others, thou condemnest thy self, and art come under the chain of darkness, in all thy Curses and Blasphemies, against the divine and spiritual Light of Christ Jesus, who according to thy own writing canst not discern Reporters.

Mugl. *And whereas thou saist, thou art a Witness of the Spirit, and givest the Sentence of Eternal Damnation.*

Answ. In this thou manifestest another Lye, for thou hast manifested not the Spirit of discerning, as before mentioned, and so thy spirit to be a dark lying spirit, and so in condemning another, thou hast condemned thy self, and thy own words will be thy burden.

Then again *Muggleton,* thou saiest, *Thou accusest no man of sin.*

Yet in a few Lines after thou accuses the *Quakers* of sin and blasphemy. Here thy own spirit hath given thee the lye, which is found in thy mouth. In the same *Page 73* in manifesting a spirit of darkness and lyes, and not of God; and therefore hast thou judged and condemned a People, which Judgement comes upon thy self and touches them not; so thy Spirit is a Spirit of presumption and cannot judge in Spiritual matters, which thou so much boastes of.

Muggle. Thou saiest, *Thou judgest as the Prophets and Apostles did.*

Answ. In this thou hast manifested another lye. The Apostles said, *Bless and Curse not.* And *Peter* saith, *Out of the same Fountain there cometh not sweet Water and bitter, blessings, and cursings,* which come out of thy muddy Fountain, and from a lying Spirit.

Mugl. Thou saist, *God hath given thee to know the Law, and Book of Scriptures, more than all them men of the World hath this day.*

Answ. This is *Lucifer* like, who art ignorant of the Spirit of God, and contradicts them. See in the same *Page* aforementioned, who goest contrary to the Scriptures, shewing another Spirit then they did that gave them forth, so art of the Serpent that cursed Spirit whose mouth is full of Cursing; and leads People into new Fangles and Imaginations.

Mugl. Thou saiest, *The Scriptures stand upon the true God and right Devil.*

Answ. The Scriptures of Truth were given forth from the Spirit of God, and not from such an earthly lying spirit as thine is. The Scriptures of Truth which speak of God, and his People, and of the wicked One the Devil, and of wicked Men, &c. But where doth the Scripture speak of a right Devil?

Mugl. Thou saiest, *No* Quaker *can have any state of Eternal Life that denyes Christs Flesh and Bones which Suffered, &c.*

Answ. Here are more of thy Lyes, which proceed from the lying spirit of Satan, The *Quakers* are Witnesses of Christs death and Suffering, and do not deny his Flesh and Bones, who remain in the Heavens until the restitution of all things, and they are Heires of the power of an endless Life; and are flesh of his flesh, and bone of his bone: and so thy lying spirit thou hast manifested, and thy ignorance of them, and of the Spirit that gave forth the Scriptures.

Mug. And thou saiest, *Those that receive the Commission of the Spirit judge of men and womens Spiritual and Eternal state; and thou saiest, that God hath made thee chief Judge.*

Answ. Here thou boastest thy self and seemest to strengthen thy fleshly Disciples, and hast brought thy self under the judgment of Christ, who saith, *Bless and Curse not,* who is the chief Judge, and judgeth righteously, but thou judgest with a lying Spirit, for Christ is the chief Judge, but thou saiest, *He is not within thee, but without thee;* who callest thy self a chief Judge, who must know thy own condition before thou canst know others.

Mugl. Thou saiest, *God hath given thee the Book of the Law, which is the Scriptures, into thy hands.*

Answ. By that Law thou art judged out of thy own mouth, which saith, *Bless and Curse not.* And this is another of thy lyes, and thee and thy Disciples know not the Spiritual and Eternal State of men and women, and so cannot judge but amiss of them with your lying spirit; for thou who callest thy self a *Witness,* being a lying spirit, thou canst beget no other but a lying spirit in thy Disciples, and the lying spirit knows not the condition of its self nor others.

Mugl. Thou saiest, *Thou hast seen some of thy Disciples have passed sentence of Cursing upon others, and it hath turned back again upon themselves.*

Answ. This we believe, That both thine and thy Disciples sentence is turned, and will turn back again upon thy self, and upon thy Disciples; and all the dark sentences you have or shall pronounce with your lying spirits.

Something in Answer

And *Muggleton* saith, *Peter was chief Judge among the Apostles; so there must be one particular man among them to be chief in all places; so* John Reeve *and himself were chosen.*

Answ. Here thou hast contradicted thy self again, for thou saith, There must be One in all places, and thou hast set up Two. And another lie thou speakest, of *Peter* being the Chief of the Apostles, so chief judge. Read in the *Acts* and thou mayest see it was *James* that gave the Sentence in the Council of the Apostles concerning the Churches, and not *Peter:* And this thy Lye concerning *Peters* being Chief, is contrary to the Spiritual Law of Christ Jesus, who saith, *They shall not exercise Lordship one over another, for they are Brethren;* that was the way of the Gentiles to do so, and the Pharisees, which he reproved: which is the way now of *John Reeve* and *Muggleton.* And here is thy ignorance of the Scriptures sufficiently manifested, and thy Spirit of Error in perverting of them, and hath brought thy self under the Judgement of Christ and his Disciples, and all the Faithful, to be a lying spirit, and a false witness, and hast ensnared thy self in thy words, who wouldest set thy self up like a Pope.

And thou lyest, and callest thy Commission to be the *Commission of the Spirit of God,* and scoffest and mockest at the Divine and Spiritual Light of Christ in the People of God called *Quakers,* which is and will be thy condemnation, together with all thy curses, and blasphemies, and lies in thy third page.

Now where *Muggleton* goes about to make people believe that *Cain* was not begotten by *Adam,* as he was flesh and bone, which shews another spirit of Error, and not that Spirit that gave forth the Scriptures, for *Evah* saith, *I have begotten a man from the Lord;* and thy false witness, and thy lying spirit, makes as though *Cain* should be begotten by the Reprobate Angels. And the Scriptures saith, Adam *knew* Evah *his Wife, and she conceived, and brought forth a Son, and called his name* Cain; and she said *She had gotten a man from the Lord.* And thou speakest as though he were begotten from the Devil, and by him. So thou hast manifested, who is thy Father, the Serpent, thou speakest of.

Mug. Thou sayest, *That God created the person of the Serpent, who was more glorious then the holy Angels.*

A. Where findest thou a Scripture for this? thou hast presumed above what is written. What is the Serpent above the Angel of the Covenant, and above the Angel of his presence, and above *Michael* the Arch Angel, and above the Angel that flies through the midst of Heaven with the everlasting Gospel to preach? Was not *Adam* and *Evah* set above the Serpent before they fell, when they were set above all that God made? And thou saist, *That* Edward Bourn *is the Seed of the Serpent,* in thy rage, because he hath witnessed against thy Lyes, which thou callest *Pure Truth,* which is contrary to the Apostles and to Christ.

And *Muggleton* saith, *That he and* Reeve *are the Last Witnesses of God on the Earth.* And saith, *He hath Cursed* Edward Bourn, *and Damned him Soul and Body from the presence of God and his Angels;* And then he scoffes at the Divine and Spiritual Light of Christ within. See his 6th *Page.*

Ah poor Creature, thou art guided with the spirit of darkness, that knowest not thy own condition, who art full of darkness and errour, lyes and rage: *For God hath not left himself without witness in the Earth; and there are three that bear witness in the Earth, the Spirit, the Water and the Blood;* and *Muggleton* is but one, for *Reeve* is dead, he saith: And they that have the Water, have the Spirit, and have the Blood which are the Witnesses; *And keep the Testimony of Jesus, and love not their lives unto death,* as *Muggleton* did, else how got he out of *Darby* Prison for his Blasphemies? How shuffled he out of *Darby shire,* when he was touched a little with the Powers of the Earth; but he knows the People of God will use no violence to him, and therefore his is so liberal in his Curses and Damnings, even of the Souls of People, though he knows not yet what it is; who hath shewed another Spirit than Christs, and his faithful Witnesses the Apostles, who say, *Bless and Curse not,* but thine is a Curser. But *Edward Bourn,* who is in the divine Spirit and Light of Christ, thou canst not Judge nor Curse, who knowest not his condition nor thy own; but they are turned back upon thy own head, and sealed with the Spirit.

Mugl. Thou saist, *The Light of Christ which the* Quakers *speak of, will vanish away like the Smoak, and come to nothing.*

Answ. We say as Christ saith, *He is the Light,* and his divine and spiritual Light will be thy Condemnation, as in *John* the third, but thy Cursings, and Damnings, and Lyes, will be all Fuel for to kindle the Fire of Hell against thee, and the Light of Christ will abide when all thy Lyes and Smoak is condemned by it.

Mugl. And thou saiest, *That the* Quakers *will have no person of Christ at all.*

Answ. This is another of thy lies, for we say as the Apostle said, who spoke in the Person of Christ; and thus thou addest lie to lie. But thou that hatest the Light, what hast thou to do to talk of the Holy Ghost, or Christ, or God, which hatest his Light, and art not reformed.

And whereas *Muggleton* saith, *The Quakers were of the Ranter.*

Answ. I say, *Muggleton* and his Disciples might have taken that to themselves, who say, *The Soul is Mortal,* and scoff at Christ's being within, and by their false witness would cast a blemish upon them that are of the righteous Seed; but they are far enough above it, it touches them not. And *Muggleton* is offended, because some of the People called *Quakers* have been Sword-men and Ranters. Let *Muggleton* look among his own Disciples and see if none of them have been Sword-men and Ranters: and are they not so still? And if them that are *Quakers* were some of them *Ranters,* they have forsaken their Vice, and broken their Swords into Plow-shares, which I hardly believe that any of *Muggletons* Disciples have done it yet. Thou mayest find fault with *Peter,* which had a Sword, and the *Jewes* which were Sword-men, which after *Peter* was to put up his Sword by the command of Christ, &c. and the *Jewes* also when they came to the Kingdom of Christ, as *Peter* did; and we are of the same Faith of the Apostles, and Church in the Primitive time, who were to love one another, and enemies also.

And thou makest a large discourse of the Mortality of the Soul, and sayest, *It's Mortal,* when the *Quakers* queried of thee, Whether it were Immortal or no? And in stead of answering, thou railest, and callest them *Devils,* not worthy to be answered to, as touching the Soul; and callest them deep Secrets, &c.

Now all People may see whether this be an answer by one that professeth himself to be a Witness, and can Interpret Scripture; whose evil words hath corrupted his manners; but this hath manifested thy insufficiency and thy ignorance. If they had been Gainsayers, thou shouldst have convinced them; in stead of that thou fallest a cursing of them, and callest them, *The Children of the Serpent:* Who art one of the Spirit of the World in thy Judgement, judging the Children of the Light, of the Most High, with thy dark spirit, contrary to the Spirit which gave forth the Scriptures, which was to convince gain-sayers, and to be ready to give a reason of the hope that was in them.

Mugl. And thou saiest, *That Christ is not in the Quakers.*

Answ. And why; because they bear testimony against thy lying spirit, and because the *Quakers* say, they are in the Spirit of Christ before Antichrist was; these are exceeding lies.

Mug. Saith, *Antichrist hath been ever since* Cain *in the world, Page* 15.

Answ. Here all People that will not stop their eyes, that have the least spark of truth to guide them, and are guided by it, may comprehend *Muggleton,* for you know, *That Christ was before the world began;* yea, before *Cain* was, and so before Antichrist was. Christ was glorified with the Father before the world began; and the *Quakers* which have the Spirit of Christ, comprehend *Muggleton* with his lyes and his lying spirit, together with all his Cursings, and his Damnings, and hath Judged him with all the Spirit of Christ, and there the sentence is gone over his head.

Muggleton saith, *That the* Quakers *Christ hath never a Body, which they have gotten within them.*

Anw. Here is more of *Muggletons* lies, who scoffes at Christ within, which we and the Apostles preached, warning every man, and presenting every man perfect in Christ Jesus; and Christ whom we preach in you, the hope of glory. And thus the false witness scoffes at Christ within; and Christ, we say, hath a Body, for that which descended ascended, and hath a Spirit, and the *Quakers* are of his Body, and as the Scripture saith, *A Body hast thou prepared me.*

Muggleton Jeers, and saith, *The* Quakers *are sent by a Light within them to preach, &c.*

Answ. In this thou hast shewed thy ignorance of the true Commission: that which gives the knowledge of the glory of God in the face of Christ Jesus is the Light within in the heart, *2 Cor.4.* that which makes manifest is Light, and they are Ministers of the Spirit and not of the Letter.

And Muggleton saith, *Reason the Devil, thinks to have a Reward from Heaven, for he will preach in his Name, and cast out Devils in his Name, &c.*

Answ. What is the Devil dividing himself? Where was the Devil called *Reason* in the Scripture? And dost thou not say in another *Page* thou wilt shew People thy Reason without any distinction, and then thou judgest thy self out of thy own mouth to be the *Devil Reason.*

And again People may see thy ignorance, that they that had cast out Devils & preached in his Name, it was by the Power of God, which they were departed from into the lying spirit which thou art in; and so departing from the Power of God in the Iniquity, Christ bids them depart from him, and this is thy interpreting of Scripture. Here again thou hast sufficiently manifested thy spirit, which is comprehended by the Truth.

Muggleton saith, *The World can hardly bear his Message.*

Answ. Yes; they that be in the same spirit of Cursing will bear thee, who, it seems, have been in this Cursing Damning spirit a matter of eleven years, and the world will love her own.

And Muggleton saith, *His mouth is full of Cursing, and that is his Commission, &c.*

Answ. It may be *Muggleton* may frighten some evil Consciences, in whom his cursed Spirit may enter, and terrifie them that are ignorant and disobedient to the true Spirit of Christ, which saith, *Bless and Curse not;* who is the same yesterday, and to day, and the same for ever.

And *Muggleton* saith, *He rejoyceth in his Cursings, and them that he doth Curse and Sentence, shall never see any other God or Judge.*

Answ. How now *Muggleton,* Art thou become God and Judge? Must not all appear before the Judgement seat of Christ, to have their Sentence and Reward from him, whether they have done good or evil? And every eye shall see him. What will *Muggleton* give all the Prophets and Apostles the lye? Do not all see him here to be in a lying spirit, and not in the Spirit of Christ nor the Apostles, nor hath he the mind of Christ, but is comprehended here to be of another mind.

And Muggleton saith, *Because he hath passed Sentence upon the* Quakers, *They shall never grow to have more experience in Visions and Revelations, but shall wither.*

Answ. Here are more Lyes of *Muggletons,* for the Truth spreads, yea and will spread over the World more and more, as thousands can witness since *Muggleton* began to Curse, who hath been a Curser these eleven years, or thereabouts. And all the Curses that thou hast cursed upon several that thou hast named, they are clear over thy spirit, yea, in the Spirit of God, before they cursing spirit was, who are redeemed by Christ, who became a Curse, and hath redeemed from under the Curse.

And Muggleton saith, *That Scripture is nothing to him, wherein Christ saith,* Bless and Curse not; *and saith, That was before Christ was ascended.*

Answ. Here again *Muggleton* shews his Ignorance of Scripture and the spirit of Errour; for Christ said, *Bless and Curse not,* to his Apostles, which command they practiced after Christ was ascended, and bid them lay away Cursings, &c. And so he would make that Christ was not the same to day as he was yesterday, and so for ever. Thus he shuffles up and down, whose cursed spirit is like unto his doctrine, and that power which was given to *Peter* was given to the other Apostles, to bind on earth, and to loose, &c. And *Peter* was not made Head, as thou lyingly sayest: But thou wouldest be like a Pope.

And Muggleton saith, *That* Peter *and the rest of the Apostles were not tyed to the words of Christ, after they had received their Commission.*

Answ. Here all People in the Truth may see and comprehend thy spirit, because Muggleton is gone from the words of Christ, and is not tyed to them, but to his own Curses; yet he belyes the Apostles, and saith, *They were not tyed to his words.* So his own lying will not serve his turn, but he must belye others, and make People believe that the Apostles were not tyed to the words of Christ, as though they preached themselves as he doth; for they preached what they had heard and seen of him, and what they had handled, and preached not themselves. How canst thou publish such lies in Print without blushing.

And then *Muggleton* boasts of his wisdom above all men in the Scriptures, wherein he shews his ignorance, and that none can know nor interpret the Scriptures but himself; wherein thou hast shewed thy ignorance sufficiently to all that do not stop their eyes.

And *Muggleton* saith, *That none must be Ministers, or Messengers, or Embassadors of Christ, but such as are authorized of* John Reeve *and himself.* And then he Scoffes at the divine Light of Christ within.

Answ. Thou hast manifested thy insufficiency enough either interpreting or knowing the Scriptures by thy lying spirit. And every one must approve themselves to God, for to him they must give an account, and not to *Muggletons* lying spirit, and *John Reeves.*

And *Muggleton* saith the words of Christ over again, which was spoken to the Apostles, which is, *Bless and Curse not;* and saith, these words be nothing to him, yet he saith, *If any man preach any other Gospel, let him be accursed, then the Apostles preached.* So here any man may see how he hath confounded himself again, for the Apostle saith, *Bless and Curse not.* So *Muggleton* here hath brought the Curse upon his own head, who rejoyceth in his own Cursing.

And Muggleton saith, *The Quakers Judgement is from the Letter of this Scripture without them, or else from the Light within them, and this is not worth a straw.*

Answ. Mark this mans discerning, together with his unsavoury words. *Their Judgement* (saith he) *is either from the Scriptures, or from the Light within, and this* (saith he) *is not worth a straw.* But whither it is from he hath not manifested. But his Judgement is neither from the

Something in Answer
69

divine Light within, nor from the Letter of the Scriptures, his cursing and damning men and womens Souls to Hell. We have tryed his spirit, and the Quakers Judgement is from the Spirit that gave forth the Scriptures; the Spirit of Christ which was before Scripture was in the divine and spiritual Light of Christ within.

Muggleston saith: *The Quakers deny the Son to be a person in the Form of a Man, which suffered death, and is risen, &c.*

Answ. These are more of thy lyes, for we own the Son of God and his Flesh, Bone and Blood, who was Crucified, and laid in the Grave, and Rose again, and sits at the Right Hand of God, and as Members of him; and therefore thou utterest forth thy folly, and thy Lyes and thy shame to cover thy self.

And because the *Quakers* say, Christ is the express Image of the Fathers Substance, and they own the Father and the Holy Ghost, and they are flesh of his flesh, and bone of his bone, and they have the mind of Christ; *Muggleton* saith, *This is a Riddle to me.*

Answ. We do believe it, that this is a Riddle to the Lying Prophet and false Witness, that yet boasts of knowing the Scriptures, but is ignorant of them, and interpreting the Scriptures, and the knowledge of Christ, which now is become a Riddle to him, which is God manifested in the flesh, seen of Angels, believed of in the Word, and by us who are of his flesh and bone.

And *Muggleton* thou speakest of some *Eastcheap,* and one thou callest a *Lubberly fellow,* that denied Christs flesh and bone, but this is like the rest of thy lies, together with thy evil spirit that despiseth Gods workmanship.

Muggleton saith, *That the person of Christ, nor his Essence, cannot be in the World, nor in the* Quakers, *nor in Himself, who is a chosen Messenger of him.*

Answ. If the Being of Christ, or his Essence, or Nature, or Power be not in thee which is in his Saints, and was revealed in the Apostles, that spake in the Person of Christ, thou hast manifested thy self to be no Minister of him.

And Muggleton saith, *He could never find any* Quaker *that would own God to be a Person in form of a Man, which shews the* Quakers *darkness.*

Answ. Here *Muggleton* the Prophet hath shewed his Ignorance of the Scriptures, for the Scripture saith, *That God is a Spirit,* And Christ saith, *That a Spirit hath not flesh and bone as I have.* And, *God fills*

Heaven and Earth; God saith so of himself. Herein thou hast shewed thy ignorance and darkness.

And Muggleton saith, *That Christ hath a distinct Body of flesh and bone of his own.*

Answ. Is Christ distinct from his Saints? then how come they to be of his flesh and bone? But this is a Riddle to the Prophet *Muggleton.*

And Muggleton saith, *The Quakers blaspheme, in saying, according to the flesh Christ was of* Abraham, *and of* David, *&c. for they were* Jewes *that persecuted Christ.*

Answ. In this thou hast shewed thy Ignorance of Scripture; and as for the Blasphemies, they are from thy own lying spirit, for according to the flesh he was of *David, Rom. 1.3. For the Lord hath sworn with and Oath, that of the fruit of his loynes, according to the flesh, he would raise up Christ. Which took not upon him the nature of Angels, but the Seed of* Abraham. *Of whom are the Fathers, and of whom concerning the flesh Christ came,* Rom.9. And Acts 2. *He took not upon him the nature of Angels, but the Seed of* Abraham. And though the *Jewes* had transgressed the Law of God and the Prophets, and gone into the evil Seed, and turned against Christ; yet this altereth not the fulfilling the Prophets Prophecies of him, nor Gods words, that saw of whom he should come; though thou in thy darkness and evil nature of the transgressing *Jewes* knowest him not, nor his generation, no more than they did being out of the Faith of *Moses* and the Prophets, and Apostles, as the *Jewes* were.

Muggleton saith, *This Body of Christ, which is the only God;* Yet contradicts himself again, and saith, *The Quakers know no other Christ but according to the flesh, that is, according to the Seed of Reason, and Reason is the Devil he saith.*

Answ. Here may all see thy darkness and confusion: For God is a Spirit, and God is in Christ, who prepared Christ a Body; there cannot be Christ without God, for Christ signifies, *the anointed God.* And the Quakers do know Christ in the flesh. And the Apostle saith, *They had known Christ after the flesh, but henceforth they would know him so no more.* And most of thy talk of him is about his flesh, and art ignorant of what thou talkest, or what thou affirmest; and Christ his Body is above the Devil, for his flesh saw no corruption, which is a Mystery to thee who art full of darkness, even in the very Pit of it I feel thee; and the Spirit of God is over thee, and Christs flesh and his body is over thee, who art as ignorant of it as thou art of the *Quakers* Principles.

Muggleton saith, *The Scriptures take no notice of the outward body of flesh.*

Answ. Here dost thou not give thy self the lye again? Didest thou not say before, it spoke of the Body of Christ, his flesh and his bone? And doth it take notice of no outward bodies of flesh? and also doth not the Apostle say, *Your Bodyes are the Temple of God;* and, *Glorify God in your Bodies and Spirits, which are the Lords?* And *Your Bodies are not for Fornication? And a Body thou hast given me, to do they Will, O God? Christ was manifested in our mortal Bodies.* And what? can Muggleton see no Scripture that takes notice of outward Bodies. Yet the Prophet *Muggleton* saith, he hath all Scripture given into his hands. This is one of *Muggletons* Ranting Principles.

Muggleton saith, *The* Quakers *make no distinction betwixt the Person of Christ, and the Light of Christ.*

Answ. This is another of thy lies. For he suffered according to the flesh, and rose again by the same power that quickned us, who enlightneth us; yet we say, *That Christ is the Light of the World, and enlightens every man &c.* and God is Light, and was in Christ, and the Light gives the knowledge of him, which thou scoffs at.

Muggleton saith, *The* Quakers *Christ is an Imaginary Christ, because they say, according to the flesh he is of* Abraham, *and of* David; *and* Abrahams *Children according to the flesh are of* Cain.

Answ. Here again are thy lies, who art the lying witness; Was not *Jacob, Isaac,* and *Samuel,* and the Prophets, of the Seed, and of the Flesh of *Abraham?* Did not Christ take upon him the Seed of *Abraham;* and not the Nature of Angels, but the Seed of *Abraham?* This is thy interpreting with thy dark spirit, and with thy ignorance. Now those Jews that did not live in the Spirit, to the Law of God, as the Prophets, *Abraham, Isaac,* and *Jacob* did, but were persecutors of such as were in the Life and Faith, those were of *Cain,* and in his Nature.

Muggleton saith, Solomons *writings are no Scripture, which you bring to prove your Scripture Light, and knowledge of Christ by, for* Solomons *writings are no more then the* Apocrypha.

Answ. It's like that all Scripture is no more of authority to thee, then *Solomon* and the Apocrypha, for *Solomon* saith, speaking of Christ and the Church, *He was with him before the Hills were setled; and was by him when all things were made;* but thou hast manifested another Spirit, which differs from *Solomons,* shewing thy ignorance of his words.

Muggleton saith, *That none can interpret Scripture but himself, and none knows God and Christ but himself, and he is made Judge of Scripture.*

Answ. This is all self, who hath manifested thy self to be out of the Spirit that gave forth Scripture, in a Spirit that hath uttered forth these lies, who hast them from thy Father the Devil, and not from God; this is the Word of the Lord to thee.

Muggleton saith, *The* Quakers *have no understanding from God and Christ, but the dead Light, from other mens words, and then he follows on with railings.*

Answ. These are more of thy lies. Our knowledge is from the Father, and Christ, and the Holy Ghost, which leads into all Truth, and so our understanding is by the Spirit, and not from others dead Letters and mens Words; who are come to the Just mens Spirits, and God the Judge of all, yea, and are lead by the Spirit that gave forth Scriptures, which is before it was; by which we comprehend both *Muggleton* the lying Prophet and Witness, and his Father.

Mugl. saith, *The Quakers were never sent from God without them, but only a Light within them; and though it be the Light of Christ, yet it will not give them the knowledge of God, but will perish.*

Answ. Did you ever hear such lies from one that calls himself a Prophet, and the Last Witness? who hath manifested himself and his Father, who is a Lyar from the beginning. What, will not the Light of Christ give the knowledge of God? Doth no he here give the Apostles the lye? who say, *The Light that shineth in their hearts will give them the Light of the knowledge of the glory of God in the face of Christ Jesus.* 2 Cor. 4.

And also *Muggleton* blasphemously saith, *That this Light of Christ will perish.*

Answ. This will be his condemnation, and shews his ignorance of the Scriptures; For, *He that believes hath the Witness in himself.* And with the heart he believes, and then Confession is made unto Salvation, which is Christ. So, can any be sent of God, but first he must have it in his heart, before confession to Christ, his Salvation, be made, and preach him? Doth any man know the things of God but the Spirit of God? And doth not the Scripture say, *That God will walk in you, and dwell in you?* This is all without *Muggleton,* who is without God in the world, who scoffes at the Light within, but this Light will be his condemnation, *John 3.*

Something in Answer

Mugl. Saith, *Those men which spoke forth the Scriptures, knew what the Light of Christ was, but knew nothing truly what the Light of Christ is.*

Answ. Here is more of thy confusion, and lyes, and contradictions; Can man know the Light of Christ what it was, and yet know who doth enlighten every man that cometh into the world, with a saving Divine Light, which is the condemnation of every one that hateth it; had we ever seen Letter of Scripture, or any man: and therefore the false Prophet is ignorant of us, and our Commission, of speaking in the Power, and Spirit, and in the divine Light of Christ, had we never seen Letter of Scripture nor man.

Muggle. Saith, *That the Light within will avail nothing, for there are but three estates;* Egypt, *the* Wilderness, *and the Land of* Canaan.

Answ. Here are more of thy lies, and confusions, and ignorance of the false Witness and Prophet, who followeth his own spirit to say, *That the Light will avail nothing: For, the Light of Christ gives the knowledge of the glory of God in the face of Christ.* And *believing in the Light, they come to be children of the Light.* And thou givest the Apostle and Christ the lye, and sayest, *It will avail nothing.* Who art worse than the *Pharisees,* and like unto the *Ranters,* and all other Professions, and become darker than some of them. And what, is there nothing but *Egypt,* and the *Wilderness,* and *Canaan* in man? thou saiest, *There is none but these three states.* It seems thou hast not found *Babylon* in thee, that is not yet discovered to the false Prophet, and false Witness; and the Prophet hath not seen *Sodom* yet, neither hath he seen *Judas, Ishamael* nor *Cain,* nor prophane *Esau,* not the cursed Speaker the Apostle speaks of: And much more might be spoken to the blind Prophet and false Witness, which he might see in him, which the *Quaker,* as he calls them, have seen and comprehended, *Page 27.*

And *Muggleton* saith, *The Quakers propounded Questions to him that they could not answer themselves; which,* he saith, *he never propounded any, but he could answer himself.*

Answ. This is *Muggletons* shuffle, in stead of Answering thy Queries, we know thy Answers are a company of Railings and Cursings.

This Devil, saith Muggleton, *spoken of in Scripture, is nothing but the spirit of Reason, that kild the Righteous in a killing power.*

Here you see *Muggletons* Judgement and Spirit; For, to say, *The Devil, who is Reason, kild the Just;* For he it is that leads to judge unrighteously, and to do unjustly; and unreasonable men that have not the Faith that is from thy Father the Devil, who puteth Reason for Unreason, and so Light for Darkness; and unreasonable, men have not faith. Shewing, that a reasonable man hath the Faith of the Elect; And so now by *Muggletons* Argument, *it was Reason that kild* Abel, and Reason that doth all unreasonable things; and it was Reason that led People to steal, to cozen, and to cheat, to do unjustly and unrighteously. For this is *Muggletons* Commission, to *Curse*.

For saith *Muggleton, Who is a Prophet and the Last Witness? who hath a Commission to Curse? The Devil,* he saith, *hath no other spirit but Reason.*

So he hath clearly manifested his spirit to be of the unreasonable, and so a false Prophet, and a false voice, from the Devil, the god of the world, which was a lyar from the beginning, and an unreasonable one; for all they that went into the Devils Power, and had not the Faith, were unreasonable, seeing it was the Faith that made People unreasonable; but this is *Muggletons* work he hath from his god of the world. And the Apostle saith, *People must give a reason of their Faith,* then *Muggleton* saith *They must do it by the Devil,* for he calleth the *Devil, Reason,* without distinction. Was there ever heard such Blasphemy!

Mugl. And he saith, *It was the very God-head-Life that suffered Death.*

Answ. All may see *Muggletons* darkness, here again, of God, and Christ. For Christ he suffered in the flesh; he did not dye as he was God, for if he had died as he was God, why did he cry, *Why hast thou forsaken me?* So he suffered as in the flesh. And much more might be said to this, which would be a Riddle to *Muggleton, Page, 29.*

Mugl. Saith, *He knowes that the Quakers do not regard to look into other Writings but their own; therefore he leaves them to the conceited Light of Christ within.*

Answ. Here are two more lyes from the scoffing Prophet. As for others Writings, we have tried them more than thee, or any other People have done, for we do try all things; and thou who art so full of darkness within thee, canst not abide the Light, but art one of them that hated the Light, and callest the divine and spiritual Light of Christ within, *a Conceit;* which will be thy eternal condemnation, whose Cursings hath blinded thee.

And *Muggleton,* thy Cursing *Samuel Hutton,* and *William Smith,* and Damning their Souls and Bodies, and saying, *Your Light within, and your God without, cannot deliver you from my Sentence.*

Answ. Poor silly Captive, who knows not what the Soul, nor God, nor Christ, nor his Light, nor his Life is; and in that thou hast Damned others, thou hast damned thy self; so a clamorous Woman hath plucked her own house upon her own head; but Christ the Light, which is manifested within, will bruise thy god of the worlds head, though he be a Prince of darkness, and God through Christ hath delivered us, and set us above all Curses and cursed Spirits, Glory to his Name for ever, and thy Cursings and Damnings go away like a smoak, and turn back into thy own Bowels and Temple, which is filled with it; and we can try Spirits, and have tried thine to be as bad as any in the world.

Muggleton saith, *The Quakers have done much good, they have cast out Devils, and yet they are of the Seed of the Serpent.*

Answ. What contradictions are these, *Muggleton?* the Devil is out of Truth, there is no truth in him, but speaks of himself, as thou dost, he is a lyar from the beginning; for he that doth good is of God, and the *Quakers,* thou saist, *have done much good,* and therefore they must be of God, and not of the Serpent (as thou saiest they are) but this, *Muggleton* the Witness cannot see *Babylon* in him here.

Though *Muggleton* pretends God, yet he is of his Father, who is a Lyar from the beginning; thy language betrayes thee, the Devil doth evil; he that is of him, like thee, is the same. He that is of God, as before-said, doth good, for they that have the least spark of the divine Light ruling in them, can judge both thy spirit and thy words, to be of thy Father, that is out of Truth.

Mugg. saith, *God, the King of Heaven, is not in the world at all.*

Answ. Here are more of thy lyes, for thou dost confess that Christ is God; and *John* saith, *He was in the world, and the world knew him not.* Here thou hast given *John* the Evangelist the lye. And yet in another place, thou sayest, *That thou art John Baptist.* See what lyes and confusion is this. And the Apostle saith, *He is in all, and through all, and above all, God blessed for evermore.* And, *Is there any voyce or language where he is not.* And the true Prophet saith, *He fills Heaven and Earth.* But the falst Prophet saith, *God, the King of Heaven, is not in this World at all.* But the true Prophet saith, *He beholds all the actions of men, the evil and the good.* And *David* saith, *If he were in the nethermost Hell, he was there.* But *Muggleton* knows not that yet, who manifests his darkness and his ignorance of the Region of all the holy men of God, of their Circuit and Passage, who passed through the paths of Hell, and Death, and saw through depths and heights, *Page. 39.*

Mugl. Saith, *There is great need that God should make some mortal man Judge of the Quakers,* whom he calleth, *A cursed Sect.*

Answ. This mortal man is *Muggleton* the false Witness, so no spiritual man, for the *spiritual man judgeth all things;* and so this mortal man judgeth with his mortal spirit, and mortal judgement, and a mortal witness, and a mortal message, with a voice from his Fathers dark spirit the Devil, and yet this mortal man *Muggleton* is Judge, is the Last witness; so he is Judged out of his mouth, that he cannot judge all things, for it is a *spiritual man that judgeth all things.*

And as for *Muggleton* saying, *The cursed Sect of Quakers.*

Answ. They who are in scorn called *Quakers,* are it the power of God before Sects were, who comprehend thy mortal judgement. Yet *Muggleton* in another place commends the *Quakers,* and after he curseth them, soul, and body, and spirit to all Eternity; this is *Muggletons Babel* and Confusion, who will sink himself with his Curses, and lay more upon himself than he can bear at last, when his fuel is set on fire; and the *Quakers* will be clear of him.

Mugl. Saith, *A Commission is given to him and* John Reeve, *by the voyce of words from God.* And then *Muggleton* contradicts himself and saith, *God hath spoken to* John Reeve, *in* 1651. And so *Muggleton* doth not say he heard it from God, but from *John Reeves* mouth, he must be his mouth; and before *Muggl.* said, *he had it from God.* O *Muggleton,* is thy jugling found out! And *John Reeve* should be the last Messenger and Witness. Here *Mug.* gives *J. Reeve* the lye; for he saith, *He is the last Witness;* and *Mug.* saith, *If he should dye, his disciples should be witnesses, what contradicted thy self against* Muggleton. But you must take notice it must be some mortal man that must be raised up, and what must be his Message but to curse, we have enough of them *Muggleton* raised up already; but that which thy spirit begot are Cursers and not Blessers, so not the Witnesses of Christ; so this voyce was but a whispering of Satan, which came to *John Reeve,* which *Muggleton* is one of his Emissaries, which publisheth his Charmes, *Pope-like,* with Bell, Book and Candle.

And *Muggleton* saith, *That he and* John Reeve *were chosen as* Moses *and* Aaron. And saith, *If it should be objected, that* Moses *did Miracles,* he saith, *there is need of Faith to believe, to have Miracles from him.*

Answ. Moses did Miracles though there were no Faith in *Pharoah,* unto whom he was sent. This is a weak Argument indeed, as to shuffle off his Commission, that is before all the Apostles, as he saith; but what miracles hath been wrought amony thy Disciples, who do believe, whom thou boastest of in thy lying Pamphlet, that thou hast spread so far up and down the world, and thy lying Commission. What, is there no miracle, not no signe, not so much as the sign of *Jonas* amongst you? No, they may say, thy work is to cover people with darkness and Curses.

Muggleton saith, *The Quakers hearken to the Light within, but they despise the Body and Person of Christ without them, and so they are Anti Christ, &c,*

Answ. Here are more lies of the false Prophets. For Christ that died at *Jerusalem,* his Person we own without us, who is manifested within us. The Light of Christ Jesus, by which we have seen of his Glory, and speak in his Person. And this Light of Christ hath condemned thee, who art choaked with evil, and malice, and envy against Christ; thou that speakest so blasphemously against his Light, speakest against Christ, for het that his Light hates, hates him, and he that denies the Light denies his Person. And we must tell *Muggleton,* that *Solomons* Books in the Bible, are good Scripture though he despiseth them as not good, he being not in the Scripture of *Solomon* that gave them forth.

Muggleton saith, *It is in his power to acquit and condemn, yet God cannot reverse his sentence.* And *Muggleton* saith, *He curseth not until they judged him first.* Yet in another place he curseth all the *Quakers,* and condemnes, that they should never be saved in the state they live in. And so see his contradictions, how he sets himself above God.

And *Muggleton* saith, *That is* Darby-shire *he fled the Devils malice,* meaning the Magistrates; and yet he said before, *he Cursed none but the Devil.* It seems the Devil made *Muggleton* fly here, he was too strong for him; he was not able to withstand the Devil, it was but reason he should be cast into Prison, for *Reason is the Devil,* thou saiest; so thou canst not say it was unreasonable, according to thy own judgement; for if they had whipped thee or beat thee, it is but reasonable, for *Reason* is the Devil still. If they had kept thee in Prison until this day, it is but Reason still; why dost thou say it is the Devils malice. And so all the Blasphemers, and false Swearers, and Cursers are but *Reason,* that is *Muggletons* Doctrine, his Devil is *Reason.* Thou canst not say that any judgeth thee falsly, for its Reason. *Reason,* thou saiest, *is the Devil;* and the *Quakers* are not deceived with other mens Commissions as thou art; for what hast thou but *Reeve's* dead Commission for thy Cursings? and we receive not our Commission from the dead Letter, mens dead Commissions and Words, but from Christ and God, through whom onely thou saiest thou hast received a Commission from God, and another –while from *Reeve;* so receiving it from *Reeve* why not from dead mens words, for all is one *Muggleton* which thou hast taken up from *Reeve,* which came from him which was out of Truth, judged from the Spirit of Truth; he and thy

Commission, and thy lyes; and so hast sufficiently proved thy self to be a false Witness, and Prophet, and Embassador.

Muggleton and *John Reeve were chosen Chief Witnesses,* and to prove it he saith, *Peter was chosen Chief Judge.* And he saith, *That Christ doth not teach every man particularly by his Spirit now; and Interpretation of Scripture doth not belong unto Christ, but to* Muggleton, *for none can Interpret Scripture but himself. and neither doth any know the Scriptures but himself,* Page 60.

Answ. Here people may see *Muggletons* Blasphemies and Lies, for *Peter* was not Head of the Apostles, and chief Judge; but they were Brethren; and as I said before in the *Acts,* it was *James* that gave counsel among the Apostles, and it was Christs command that they should not exercise Lordship one over another as it was among Heathens, but this Heathen *Muggleton* would have Lordship, for Christ was chief Judge among the Apostles. And the Prophet saith, *All the Children of God shall be taught of God.* And can they be taught of God, *Muggleton,* and not hear his voice, and the manifestation of the Spirit of God is given to every one to profit withall; so thou hast denied Christ, and the New Covenant, which is, *That all shall be taught of God; and ye shall all know him from the least to the greatest, and shall not need to say, know the Lord, for he will poure out his Spirit upon all flesh, and his Sons and Daughters shall Prophesie,* mark, *all flesh.*

And as for thy exceeding lying against Christ, who saist, *It doth not belong to him to interpret Scriptures;* now mark, people, his Blasphemies and Lyes, do not ye see and comprehend his false spirit, for doth not Christ say, *That his Spirit of Truth, which he sends shall lead them into all Truth?* Did not he come to fulfil the Scriptures? and doth he not say, *That he opens and no man shuts?* And doth not *John* say, *No man was found worthy to open the Book but the Lyon of the Tribe of* Judah? And was not *Christ Anointed to Preach?* And many other Scriptures, which the Spirit of Truth hath given forth, might be instanced. For is there any thing to be known of the Scripture, which are the things of God and Christ, but by Christ? and so, Is not he to have the Glory in all? And as for *Muggletons* Interpreting of Scriptures by the lying spirit, which never gave them forth, hath sufficiently manifested his insufficiency in that, and so thou art neither messenger of the Letter nor of the Spirit, who callest thy self *A Chief and Last Judge.* But they that be in the Spirit of Christ comprehend thee and thy Judgment, who see Christ to be the First and the Last Judge, whose stone is fallen upon thy head, and will grind thee to powder.

And the *Quakers* do not say as *Muggleton* lyingly doth, *That reading over of other mens Conditions, or Words, or Letters, or Scriptures, will make a man a Minister;* For they are neither a Witness nor Commissioned according to the Scriptures, nor them that gave them forth, though thou boastest in the presumptuous spirit, and evil, *That thy Commission is higher than the Apostles,* which thou canst do not otherwise than lye to make it good, because thou goest contrary to them all; for Christ is the Chief Judge, ordained of God, which thou blasphemest against his Light in People, and dost not only blaspheme against it, but him.

And also *Muggleton* falleth a railing against the *Quakers,* and calleth them *Blind,* because they let him see how much contrary to Scripture he is, by his false Commission and Witness; and the Jewes were out of the life of the Law and the Prophets, that were against the Apostles, for the Apostles proved by the Law and be Prophets, what they spoke, so cannot *Muggleton;* and thou art as ignorant of the true God as other men are; and so the *Quakers* do bear their Testimony, and have the Testimony of Jesus against thy false Commission and Lyes, and it is the Spirit that led them to give forth the Scriptures by which they are seen again.

And *Muggleton* seems to be offended because the *Quakers* do not Print his Lyes; and saith, *It would have saved him trouble and charges.*

Answ. No, it is the Truth that we mind, and for Truths sake have we written this in answer against thy Lyes, which will pursue thee, and will gather up thy Lyes and Blasphemies into Bundles for the fire.

Muggleton satih, *He wondred what Lord it is the* Quakers *are so bold in.*

Answ. Muggleton saith, *He knowes the right Devil, and the right God;* and yet he saith, *He marvels what Lord he is.* Well People, this is the mortal man Judgement, *Muggleton,* but we do not marvel at the false Prophet *Muggletons* marvellings, who comprehend him and his god of the world.

Muggleton saith, *There is no God nor Christ but what is within the* Quakers; and yet he saith, *There is no God nor Christ without them that can deliver them from his Curse.* How now *Muggleton? Bable again!* What Confusion and Contradiction is this? And the Prophet *Muggleton* with his breath can blow away their Lord.

Answ. That Christ which Suffered, and Rose again, and Remains in the Heavens, which is manifested in his People; that God which is over all, in all, through all, and above all, blessed for ever, this is he who *Muggleton* saith, *He can blow away with his breath;* whom the *Quakers* own, which for his Blasphemies will have his sentence and reward from the living God, &c. As for thy foul breath, which comes from the souls spirit of thy father, which is the god of the world, whose head is bruised by Christ, and the *Quakers* are over.

Muggleton saith, *He must be as* Peter, *and a true Shepherd layes down his life for his Sheep.*

Answ. But thou runst away from thy Sheep in *Derby-shire* when thou saidst, *The malice of the Devil made thee fly;* and thy Judgement will stand against the *Quakers,* as thy god of the world doth, which will have an end.

And *Muggleton* saith in his rage, *That God hath made him a Judge of the Light of Christ within you, and of the Infinite Spirit which ye call God;* Ye he saith, *he is a* John Baptist *to prepare the way.*

Answ. John Baptist was not a Judge of the Light of Christ, neither doth he say he was a Judge of God and Christ within, and the Infinite Spirit which Blasphemous *Muggleton* doth, who is of another Spirit then the Prophets and Apostles, who said, *God should dwell in you: and the Light that shined in your hears, &c.* And so its very like thou dost judge like *Pharoah,* and the Heathen, and the Jews, of God and Christ; and thy god of the world hath made thee a Judge: But both thee and thy god are judged by God, and Christ, and his Life, and his Infinited Spirit which dwells in his People. We must tell thee *Muggleton,* he cannot judge us, nor God, nor Christ, but with his evil thoughts, and his Judgement doth not touch us, and we are clear from his Judgement; for that which thou hast Judged is thy Judge, and hath Judged and Condemned thee, the Witness in thy Conscience shall answer it.

Answ. Muggleton falls a railing against the *Quakers,* and calls them *Proud and Stiff-necked.* Why *Muggleton,* didst not thou say, *The Neck of the* Quakers *was broke,* and now, *they are so stiff-necked thou canst not bend them?* It seems those that tremble at the Word of God trouble *Muggleton,* and torment him, as in *Page 52,* and thou dost not know the *Quakers* Doctrine, who art in the Spirit of witchcraft; thou speakest like unto thy Brother *Robins.* And *Muggleton* is troubled because the *Quakers* cry against the Pride of the World, so thou must needs uphold the Kingdom of Pride which is the Devils. Thou speakest must of *John Robins,* and the Sprit of Antichrist running through the Bodies of the *Quakers,* and saist, *they are all fighters against God, and have gotten a Christ within them, and that no man can almost tell how to deal with them,* Muggleton saith.

Answ. What *Muggleton,* more lyes and contradictions? Doth Christ fight against God? the spirit of Antichrist that is in thee doth not know how to deal with Christ, and God that dwells in his People; For Christ and God are one, which comprehend both thee and *Robins* to be the fighters against God and Christ, who will grind you to powder.

And thou saist, *The Quakers deny the Resurrection.*

Answ. That's another lye; they do own the *Resurrection of the Just and the unjust;* and therefore thou that art of the nature and seed of the Serpent, as thou speakest to the *Quakers,* fightest against Christ, who will bruise thee to pieces in thy false Messages; and again that which God works in man according to the Doctrine of Christ and the Apostles, thou art against, who said, *God will dwell in man, and Christ will dwell in man;* at which thou railest so much, because thee and thy Father cannot get your lodging in the *Quakers.*

Muggleton saith, *If he had lived in the dayes of Christ, he should hardly have found his name recorded in the Law and Prophets; and the Scriptures are given into* Muggletons *hands, none must interpret them but himself.*

Answ. Here is thy ignorance again manifested, of the false Witness and Prophet; Was not Christs Name written in the Law and Prophets? yea, and after the Law too. Read *Jacobs* Prophesie to his Sons, and read in *Isaiah's* Prophesie. And doth not Christ signifie *Anointed,* and Jesus *a Saviour?* See if thou canst not find this Name in the Old Testament, in many places. *Muggleton* is not in the Spirit that gave forth Scriptures, but being in a blind spirit, and following his own spirit that can see nothing, like a blind Prophet, yet he saith, *that he is made Judge of the Scriptures,* who is Judged by the Spirit of God that gave them forth; and so we can try thy Doctrine with the Light of Christ Jesus, which thou hast Judged, which is thy Condemnation.

And thou saist, *Thou condemnest our Christ and Light,* which is thy Judge and Condemnation, and wouldest have all people believe in thy Doctrine of Lyes. And *Muggleton* saith, *The* Quakers *think to have Eternal Life in the Scriptures.* This is another of the false Prophets Lyes, for our Eternal Life is in Christ before Scriptures were.

Muggleton saith, *Dorthathy,* which is one of his hearer, *is not to judge of his Doctrine, neither hath she power to try his Doctrine,* neither will *Muggleton* allow her to try it.

How now! *Muggleton* hath made himself a Pope, People must believe Implicitly; this is contrary to the Apostle, that saith, *Try all things,* &c. and commended the *Bereans, that did search to see whether these things were so or no.* But we saw before where *Muggleton* was, that he would not have his Doctrine questioned, nor tryed; for it is his Disciples did but question him, or try him and his Doctrine, and let him see his Lyes, he would fall a Cursing of them, but he must have them to be his Slaves and Vassals, to sow his Seed; and so this is fulfilled, *Such as are overcome by him, are brought into bondage;* for he saith, *He Judgeth none but such as Judge himself;* but a Lye is found in his mouth, in this, as you may read *Page 51.* But though he will not suffer his Disciples to try him, nor to judge him, whom he hath darkned and lead from the Spirit of Truth, and the Light of Christ within them, and scoffs at God and Christ dwelling in man, that he might fill them with the Serpentine Seed, and his poisonous Inchantments and Witchcrafts, yet the Spiritual man doth try *Muggletons* Doctrine and Commission, and we have power to examine and try by the Spirit and Power of the Living God, both to judge and try, and can say that the *Spiritual man judgeth all things, yet himself is judged of no man;* for they cannot judge him indeed; and the false Witness with his Commission will be cut down with the Spirit, the Word of God; for *Muggletons* Barn is but as the Stable to Christ the Seed, and thy sword and *Cains* weapons will turn into thine own head, and into thine own Bowels.

And *Muggleton* saith, *The* Quakers *despise their fellow-creatures.*

Answ. Here again thou addest lye unto lye, for the *Quakers* love all Creatures, as they are the Creatures of God, and have respect to that of God in all; their fellowship lyes in the Spirit of God.

And *Muggleton* saith, *That there is never a Minister of Christ, said to authorized from God, without him, or man without him, for the Light of Christ within never made any Minister of Christ;* and then thou railest and callest the *Quakers, Blind.*

Answ. To which we Answer, and say, That the knowledge of God is within, and none knows God but knows Christ, and no man knows the Father but the Son, and he reveals him, and when the Son is revealed in Man, he preaches him; but this is without *Muggleton*, and such as are made Ministers by him, but such as are made not of man, nor by man; but *Muggleton* is authorized by *John Reeve*, who hath received his Commission to Curse from the evil spirit, and not from the Spirit of Christ in the Apostles, which saith, *Bless and Curse not.*

Muggleton saith, *That* Moses *and the Prophets had no other Scripture to Interpret but their own Prophecies.*

Answ. What canst thou not see the Law *Muggleton?* Had not they the Law to interpret, as well as their own Prophecies? Much more might be said to it, but it is like the rest of thy Ignorance.

Muggleton saith, *The Apostles Commissions were of the Blood, and this was the Gospel of Christ.*

Answ. Their Commission was, that they were Witnesses of his Resurrection as well as of his Blood, and of the Flesh of Christ, and of his Bones, as well as the Blood; but *Muggletons* dark spirit will limit it to the Blood, and they were Witnesses of the Gospel which was the Power of God.

And then *Muggleton* saith, *He knows more spiritual things then either the Prophets or Apostles did since the beginning of the world; and he knows more then any to the world end.*

Answ. Here he manifests his Pride and Presumption, and his Ignorance, as afore mentioned, *Muggleton,* thou shouldest have let another have praised thee, and not have praised thy self, whose knowledge is contrary to the Prophets and Apostles and Christ Jesus, who hast exalted thy self above all that is called God, who art one of them that boast they know, but know nothing as they ought to know. And thou saist, *Thou hast an understanding of the Scriptures above all men;* here thou exaltest thy self above Christ, for he is a man; but the man Christ Jesus will bruise thee to pieces, which is mainfested in his People.

Muggleton saith, *He never cursed any through envy and malice;* and he saith, *He never cursed any, nor judged any, till they judged him.* What is this but envy and malice; for Christs words are, *when they Curse, do you Bless.* But *Muggleton* hath proved himself to be of another Spirit then Christ and the Apostles, and so it is comprehended and judged, and so thy Power, and thy Commission, and thy god of the world, from whence it comes, is judged, being the same as ever rose against Christ, and the Prophets, and Apostles since the world began, &c. As for thy sentence and curses, they go to the Pit with thee, from whence they came; they are nothing to us, we are clear of them, neither thy Blessings nor thy Cursings.

Muggleton saith, *He hath a Pardoning power and a Damning power, which he received from* John Reeve, *and he would not have Curst him* (meaning Muggleton) *to all Eternity if he had not yeelded obedience to* Reeve.

Answ. Here it seems *John Reeve* frighted *Muggletons* evil Conscience, by that means he received that cursing spirit, which presumptuously he hath followed these many years, and so received this cursed doctrine and spirit; and then, it's like he received *John Reeves'* Blessing, and here he became Pope-like, with his evil spirit to pardon whom he will; and such as flatter him, he Blesseth, and such as judge him, he Curseth, as he hath said. And here people may see the ground and rise of this dark spirit, out of Truth, comprehended by it, and judged into the Pit with its motion, Commission, and false Witness, who hath so often blasphemed against the holy Spirit; who saith he is an Accuser, a Judge, and a Witness, and a great deal of Rambling stuffe, about outward Judges, and Laws, and Juries which he is ignorant of; as in the Scripture, who is like unto the Servant that Christ speaks of, who art the Accuser of the Brethren, spoken of in the *Revelations,* cast out into the Earth, therefore thou ragest. Christ said, He did not accuse the Woman taken in Adultery. And Christ said, *John 5. Do not think I will accuse you to the Father; there is one that accuseth you,* Moses, *in whom ye trust:* But this is little to *Muggleton.*

Muggleton saith, *He is in rest and Eternal happiness.* And yet *Muggleton* and *John Reeve* say in the Book called, *A Transcendent Spiritual Treatise,* That, *this Book was penned by a sinful man.*

Answ. How now, what *Muggleton* and *John Reeve,* what, a sinful man in perfect rest and happiness! Can a sinful man give out heavenly and spiritual Doctrine? See the 37 *Page* in thy *Transcendent Spiritual Treatise,* and see thy *Page 41.* of the *Quakers Neck-broken,* and there mayest see thy contradictions, lyes and confusions: for the perfect rest is *Christ;* Imperfections are in *Adam* in the fall; and if Christians have persecuted by National Laws, and God had Witnesses in the Earth for three hundred years after Christ as *Muggleton* and *Reeve* say, that all spiritualized Christians were persecuted, and yet God never had a Witness until *Muggleton* and *Reeve* came; so all the Martyrs that kept the Testimony of Jesus, are judged by *Muggleton* and *Reeves* lying spirit: but the Martyrs stood to their Principle, and did not fly from the Devil as *Muggleton* did out of *Derby-shire.* Read through the Book of Martyrs, and read in his own Book, and ye many see how he hath confounded and contradicted himself. And thou sayest in the 76. page of thy Transcendency, *That the Soul of* Adam *was of a Divine Nature,* and yet another place, *That the Soul is mortal.* What contradictions are here *Muggleton?* But it is like the rest, his Divine mortal: But thou art ignorant of Christs words, who says, *If they can kill the Body, yet they cannot kill the Soul.* What a carnal Judge? a poor mortal man, as thou sayes, God hath raised up.

Mugglet. Again, thou sayes in thy *Transcendency, The sayings of* Solomon *are pure Truth;* and yet thou saiest, in thy *Neck of the Quakers broken,* That *Solomons Books are Apocrypha.* What a contradiction is this? Apocrypha is not of Authority; Is pure Truth darkness, and like the rest of the fruits of thy dark spirit.

Mug. And thou saiest, *Though men believe they have two Spirits in them, yet there is but one in mens bodies,* in page 19. of thy *Joyful news from Heaven.*

Answ. Here thou hast manifested thy self to be of a right principle with the *Ranters;* This is a ranting principle indeed. I believer there is something in thy self, and in all men, and in the Scriptures will witness against thee, which saith, *That the flesh was against the Spirit, and the Spirit against the flesh, and they are contrary,* and so not one.

Muggleton and *Reve,* in page 47. of their *News from Heaven,* say, *That the Spirit and the Soul is not capable of dying,* and say, *Why wouldst thou suffer thy self to be overtaken with sudden death? And why art thou so foolish as to suffer thy self to be over-topt with death?*

Answ. This is the cry of the *Wild Irish;* this is not the cry of *News from Heaven,* but the cry of thy *dark spirit;* What can a false Prophet, and a false Commission, and a false Testimony, which comes from his Father, which is out of truth, being otherwise.

Muggleton and *Reeve* say, *That Christ shed his blood for the sins of the Elect, and when Christ said,* My God, my God, &c. *This God that Christ meant, was* Elias, *and you must understand the reason why Christ is onely God, &c.*

Answ. Here in this thou hast shown thy darkness and ignorance of the Scriptures, and the Spirit that gave them forth, like unto the *Jews;* for the Scripture doth not say that it was *Elias* the Prophet that Christ cryed unto; for no where in the Scriptures, by all the holy men of God, nor Christ, nor God, is *Elias* the Prophet called God: Here thou hast judged as the *Jews* did. And *who shall lay any thing to the charge of God's Elect?* Saith the Spirit that gave forth the Scriptures, *It is God that justifies:* but thou hast charged them with sin, and manifested thy self not to be of God. *Christ tasted death for every man,* and dyed not for the Elect onely, as thou speaks of; and *he was an Offering not for our sins onely, but for the sins of the whole world.* Here is thy ignorance of the two Seeds, but this is the reason which thou wouldst have the Readers to understand. And before *Muggleton* said in his other Book, that *Reason was the Devil.* So according to thy own Argument, we must understand by the Devil the things of God, and know Christ Jesus by the Devil; for in thy 34, and 37. pages, thou speaks of Reason without dinstinction; and Reason being the Devil according to thy Judgment, and thy Prophesies, are all from him, according to thy own Judgement. The reason why thou sayest mens bodies are in Death, and in the Grave, and do not stink, and come to dust; this leaves little answer, for it is by thy Reason which thou callst the Devil, and he was a lyar from the beginning, and was the Father of it, of whom thou art; and so the Grave-makers may answer thee the rest, as touching peoples bodies.

Mug. Thou sayest, *Three hundred years after Christ, nor since, there hath been a Minister, or Messenger of Christ;* and this he declares and affirms; and then after again thou declarest and affirmest by

Revelation, *That it is fourteen hundred years since there was a true Minister.* Here thou contradictest thy own Revelation, and hast shewed thy lying Spirit: for 1400. and 300. years, makes 1700. Here is about forty years difference, according to thy own lying Spirit and Revelations; and many such contradictions, falsities, and confusions thou hast in all thy Books, which a man might make a large Volumn of, in letting thee see thy contradictions; but they are so clearly seen and judged of by all the Righteous, that they are not worthy of Writing nor Printing such a pack of nonsence and confusion, worse then the very Priests Books; for this is done for Truths sake, which, as I said before, will pursue thee and find thee out in all thy holes and corners, and will arraign thee to thy condemnation, for thou hast judged neither according to the Law of God nor Scriptures, nor the Laws of men, but according to thy own dark spirit; for the Spirit of God exhorts men to repent, and reproves, and rebukes before he judges; but thou in thy fleshly, rash, heady, hasty passion followest thy own spirit, and with it judgest that which is thy condemnation: so in judging another thou hast judged thy self, who art seen with the holy Spirit of Christ Jesus to be vain; whose Commission, Prophesie, Witness if for condemnation, and condemned and judged with the Spirit of Truth; and over thee is the true and faithful Witness Christ Jesus, the Corner-stone set, which will grind thee to powder. Fare thee well. And in Christ is his People that reign over thy head, that can rejoyce and raign over the head of the Curser.

> *Edward Brown,* whom thou hast curst and damned, who is far Above thee and thy father, in him that redeems out of the Curse, And destroys thee and thy father both.

Something in Answer to Thomas Fuller, in his Church-History, to that which he writes to Baron Brook, wherein he Rayles against the Quakers.

First, He saith, *They cast of their Clothes, until the Cold converted them to more Civility.*

Answ. This doth not become *Thomas* to record Lyes. For the people that are in scorn called *Quakers,* it was not the Cold that converted them. And why dost not thou record *Isaiah,* and judge him that went naked and barefoot three years together, as one of them (thou in scorn callest *Quakers)* did, being moved of the Lord? Which was a sign or figure of all your nakedness, and the rest of them.

Secondly, Thomas *is offended because the People, which he in scorn calleth* Quakers, *say to one single person, Thee, and Thou.*

Answ. If *Thomas* had not shewed himself ignorant of the Scriptures, and forgotten his *Accidence* and *Grammer* he learned (if any) he would have seen in the Scriptures, from the highest to the lowest, that the People of God used the word, *thee* and *thou*. And if he had spoken *you,* when he should have spoken *thou* in Latine, his Master would have gon near to have whipt him. And then *Thomas* falls a begging to the (then present) Powers, like unto the *Jewes* against the Apostle, *Help men of Israel,* to Persecution. And *Thomas* his envy hath so choaked him that the hath forgotten what is said in the Lords Prayer, *viz, thy,* and *thee, &c.* And he saith also, because they use the word *thou, &c. They speak evil against Dignities, and against Ordinances of God, &c.* and saith, *God grant that they may be seasonably suppressed.*

A. Here thy envy and malice is seen again, *Balaam*-like, for it was the language of the Righteous, and no man found fault with it, to Superiour or Inferiour (as *thou* and *thee*) and Gods Ordinances they do not deny. And whereas thou callest upon God for the suppressing of them who inventest lyes, and then criest for help against them. But the living God, whom we serve, hears not the prayers of the Persecutor nor Lyar.

And *Thomas* saith, because thy use the word *thou* to a Superiour, *Here their Honours lye at the mercy of mens moutes; so if they grew numerous, hereafter they will question the wealth of others, and condemn them for covetousness.*

If all *Thomas* his History be like this, tis worth little to be credited, who begged Persecution of *O. Cromwel,* and when the King came in, turned to his Surplice. And if the honour due to Superiours lye in giving the word *you* to a single person, then thou mayest find fault with the Apostles and the Prophets, who said *thou* and *thee* to them; and so did the Prophets. But why doth not *Thomas* find fault with the *Accidence* and *Grammer,* and with them that translated the Scriptures, which did translate them Singular and Plural. See the *Quakers Battledor,* given forth for you to learn in.

A. As for your outwrd wealth we seek it not; but covetousness is reproved by the Spirit of Truth. And whereas thou art afraid we should grow numerous; we tell thee that God will spread his Truth abroad, and gather his Elect from the four Corners of the Earth. And the honour that all men are to be honoured withall, even Superiours, is not the word *you* to a single person, but to esteem every man, and those that rule well, to have double esteem, and this is the true Honour, and such as do so will hurt no man. And *Thomas* is angry because they tremble at the Word of God; he therein shews his ignorance of the Scriptures, and of the holy men of God, and such as be regarded of the Lord, who saith. *This is the man I do regard, who is of a contrite and broken spirit, and trembleth at my Word,* as in *Isaiah* may be read. And thou art like the persecuting *Jewes,* that despiseth them that trembled at Gods Word; but such the Lord often cutts off, and shortneth their dayes for the Elects sake.

Somthing in Answer to Samuel Clarke, who calls himself a Pastor, in his Book called, A Looking Glass for Saints and Sinners.

Wherein he mentions the People of God (called *Quakers*) and numbereth them among them among the Scismaticks, and Hereticks, wickedly; and he instanceth one *Gilpine* about *Kendal* in *Westmerland,* that somtimes came among the said People, which after the Priests had poysoned, and turned him to be a Souldier, who raised up many lies against the said people (called *Quakers*) which he and his brethren put for truths, which this *Gilpine* went from the people (*called Quakers*) and became one of theirs, and run out to bad actions, which if we should go to reckon all the bad actions of all their people, we might make a very great Volumn: But this *Clarke* (that calls himself a Pastor) might have looked in the *Quakers* Answer to the Priests, and the said *Gilpin,* wherein they manifest their lies and slanders against the said People; but in stead of that, he's scoffing at the Light, and the Cross of Christ, and Prophesie, and of hearing the voyce of God and Christ, and yet he blusheth not to call himself a Pastor, and takes upon him to set forth an Abridgment of the Book of Martyrs, and a Mirrour or Looking-glass of Saints and Sinners; which makes them all questionable and unvaluable to the Faithful, as seeing his envy and rage in his scandal and lies against the people called *Quakers,* thrust into his said Book, not having quoted any Author, as Historians use to do: therefore they lie upon his own head. But we perceive the thing that troubles *Clarke,* was, because the Ministers of *England;* were proved to be false Prophets, and Priests of *Baal,* which in that day 1663 (nor since) they could never prove themselves otherwise: For read those Scriptures of the Kings, and see how like they were unto them in visage and practice; For above three thousand of the said People (called *Quakers*) were persecuted by them in their day, and some even unto death; which is an evident mark of Hereticks and Priests of *Baal:* for Christ Jesus saith, *Love one another, love enemies;* and Christ's Ministers keep his Command, because they love him. But *Samuel Clarke* scoffs at this Doctrine, who neither he nor his company could ever get from under these Scriptures following, As teaching for handfuls of Barley and pieces of breadk, *Ezekiel* 13 & 14th chapters; and of bearing rule by their means, *Jer.* 5. and greedy and dumb dogs that never have enough, seeking their gain from their quarter, *Isa. 56, & Micah 3.* the chapters throughout, & *Matth. 23,* and *Ezek. 34.* most of the chapter concerning the false Pastors, and *I Tim. 3.* and *Rom.* 16.18. and the Epistle of *Jude* and *2 Peter 2.* chap. Throughout, & *Malachi* the ad, where the Curse is from God pronounced against you; and your blessings cursed, and your seed corrupt, and dung spread upon your faces in your solemn feasts: All which Scriptures, with many more, you could never answer; and *Gal.3.20.* with *I Cor. 2, &c.*

THE END.

The New Witnesses proved Old Hereticks:

OR,

Information to the Ignorant; in which the Doctrines of *John Reeve* and *Lodowick Muggleton*, which they stile, Mysteries never before known, revealed, or heard of from the Foundation of the World, are proved to be mostly ancient Whimsies, Blasphemies and Heresies, from the Evidence of *Scripture, Reason*, and several *Historians*.

ALSO

An Account of some Discourse betwixt L M. and my self, by which his Blasphemous, Ignorant and Unsavory Spirit is clearly and truly manifested, in Love to the Immortal Souls of those Few, who are concerned in the Belief of his Impostures.

By a Living True Witness to that One Eternal Way of God, revealed in the Light of Righteousness, W. Penn.

Now as Jannes and Jambres withstood Moses, so do these (Reeve and Muggleton) also resist the Truth, Men of corrupt Minds, reprobate concerning the Faith. But they shall proceed no farther, for their Folly shall be manifest unto all Men, as their- also was, 2 Tim. 3, 8, 9.

To the READER.

READER,

Amongst the many strange Pretensions, that have been made to Religion, and the Authors and Abettors of variety of Sects, through every Generation, from the most primitive Christian Times, there has not appeared (though not a less formidable yet) a more compleat Monster on the Stage of Controversie and Opinion than this of John Reeve and Lodowick Muggleton, Brethren and Associates in the blackest Work that ever fallen Men or Angels could probably have set themselves upon: What many Ages singly were infested by, we are assaulted with at once; and as if the scattered Limbs of Heresie had rallied and re-enforced themselves for a new Combate; no sooner was the Glorious Truth appearing, than they were ready to make their utmost Opposition, either by their Enchantments, to delude the Souls of some; or through their unparallel'd sottish Folly, to scandalize the World in general against all Religion, as ridiculous; and amongst others, the true as also Fabulous: Yet the Lord God of Eternal Power, whose Thoughts and Ways are not as Mortal Men's, but Infinite and Almighty, like himself, having decreed the Redemption of the fallen Souls of Men, by the Illumination of their Understandings, and Quickening of their Minds, dead in Trespasses and Sins, by the living powerful Operation of his own Eternal Spirit of Holiness, did appear in so great Glory and Majesty, that those Fogs and Mists, which began to over-spread the Earth, were soon scattered, and the Everlasting Light arose, and hath effectually shined forth unto the Convincement and Conversion of Thousands from the Ungodliness of this present evil World, and the Fruitless Religions that are protest therein, to live a Sober, Heavenly, Righteous Life and Conversation.

But alas! Some few have strayed by the Way, one hither, and another thither, for want of that Subjection and Holy Watch they ought to have lived in, unto the Blessed Living Truth of God: And as many Snares have been presented to delude, so amongst others, their sottish Imaginations have not been without the Power of a Temptation, and too effectual upon some, the Lord knoweth, which though their Number be but very small, yet the Concernment of their Immortal Souls is great: For who living, that have tasted of the sure Mercies of God, and enjoyed of the Reward of Faithfulness to the Truth, but must needs Pity, Sorrow and Lament on their Behalf; some that might have run well, and would not; others that began to do it, and Satan hindred?

No sooner were Adam and Eve made sensible of the Blessedness of their Innocent State, than the Serpent endeavoured to beguile them; How? by preaching Righteousness, Holiness, Watchfulness and Godly Fear, as without which none should ever see the Lord? No, nothing less, but by Idle Dreams, Luciferian Thoughts and Exalted Imaginations, above the lowly Awe and Fear, they ought to have lived in towards their Almighty Creator: And thus in some Measure hath it fared with a few unhappy Souls, that have been beguiled by these Impostors.

I shall not altogether make it my Business to confute their Tenets; but since they more than once, with an intolerable Pride, boast of these Things, as New Revelations, and challenge the whole World to disprove them, and upon this single Credit it is that their credulous Adherents are so mightily perswaded of their Patrons Sincerity and Infallibility (it being their first Lesson at entrance, To abandon all Scripture or inward Witness) And that Muggleton to my Knowledge, in his Discourses, and otherwise, makes it his brag, That he not only knows more than all Men ever did or shall know to Eternity; but that the Doctrines Reeve and he say they are deputed to declare (by Virtue of an immediate oral Commission from God himself.) are such divine Revelations, as were never known to Men or Angels before them.

And consequently, since their Followers have nothing for Proof besides their bare Assertion (which is most arrogant and false (for they deny all inward Witness) It will appear both reasonable and necessary, that by an external Judge and Witness they should be tryed, and if upon their Arraignment at the Bar, they be found only to have patcht up old Phantasms together, and published them under the Name of Transcendent Spiritual Treatises, Divine Looking-Glasses, and the like; I hope they will be judg'd by every sober Person to be both horrible Impostors, and their Commission to be a meer Counterfeit.

The New Witnesses Prov'd Old Hereticks, &c.

I now proceed to perform what has been promised by most Undeniable Proof.

First, Reeve and Muggleton declare as a great Secret to the World, That God is not an Infinite Spirit in every Place at all Times (contrary to the Scriptures, which say, He measures out the Heavens with his Span, nor can the Heaven of Heavens contain him) but against Men and Angels, and by Authority from the Holy Spirit (to use their own Words) God is but in the Shape of a Man; and that Man, in respect of his Body, is the Image of God. Trans. Spirit. Treat. pag. 15. Div. Look. Glass pag. 3, 4. That this is against Scripture we prove.

First, There is none like to the God of Jeshurun, who rideth upon the Heaven inthy Help, and in his Excellency on the Sky: The Eternal God is thy Refuge, and underneath are the Everlasting Arms, Deut. 33. 26, 27.

If the God of Jeshurun be the true God, and none be like to him, then cannot Man's bodily Shape be the Likeness of the true God; consequently, if Muggleton's God be in the Likeness of Man's bodily Shape, he is not the True God, because he is not that God of Jeshurun, which none is like unto.

Again, If the Almighty God were but of the Dimension of a middle statured Man, how could he be said to ride upon the Heavens and the Sky; and to have his Everlasting Arms under a People, many of whom are singly bigger than himself; for by Muggleton's Principles, We are still to keep to the Literal Sense.

Secondly, But will God indeed dwell on the Earth? behold the Heaven and Heaven of Heavens cannot contain him, 1 Kings 8. 27.2 Chron. 2. 6.chap. 6. 18.

If the Earth, on which dwell so many Millions of Men, be not able to receive God, as he is, and in Comparison of limiting him to any Place, (suitable to such a Body as Muggleton faith he hath) the very Heaven and Heaven of Heavens cannot contain him; Certainly this immense and infinite Being must be of a larger extent, than the Proportion of a mortal Man, his own Creature.

Thirdly, Who hath measured the Waters in the hollow of His Hand, and meted out the Heaven with a Span, and comprehended the Dust of the Earth in a Measure, and weighed the Mountains in Scales, and the Hills in a Balance, Isa. 40. 12.

He that cannot measure the Waters in the hollow of his Hand and mete out the Heaven with his Span, and comprehend the Dust of the Earth in a Measure, and weigh the Mountains in Scales, and the Hills in a Balance, is not the true God; but a God of Man's Stature can never do that; therefore the true God is not such an one, neither can such an one be the true God.

Fourthly, To whom then will ye liken God? What Likeness will ye compare unto Him? The Workman melteth a Graven Image, and the Gold-smith spreadeth it over with Gold: Have ye not known? have ye not heard? hath it not been told you from the Beginning? have ye not understood from the Foundations of the Earth? It is he that sits upon the Circle of the Earth, and the Inhabitants thereof are as Grass-Hoppers, that stretches out the Heavens as a Curtain, and spreads them out as a Tent to dwell in. Isa. 40. 18, 19,21. 22.

In this Passage is a most pregnant Overthrow of this vain Opinion.

1. That God of whom Man can make a Likeness, is not the true God; but such an one is Muggleton' s, therefore not the true God.

2. If God was of Man's Figure and Stature, then Gold-smiths were able to make His Likeness; but this the Scriptures utterly deny, and ask, what likeness will ye compare unto Him? Therefore God is not in the bodily Shape of a Man.

3 God by his Prophet disdained all such vain Conceits, and left any should think so meanly of Him, he gives his own Character, Have ye not heard? hath it not been told you from the Beginning? It is he that sitteth on the Circle of the Earth, and to whom the Inhabitants thereof are as Grass-Hoppers; who stretches out the Heavens as a Curtain, and spreads them out as a Tent to dwell in.

Fifthly, God is a Spirit, and they that worship him must worship him in Spirit and in Truth, John 4. 24.

If God be a Spirit, he is either a finite or an infinite Spirit; a finite he cannot be, and be God; therefore an infinite one.

If God be an infinite and immense Spirit (which are Terms reciprocal) then not a Body of a little more than five Foot high, as blasphemous, ignorant and sottish Reeve and Muggleton darkly imagine; but the only wise and invisible God is that infinite Spirit, therefore not con-in'd to any bodily Shape.

Sixthly, For what the Law could not do in that it was weak through the Flesh, God sending his own Son in the Likeness of sinful Flesh, for sin condemned sin in the Flesh, Rom. 8. 3. But made himself of no Reputation, and took upon him the Form of a Servant, and was made in the Likeness of Men, Phil. 2. 7.

By the Likeness of sinful Flesh, and was made in the Likeness of Men, we understand and grant Christ's taking upon him not only the

The New Witnesses

Shape of a Man, but the Flesh and Blood of a Virgin; the Question will then be this, Whether Christ had this Shape before he took it? If he had, he took it after he had it, which is absurd; if not, he was before he had it; and if he was before he had it, either he was like his Father, or he was not; if not, then not his Son; if he was, then because the Scripture declares him to have taken upon him the Likeness of a Man, which supposeth him to have had a Being before he took it: God is not in the Likeness of sinful Flesh, nor made in the Likeness of Men; but is the Divine Immortal Substance, of which Christ was the express Image before he took upon him the Form of a Servant, or was made in the Likeness of Men, which take Notice are both joyned together, as Expressions of his Condescension, as the following Verse also shews; and in being found in the fashion of a Man (as being a new and uncouth Thing to him) he humbled himself, and became obedient unto Death, &c. This was in the Day he took upon him the Form of a Servant and likeness of Man, making himself of no Reputation; and not whilst he was in the Form of God, when he thought it no Robbery, to be equal with God.

In short, If that only makes equal with God, which is found in the Form of God; then that which is in the Form of a Servant, and in the Likeness of Men, is not in that State equal to God; and if that be so, as it is, if Scripture be true, certainly there is ground to believe, that Reeve and Muggleton are not a little out of the Way, in asserting, That God's Form is the Pattern or Image Man's body was made by.

But here I expect to meet with an Objection, that it may be fit to remove, as that only one which can carry any Colour of an Answer with it.

Object. Most of those Scriptures, especially out of the Prophets, only intend to shew God's Sovereign Power, and not that he is not a Person, as I assert him to be. Thus far Muggleton and his Company.

I Reply, All Scriptures either import a literal or a mystical Sense, and either would serve us against this false Witness; if he says they should be construed mystically, I will tell him, that he must give us the same Liberty in that Place to do the like, Let us make Man after our own Image; for they only collected from that Passage God's Image by Man's Likeness; but in many of the Places urged by me, those Members, which in a literal Sense denote a Body like to Man's, are particularly mention'd: We will never allow him to allegorize the more literal, and literize the more allegorical; if the one must be literal, let the other he so too, especially there being more ground for it.

To Conclude, if he will interpret God's Hands, and Arms, and Span to signifie his Power, as is most true; then will I also explain God's Image to be Holiness, which is also true. But if he will have it, that because God made Man after his Image, and that Man has an Head, Eyes, Nose, Mouth, Ears, Hands, &c. Therefore God has such too, I will infer, because the Scriptures say, He span'd the Heavens with his Right Hand, and rid upon the Circle of the Earth, That he really and bodily did so span the Heavens with a great Hand, and rid with a mighty Body upon the Circle of the Earth; which how ridiculous and false soever it is, is as true as Reeve's or Muggleton's Conceit: Thus far indeed they would be in the right, by such a Consequence, That Almighty God would have a Body, but they would grosly lye in the Dimensions of it, who say, 'Tis no bigger than a middle statured Man. Thus much, if not too much upon this Piece of old vain Anthropomorphitism.

That this idle Opinion is against that Understanding which God has given Men to judge of the Difference of Things, we also prove.

First, If God were a Person of Man's Stature, it would destroy his Ubiquity or Omnipresence, which is one of his most Divine Properties, rightly attributed to him: For, how is it possible so inconsiderable a Body can be at all Places at one and the same Time, by which to see and understand all Things, or to administer Strength and Comfort to his scatter'd Flock throughout the World?

Secondly, If they would say, he is present by his Spirit (as read Reeve's Epistle to his Divine Looking-Glass) I affirm against all Muggletonians upon Earth, That then not that Body, but that Omnipresent Spirit is the truly Infinite God.

Thirdly, But I would fain know how God and his Spirit can be divided or separated; Can any Man be truly such, whose Spirit is absent from him? What Body is a living Body without a Spirit, any more than Faith can be living without Works? How then can God's Body, no bigger than a Mortal Man's, be contained in Reeve's and Muggleton's conceited Heaven, and his Spirit every where? Where God's Spirit is, God is; he can never be divided from his own Life and Spirit; for God is that Spirit, or that Spirit is God; they are synonimously or equivalently to be taken. This the Apostle believed, when he told the Athenians, That God was nigh to every one of them, and in him they lived, moved, and had their Being.

Fourthly, How was it possible for Reeve to hear God speak with a Voice of Words from beyond the Stars, as one Body speaks to another, and no Body hear besides himself, nor the visible Firmament or Air to receive any Alteration or Discomposure, as ever was when Voices of Words have been uttered, whether to Moses, or of Christ, or otherwise? If any say, It was a spiritual Voice, such talk sottishly; no Carnal Ear can hear a Spiritual Voice, as Reeve himself teacheth, p. 47. T. S. T. concerning which something may be fitly hinted elsewhere.

Fifthly, But I would add from their wicked Principles, That if Man be God's Image, in Reference to his Body, then, because Reeve and Muggleton declare that a select Number of Men's Bodies and Souls are pre-ordain'd to be eternally damned, therefore God has decreed his own Image to Everlasting Vengeance, and that to glorify himself too; which one Horrible Impiety I desire all to weigh, and then there needs no farther Undertaking to his Confutation.

The New Witnesses

That this is Old, and also Exploded Heresy, I prove.

This wonderful dark Secret is to be read in Theodorus of Heresy, the 4th Book, and 10th Chapter, where he speaks of one Audaeus, who liv'd in Caelosyria, in the Time of Constantius the Emperor, and grounded his Conjecture upon these Words, Let us make Man after our Image. Also several Monks inhabiting Aegypt conceited the God that made Heaven and Earth to be no bigger than a Man. Of which Opinion, with Muggleton, was one Theophilus of Alexandria, and others, they were called Anthropomorphites, as may at large be seen in Eusebius Pamphilus's 6th Book and 36th Chapter; also in Socrates Scholasticus in his 6th and 7th Books: This was about the Year after Christ 403, and One Thousand Two Hundred Sixty Nine Years since.

Secondly, Their second Secret is, That God did not create the Heavens and Earth out of Nothing, but the Substance was with God from Eternity, T. S. T. Page 12.

That this is also inconsistent with Scripture we prove.

First, In the Beginning God created the Heavens and the Earth, and the Earth was without Form and void, Gen. 1. 1, 2.

If they were created before they were formed, as saith the Place, then Creation and Formation are not one and the same Thing, as Reeve and Muggleton assert in their Transcendent Spiritual Treatise, p. 16. so that either the Authority of Scripture must be denied, or else Creation is first a bringing forth of the Chaos or rude Substance, and Formation the Disposition of it into such Parts, and Designation unto such Ends or Services, as that all-wise Creator might think most befitting his great Work. Enough might be said on this one Particular to confute all with whom the Scriptures remain of any Force.

Secondly, Hearken unto me, O Jacob, and Israel my called; I am he, I am the first, I also am the last; my Hand also has laid the Foundation of the Earth, Isaiah 48. 12, 13.

To be first, and to have laid the very Foundation of another's Being, supposeth that Thing neither to be before it, nor so much as in Time equal with it; and therefore denotes Priority and Superiority: Wherefore thus I argue, If God was before so much as the Foundation of the Earth was laid, then was neither the Earth, nor Foundation of it, from Eternity with God. But the Text affirms, That God was first, or before the very Foundation was ever laid; therefore neither the Earth, nor Superstructure, as to it's Form, nor yet it's Foundation or first material Principle was Co-eternal.

In short, Nothing can be said to create any Thing that is equal in Time with it, because such Creation supposeth the one to receive it's Being from the other: and since God gave it's Foundation, or first Bottom, the very material Principle, it follows, there could be no Co-eternity betwixt them.

Thirdly, ——— And the Word was God: All Things were made by him, John 1. 1.3.

If all Things were made by him, then both Heaven and Earth, because they are Part of all Things, were made by him; but the Place says, all Things (or whatever has Being) were made by him; therefore all Co-eternity of Earth or Heaven with the Everlasting God is excluded and refuted:

To this answers that Passage of the Apostle Paul in the Acts, God that made the World, and all Things therein, &c.

Fourthly, To conclude this Head, For by him were all Things created; and he is before all Things; and by him all Things consist, Colos. 1. 16, 17. And thou Lord in the Beginning hast laid the Foundation of the Earth, and the Heavens are the Works of thy Hands, Heb. 1. 10.

That which had a Beginning, which was made, and which was and is upheld by another, neither can have been contemporary nor co-eternal with that from which it received it's Being; but that did the Heaven and the Earth, and from Almighty God, as the Place proves: Therefore not Co-eternal with him.

Nor can their idle Shift any Ways secure them from the Dint of these Scriptures, nor the Arguments built upon them, viz. making is fashioning, so God made the Heavens and the Earth, as a Carpenter makes a Door or a Chest; he fashions it of Wood, but he does not make the Wood: A Distinction fitter for Bedlam, than Men pretending to be in their Wits: Can any rationally think, that when God is said to lay the Foundation of the Earth, and to make the Heavens, and all that live therein, that he only fashion'd them up? Who made the Trees, Plants, Beasts, Fowls, Fishes, and rational Creatures? Do they strain at a Gnat, and swallow a Camel? Can they think that it was harder to Almighty God, to create out of Nothing the more inanimate or lifeless Part of Heaven and Earth, than to compose that Variety of excellent Creatures, and to infuse that great Spirit and Soul, by which they are respectively instincted or acted.

But how pertinent his Distinction is betwixt fashioning and making, we will manifest by that remarkable Passage to our Purpose in Paul's Epistle to the Philippians, Chap. 2. And being found in Fashion as a Man, he humbled himself, &c.

Was Christ a real Man, or not? If not, then Reeve's and Muggleton's Fleshly Mortal Notions, of the Immortal Son of God, fall to the Ground; if a real Man, then to be fashion'd may import to be, and the Fashion of a Thing passeth for the Being of a Thing.

Of what Value now their Distinction is, they may consider if they please.

But this Opinion is also against Reason.

First, It is the Nature of what is Eternal, or from all Everlasting to be Infinite, Unalterable and Almighty; for it oweth no Original or Preservation to another, and is equivalent in all other Properties to Eternity: Now where there is not Proportion, it is highly to be suspected, That there is no such Thing at all; but is a mere Chimera, and real only in a Fiction.

Secondly, That there is no Resemblance is manifest, the whole visible World is full of Time, inconsistent with Eternity, as having Beginning and End; the Heavens have their set Motions, the Earth her distinct Seasons, in which are various Revolutions, -and both filled with divers Temporary Agitations and Motions: Therefore it is impossible that Heaven and Earth could have been from Eternity, which are so filled with and made up of all the Instances of Time and Mutation; for should they, The Sun must always shine, the Rain descend, the Tide flow, the Winds blow, the Winter last, and every Alteration that is in Time be perpetual.

Thirdly, It is utterly impossible, that Temporal Beings could receive their Sustenance and Growth from what is by Nature Eternal; there being as great Contrariety, at least, Difference between them, as there is betwixt visible and invisible, Spiritual and Carnal Things.

Fourthly, Such as is the Food, such should the Life be; now if this visible World should be Eternal, then the Food that springs from it should nourish to a Life as Eternal as that World which does produce it. Nay, since Man's Body was made of the Earth, we might well infer, That Man's Body, as so made, is Eternal; and if Eternal, as such, not Mortal, which Experience tells us is an idle Tale. But let this suffice at present.

But that this Conjecture had other Founders than Reeve and Muggleton, I prove, and that by two Instances.

Augustine says, That there were several that affirmed, That the Water was not made by God, but was Co-eternal. Next, a certain Sect called Seluciani taught, That the Substance of the Creation, or whereof the World was made, was not made by God, but Eternally with God (then no Creature, and then God) as may at large be read in the said Augustine's Book of Heresies; this Heresy reigned about Anno 300 after Christ. To say nothing of that known Philosopher Aristotle, who was sometimes Idolater, sometimes Atheist.

Thirdly, The third Secret, which only was revealed to Reeve and Muggleton, if we will believe them, is, That the Soul of Man is generated or got by the Man and Woman with the Body, and that the Body and Soul are inseparable. T. S. T. p. 42.

That this is contrary to Scripture Testimony, I prove.

First, And the Spirit to God that gave it, Eccl. 12. 7.

No Carnal Generation can bring forth a pure Spirit; External Matter producing only External Matter of it's own Kind.

But the Soul of Man is a Spirit, as the Words express it in Reeve's and Muggleton's own T. S. T. p. 44. Therefore no Man gets the Soul or Spirit of a Man when he generates the Body.

Secondly, That which returns to God came from God; but the Soul of every Man returns to God, and consequently came from him.

I omit mentioning more Scriptures, because the following Principle being a Consequence of this; what I prove there is proved here, namely, The Immortality of the Soul, against their Atheistical

Assertion, of the Soul's Mortality with the Body: For where there is no Corruption, there could be no proper Generation; and if the Soul be Immortal, it was not descended of Mortal Race, or begotten of elementary visible Matter.

That this is against all Right Understanding, I prove.

First, Such as is the Soul, such must that be which produceth it; but it is Spiritual. Now that which generates the Body of Man, being only and meerly visible Matter, it cannot produce or generate an intellectual Soul or Spirit.

Secondly, If Man got the Soul, then would that Soul be as well the Image of the Father as the Body, and partake as intirely of the Father's Nature and Disposition in all Respects: But Experience shews us, That Sober Parents have Wild Children, and Religious Children Debauched Parents; therefore Parents do not generate the Soul.

Thirdly, If Soul and Body be inseparably generated, then the Sexes as well belong to Souls as Bodies; the which as it is absurd, so would there be Men and Women in that very Distinction to all Eternity: And who ever read of She Souls or Female Souls?

Fourthly, If Soul and Body were intermixedly and inseparably generated by Man, then in all Anatomies it were no more difficult to find out the Soul than any other Part: and in Case of Opening or Dissecting of Living Men, as I have at the University seen living Beasts by Anatomists, it would not be impossible, but rational, that one should behold the very Thoughts, Purposes, and Intents of such Men's Hearts and Souls. But because this were most Vain, we shall conclude, The Soul is not generated with, nor inseparable from the Body, but of an immaterial Nature.

That this is no newer than the rest, and was esteemed Heresy in the Primitive Times, I will Evidence.

There was a Sect called Luciferians, from one Lucifer of Sardinia, and the Ter who held, That the Soul was transfused by Generation from the Parents to their Children, and that the Soul is of the Flesh, and Substance of the of which reed Sacrates Scholast- in his 3d Book, and 7th Chapter; also Augustine of Heresies; and Theodorus, his 3d Book and 5th Chapter, about Anno 350.

Fourth, The Fourth sublime Mystery of those Phantastick and Imaginary Persons is a Consequence of the formet, namely, the Mortality of the Soul, That the Soul and Body go to Dust, and rise together at a General Resurrection. T. S. T. p. 43, 44.

That it is consistent with Scripture, I prove.

First, And the Lord God formed Man of the Dust of the Ground, and breathed into his Nostrils the Breath of Life, and Man became a Living Soul, Gen. 2. 7.

If the Breath of Life made a dead Body live; then the Privation of the Breath of Life, makes a living Body dead; since the Life it has was from and is whilst that Breath inspired remains in it; and if so, then not the Soul, but the Body dies.

2. This is farther prov'd thus, If it was living Breath before it entered into the Body, it must be living Breath after it is withdrawn from the Body; since the Body makes no Alteration upon it, but it upon the Body; as from a life-less Heap to a living Body, and from a living to a dead Body again.

3. Though some of those Things which are living may die, because they live by the borrowed or lent Life of another; yet every Life, as Life, cannot die; for since Life and Death are contrary, as Light and Darkness, because very Light can never in itself be utterly extinguish'd by Darkness, so as to become very Darkness, nor Truth Untruth by Error, it is impossible that the Breath of Life, or Soul of Man, can suffer Death, as here understood; for that were very Annihilation itself, or being from an intelligent Something made Nothing.

Secondly, And he cried unto the Lord, and said, O Lord my God, hast thou also brought Evil upon the Widow with whom I sojourn, by slaying her Son? And he stretched himself over the Child Three Times, and cried and said, O Lord my God, I pray thee, Let this Chila's Soul come into him again: And the Lord heard the Voice of Elijah, and the Soul of the Child came into him again, and he revived, 1 Kings 17. 20, 21, 22.

If the Soul was withdrawn when the Body lay dead, as the Place proveth, then the Soul lay not dead from all Motion, Life and Heat, in the Body, as one inseparable Lump. But the Soul was separated, and when it did return, according to Elijah's Prayer, and had resumed it's forsaken dead Body, it revived the Body again; therefore the Soul died not with the Body, nor at all; inasmuch as if it had died, when separated, it could not have revived the dead Body, when returned.

In short, This Place most expresly proves, 1st, The Bodie's Death, from the Soul's Separation: 2dly, The Soul's certain Departure from the Body: 3dly, The Soul's living after Separation.

Thirdly, Then shall the Dust return to the Dust, as it was; and the Spirit to God, that gave it, Eccl. 12. 7.

This Place very evidently harmonizeth with the former, and is a pregnant Instance to the Consutation of that Atheistical Opinion, and as pertinent here, as where mentioned. For, as Man is composed of Body and Spirit, so they have two Originals; the one from below, Dust; the other from above, the Breath of Life; They have also two Dooms, the Dust to the Dust, from whence it came; the Soul to God, from whence it came, to be by him sentenced to the Blessed or Cursed State for ever, according to the End of that Chapter, For God will bring every Secret Thing to Judgment; from whence I argue,

1. That only can properly return to Earth that came from it, that is, Dust. But the Soul never came from Dust nor Earth, as Reeve and Muggleton affirm, p. 45. T. S. T.

Therefore it is impossible that the Soul can truly be said to return to the Earth.

2. That which returns to God is what more immediately and eminently came from him, and that cannot die.

But the Soul doth return to the End aforesaid.

Therefore the Soul came from him, and dieth not, neither can it with the Body return to Dust.

Fourthly, Be not afraid of them that kill the Body, and after that have no more that they can do, Luke 12. 4.

If Reeve and Muggleton speak Truth, then he that kills the Body kills the Soul too; for he cannot kill the one without the other.

But Christ Jesus, the Author of Truth and Salvation, saith, The Body may be killed by Man, and the Soul remain alive; therefore Reeve and Muggleton are Lyars against Christ and his Doctrine.

The Body's Death is Natural, the Soul's Spiritual; Man's Power extendeth but to one, and consequently the latter is independent of the former.

Fifthly, For me to live is Christ, to die is Gain; but if I live in the Flesh, (or Body) this is the Fruit of my Labour: yet what I shall chuse, I wo- not; for I am in a Streight betwixt two, having a Desire to depart, and be with Christ, which is far better, Phil. 1. 21, 22, 23. From whence I plainly argue,

1. If to die was Gain, then he was not to enjoy less of that Divine Consolation which he had living, since to live was Christ. But he that has lain Body and Soul One Thousand Six Hundred Years in the Grave, and may for ought we know One Thousand Six Hundred more, must needs have lost not only a little, but all that he enjoyed Living, instead of farther Gain: Therefore I infer, Their Principle of the Soul's Mortality is contrary to the Testimony of the Apostle; for with him to die was Gain. That this was the Apostle's Sense, I proceed yet farther to make appear from his own Words.

2. The Reason of his Streight was, Whether to live to serve Christ, or die to enjoy him: But this had been no Streight, if he was to lose what he had, and not to enjoy him after Departure in any Sense, as the Dead don't; therefore it was not the Apostle's Judgment, though it is Wicked Reeve's, and Blasphemous Muggleton's, That the Soul is deprived with the Body by Death, of all Divine Enjoyments of God, or Punishment from him, 'till the Day of Resurrection. For the Apostle counted it far better, to depart, and be with Christ; which had been a Vain, if an Inobtainable Desire, as would follow from their Anti-Scriptural Opinion.

Sixthly, And when he had opened the Fifth Seal, I saw under the Altar the Souls of them that were slain for the Word of God, and for the Testimony which they had held; and they cried with a loud Voice, saying, How long, O Lord, Holy and True, dost thou not Judge and Avenge our Blood on them that dwell on the Earth? Revel. 6. 9. 10.

If their Souls liv'd after their Bodies were slain, then they did not die together;but the Scripture proves, their Souls lived after their Bodies were Slain: for they cried for Vengeance on the Blood-thirsty

Inhabitants of the World; therefore Souls are not Mortal, as Bodies are.

In short, Their Bodies were Slain, their Souls were alive; their Bodies were in the Grave, their Souls under the Altar, worshipping God Day and Night for ever and ever.

That this is against Reason, I farther prove.

First, There is nothing Mortal that is not Elementary, or composed of visible Matter or Substance; but the Body is that only Part of Man, which is so composed. And consequently, the Body is the only Mortal Part of Man.

Secondly, That only can be subject to visible and material Generations, Agitations, Motions, Privations, Diminutions, Increases, Alterations, Operations and Corruptions, which is of a Visible, Elementary, and Corporal Substance, (for an Invisible none ever saw subject to any one of them) but of such is the Body, and not the Soul (by Reeve and Muggleton their own Assertion, of Man's Nature to be of the Faith which is God's Nature.).

Therefore the Body is subject only to Generation and Corruption, and not the Soul, That the Soul is not of the same Nature as the Body, I thus prove;

Thirdly, That which is intellectual, which in it's pure Nature knows, comprehends, governs and orders all visible, elementary and corporeal Beings, and yet is Invisible, Spiritual, Rational, and Internal (as is manifest from it's Heavenly Meditations, it's secret Thoughts, it's serious Reflections, acute Memory, and profound Reasonings about the Causes and Effects of all Things) cannot but be of a Nature more refined, excellent and noble, than to fall under the same Generations, Revolutions, and Corruptions, those inferior visible Beings are subject to. But such is the Nature of Man's Soul, as daily Experience manifests to all that will not wilfully Blind their Eyes; therefore though Man's Body be Mortal, as being of that grosser Substance and Elementary Nature, yet his Soul is of -n immortal Nature, and can receive no Alteration of Being by any that may or can happen to the Body, which is but a Well-Organiz'd and disposed Instrument for the Soul to exert or put forth her self by, according to the good Pleasure of God, and that creaturely Prudence necessary to be eyed in and about all Worldly Concernments.

Thus much and enough to this Point.

That this is as Grey-headed as *Atheism*, we may suppose; and that it is not only their only Revelation I prove:

John the 22th Bishop of Rome, and some in the Countries of Arabia, held this very Doctrine, affirming, That Souls and Bodies dyed and rose together; of which read Origen, and Eusebius Pamphilus, lib. 6. chap. 36. nor can any be ignorant that converse with Story, that long before, since, and at this Day, where Reeve and Muggleton were never thought on, this wretched Opinion is but too rise, Anno 249. 1423. Years since.

Fifthly, But their most admirable Secret of all is, That God descended with his Body in the Shape of a Man, and dissolved himself into the Virgin's Womb, and so brought forth himself a Man, who af-r he had lived to such an Age, was Crucified, and really dyed, or ceased to be either God or Man for Three Days and Nights: T. S. T. p. 23 to 30.

That this is in three Particulars highly inconsistent with Scripture I prove.

First, God did not so transmute his Divine Nature into Fleshly Mortal Nature.

1. Your Father Abraham rejoyced to see my Day: Then said the Jews unto him, Thou art not yet Fifty Years old, and hast thou seen Abraham? Jesus said unto them, Verily, Verily, I say unto you, Before Abraham was, I am, John 8. 56, 57, 58.

If that which was before Abraham, and yet then in being the same, was God, as none that own the Scriptures do deny; then because that outward visible Body was not before Abraham, that was not God: The first all grant, the second none reasonably doubt; for Christ was crucified about the Three and Thirtieth Year of his Life: And then I hope none will believe the Eternal Deity was Transmuted, or Transubstantiated into that Visible Body; for so Christ's Answer would not have been true: for that mortal Body, which say Reeve and Muggleton was the Eternal God, had a Beginning, and was of that Age the Jews said it to be.

2. Whose are the Fathers, and of whom as concerning the Flesh Christ came, who is over all, God blessed for ever, Rom. 9. 5.

If Christ, as concerning the Flesh, was not God, as the Text manifestly implieth (by a Distinction betwixt his Appearance in that Body of Flesh, and his Divine Essence or Being, with their Originals) then that fleshly Body was not God, or the Eternal God was not Substantially Transmuted into that Fleshly Body.

Secondly, Neither could Elias be God's Deputy to transact in his stead the Affairs of Heaven, during that Journey which these Impostors affirm God to have taken, from any Scripture Evidence.

1. For my Father is greater than I, John 14. 28.

And he kneeled down and prayed, Father, if thou be willing, remove this Cup from Me; nevertheless; not my Will, but thine be done, Luke 22. 41, 42.

If Elias was that Father which Christ spake of, and prayed and cryed to, as Reeve and Muggleton assert; then either he that cryed to him was not God, but Elias really God (and so they both contradict their own Doctrine, who tells us, That he that was born of the Virgin, and dyed on the Cross, was the Everlasting Father) or else, that which needeth and crieth for Help of another, was greater than that, which was able to succour and deliver it; which how absurd it is, let all sober

The New Witnesses

Men judge: Therefore he to whom he cry'd and pray'd in all Streights, and whom he had affirmed to have received all his Doctrine and Commission from, and who was greater than all, was the only true God, and not any glorified Creature. For God could not leave Elias his Deputy, and not leave him his Power, which if he did, he left Himself; since without his Almighty Power he were not God.

Secondly, I thank thee, O Father, Lord of Heaven and Earth, because thou hast bid these Things from the Wise and the Prudent, and revealed them unto Babes. Mat. 11. 25. The Hour is come, glorifie thy Son, that thy Son also may glorifie thee. And this is Life Eternal, to know thee, the only True God, and Jesus Christ whom thou hast sent. And now Father, glorifie thou me with the Glory which I had with thee before the World was. John 17. 1,3,5.

On this Place I raise these three brief Arguments;

1. If Elias was not the Father of our Lord Jesus Christ, nor Lord of Heaven and Earth, but a created Being, as all confess, then it was not unto Elias that Jesus returned that Heavenly Thanks-giving, but to his own Father, greater than all, who is Lord of Heaven and Earth.

2. If he to whom he prayed be that only true God, and that to know him, and Christ Jesus whom he hath sent, be Life Eternal, then was it not Elias to whom he prayed, because all grant, that he is not the only true God, nor did he so love the World as to send his only begotten into the World, that through believing in him it might obtain Eternal Life. This most plainly knocks down all Conceit of a Deputed God, that Christ should pray unto, because, supposing that such a Thing could be, yet he could not be that only true God, whom to know were Life Eternal: But this to whom Jesus prayed, who say Reeve and Muggleton was Elias, saith Christ Jesus, was the only true God, whom to know is Life Eternal.

3. This God to whom Christ prayed, that he would glorifie him, was the same Eternal God with whom he had Glory before the World began; but Elias was Two Thousand Years or more after the World was made, inst-d of being before the World began; and consequently, Elias was not that God and Father, unto whom the Lord Jesus made his Supplications.

Object. But Muggleton will tell me, That Elias was enthroned with that God-like Power, Glory, Wisdom and Majesty, that rendred him all that which was needful to make able to answer all those Petitions, and what ever else was necessary.

Answ. If the Majesty, Power, Wisdom and Glory of God were left with Elias, I would fain know what God had to dye with; for 'tis his Power, Glory and Divine Wisdom that makes him God- If Elias had them, God left himself destitute of what made him God: For how can a Man leave his Properties alive behind him that truly Man him, and yet he said to dye in Reeve and Muggleton's Sense, which is, That all those Faculties and Properties dye with a Man? Would one not rather say, that such an one does not dye, because that which makes him a true Man lives: So that their Conceit is spoiled in the over-turning of this one Thing; for, show the Impossibility of God's dying, and yet leaving his Power, Wisdom and Glory with Elias, and the whole Fabrick, filled with their many Chambers of Imagery, will fall to the Ground; for, say they, without a God's dying, and becoming from Immortal Mortal, and from Mortal, Immortal again, the whole Heaven and Earth would be out of order, and no Right Knowledge or Salvation can be procured or arrived at.

Much might be urged from many other Scriptures, as that God raised him, and that he is set down on the Right-Hand of the Most High, but let this suffice.

Thirdly, Nor is there any Thing in the whole Scriptures of Truth, that so much as incourages any to believe the Mortality of the Immortal God.

1. Even from Everlasting to Everlasting, thou art God, Psal. 90. 2.

He that was from Everlasting, and is to Everlasting, never ceaseth to be, as that which dyes doth; but the true God was from Everlasting, and is to Everlasting; therefore Reeve and Muggleton's Mortal God is not the true God; or, the true God never ceaseth to be.

2. Hast thou not known, hast thou not heard, that the Everlasting God, the Lord, the Creator of the Ends of the Earth, fainteth not? Isa. 40. 28.

He that could never faint, could never dye, because Death is more than a Degree beyond fainting (though fainting be a Temporary withdrawing of Life) but the true God and Creator of the Ends of the Earth never could faint; therefore the true God could never dye.

3. And one of the Malefactors said, Lord, remember me when thou comest into thy Kingdom? And Jesus said, Verily, verily, I say unto thee, To day shalt thou be with me in Paradise, Luke 23. 42, 43.

If Christ, the Author of all Truth, spake Truth, as most unquestionably he did; then both himself and the Malefactor were in Paradise that Day, and consequently, it was utterly impossible that they should both dye from all visible and invisible Life, Sense, Understanding and Enjoyment. But I hope, none are so impudent as to say, Christ spake not the very simple Truth, and so would have deceived the poor Man; and yet I know not how far Muggleton will go in this Matter, since he told me, that Moses in his Discourse of the Creation, set the Cart before the Horse; and that if Paul were alive, he would reprove him, and so censure that Holy Spirit by which he wrote.

Therefore it was not the Eternal Deity that suffered Death, but the Body of outward Flesh, subjected to all those natural Passions of Heat, Cold, Hunger, Thirst, Life and Death (as ours are, sin only excepted) which the Eternal Infinite Creator had provided, through which to manifest his Everlasting Wisdom, Counsel and Mercy for the Redemption of Mankind.

That these three Branches of this sottish Opinion are all of them greatly repugnant to that Understanding God has afforded Men to measure and distinguish Things by, I prove.

First, It was impossible for God to transubstantiate himself from an Immortal Deity to a mortal Man.

1. It must suppose God's begetting himself, which is absurd, and impossible since being begotten, supposeth him to have had a Beginning (that gave Beginning to all) and to beget, supposeth him to have been before he was begotten, and so before he was.

2. Such as is the Begetter, such must the Begotten be: We see, Men get Men; Horses, Horses; Fish, Fish; and every Seed has it's own Body, as say Reeve and Muggleton; then, by good Consequence, the Immortal God must have begotten himself an Immortal God, one that could not dye by the Hand or Cruelty of his own Creature.

3. It is as impossible for God to become a Creature, or to dissolve his own Infinite, Immortal, Eternal Nature into a Finite, Mortal, Created or Generated Nature; as for a Mortal Created Nature to be refined, preferred, and transmuted into an Infinite, Immortal, Creating Nature. In short, It is as impossible for God, as God, to become a dying Man, as for a dying Man to be changed into an Immortal Eternal God: They are reciprocally impossible and Blasphemous.

Secondly, It is absurd, and untrue to affirm, that Elias was God's Deputy, and he to whom Christ prayed when in that Body of Flesh.

1. He that is Infinite, is every where, and circumscribed to no particular Place; but Scripture, Reason, and Reeve and Muggleton (yet they are seldom of one Mind) own and declare the Infiniteness of God, therefore God is every where, and if every where, then not excluded Heaven, the Habitation of his Throne, and consequently Elias was not God's Deputy, neither was it any ways needful that he should be.

2. That which in any Sense may be said to want, is not God, who is all in all to himself; but who needed a Deputy, neither was Omnipresent, nor Almighty, and therefore not the only True God.

3. Either Christ did not stand in need when on Earth, or he did; if not, then he was not sincere in his Supplications; if he did, then the Omnipotency was with Elias (he that supplies Wants is greater than he that is supplied) and consequently, he that cried was not that Everlasting God and Father, but Elias.

4. Elias was not so considerable as Moses, who was the first Grand Commissioner of God's Dispensations to the Sons of Men (as Reeve and Muggleton affirm) why then should Elias be preferred to Moses, a meek Man, Israel's Leader; and who said of Christ himself, That a Prophet like unto me shall the Lord your God raise up unto you, him shall you hear in all Things (then not Reeve and Muggleton in any new Thing) 'Tis strange therefore, that Moses was not rather of the two, elected to represent him in Heaven, who was a Figure of him on Earth. But though Reeve would not tell us so, I am of the Mind I know the Reason of it, namely, That Christ did not call, Moses, Moses, but Eli,

Eli, when upon the Cross; and I am perswaded he had no other Ground for that Conceit, not considering that Eli, Eli, are Hebrew Words, importing no more Elias, Elias, than they do Moses, Moses, but My God, My God, as the Place expresly shews us.

Much more might be said, but let this serve.

Thirdly, That the Immortal God could never Dye, or cease to be, is manifest, and the contrary Blasphemously False.

1. If God was he that made all Things, and by whom they are upheld, as all believe, that believe there is a God at all, then had he ceased to be, the Created had ceased to have been upheld; and consequently all had fallen into it's first Chaos, or else the World can subsist without Him.

2. That he, whose Nature it was never to have Beginning, and ever to live without Variation, could never become so contrary to his own Nature and Being, as to change, dye or cease to be; but such was the true God, therefore he never dyed.

If Saints live, move, and have their being in God, as say Reeve and Muggleton, pag. 201. D. L. G. then either God never dyed, or there were no Saints when the Jews Crucified Christ, or the Saints dyed too. They deny them all; they say, God Died, and there were Saints, and they Lived, Moved and had their Being in God, though Dead; which how all, or any of them can hang together, let sober People judge.

4. If God died, who lived, and by whom? For nothing can live of it self, that had beginning from, or Dependence on another, as had all the visible World on God; therefore because all lived, and was preserved, that had it's Being from God, He from whom they had their Being, could not be annihilated whilst they remained in Being.

5. If God was raised by Elias, then either Elias was the True God, or Elias the Creature was stronger than Jehovah the Great Creator. Let this serve to confute, and for ever to overturn these idle Chimeras of those filthy Dreamers Reeve and Muggleton.

That this Blasphemous Conceit of the Immortal God's Mortality, is not new, I shall make appear.

First, Valentinus is said, openly to have published at Rome, That Christ brought a Body down from Heaven, and that he after some Time passed through the Virgin's Body again. Noetus affirmed, That the Father, Son and Holy Ghost were Flesh, or that one Person of the Son of Man, or that Person so long since at Jerusalem, to be Father, Son, and Spirit; and that when he suffered on the Cross, the Father, Son and Holy Spirit died. See Euseb. his 4th Book and 10th Chap. Ireneus. Epiphanius Heres. 31. & 57. about Anno 150. which is 1522. Years since. What Stange New Revelation this is!

Lastly, I May mention another of their Tenets, held at this Day by all Calvinists abroad, and of several Sects in these Nations; namely, Predestination, or that God from all Eternity, without any other

Inducement than his own Pleasure, hath decreed some for Salvation, and some for Damnation; contrary to which, all their Obedience or Rebellion shall be in vain, to alter his Determination. D. L. G. p. 72, 73, 74.

That this Principle is Accurst by Scripture I prove.

First, The Righteousness of the Righteous shall be upon him, and the Wickedness of the Wicked shall be upon him; but if the Wicked will turn from all his Sins that he hath committed, and keep my Statutes, he shall surely live, he shall not dye, Ezek. 18. 20, 21.

1. If Righteousness or Wickedness are the Grounds of God's Rewarding or Punishing the Souls of Men, then is there no Predestination previous, without Consideration had to their Works; but the Text affirms this most plainly; therefore such Dec-ees are denied and disowned.

2. If Man may turn from his Righteousness and Wickedness, then are the Means no more inevitably Predestinated for Men to use, than before-mentioned; but Men may turn from either, and accordingly they will be rewarded; therefore no such Predestinated Damnation or Salvation.

Secondly, For it is good and acceptable in the Sight of God our Saviour, who will have all Men to be saved, and to come unto the Knowledge of the Truth, 1 Tim. 2. 3, 4.

If the Apostle writ by the Spirit of God, that gives to know the Mind of God; then it was the Good Will of God, that all Men, not excluding any upon a Predestination, should come to the Knowledge of the Truth, and be saved: And consequently, there is no Predestinated Restraint upon Men's Understandings, from knowing the Truth, nor fore-appointed Bar from their enjoying the End of such True Knowledge, even the Salvation of their Souls.

Thirdly, The Lord is not slack concerning his Promise (as some Men count Slackness) but is long-suffering to us-ward, not willing that any should perish, but that all should come to Repentance, 2 Pet. 3. 9.

The Long-suffering of God either related to the Elect, or Reprobate, or Neither.

Not to the Elect, because there is no need of fearing their Perishing.

Not to the Reprobate, for there is no Possibility of their Repentance.

Therefore to neither; and consequently, either the Place is spurious, or deceitful; or else those Kinds of Elections and Reprobations are meer Phantasms. Let these few Instances serve, of those Hundreds that might be mentioned, most expresly to confirm the same.

That this is highly inconsistent with Reason, I briefly prove.

First, it renders God most Unwise, to make so many Thousand Creatures on purpose to Rebel against him, to Kill, Lye, Steal, Blaspheme, and commit all manner of outragious Wickedness, to the grieving of his own Spirit, the making him Repent he had made the World, and obstructing of his Glorious Work of Reformation.

Secondly, It greatly disparageth his Justice, which consists in proportioning Rewards and Punishments to the Good and Evil Works of Men, and overturns both, by making their Eternal States necessary and unavoidable upon a Predestination, without any Regard to their Works; so that Man is damn'd for not doing what he can't do, any more than it is possible for him to break an Almighty Decree.

Thirdly, It quite destroys his Mercy, and renders him the most Cruel of all Beings; for instead of not being willing, or desiring the Death of a Sinner, He is here made to desire, and take Pleasure in it too; nay, so Essential is this unutterable Cruelty to his Glory (as say the Asserters of this Opinion) that it would be lessened or eclipsed without it: O infamous!

Fourthly, But above all Things, it strikes at the very Root of God's Rectitude, and Faithfulness, and makes him worse than the worst of Men and Devils: For whilst he says, Your Sins have kept Good Things from you; as I live, I delight not in the Death of a Sinner; Repent, and Iniquity shall not be your Ruin; How long would I have gathered you, and ye would not? But now God commands all to Repent; God is no Respecter of Persons, but they that fear him in every Age shall be accepted, &c. with many more. They make him but to complement with wicked Men, and speak them fair in Words, meaning nothing less in his Heart, having Pre-Ordained them to Eternal Wrath.

Fifthly, This Principle would defile his eternally inherent Holiness, by making him as well the Father of Sin, as of Destruction; for Men are either damned for something, or for nothing; if for nothing, that were most Wicked in these Predestinarians

Account, then for something: And what is that? Sin: Very well: And how came they to this Sin? They committed it: And how came they to do so? They would do it. Why? Could they have avoided it? By no Means. Where's the Difference then betwixt being Damn'd for not doing what they could not, and doing nothing? The Predestination was not, that all Evil Men, that wilfully withstood Mercy, should be Damned; For they were Ordained never to receive it; but that such a Number, consisting of such and such particular Persons, should Unalterably and Unavoidably be Damned, only to Glorifie God.

Sixthly, But this would stain the Glory of the Almighty, in that neither in himself, nor from the Redemption and Salvation of the Souls of Men, his Glory is great enough, unless it be compleated in the Eternal Destruction of far the greatest Part of Mankind.

Seventhly, This destroys all Good Works; for, may all say, Neither can my Good nor Evil Works make one Hair white or black, add, or diminish, in reference to God's unalterable Decree; and therefore will I give my self unto the Liberty of the Flesh, and enjoy the Pleasures of this Life, whilst I can have them.

Eighthly, It destroys all Government, since who cares how desperate he is, or what Injury he does, who conceiting to himself his

The New Witnesses

Post is pitcht, his State set, and that unchangeably; but breaking all Laws, takes his Revenge on what would bring him to condign Punishment for his Exorbitancies.

To conclude, and come somewhat closer to the Persons concerned: What signifies their coming to call them to Repent, that cannot be saved if they do? Or to warn such to Repent that cannot be Damned? What signifies their Commission? Or their Cursing, or Blessing? For can they Bless him to Life, that is Ordained before-hand to be Damned? Or can they Curse him to Death, who is Pre-ordained to Eternal Life? If therefore Men are Pre-ordained to Salvation or Damnation, to what Purpose should any fear their Curse, or prize their Blessing, since neither can alter or change the Condition of any Person; and what more contrary to the Mind of the Merciful God, who is willing that all should come unto the Knowledge of the Truth, and be saved?

That Antiquity both knew, and abhorr'd this Opinion, is manifest.

Read Josephus, in his 18th Book of Antiquities, and second Chapter. Also Epiphanius, in his Preface to his first Book of Heresie. Again, Eusebius, in his fifth Book, Chap. 13. and Socrates in his first Book, and Chap. 17. and you will be fully informed of the Abettors of this dangerous and wicked Opinion, namely, a Sect of the Pharisees; also Florinus and Blastus, against whom Ireneus, Bishop of Lyons in France, wrote two Epistles, and a Book call'd Ogdous, wherein he tells Florinus, "That when himself was a Child, and with the famous Christian Polycarpus, who conversed with John that conversed with Christ, he remembred him to be busie about the Emperor's Court; and farther tells him, That had the Apostle John but lived to have heard that Damnable Doctrine, which makes God the Author of Evil, he would have said, Good God, unto what Times hast Thou reserved me! And tells him, That in publishing so wicked an Opinion, he had declared that which all the Hereticks before had never durst to pronounce plainly," with much more to this Purpose, against him.

The Sect called Manichees, from one Manes, held, and promoted this Opinion of Fatal Destiny, who, Muggleton-like, is reported to have called himself Christ and the Comforter, and published the Work of one Buddas in his own Name, calling it, A New Dispensation; all which, Reader, I assure thee, Histories do inform us, to have been known in the 2d, 3d, 4th, 5th, and 600 Years after Christ, which is above a Thousand Years since: In which Time, many were the impudent Spirits that assum'd to themselves as great Authority as Muggleton in Reeve's Absence doth at this Time; namely, Simon Magus, who had so far possess'd the Romans with his Sorcery, of his (pretended) Divinity (calling himself to the Samaritans the Father; to the Jews the Son, to the Gentiles, the Holy Spirit) as that the Heathens erected a Statue or Image of him, in the Time of Claudius at Rome, having this Inscription, Simoni Deo Sancto, to the Holy God

Simon. Next, one Helen a Woman, that accompanied him, whom he called the Principal Understanding, much like Muggleton's Daughter, who, Reeve said, Should be the Chiefest of Women. Eusebius in his 2nd Book, and 12, 13, and 14th Chapters. After this, one Menander, said to have been a Sorcerer, and the Disciple of Simon, went up and down, deluding

filly credulous People, by affirming to them, He was the Great Power of God, come down from Heaven, and that all were to believe in, and be Baptized in his Manner, or they could not be saved, but those that did, should never dye. Read Eusebius in his 3d Book, Chap. 23. Ireneus, Book 1. Chap. 21. Epiphan. Haeres. 22. Again, Carpocrates is reported to have (like Reeve and Muggleton) patch'd his Opinion (who was so Vain-Glorious as to affirm he knew all Things) out of Simon, Menander, Nicholas, (from whence came the Nicolatians in the Revelations) Saturninus, Basilides, &c. and see Epiphan. Haeres. 27. also Augustin of Heresies. Again, we find that Eusebius tells us of one Montanus (whereof Montanists, or Cartaphrygians are called) who taught in Phrygia, that he was the Holy Ghost, as may be seen in the 5th Book of Eusebius, 13, 14, 15, 16, and 17th Chapters. Also that one Buddas affirm'd, That he was born of a Virgin, (as true as Muggleton's being the Last Witness of God.) This Buddas writ a Book, and in his swelling Pride, styl'd it Mysteries, much like the Whimsies of Reeve and Muggleton, in their Transcendent Spiritual Treatise; next, he wrote a Book, called The Gospel, of the Nature of Reeve and Muggleton's Divine Looking-Glass: His End was to break his Neck: 'Tis to be fear'd that a worse will be miserable Muggleton's, even Torment of Spirit, as Reeve is said to have left the World in. To conclude, Noetus, the Ring-Leader of that Great Mystery, (never revealed till within these Twenty Years, says Reeve and Muggleton) namely, the Godhead being a Man, and so absolutely Flesh and Blood, as that when the Body dyed, the Godhead ceased, and lay under Death's Power three Days and three Nights. He, through the Height of his Imaginations, called himself Moses, and Aaron his Brother, as Reeve called himself and Muggleton, T. S. T. see Epiphanius Haeres. 57. By all which, Reader, I am not without Hopes, but it does appear, how falsly, and with what Treachery, these Persons have dealt with poor filly People, who not being satisfied in what they did know, have pin'd their Faith on the Sleeves of such as told them Things they did not know, and so have been given up to believe a Lye: For what is more evident, than that in this very Trial he, and his deceased Colleague, are found Guilty of Error, Treachery, and great Deceit: Therefore, Reader, delay not to pass the Just Sentence of Impostor and Counterseit upon them, and their Commission, who would raise to themselves a New Sect out of the Ruins of Old Heresies, and that under the Pretence of Choice Revelations, wherein there is no Proof beyond their bare Assertions, and to make them pass, forge an Authority from Heaven (which loaths both them, and their Lyes) to back and recommend them as unheard of Mysteries.

The New Witnesses

O! fell not thy Reason, whoever thou art, enslave not thy Judgment, nor rob God's Light and Grace of it's Office, to guide and teach thee in the Denial of those Evils that are to be forsaken, and in embracing whatsoever ought to be followed: Bring not thy self under the Power of an ignorant, arrogant, blasphemous, and sottish Man, but remember that God Almighty, who cannot lye, hath promised, That in the last Days he would be the Teacher of his People by his Spirit of Truth, and where is the Habitation of the Most High, but in the Contrite and Humble Hearts of Men? For whatsoever may, or can be known of God, is manifested within, who having illuminated all, and given to every a Man a Talent, into it, Reader, have thy Mind retired, and wait to have it subject thereunto, and thou shalt come to know him (whom to know aright is Life Eternal.) But as I have plainly shown their abominable Cheat, in obtruding Old Fables for New Revelations upon People (whereby I have discharg'd the first Part of my Promise) so for a Confirmation of my Judgment concerning Muggleton, and to accomplish this abridg'd Discourse, take my following Relation, with the same Impartiality that I give it thee.

I have been twice to visit Lodowick Muggleton, and at each Time I staid too long to repeat all, or the very Words which passed betwixt us; yet shall I faithfully write something of the Matter and Words, as near as I at present do remember them.

Penn. Art thou the last Witness that ever shall be?

Mug. Yes; and there shall never be another.

P. Who sent thee?

M. God spoke to John Reeve, and he spoke to me.

P. Is that all thou hast to produce, only J. R 's Word for it? This he avoided.

Again, P. Thou sayst God did not create the Earth and the Heavens, he only fashion'd them; making them Co-eternal with God; but Moses said he did: Let me see a Bible.

M. Moses put the Cart before the Horse.

[This I bore for the next Question's Sake.]

P. Paul the Apostle, who also wrote, by the Inspiration of the Holy Ghost, saith God created all Things, or made them; and the World is a great Part of all Things: Besides, if it was before he made it, in this Sense, Must it not be God? Since nothing which is uncreated can be a Creature.

M. If Paul were living, I would have reproved him for that: Come not here to dispute, but believe, I say it, that's enough.

P. Canst thou reprove the Holy Ghost; for he spake by it?

M. Yes.

P. That's Blasphemy; besides, if thou sayst it, must I therefore believe it, because thou sayst it?

At this he grew inraged; and but for an Acquaintance by, and a Friend of his, I had doubtless been Curst at that Time.

The next Time I came (with a Friend in Company) I found him sitting by the Chimney-Corner, quaffing with some of his Followers and Benefactors, as what we saw before us did Evidence. My first Salute was thus:

P. How is it Lodowick? Methinks thou look'st with thy old threadbare black Suit, like a sequester'd begging Priest.

M. I am a Priest.

P. Art thou? Of what Order?

M. The Order of Aaron.

P. Aaron! Where be thy Bells then?

M. I have them in the Mystery.

P. Mystery! For Shame, don't talk of a Mystery; for there was no such Thing that did belong to that Order; Things were altogether External, Typical, and Figurative: Methinks this were enough to show, that thou art no Ways concern'd in any Christian Commission, who art not a Priest after the Order of Melchisedeck, but Aaron, whose Priesthood is at an End, as said the Apostle to the Hebrews, ch. 7. so that thou hast Unchristian'd thy whole Commission, and brought it under the Law of a Carnal Commandment; and therefore hast no Part nor Portion in the Power of an Endless Life, as saith the same Apostle. He interrupted.

M. Have a Care, Life and Death's before thee; therefore chuse Life and live, &c.

P. But Lodowick, thou pretendest to know the Dimensions of God, how high may he be?

M. Betwixt your Height and his, (meaning a Friend then present.)

P. O Abominable! Well, L. Muggleton, God will blast thee for ever, thou Presumptuous and Blasphemous Wretch, If thou turnest not from thy Wickedness, with much more.

M. Thou shalt be Damned, God has decreed thou shalt be Damned; thou art of the Seed of the Serpent.

P. Why then didst thou set Life and Death before me just now, (saying thou hadst more Mind I should be saved, than any of the Quakers) if I am ordain'd to be damn'd? Is it not great Deceit, to exhort a Man to chuse what he cannot have, though he bid for it, and to refuse that which he is unable to avoid? But Muggleton, I will not say, that I serve such a God; no, my God never ordained thee to be damned, whether thou dost well or ill: This destroys all Rewards and Punishments, and makes Evil and Good unavoidable.

M. I would not give a Pin for that God which would save us both, now I have Damn'd thee.

P. Why dost thou talk of a God; for thou sayst, Thy God can dye; did the Immortal God ever cease to be?

M. I would not give a Rush for that God which can't dye.

P. I say, thou and thy God shall to the Pit, from whence ye came, where is Death and Darkness for ever: How can God cease to be, and yet be God; since if he ceast, every thing that remained in Being, must

The New Witnesses

have been greater, since below ceasing to be is nothing? But suppose this Nonsense and Blasphemies; how rose he again?

M. God left Elias with Power.

P. Then Elias was greater than God; for that which raiseth, is greater than that which is raised; but if the Power never dyed, the Power was God, and that which dyed, not God: O, Hellish Impudence and Blasphemy! O, Muggleton, thy End will be Destruction.

M. W. P. I say thou art a Damned Devil; remember Thomas Loe, who was the wickedest Devil that ever I knew, who never went out of his Bed after I Curst him.

P. Thy Curses are under my Feet; Thomas Loe was known to be an infirm Man in his Natural Constitution (as well as by his great Labours) for near these sixteen Years, who is gone to rest: But art thou not ashamed to say, he never went out of his Bed, who was as well as he used to be, and often after abroad? And when he fell sick, was often up, and changed his Lodging before he dyed, having been ill three Weeks. Is this thy infallible Spirit, that thus suggests Lyes to thy self and others?

M. I heard so.

P. Is that enough for one that pretends to be the last Witness of the High and Mighty God, to say for a Lye, I heard so? Cover thy Face for Shame.

M. He writ me a Curse, and he writ a very good Hand too; but for all that he was a Damned Devil, and thou W. P. art as arrant a Devil as he, and you shall be Damn'd together.

P. Lodowick, in this thou hast told another Lye; for it was an Apprentice that writ it: Where is thy Unerring Spirit now, thou Vile Impostor? And for being Devils, and Damn'd together, God rebuke thee; only this know, that I am willing to go where he went, and whither thou canst not come, without great and unfeigned Repentance.

M. Just so, many of you Quakers have dyed after my Curse, amongst others, William Smith.

P. This is a notorious Lye; for the Man is yet Living: Well, Muggleton, God will reckon with thee for all thy Wickedness.

M. Thou art a Cheat, and a Deceiver, W. P. (my Friend spoke)

G. W. Muggleton, have a Care what thou sayst; for though it is our Religion to forgive Injuries; yet perhaps his Friends would question thee, and make thee prove it.

M. I care not a Fart for him, nor his Friends, nor the Greatest Man in England.

P. Thy black Mouth is no Slander; but know, Muggleton, That from my Youth I have sought God, and dared not willingly to abuse a Worm: And as my Friend has said, thou knowest there are Laws, other People make use of to vindicate their Credit by, but I forgive thee; thereby thou may'st know the Difference betwixt our Gods, and our Religions; thou revilest, and passest Curses upon me, I freely forgive thee.

M. I care not a Turd for you, nor the Law neither.

This, with many more unfavoury soul Expressions sell from his Mouth. He also affirmed, That God never gave a Law but to Devils; and that Moses and the Israelites were so. I askt him if he received a Law? He said, Yes. I askt him for whom? He said, For the People of these Nations to whom he was sent. I told him, Then that render'd both himself, and those to whom he was sent, Devils by his own Assertion.

In short, such Impertinency, such Blasphemy, such sottish Nonsense, and such unsavoury ill-bred Expressions, I don't remember to have heard from the Mouth of any Man, pretending to Religion. If this be your Prophet, (you that believe in him) your Last Witness, the only Messenger of the Spiritual Dispensation, and Grand Commissioner of Heaven, whom all must credit, or be damned: For Shame, own not so manifest an Impostor, so soul a Wretch, so ill an Example; his Arrogancy, his Ignorance, his Sottish Life, his Cowardliness, and finally, his abominable Lying Spirit is far from the Holy, Patient, Suffering, Self-denying, and Heavenly Life of Christ and his Apostles, who being Reviled, Blessed. I therefore intreat, nay, warn the Reader hereof; and to fear the Infinite Almighty God, whose mighty Judgments (for Sin in the Consciences of Men and Women) are come; and not to Worship this Beast, nor any Evil Thing, by bowing to his dark Imaginations: For know of a certain, the Time is at hand, when every Word, Faith and Work shall be tryed, that they who believe the Truth, and live in it, may have Rejoycing in themselves, and not in another; when Muggleton's Airy Stories (which may perhaps swell and puff up the Minds of silly People) shall vanish; and such as have made his Lyes their Refuge, shall be swept away, and their Place not be found among the Living. Therefore mind the Light, the Grace, the Gift of God in yourselves, which leads to Repentance, and all manner of Godly Conversation (a Thing Muggleton meddles not with) that by it your Hearts may be sanctified, and settled in the Belief of the Truth, as it is plainly revealed to every Particular in Christ Jesus,

Shall you obtain a sound Understanding, and possess the Habitations of true Peace, when Muggleton and his obstinate Brats shall howl in the Lake that burns with Brimstone and Fire for ever and evermore.

W. P.

John Reeve and Lodowick Muggleton, Contradicting Themselves, and One Another.

It can be no Wonder unto such as have impartially read thus far, that these Men should contradict themselves, and one another; who are filled in their Discourses (or rather Ravings) with nothing sober and consonant; but Confusion heap'd upon Confusion, to the astonishing of every Man that is in earnest about Religion, and has any due Fear and Reverence for God; but because they lay it down, as the Mark only of the True Commissioners of Heaven, in nothing to Jar or Contradict, I am the more induced to add to my own Pains and the Readers, a Comparison of their Contradictions.

Doth not this Demonstrate those to be the Commissionated Witnesses of the Unerring Spirit, that are endued with a Divine Gift, to write a Volume as large as the Bible, and as pure a Language as that is, with as much Variety of Matter, without looking in any Writing whatsoever, or Having any Real Contradiction in it, R. & M. Div. Look Glass, Page 112.

Contradiction I.

Therefore it is written, Dust thou art, and unto Dust thou shalt return: When the Lord spake those Words, he did not speak to the Flesh, or outward Form, or Body of the Man; but he spake to the Inward Spirit or Soul, that understands the Words of a Spirit. Look in his Transc. Spiritual Treatise, p. 44.

Wherefore it may be queried by some, What was that which entred into the Dust, and brought forth Angelical Bodies; was it any thing else, but the Divine Nature of God Himself? Unto this Curious Query, from the true Light of Life I answer, That neither the Spirit of Angels, nor any other Creatures were formed of the Divine Nature; but the Souls of Adam and Eve only, His Divine L. Glass, p. 8.

Animadversion I.

If that which returns to Dust, cannot be said to return to Dust, unless it first came from Dust; then, if the Soul returns to Dust, it consequently came from Dust; and if from Dust, then was it not formed of the Divine Nature, as on the other Side is affirmed, and therefore a Contradiction.

Contradiction II.

Again, I declare, That when the Elect are Glorified, they are absolutely of the very same Glorious Nature, both in Spirit and Body, as God is. T. S. T. p. 46.

Therefore the most Wise and Holy Creator created the Bodies of Angels Spiritual, and their Natures Rational; and he made the Body of the Man Adam Natural, and his Soul Spiritual: For, if their Spirits and Bodies had been both of the Divine Nature, then it would have been impossible for them to have been capable of any Sin or Evil, any more than the Creator Himself;; for what would have been formed, but Creators only, instead of Creatures? D. L. G. page 9, 10.

Animadversion II.

If to be in Body and Spirit, Spiritual, be to be Creators, then Gods; and if the Saints are to be of the same Body and Spirit, then they are to be Creators, and consequently Gods; which is absurd: For if the Reason, why Man was not at first made all Spiritual, but the Soul Spiritual, and the Body Natural, was, because he had been a Creator, as they say, which was impossible; then, if Man is to be of the same Body and Spirit that God is, as they affirm; Man is to be a Creator in the next World. Monstrum Horrendum!

Contradiction III.

If the very God-head had not died, (that is) If the very Soul of Christ, which is the Eternal Father, had not died in the Body, or with the Body, to quiet or satisfy the Cry of the Guilt of Sin in Men's Spirits, all Men would have perished to Eternity: Thus the Father and the Son was but one unseparable Person in Immortal Glory, from all Eternity; and became, in Time, one unseparable Person in Mortality. T. S. T. p. 25, 26.

If Angels and Men had been both of God's Divine Nature in their Creation, then instead of their being capable to be changed into an higher or lower Condition, at the Divine Pleasure of the Creator; would they not rather have been Unchangeable Creators, than Changeable Creatures? D. L. G. p. 9.

Animadversion III.

If the Reason why Men and Angels are not of the Divine Nature, be, That they are subject to Change, and that if they had been made of it, they would not have been capable of Mutation into lower or higher Degrees, at Divine Pleasure; then because God is of that Divine Nature, it is consistent with his Nature to Change, or be Transmuted, as they often speak, from an higher State to a lower; and so, their whole Conceit of the Deity's Mortality, is Vain, and by themselves Contradicted.

Contradiction IV.

Again, Many seeming wise Men do imagine the Lord to be a Vast Spirit. D. L. G. p. 16.

Others blasphemously say, that the Spirit of Man is God, and that the Body only dies: These say also, God is an Infinite Spirit. T. S. T. p. 44.

The New Witnesses

Is not that Infinite Spirit, and it's Glorious Properties, but only one Essence, or God-head Substance? D. L. G. p. 106.

You may know, that all Things are possible and very easy for an Infinite Spirit to bring to pass. D. L. G. p. 114.

Animadversion. IV.

It can be no Crime, for any to believe, God to be an Infinite or Vast Spirit, as one while they would have it, whilst presently they call the God-head Substance, an Infinite Spirit, and confess all Things to be possible unto an Infinite Spirit. O Gross Contradiction!

Contradiction V.

I say, In the Great and Notable Day of the Lord, by his Decree, they shall every one of them rise out of the Dust together; not with the same Bodies that died, because there was somewhat of God in those Bodies. T. S. T. p. 11.

So likewise that Infinite Spirit abiding within the glorious Body of Christ, is so unspeakably fiery Glorious, that no Created Spirit of Man nor Angel is able to bear the In dwelling Essence of it. D. L. G. p. 69.

Animadversion V.

If something of God dwells in this Life in the Souls and Bodies of Men, then it is not so fiery Glorious, but it may abide in them, and they not be consumed: For God's Nature or Essence is irreconcileable to nothing but Sin; the Righteous shall behold him Face to Face: So that one while, God dwells in Men; another while, if it should be so, Man would be consumed. Behold the Self-Opposition of these Miserable Witnesses.

Contradiction VI.

How can any Rational Wise Man possibly think, that Man, or any other Living Forms, should ever be without a Glorious Creator, to give them their Beings at first. D. L. G. p. 16.

This was the Creator's very Case in the Matter of Creation; and who dares speak against it? no Spiritual Wise Man, I am sure, only some Lustful Persons, may dispute against it, though it be contrary to their own Reason, when it is sober. D. L. G. p. 12.

I confess, it is not only contrary to Reason, but far above all Reason's Reach, truly to understand the Mysteries of the Creation. D. L. G.

Animadversion VI.

If an Appeal be made to rational Men, concerning the Creation by a God, and if it be contrary to sober Reason not to believe so, then it is not far above, nor contrary to all Reason, to understand the Creation; for else, why is it rendred by them so agreeable to Reason, and an Appeal made unto Rational Men concerning it?

Contradiction VII.

Again, For your Information, in whose Persons, the Lord by his Holy Spirit Delights to dwell. T. S. T. p. 22.

Whoever thou art, that boastest of a God, and a Christ, and his Ordinances, and of a Glory to come without thee, in the Highest Heavens; if thou should'st be left to the Pride and Envy of thy Formal Spirit, to condemn the Invisible Teachings of the Lord Jesus Christ in his Innocent People, because they are contrary to thy Opinion; I say, from the Everlasting Emanuel, That thou art also but a Reprobate. D. L. G. p. 68, 69.

For in him dwelleth all the Fulness of the Godhead bodily, and from his Fulness we all receive, and Grace for Grace. If Christ, or his Spirit, were within Men when they uttered those Words, all Faith or Hope, in Reference to Eternal Glory was vain. D. L. G. p. 67, 68.

Animadversion VII.

If Christ delighteth to dwell in the Persons of his People, by his Eternal Spirit, and that he thereby teacheth their Souls what he requires from them, as say they; then it is not in Vain to believe or hope, though Christ, or his Spirit, were within, as they also say: nay, they affirm; That the Souls of the Redeemed is the Throne of God, on which he now sits, D. L. G. p. 46. And therefore, though Christ, or his Spirit were in Believers, yet that would not make their Faith and Hope Void; Why? Because they stand therein.

Contradiction VIII.

Is that Eternal Spirit, in it's Heavenly Virtues, any Thing else, but Immortal Crowns of bright burning Glories? Tho' the Eternal Spirit, be that Invisible God, that by the Power of his Almighty Word hath created all Things; and though all Power, Wisdom and Glory proceeds only from an Invisible Eternal Spirit, D. L. G. p. 106.

Can this Infinite Spiritual Glory, be sensible of it's Divine Excellency, or be a perfect Blessedness, except he hath a distinct

Body, suitable to his Eternal Spirit; yet without a Body, Face, or Tongue, or a Majestical Person, like unto Earthly Monarchs, he could not possibly have spoken distinct Words, nor his Glory have been perfect. D. L. G. p. 106.

Animadversion VIII.

If that which is requisite to define or render God truly such, be singly attributed to the Eternal Spirit, without the Mention of a Body, then is the Eternal Spirit the Invisible God, as they themselves prove. If the Eternal Spirit be nothing else than Crowns of Immortal Glory, and that it is the Invisible God, whose Power created all Things; and if all Wisdom, Glory and Power proceed only from this Invisible Eternal Spirit, as they say; then not unto a Body, but unto that, who alone has all Power, Wisdom and Glory, is the Godhead to be ascribed; but that is unto the Invisible Spirit: And if the Eternal Spirit be thus qualify'd, how possibly can it's Glory be eclipst for want of a Body, Face, or Tongue? Is the Eternal Spirit Crowns of Immortal Imperfect Glory? And how can all Glory alone be given unto the Spirit, whose Glory is Imperfect, without a Body? He should have said, From the Spirit and Body alone proceedeth all Glory, &c. But this Confusion is like the rest.

Contradiction IX.

Moreover, You may know, That those Men called, Independents, Anabaptists, Presbyterians, are the Literal Apostolical Jews. D. L. G. p. 191.

Furthermore, Those Anabaptist, Presbyterian Men, which hold it lawful to persecute Men, in their Persons and Estates, upon a Spiritual Account; I say from the Eternal Spirit, That they are for the most Part, the Off-spring of those bloody-minded Jews that Crucified the Lord of Glory upon the Account of Blasphemy. D. L. G. p. 192.

Animadversion IX.

That Exception should have been made before: for, if those that are called Independents, Presbyterians, and Anabaptists, are Apostolical Jews, and yet such as are for Persecution for Conscience, are of their Race that put Christ to Death, then they are not of the Apostolical, but Mosaical Jews: But how can they make that hold together? The Apostolical Jew, is one, not outward in the Letter, but in the Heart, and in the Spirit; if so, either they are Independents, Presbyterians, or Anabaptists; or else those three Opinions are come to be of theirs, since at the Distance they stand, they cannot be under the same Covenant and Circumcision. But to be short, By their declaring them (whilst not their Followers) Apostolical Jews, we may conclude, That

Reeve and Muggleton count themselves none of them, but Men of another Dispensation; and therefore not of the Circumcision in Heart, which is not according to the Letter, but the Spirit; beyond which Dispensation, all other Pretensions are Imaginations and vain Exaltations.

Contradiction X.

It is not thy Natural or Allegorical Whimsies, that can blind the Elect, nor pacify the Judge of Life and Death within thee. D. L. G. p. 268. And now I desire no other Witness, to bear Record in the Consciences of Men to this Epistle, whether it be Truth, or no, but the Everlasting Jehovah, or Eternal Spiritual Jesus himself. D. L. G. p. 208.

Again, If every Man have the Spirit of Christ living in his Conscience, as many Men vainly imagine; What then is become of the Spiritual Body of that Jesus that ascended into the Throne of his Glory, in the visible Sight of Men and Angels? D. L. G. p. 68.

Animadversion X.

If the Judge of Life and Death be in Man, then Christ unto whom all Judgment is committed, is in Man, to justify or condemn him; therefore Christ, or his Spirit, or both are in Man, and consequently, it is no Impediment to, nor Denial of Christ's Ascension with a Glorified Body: Neither is it vain to believe, that the Spirit of Christ lives in the Consciences of Men. Observe their Folly, The Judge of Life and Death is within thee; Again, It is vain to imagine, that the Spirit of Christ lives in Men's Consciences: Thus they say and unsay almost in a Breath. But above all, That the Everlasting Jehovah, and Eternal Spiritual Jesus, should be in Men's Consciences the true Witness, and yet not be in Men: Who can understand this strange Riddle?

Contradiction XI.

But you may say, Did God the third Day arise from the Dead, by his own Power, or by the Power of his Deputy, Elias? To which I answer, He by his own Decree, and Spiritual Compact, with Elias, and by that Spirit of Faith, in his Innocent Body, the which Faith died in his pure Body, and quickened immediately, and brought forth that Natural Innocent Body, out of the Grave, a pure Spiritual Body. T. S. T. p. 32, 33.

Therefore whosoever saith, that any other Body ascended into Glory, but that very same Body of Flesh and Bones that suffered Death upon the Cross, he is an Antichrist, and in utter Spiritual Darkness. D. L. G. p. 15.

Animadversion XI.

If the Body died a Natural Body, and was brought forth, a Spiritual Body; then, unless that Spiritual Body laid down it self, and resum'd it's Natural Body, as at the first, it could not be the very same Body, of Flesh, Blood and Bones, that Died, which Ascended; but it must have been a Spiritual Body. In short, If Natural and Spiritual be not all one, as say they else-where in these Contradictions, then was it no more the same Body, than Natural is Spiritual, and Mortal Immortal, upon their own Principles; and consequently, Reeve and Muggleton are the Antichrists, and in utter Darkness.

As for the Three-fold Answer he gives to the Objection, it is wretchedly Blasphemous. 1. God's Decree. 2. His Compact with Elias. 3. His own Spirit of Faith. To the first I reply, What did the Decree avail, when the Power was in another, and when he that made it, was dead? To the second I return, That God's Rising lay on the Side of Elias's Honesty, in performing Obligation, and keeping Covenant, and not in any other Thing. 3. As to that Spirit of Faith, they confess it died, if so, how did the Faith raise him? Besides, In whom should God have Faith? In Himself? He was dead; In Elias? He could not exercise it, when in the Grave. Again, He that believes, enjoys not fully; and has Confidence in one Greater than Himself; but God wants nothing, and can have no Object for Faith, and therefore no Faith. O the Unparallelled Sotrish Folly, and Raving Conceits of these Men!

Contradiction XII.

So likewise, I positively affirm, against all Gainsayers under Heaven, That I John Reeve am the last commissionated Prophet, that ever shall declare Divine Secrets, according to the Foundation of Truth, until the Lord Jesus Christ appear on his Throne of Glory. D. L. G. p. 119.

A True Interpretation of all the chief Texts and Mysterious Sayings, and Visions opened, of the whole Book of the Revelations of St. John; wherein is unfolded, and plainly declared, those wonderful deep Mysteries, and Visions interpreted, concerning the True God, the Alpha and Omega; with Variety of other Heavenly Secrets, which hath never been opened, nor revealed to any Man, since the Creation of the World to this Day, until now: By Lodowick Muggleton, &c.

Animadversion XII.

Who shall we believe of these two? they both pretend the same Commission, and yet contradict: But how can any Credit be given thereunto? when (though Reeve says, he was awake, at the receiving of it, yet presently after tells us, that) he knew not, whether he was an Immortal God, or a Mortal Man: What ground is there for any Belief, of what Reeve himself was so far from a clear Knowledge of, as that he was not more unable to resolve, whether he was an Immortal God, or a Mortal Man: than to know the Truth of all his Revelation? O, the Willingness in Men to be blind! Certainly if the Devil himself should, as a Devil, seek Proselytes, some would follow him.

A few Additional Observations upon some Passages, of John Reeve and Lodowick Muggleton, in the before-cited Books.

The Spirit of Faith and Love, infinitely in the Glorious Person of God, overfloweth as a Fountain, continually with Revelation of New Heavenly Wisdom, from whence flow New Joys, and Glory to Himself, T. S. T. p. 46.

Observation, That unto which any Thing may be added, cannot be said to be Perfect, and consequently cannot be God; but he unto whom Wisdom is renewed. wanted that Wisdom before he had it, and consequently was not Perfect, and therefore not the True God; unto whom there is no Encrease of Wisdom, Power or Strength; but was and is, and will be for ever the same Unalterable Being; Infinite in Wisdom, Power, and all other Divine Excellencies, without any Diminution or Addition.

The Reason why Men's Bodies in Death, or after Death, do Rot or Stink, in the Grave, and come to Dust, is, because there was Sin in their Bodies; whilst they lived; but on the contrary, if Men had no Sin in their Natures or Bodies, they might Live and Dye, and Naturally Rise again, by their own Power, in their own Time, T. S. T. p. 33.

Observ. O the exceeding Folly and Blindness of this sottish Man! Why should Sin only cause the Body to Rot, Stink and go to Dust? Does not the Scripture, and Reeve himself, in his T. S. T. p. 44. give another Reason, namely, That what came from Dust, is that which must go to Dust? Besides, If the Flesh of Beasts, is capable of Dying, Rotting, and going to Dust, who never sinn'd, why should not Man have Dyed, and gone to Dust, though he had never sinn'd? For though there is a vast Difference betwixt Men and Beasts, in reference to their Souls, and Bodies too, so far as may concern the Distinction of Kinds; yet as to their being lyable to one and the same External Casualties, and Sufferings, by Hunger, Thirst, Sickness, Death and Corruption, no Man can rationally contradict: But above all, this deserves our Observation, That since Reeve is Dead, Rotten, and gone to Dust, he was not cleansed from Sin, as he is said to have pretended; but by Reason of his Wickedness, Death holds him in the Grave, and consequently, he cannot have been God's last Witness, whose Witnesses he hath always cleansed from that, against which they were to Witness. And it is farther evident, That Sin is not the Cause of Men's Bodies crumbling into Dust, from Reeve's own Words, who

The New Witnesses

saith, The Most High God, by his Unsearchable Wisdom, hath Decreed, that all Light of Life in Man, shall become Dead, Dust, or Earth, D. L. G. p. 17. So that God's Decree, and not Man's Sin, in his own Sense, must be the Reason of such Conversion and Corruption.

Therefore you may know, that the Lord's Reasoning with the Jews, was only by his Prophets, which were Rational Men, like unto themselves, which were sent to Convince those stony-hearted Jews, by declaring the Glorious God, and his Spiritual Truth unto them, in the Balance of their own Reason, D. L. G. p. 117.

Observ. It is remarkable, with what unusual Nonsense, and Contradiction he proceeds, in his whole Affair, since herein he Contradicts one of his main Foundation Principles; namely, That God hath not in his Glorious Spirit, one Motion of Reason inherent, nor yet the Elect of God, as may be seen, D. L. G. p. 18. and T. S. T p. 17. Whereas it's manifest unto all Men, who would not deny themselves the Use of their Understandings, That none can properly reason of any Subject, unto whom Reason cannot be, or is not inherent; so that if God, did both Reason with the Jews, and his Prophets were Rational Men, then may we safely conclude, That Reason is Inherent, to God, and his Elect Children; and that Pure Reason is not inconsistent with, or distinct from the Nature of Love and Faith; not only, because it is most rational to believe in, and love God most uprightly; but because John Reeve himself (that great Enemy to all sober Reason) makes it the Balance, in which the Prophets Declaration of the Glorious God, and his Spiritual Truth, should be weighed.

Again, I declare from the Holy Spirit, The Lord spake by Voice of Words to his Three Commissioners, which he hath sent unto the World; yea, I know God the Father spake unto Moses, as a Man speaks unto his Friend; and I know, that God spake unto the Apostles, in the Person of his Son, because I know the Lord God spake unto me in the Person of the Holy Ghost; only the two former Witnesses, saw the Person of God, in Part Visibly, but I saw the Glory of his Person Invisibly, or within me, because I am the Messenger of the Holy Invisible Spirit, T. S. T. p. 35.

Observ. Upon all this I make my following Observations, as regular as this Irregular Confused Matter, will permit me.

First, Then I would fain know, how he came to this Mighty Confidence in God's speaking to Moses; for it is in no part of his Commission; and Muggleton says, Moses set the Cart before the Horse; and they both of them despise the Scripture, in Comparison of their own Writings.

Secondly, Though God might speak in the Person of his Son to his Apostles, yet I utterly deny, upon Reeve's Principles, that the Lord Jesus could speak unto him, in the Person of the Holy Ghost, because this would necessarily imply a Trinity of Persons, which is by him elsewhere absolutely denied; therefore the Lord Jesus could speak to him in no other Person, than his own, if at all.

Thirdly, If God spake to J. Reeve by Voice of Words, because he affirms him to have so spoken to Moses, and the Apostles; then may we plainly infer, that God should as well have shewn his Person unto J. R. as he believes him to have done to Moses, and the Apostles, since if he did not decline to utter Words to the Carnal Ear, in this third Commission, as is pretended, any more than in the two former, there is no Reason in the World, why John Reeve's Carnal Eye should not have had equal Priviledge with the former Commissioners, in visibly beholding God's Person also: but since he makes God so to differ in the one, we ought the less to believe him in the other; that is, If his Carnal Eye could never see Him, because of the Spirituality of the Commission, his Carnal Ear could never hear him, for one and the same Reason; therefore all a Counterfeit.

Fourthly, Suppose he had seen the Glory of God's Person within him, yet that had been impossible, unless God's Person had been within him, since his Person and his Glory are insepaxable, as he largely affirms, D. L. G. p. 106. and if so; how manifest a Contradiction is it to several Places of his Writings? particularly this, he Spirit or Person of Christ, may fitly be compared unto the Face of the Natural Sun; you may know, that the Natural Spirit of the Sun, is so exceedingly Fiery Glorious, that no created Thing, that hath Natural Life in it is capable of it's in-dwelling Brightness, but it's own Body or Face only: If this be true, then Reeve could not behold the Glory of God's Person within him.

Fifthly, But let us suppose, that by Reeve's Principles, the Glory of God's Person, may be beheld, yet it is highly against them, that it should be beheld within; for if the Body and Soul of Man, are one individual and inseparable Substance, as he says they are, then can there be no Invisible Eye, distinct from that which is Carnal, to behold an Invisible Glory; and if so, then could Reeve never see God's Glory Invisibly within him; and consequently, he had no Commission: But out of his own Mouth he is prov'd a Lyar and Impostor. I shall conclude the whole with Queries to L. Muggleton, and his Companions.

Ten Queries Propounded.

I. If J. Reeve and L. Muggleton were the two True Last Witnesses, mention'd in the Revelations; How comes it, that they bear not the same Testimony, when risen, that was born before the slaying of the Witnesses; since they were nor other Witnesses, that rose, than those that were slain, and consequently, the Testimonies no more vary than the Witnesses themselves?

II. If they be the same Witnesses, should they not have Prophesied, 1260. Days, that is Years; and have been slain Three Days and an

The New Witnesses

Half in spiritual Sodom and Egypt, where our Lord was crucified, and then have risen from the Dead?

III. How did they Prophesie so many Years? How were they (Visible Witnesses) slain in spiritual Sodom and Egypt, where Christ was crucified? Does not this show the Witnesses to be Spiritual and Mystical, like the Place in which they were slain, (the Hearts of Men) and their Death to be the same? And were they ever such Witnesses, so slain, so long slain, and in that Place, as in the Revelation exprest?

IV. If they be the same Witnesses, were they not to Live, and Dye, and Rise together? Has not Reeve been Dead many Years?

V. If they were the True Witnesses, When did they shut the Heavens, that it Rained not, turn Water into Blood, and Smite the Earth with Plagues?

VI. If John Reeve was the Moses, or Principal Understanding; and L. Muggleton the Aaron, or Mouth only, as says Reeve; then whether Muggleton be any Thing, but an Empty Mouth, now his Understanding, Moses, is gone?

VII. How can Muggleton, upon Reeve's Principle, be a Witness or Commissioner for God, who confesseth, He never had any Commission by Voice of Words, but from Reeve only, whom he trusted; though Reeve himself affirms, That there is no True Commission, but by Voice of Words to the Party sent?

VIII. Whether Men's Trusting upon Muggleton (who relied upon Reeve) without any Internal Convictions from the Eternal Spirit, be not as Sandy a Foundation as the darkest Popery.

IX. Whether, there ever was a Pope on Earth, that usurped, or exercised a more Arbitrary E-laving Power over Men's Consciences, in Imposing his Faith upon Penalty of Immediate Curse, and Eternal Damnation, than J. Reeve and L. Muggleton have done, and the last remains to do; by affirming, That whom he Curseth, God Himself cannot Bless; and whom he Blesseth, God Himself cannot Curse: Though Reeve and Muggleton have Curst, and Blest, and Curst the same Person, and that more than once?

X. And lastly, Whether upon the whole, these Men, in their Commissions, Doctrines, Jurisdictions, Sentences, Lives and Conversations, are like unto the Last Witnesses of the Lord Jesus Christ; or those Ungodly, Proud Boasters; wandering Stars; Clouds without Rain; Raging Waves, Exalted above all that is called God; Perverters of the Truth, whose Belly is their God, who Glory in their Shame, whose End is Destruction and Perdition?

Postscript.

Since the finishing of the fore-going Paper, it came into my Mind, that if I affixt a Postscript, touching the Commission it self, that might remove all Credit in the same, the rest would dye of it self. 'Tis true, this might have been better plac'd in the Front, as the best Preludium to the Discourse of it self; but it failing of that Place, I was rather willing it should go for a Postscript, than lose that Service, I am not without Hope, it may perform in Publication of it.

A Brief Examen of Reeve His Commission.

Saith he, I Declare from the Lord Jesus, That no Man can understand any Thing of those Things that are Invisible to our Natural Eyes, but by the Spirit of Revelation; therefore it is written, That Faith is the Substance of Things hoped for, and the Evidence of Things not seen: In his Transcendent Spiritual Treatise, as he calls it, pag. 16.

If these Things are Invisible to Natural Eyes, then are they Inaudible by Natural Ears, both being Capable and Natural alike: And if no Man ever can or could See them, no Man could or can ever Hear them; and if no Man could or can, then Reeve never did: And if he never heard with his Carnal Ears, for He implies so much, that denies the Power of seeing such Spiritual and Invisible Things to natural Eyes, then was his Commission a Counterfeit: For he affirmed, That the 3d, 4th, and 5th of February, 1651. He Heard God resident above the Stars, speaking to Him then in Bed on Earth, by a Voice of Words, giving to him his Pretended Commission, T. S. T. pag. 5.

In short, Four Things I recommend to the Serious Consideration of all Sober-minded People, with a Story to conclude,

1. That a Commission should be given by a Voice of Words, from the farthest Heaven to any Man upon Earth. and neither any other Hear the same, no, not so much as Muggleton Himself; nor yet the Heavens nor Air to receive any Impression or Alteration, is an incredible Thing with all Persons that are in their Wits.

2. Not only in this doth his Commission strangely vary from that of Moses, but in the Consequence thereof most dangerously, in as much as no Man living is assured of the Verity of this Commission, from any Convincing Testimony, either from without, or within him; a Credulity God himself never exacted, or expected from his Creatures: For, the Reason of God's Complaint against a Rebellious People, never was for not believing without Convictions; but because the Creation without, and his Good Spirit within, had so plentifully proved a God, and that

Fear, Reverence and Obedience which were due to Him, and yet that they were not delighted to retain the Most High in their Knowledge.

3. That this should beget an utter and perpetual Abhorrence in us of all such Impostures; do but call to mind, what an Overthrow this gives to all those famous Prophesies, of God's Tabernacling in His People, His Teaching them, pouring out His Spirit upon them, and of their beholding Him Face to Face; since in this one Conceit, all that believe it, are brought under the Verge of these Men's Imaginations, without the least convincing Ground for any such Belief, unless the Fear of their Insolent Curse.

4. To Conclude, if his Commission was after a Visible External Manner, like Moses, as he affirms, He must needs have Visible and External Miracles to confirm such a Visible and External Commission: For, to deny Visible Miracles to a Visible Commission, is to deny that Commission; and to pretend Invisible Ones, is Improper, Unnatural and Untrue.

My Story is this, and not Unknown to some of the Creditors of this Counterfeit Commission.

A Considerable Commander of the English Army, in Ireland; and but too stiff against Lay Preachers (esteemed Presbyterian) hearing in his Bed a still Voice, Requiring Him to go Preach the Gospel to the Indians, was so much amaz'd, that he question'd if he were not asleep, as Reeve did, whether He was an Immortal God, or a Mortal Man; and finding himself Awake (though he could rather have wisht it but a Dream) it greatly Terrified him; to leave his Family, Command and Station, to go Preach the Gospel (who scarcely ever adventur'd to Preach (whatever he did to Pray) in all his Life) was Matter of much Disquiet to him; till in the End, he rather inclin'd to incur the Curse that followed his Disobedience, than to leave his wonted Course of Life, and take up one so difficult to him, and in which he was so unable, as well as Unwilling to acquit himself: But it ended not so; for, I think, the next Night, or Morning, or in a little Time after, the same Voice came to him, with the same Command, which increased his Perplexity; but still, as I was inform'd, he continued a verse from such a Voyage and Enterprize, till the Third Time of his being thus Alarum'd, and then, as the Story went, he gave (for ought I know, as Freely) up to Preach to the Indians, as Reeve did to go to Muggleton, and J. Robins, &c. and I am strongly of the Mind, the Authority may have been much alike, for it proved in the End, to be the Abuse of some of his Companions, in a way of Unjustifiable Waggery and Merriment, through a Trunk, or some such hollow Thing, placed with it's Mouth or Muzzle near the Commander's Bed. What shall we say then of Reeve's Voice of Words? A Man swelled with Conceits more ready and deserving to have been abused, than the Person concerned in this Story: And concerning whom Muggleton told me, He thought Him Hot-brain'd, and Distemper'd in his Head, and that he had told him so; a Thing not hardly to be credited by such as read his Folly, Certainly God never gave a Commission yet, in that Way wherein Man's Wit or Malice could Equal it. And I would know, what one Extraordinary Circumstance attended the giving of this Commission to Reeve, that may groundedly Engage any to the Belief of it? But indeed, it was notably done of Him, to pretend an Authority of which he was the sole Judge, and Witness; and a Power to Curse all such as Refus'd his Testimony, without his rendering a Reason for the Hope that was in him. Never did the Devil more befool himself, nor any of Mankind, than in his Divulging, and their Believing of these Sottish Blasphemies.

Observations On Some Passages Of Lodowick Muggleton, In His Interpretation Of The 11th Chapter Of The Revelations.

As also on some Passages in that Book of his, stiled, The Neck of the Quakers Broken, and in his Letter to Thomas Taylor.

Whereby it may appear what spirit he is of, and what god his Commission is from.

Whereunto is added

A brief Account of my Soul's Travel towards the Holy Land, with a few words concerning the Way of knowing and receiving the Truth.

Written in tender love to Souls, in true sense and understanding received from the Lord, and with reverence to his holy Spirit and Power,

By Isaac Pennington.

Printed in the Year, 1668.

The Preface to the Reader.

    Having had a book of Lodowick Muggleton's sent me to peruse, and having been earnestly pressed thereunto by some, who had let in his spirit and doctrines, to their great hurt: in the fear of the Lord, and in the sense of his holy Spirit of Truth, and in tender love to them who had requested this of me, I cast my eye thereupon; wherein I observed very many things contrary to the Spirit of the Lord, the Testimony of the holy Scriptures, and the nature of Truth; some whereof (for the service of others) are here communicated. To which, there arose somewhat in my heart to add concerning myself, in reference to my wearisome seekings, journeys and travels after the Lord. Indeed it came upon me very freshly and livingly: and the Lord may please to make it useful to others, even to help to stay the minds and quicken the hopes of such that are fainting, as I deeply was. Now if so be any shall reap any benefit thereby, let them give glory to the Lord alone, who alone is worthy thereof. For I seek not esteem of men; but all my desire is, that men might know the Lord and the Power of his Truth, and by him be gathered into and preserved in that which is pure of him. It is the day of the Gospel, even of God's eternal power, which is risen in many hearts: for indeed the Light of the Everlasting Day of God shines gloriously, and doth conquer and shall conquer the darkness and corruption in men's minds daily more and more. O that more might partake of its virtue, and not stumble at that stumbling Stone, which the builders out of the Life and Power, in every age and generation, have still despised and rejected. O that men might seek after Christ, the Wisdom of God aright: not in that spirit and wisdom which shall never find him. For it is easy to seek amiss, but none can seek aright, save only those that are led and taught of God so to do.

Observations on some passages of Lodowick Muggleton, in his Interpretation of the 11th Chapter of the Revelations.

In page 9, he saith, [The law is not written in the seed of faith's nature at all, but in the seed of reason's nature only. (Reason, or the spirit of reason, he saith, is the devil, p. 15.)]

Observ. The sum of the law is love: even to love God above all, and one's neighbour as oneself. And this love, which is the sum of the law, and fulfils the law, God writeth in the hearts of his spiritual Seed.

In p. 15 he affirmeth [That that saying of the devil was true which he said to Christ, All the kingdoms of the earth are mine.]

Observ. The earth is the Lord's, and the fulness thereof. The devil hath no right to it. God never gave it him: but God himself is Judge, who throweth down one and setteth up another, disposing of the kingdoms of men according to his pleasure. Psal. 75.7. Dan. 4.25.

In p. 19 he saith, [There never was no enmity between the person of the serpent and the person of the woman: but the enmity which lay between them was in the two seeds.]

Observ. Is not the enemy as expressly placed by God between the serpent and the woman, as between their seeds? I will put enmity between thee and the woman, and between thy seed and her seed. Gen. 3.15.

In p. 21 he saith, [So that now God himself is not capable to dissolve himself into Seed or Nature, as he was before.]

Observ. Is God changeable? Is he one thing today, and another thing tomorrow? and can he never be any more what he was yesterday? His god may be so: but the true God is not so (I the Lord change not.): his Nature, his Seed, his Life, his Spirit, his Power is the same for ever.

Further in p. 21, he saith, [These two seeds were those two spiritual bodies which are called by the revelation of Moses two trees. Yet they were in the forms of men, and was capable, as they were spiritual bodies, to dissolve into seed or nature, and so become capable to suffer the pains of death.]

Observ. O the depth of imagination from that Spirit, which giveth imaginations to them that will receive them! He that is taught of God never learned thus, but learneth much otherwise; and in the feeling sense and experience knoweth the two Seeds, and is born of the one

Observations on Some Passages 133

and separated from the other from the very womb, I mean, from his birth of the Jerusalem which is above, which is free (from the spirit of deceit and all its imaginary knowledge) which is the Mother of all that are born of the Spirit.

In p. 22 he saith, [Knowledge proceedeth from life that hath wisdom in it.]

Observ. Living knowledge doth. But there is a knowledge which comes not from the true Wisdom; nor doth convey life but death. And such is the knowledge which he hath from his god, and holdeth forth to others: it poisons and corrupts the mind, and leads out of the capacity of receiving and obeying the Truth, as it is in Jesus.

In p. 27 he saith, [Reason can feed on nothing but what it can see with this visible eye]

Observ. That is not reason's food only, which is seen with this visible eye: but reason is in the mind, and feeds chiefly on things which the mind gathers and comprehends inwardly.

In p. 29 he saith, [I declare, by revelation from the holy Spirit, that out of these two spiritual trees came forth these two commissions, namely, the commission of Moses and the prophets, and the commission of Jesus and the apostles.]

Observ. He had said before, p. 11, that one of these trees was the tree of knowledge of good and evil (in the form of a man, p. 14) that tempted Adam. Was that which tempted Adam, the tree out of which Moses' commission came? Doth not he call this tree the serpent? (p. 30). Had Moses his commission from the serpent? Surely everyone that is of God will say, no.

In p. 30 he saith, [These two olive-trees and candlesticks here spoken of, I declare are those two commissions which came forth of these two spiritual trees.]

Observ. One of these trees he said was the very person of God himself, p. 10. That the other was the tree that tempted Adam: whereas the Tree did not tempt Adam, but the serpent tempted Eve to eat of the fruit of the tree.

Again p. 30 he saith, [Moses acted as a God in the person of the angel, or tree of knowledge of good and evil.]

Observ. Moses was faithful in all his house as a servant. Nor did he act in the person of the serpent; for the serpent was the devil, and was out of Truth long before Moses' time, and spake of his own: but Moses spake and ministered from the pure holy Spirit of Life. Was not the devil defiled, a corrupt tree, an angel fallen from his habitation, before he tempted Eve and Adam to sin and fall? And who can bring a clean thing out of an unclean? or an holy commission out of the devil?

In p. 31 he saith, [The law (speaking of Moses' law) which is just and good, doth enlighten reason to do as he is done unto, not as he would be done unto.]

Observ. If Christ may be believed, he saith otherwise: for he saith, All things whatsoever ye would that men should do to you, do ye even so to them: for this is the law and the prophets, Matth 7.12. So that the law and the prophets did teach and require this, not only for a man to do as he is done unto, but as he would be done to.

In p. 32 he saith, [The law of reason is called a law of sin and death, it being given unto reason, because reason is sin; for there is nothing doth break the law but reason.]

Observ. Those that are delivered by the powerful appearance of Christ from the law of sin and death, knows it to be another law than the law of reason, even a law contrary not only to the Life of Christ, but to the reason and understanding of a man, bringing him below the state of reason, even into brutish captivity and sensuality. Doth reason teach a man to manage his body destructively and unreasonably, as the corrupt and unreasonable law of sin and death teacheth many men? Reason is not sin: but a deviating from that from which reason came, is sin. God did not create man in sin; or make a sinful creature: but he gave him reason, and thereby made him reasonable.

In. p. 34 he saith, [The moon (Rev. 12) did signify the law of Moses, which must now be trod underfoot by the sun-shine light of the gospel.]

Observ. No not so: the law is not trod underfoot by the light and power of life, when it appeareth; but its righteousness is fulfilled in them that walk not after the flesh, but after the Spirit, Rom. 8.4. Christ did not teach men to tread Moses and his law underfoot; but brings forth that life and bestows that Spirit, which leads through and beyond the law, even to the righteousness of faith, (which the apostle Paul said) they did not make the law void by, Rom. 3.31. Therefore not trod underfoot through faith in the gospel.

In p. 37 he saith, [There was none of the prophets that were commissionated to write scripture.]

Observ. They spake and wrote as they were moved by the holy Spirit, and is not that a sufficient commission? In his book called The neck of the Quakers broken, he had scoffingly cast away the writings of Solomon from being scripture; and now he casts away the writings of all the prophets too, as being written without commission.

In p. 42 he argueth against God's being an infinite, incomprehensible Spirit, saying, [Such a great vast Spirit do not know itself, neither can this vast Spirit tell where to find or see itself; and if it cannot know or see itself, how should his creature be able to know or see his Maker, when as he cannot know or see himself?...Then would that be a vain thing which is spoken of in holy writ, where it is said, It is life eternal to know the true God.]

Observ. Here is dark imaginations indeed. He that cannot read in the Spirit, let him read that place, Isa. 40.12. according to the plainness of the letter, and see if God can be less than infinite and incomprehensible. He that knoweth the nature and Spirit of God, knoweth God, though he be not able to measure or discern the utmost extent of his being, which who can? For he is a sea of life, a sea of love, a sea of purity and righteousness, a sea of power and wisdom,

Observations on Some Passages 135

&c. but in a measure of the same life, received from him, we know him so to be; and worship him in the Spirit and life which is of him; not making likenesses of him in our minds, but bowing to him and worshipping him in his own appearances.

In p. 77 he saith, [The holy Ghost sat upon none, 'like as of fire,' but upon the twelve apostles only; neither could any other speak with tongues by inspiration, but the twelve apostles.]

Observ. This is directly contrary to the testimony held forth in scripture. For, said Peter, the holy Ghost fell on them, as on us at the beginning, Acts 11.15. And they of the circumcision which believed, were astonished, because that on the Gentiles also was poured out the gift of the holy Ghost. For they heard them speak with tongues and magnify God, chap. 10.45,46.

In p. 52 he saith, [Christ's apostles could do no miracles, neither could they cast out devils, until he was ascended.]

Observ. Did they not cast out devils and do miracles, while he was on earth? Did not he give them power so to do? See Mat. 10.8. In pp. 59 and 60 he speaking of the wild olive-tree, and the good olive-tree. [That wild olive-tree, he saith, is the state of nature or reason, the devil, which is wild by nature. That good olive-tree, he saith, was the very person of Christ, which the Gentiles were ingrafted into by faith. But the commission of Moses and the prophets proceeded from the tree of knowledge of good and evil, he acting his part in that seed, &c.] which he afore said was the serpent.

Observ. Is the wild olive-tree (the devil which is wild by nature) one of God's witnesses, or the head or root from whence any of the commissions of God's Spirit came? Did the law of God, which was against sin and the devil, come from the devil? Is not the law holy, just and good? and did it come from an unholy root? What was the olive-tree the Jews were broken off from? Read their state, Rom. 9.4,5. and 11.16,17. Was this holy Root they were broken from a wild olive-tree? What interpretation of Scripture is here? Surely from a spirit quite contrary to that which wrote it.

In p. 63 he saith [The great and high wall [about the new Jerusalem] was all that visible and external worship which was set up by Moses, which did belong to that tabernacle, &c.]

Observ. Is this the defence about the glory of the new Jerusalem? is this the wall and bulwark? Nay, nay: the power of God's salvation is the wall and bulwark, Isa. 26.1. which is a sure defence upon all the glory of this building. Isa. 4.5.

In p. 66 he saith, [The apostles should be equal in the kingdom of glory, as they were equal here in the kingdom of grace. And again, p. 67. As there should be no preheminence with the apostles here in the kingdom of grace, neither should there be any preheminence in the kingdom of glory. Yet p. 102. he saith Peter was the head of the apostles.]

Observ. Hath the head no preheminence in the body? Are the rest of the members equal with the head? is not this an absolute contradiction?

In p.78 he saith, [The commission of the apostles...was not the commission of the Spirit.]

Observ. Paul saith, they were made able ministers of the new testament, not of the letter, but of the Spirit, 2 Cor. 3.6. What is to be desired more than the new covenant? wherein life, Spirit and power is received. Now the apostles were made by God able ministers thereof: and the glory of this covenant and ministration remaineth, verse 11.

In p. 93 he saith, [Death being the first-born of the law, it went forth as a conqueror of all life, both in God and man.]

Observ. The law is holy, just and good, and bringeth forth only that which is holy. Sin is not of the law, but against the law, and the wages of sin is death. Yet neither sin nor death could ever conquer the life of God, but the unconquerable life and power have ever reigned over them. God's kingdom is an everlasting kingdom, and his dominion endureth throughout all ages, which sin, nor death, nor hell could ever conquer. That life which Christ did give up, none took from him as a conqueror, but he laid it down freely, at the requiring of the Father, knowing his glorious power was able to restore and raise it up again.

In p. 105 he saith, [The body of man is that Tophet that was ordained of old, and the spirit of reason is that king, which must abide in this Tophet.]

Observ. The body of man was God's temple before it was defiled with sin; and is God's temple again, when it is purified and purged from sin. Now him that defileth this temple of God, him will God destroy. And Christ said, Fear him who after he hath killed, hath power to cast into Hell, Luk. 12.5. What is he able to cast into Hell? why, both body and soul, Mat. 10:28. Then the body of man is not the Tophet or Hell: but Tophet is that whereinto the souls and bodies of the wicked are to be cast.

In p. 116 he saith, [Eternity did become time, and time shall become eternity again.]

Observ. Eternity did never become time, but is unchangeable in its nature, spirit, life and being for evermore: but it brought forth natural and changeable things in time, which time shall have an end.

Observations on some Passages in a Book of Lodowick Muggleton's, stiled by him, The Neck of the Quakers Broken

In p. 14 he affirmeth that [Adam had no part in the begetting of Cain.]

Observ. The Scripture saith, Adam knew Eve his wife; and she conceived and bare Cain, and said, I have gotten a man from the Lord,

Observations on Some Passages 137

Gen. 4.1. Here the holy Spirit of God attributeth the begetting of Cain to Adam's knowing his wife Eve; but L.M. saith otherwise.

In p. 15 he saith, [Whoever is partaker of the seed of Adam, may be said to have the Spirit of Christ in them, and their spirits to be in him, that is, Christ dwells in their hearts by faith.]

Observ. The Scriptures distinguish between the first and second Adam. None have the Spirit of Christ from or in the first Adam, but only from and in the second. And the old Adam's seed, spirit and nature is to be put off by him that puts on the new; and he must be born again of the immortal seed of life, who receives the Spirit of life.

In p. 17 [he calls reason the devil, and p. 29 saith, This devil so much spoken of in Scripture, is no other but the spirit of reason.]

Observ. Indeed corrupted reason is of the devil: but pure reason is of God. Man, by his fall, had his reason corrupted, and so became brutish and unreasonable: but by faith in the redeeming power he is brought out of the fall, raised from death to life, and in the new life hath the true, holy, righteous reason restored to him again, 2 Thes. 3.2. which reason is neither the devil, nor of the devil.

In p. 22 he saith, [If God be a person in the form of a man, as I am sure he is (for I do acknowledge no other God but the man Christ Jesus, who is a distinct body of flesh and bone of his own) how then can he fill heaven and earth with his presence, and get into the Quakers bodies &c.]

Observ. Solomon said in prayer to God, 2 Chron. 6.18. (which prayer God testified his acceptance of, as being from his own spirit, chap. 7:1) Behold heaven, and the heaven of heavens cannot contain thee, how much less this house which I have built? Again, Thus saith the high and lofty one that inhabiteth eternity (what is eternity?) whose name is holy, I dwell in the high and holy, with him also that is of a contrite and humble spirit &c. Isa. 57:15. Yet again it is said, Ye are the temple of the living God, as God hath said, I will dwell in them and walk in them. 2 Cor 6.16. Is it such a strange thing that God should be in heaven and in earth also? Is not the earth his footstool? and are not the feet present in the place on which they tread? Was not Christ in heaven while he was here on earth, according to his own words? No man (saith he) hath ascended up to heaven, but he that came down from heaven, the Son of Man which is in heaven, John 3.13. And cannot God be in heaven and in earth too, and also by his Spirit in the hearts of his people?

In p. 23 he saith, [to say that...Christ, according to the flesh...was of Abraham...is blasphemy.]

Observ. The apostle said concerning the Jews (whom he calls his brethren and kinsmen according to the flesh, Rom. 9.3), of whom as concerning the flesh Christ came, who is over all, God blessed for ever, amen, verse 5. Did Christ come of the Jews according to the flesh, and did he not come of Abraham according to the flesh? Now lest any should apprehend there may be some difference between according in verse 3, and concerning in verse 5, I shall add this, they are both the same in Greek. It is in both.

In pp. 24-25 he saith, [None can interpret Scripture truly, but my self.]

Observ. All that are children, to them God giveth of his Spirit: (Gal. 4:6) and they that have the Spirit, have that which interprets Scriptures truly; which they keeping to, cannot be deceived about the interpretation of them. But they that keep not to the anointing within, but receive interpretations from men without, may easily be deceived.

In p. 25 he saith, [God hath made me the judge of Scriptures.]

Observ. Let him that readeth, wait to feel the Spirit which is of God, and the Light wherein God dwells, and that will open Scriptures and the mysteries of the kingdom to him (he abiding in unity therewith, through the pure subjection thereto) and manifest to him who is the judge in spiritual matters in God's Israel.

Again p. 25 he saith further, [We the Witnesses of the Spirit do know more than Moses, the prophets, or apostles did, things of more higher concernment.]

Observ. The apostles were not the least in the kingdom, but in the glory of the day (1 Pet. 2:5) in the eternal life, in him that was true (1 John 5:20) and they had the whole counsel of God, even a ministry sufficient to perfect the work of God in the saints (Ephes. 4.12) that so they might present men perfect in Christ Jesus, Col. 1.28. And happy is he that receiveth their testimony, and cometh into and walketh in that light which their message was concerning, 1 John 1.2. & verses 5 & 7.

Yet again, p. 25 he saith, [The Quakers...have nothing but the dead letter of other men's words, whose light was but dark in comparison of that light that comes by this commission of the Spirit.]

Observ. Yes, they have much more than the dead letter of other men's words; for they witness the living Spirit, and are taught thereby and subject thereto, blessed be the Lord, who is become the Shepherd and Teacher of his people himself, according to his promise.

[And as for the apostles' light being dark in comparison &c.]

Observ. We all with open face, beholding as in a glass the glory of the Lord, are changed into the same image, from glory to glory, even of the Lord the Spirit, 2 Cor. 3.18. Again, God who commanded the light to shine out of darkness, hath shined in our hearts to give the light of the knowledge of the glory of God, in the face of Jesus Christ, chap. 4.6. In that day the woman was clothed with the sun (for as many as are truly baptised into Christ, have put on Christ, Gal. 3.27.) had the Moon under her feet, and was crowned with a crown of twelve stars, and not only travelling to bring forth, but brought forth the Man-child which was to rule all nations. They who are indeed in the Spirit, know that the Light which is now broke forth, is but the Light of the same Day which shined then very gloriously in them, who were the glory of Christ, 2 Cor. 8.23. They had the Spirit of God plentifully poured upon them, which opened to them the mysteries of the kingdom and the

Observations on Some Passages 139

deep things of God, 1 Cor. 2.9,10. And how highly soever he think or speak of himself, yet this is known concerning him, that he hath a very great journey to travel, before he can come to that measure of light that they were in, or to receive that proportion of the true Spirit that they received: For he is yet quite out of it.

In p. 29 he affirmeth, [that it was the very God-head life that suffered death.]

Observ. If the God-head life suffered death, what power was left to raise it up again? I am the resurrection and the life, said Christ; but he spake concerning that which raised Lazarus, which was of an immortal nature and could not die: not concerning the body; but the life and power of the Father, which dwelt in and was revealed through the body; which died not with the body, but remained alive to raise the body. What kind of doctrine is this, that the very God-head life suffered death, and so to make the Creator mortal like the creature?

In p. 39 he saith, [God the king of heaven is not in this world at all.]

Observ. Whither shall I go from thy Spirit? or whither shall I flee from thy presence? said David (who had the Spirit of God). If I ascend up into heaven, thou art there: if I make my bed in hell, thou art there, &c. Psal. 139.7,8. And do not I fill heaven and earth saith the Lord, Jer. 23.24. But L.M. hath affirmed contrary to these testimonies, that God is not in this world at all.

In p. 48 he saith, [I am the only and alone judge what shall become of men and women after death; neither shall those that are damned by me, see any other God or judge but me, or that sentence which I have passed upon them.]

Observ. Is he God? is he Christ? is he the only one? is there not another God another judge? (Yes we know there is another, who judgeth otherwise than he hath judged: who judgeth that to death which he judgeth to life, and that to life which he judgeth to death.) And in the resurrection of the just and the unjust, shall not both the just and unjust see him who is the judge? Read Matth. 25.31, &c.

Again, p. 48 he saith, [No man upon the earth can, or ought to judge of the doctrine of a prophet, that hath a commission from God.]

Observ. Cannot he judge, who hath the anointing? Doth not he that is a child of God receive his Spirit? and is not the Spirit of God able to judge in them that receive it? Judge not according to the appearance, (saith Christ) but judge righteous judgment, Joh 7.24. Did Christ absolutely forbid men from judging concerning him, or his doctrine and miracles, or did he not rather direct them how they might judge aright? I speak as to wise men, judge ye what I say, 1 Cor. 10.15. The apostle had a commission from God, & yet he did not bar men from judging of his words, but bid them judge: and the same apostle saith, Let the prophets speak two or three, and let the others judge, 1 Cor. 14.29. Is the Spirit of God given to and received of the believer, and shall he not therewith judge concerning spirits and doctrines and commissions which pretend to be of him, and apostles and angels, whether they be angels of light indeed, or only such as would so appear? Believe not every spirit, but try the spirits whether they are of God, 1 John 4.1. And they which are of God, love to come to the light which tries and makes manifest; but they that are not of God refuse to be tried by it. Thou hast tried them that say they are apostles and are not, and hast found them liars, Rev. 2.2. God giveth that light, that Spirit, that anointing to his which hath in it ability to try, and they ought to try therewith doctrines, spirits, prophets, apostles, and certainly find thereby that they are of him before they receive them, or else they may easily be deceived? Despise not prophesyings, saith the apostle, 1 Thes. 5.20. but yet withal though a man may not despise them, yet neither may he receive them without due trial: therefore the apostle in the next words adds, Prove all things, hold fast that which is good, verse 21.

Further p. 48 he saith, [Who do you blind Quakers think should be judge of a prophet that hath a commission from God?]

Observ. What saith the apostle? 1 Cor. 2.10. The Spirit searcheth all things, yea the deep things of God. And again verse 15. The spiritual man discerneth (or judgeth) all things, yet he himself is discerned of no man.

Yet again p. 48 he saith, [Is not a true prophet the law-giver, and ought not every one to submit unto his laws?]

Observ. There is but one law-giver, but one king, but one Lord, but one Master. All prophets and ministers from him, are but his messengers and servants, not law-givers. The law cometh forth from the king himself, from the great prophet and shepherd of the soul, to every lamb and sheep in the covenant, as it is written, All thy children shall be taught of the Lord (and I will write my law in their hearts) and so taught by this prophet (in the new and living covenant) as that they shall need no other teacher. This was once fulfilled before the apostacy (as is faithfully testified, 1 John 2.27. The anointing which ye have received of him, abideth in you; and ye need not that any man teach you, but as the same anointing teacheth you of all things &c.) and it is again fulfilled after it, blessed be the name of the holy one of Israel.

But mind, reader, what is the reason that he reviles us above all others, calling us blind, and the darkest pieces to interpret Scriptures, and the cursedst of all sects, and the like; but because we stand most in his way, because we cannot receive him as a law-giver, because we have received the true light, the true Spirit and anointing from God, which discovereth and denieth him in his very root and ground.

In p. 50 [he makes himself the judge, and the day of judgement but a day of general execution, wherein Christ shall say, Come you blessed and go you cursed. He saith there shall be no more pleading with God, but this will be all that God will say in the resurrection, Come you blessed and go you cursed.]

Observ. Yes, there will be more said. There will be the reason given publicly why men are blessed or cursed, as was testified by Christ

Observations on Some Passages 141

himself, while he was here on earth, Matth. 25.35, &c. And men shall have liberty to plead as is there expressed, verse 44. So that Christ, the great judge, is not so bound up, as he would bind him up: nor are persons, to be judged by him, absolutely bound up from considering of their sentence and pleading their cause with him; but if they have any thing to say on their own behalfs, they shall be equally heard.

In p. 60 he saith, [God doth not come down from heaven upon this earth to interpret the scriptures to men, but this was always God's practice to commissionate particular men, and furnish them with gifts for that purpose, and what interpretations of scriptures they give, it is owned of God as if he had done it himself.]

Observ. The apostle saith, Every man is to stand or fall to his own master, and bids every man be fully persuaded or assured in his own mind, and affirms, that whatsoever is not of faith is sin, Rom. 14.4,5. and verse 23. Nor did Christ deal thus, with his disciples, requiring them to receive whatever interpretation of Scripture he would give them, but he opened their understanding that they might understand the Scripture themselves, and saith the Spirit of Truth should lead them into all truth. Nor did the apostles thus deal with men, but they waited for God's opening of the true capacity in others, and were not lords over men's faith, but demonstrators of the truth of God to men's consciences by his Spirit, and as in his sight.

Again he saith, [Christ doth not teach every particular man neither by his Spirit, nor by voice of words.]

Observ. Every man that is truly begotten and new-born to God, is born of his Spirit, John 3. (There is not another begetter and bringer forth of life in the heart.) And the Spirit of the Lord, in the new covenant, teacheth all its children. It was written so of old, All thy children shall be taught of God. How taught? Why, they shall hear and learn of the Father, John 6.45. Thus the Scriptures speak: and thus it is witnessed, felt and known in the heart, blessed be the name of the Lord. For the children of the Lord are anointed with the holy anointing, with the oil of the same Spirit (the same oil of gladness, Psal. 45.7. and Hebr. 2.11.) wherewith Christ was anointed; which maketh them also of quick understanding in the fear of the Lord, and of deep insight into the mysteries of his kingdom, as they grow up in his life, and sweet innocent holy nature.

Yet again in that page he saith, [The true and right interpretation of the Scriptures, it lieth in those men that God hath chosen, anointed and sealed for that purpose, and men cannot come to the knowledge of God, nor the true meaning of the Scriptures, no other way.]

Observ. The gospel is a ministration of the Spirit and power of the endless life: and it consists not in receiving words, but in receiving the Spirit from which the good words and precious knowledge comes. And he that receives the Spirit and hath the Spirit, receiveth and hath that which openeth and giveth entrance, not only into words concerning the kingdom, but into the kingdom itself. And the apostle who had a true commission from God, was not sent to limit men to his interpretation of Scriptures; but to turn men to the Light and to the power which gives to see the Scriptures and spiritual things, Acts 26.18. And the church of Laodicea was counselled not only to buy gold and raiment, but also eye-salve of Christ, that therewith they might be enabled to see, Rev. 3.18. They had words from those that were sent by God, and much knowledge (insomuch as they seemed to themselves to be rich and full) but yet they wanted the eye-salve, which they were to buy themselves: for no man is to offer any thing, but at his own cost.

Yet again in p. 60 he saith [The opening of the Scriptures belongs unto commissionated men, and not unto Christ himself.]

Observ. In the New Covenant God himself is the shepherd, the King, the prophet, the teacher. (This is not known only from words left upon record by holy men of God; but also inwardly felt and witnessed.) The eternal Word is nigh; nigher than words from commissionated men; and teacheth more inwardly and fully, than words from men can. The same God who creates the heart anew, puts his law into the mind and heart, yea his Spirit within. Now to this the gospel ministers formerly did (and still do) direct and turn men; but did not limit them to words from themselves, or to their interpretations of Scriptures, as was said before. And as under the law men were to hear Moses: so under the gospel men are to hear Christ in all things; and he that doth not hear him is to be cut off, as Acts 7.37.

In p. 62 he saith, [Though the prophets and apostles were anointed and sealed of God for that great work, will it follow therefore that you Quakers, because you read their writings, that you are anointed and sealed of God for the work of the ministry?]

Observ. Where was this ever affirmed by them? But this they certainly know and faithfully testify, that they have received the very same Spirit in measure which the prophets and the apostles had, and minister in its name and authority and demonstration, and have the true and living seal of their ministry in many hearts.

In p. 17 he saith, [As for my mouth being full of cursing, that is my commission. And p. 18. God hath ordained me the chief judge in the world at this day to give sentence upon men and women's spiritual and eternal state what will become of them after death. Full of this cursing I confess my mouth is, and I do rejoice in it too, &c.]

Observ. When Christ pronounced judgment upon Jerusalem, he did it weeping, Matth. 24.37,38. and Luke 19.41, &c. And the true apostle knew that those that watched for the soul, when they gave up the account concerning such as did not submit to and obey the Truth, but rebelled against it and perished, they could not do it with joy, but with grief, Heb. 13.17.

In p. 69 [He teacheth his disciples to curse men to eternity, despising spirits he calls them, such he means as do not own his commission, but know it not to be of God, and faithfully testify against it.]

Observations on Some Passages 143

Observ. Christ taught his disciples to bless, saying to them, Bless them that curse you, Matth. 5.44. And the apostles said, Bless and curse not, Rom. 12.14. And Christ is the same at this day, and teacheth his Disciples so now. Yea I and many others can faithfully witness it, that since we felt the seed of blessing in our hearts, we never learned of it to curse any man, but rather to pity them and pray to the Lord for them, and direct them to the holy light, Spirit and power, whereby they might be turned from their iniquities and come into the blessing, as Acts 3.26. And though he pretends that those whom he curses, have sinned the sin against the Holy Ghost, and are devils; yet that is but the judgment of his spirit, not of God's Spirit: for they are in that which keeps from grieving God's Spirit; much more from sinning the great and unpardonable sin against it.

In p. 63 he saith, [Neither do I curse any until he judge me first.]

Observ. Feel, ye that have true sense and understanding, what moves him to curse.

In p. 73 he saith, [If the witness that informed me did not witness truth, then the sentence which I have passed upon them shall be of no value.]

Observ. How often hath he affirmed his judgment to be infallible, and such as God himself could not reverse? But here, it seems, it is such as may be passed by hearsay, and depend upon the witnesses' words: so that if the witness that informed him spake truth, it shall stand; but if the witness did not speak truth, then the sentence which he hath passed shall be of no value. What, shall a man be commissionated and receive authority from God to judge irreversibly, so as God himself cannot pardon that man he hath judged (as he affirmeth) and yet that man not receive true sense, wisdom and understanding from God to preserve him from misplacing it, but it may be a true judgment or a false judgment according as the witnesses' information was? Ah cease deceit, and for shame be silent: thy covering is manifestly too narrow.

In p. 66 he saith, (speaking of the penalty or punishment of the laws) [If my innocency nor money will not deliver me, I must and will suffer under it.]

Observ. He hath took scope enough to avoid the cross or suffering by any laws, which might lay hold on him for conscience sake. The apostles never saved themselves by money from their sufferings for their testimony.

In p. 70 he saith, [Every man that read the Scriptures doth think to find eternal life in them, as Christ said to the Jews, and as you Quakers and others doth now adayes.]

Observ. Do the Quakers think to find eternal life in the Scriptures? did they ever teach men so? Have they not very often faithfully testified otherwise? Not in words concerning the thing, but in the thing itself, in the Word which was in the beginning and from the beginning, do they look to find eternal life. Yea and there they have found it, and do live in the life which is eternal, and the life which is eternal lives in them. This testimony hath the living seal to it (whereby it may be known by those that are truly living) and cannot be shaken. But he hath manifestly in this thing (as in several others also) discovered himself to be a false witness: and a false witness can never be a true judge. Nay alas his judgment is of and like his spirit, which manifestly is not of God; and his knowledge which he holds forth leads not to God nor to life, but to the chambers of hell and death.

Observations on some Passages in his Letter to Thomas Taylor

In page 5 he saith, [I marvel what satisfaction any man can have in his mind in believing in a Quakers' God, to tell a man that God abides in himself, and is what he is.]

Observ. Doth not God say to Moses concerning himself, I am that I am. When Moses desired to know how he should answer the Israelites, when they should enquire who sent him to them, God bid him tell them that I am had sent him, Exod. 3.14. How could the Israelites understand what God was by this? what satisfaction could they find in this answer of Moses, would this spirit say? But God is not to be known by the description of words of the earthly wisdom, but in his own feeling Spirit and life.

In p. 11 he saith, concerning the Quakers, [That which purifies your hearts, is the law written in your seed and nature, even the same as was written in the angel-serpent's nature before his fall, which is no other but the nature of reason.]

Observ. This is not a true testimony: for the light wherewith Christ enlighteneth the soul (to redeem and bring it back out of the fall) is not of the nature of reason, but confounds corrupt reason and brings it into the dust, begetting the soul into the divine wisdom and giving it to partake of the divine nature. Yea that which we are born of and purified by (as we sensibly feel and truly understand) is not the nature of the serpent's reason, but the immortal Word of God's eternal power, which doth that in us and for us, which the nature of reason never did nor can do in any.

Again in p. 11. he saith very slightingly and as untruly concerning the Quakers, thus, [As for the sins your hearts are cleansed from, they are no other but such like as these, that is to say, to keep the hat on the head before a magistrate, and to find fault with gold-lace, and a piece of ribbon, a bandstring, and a gold button, and to rend and tear gold-lace, and other lace off their clothes, and burn it, and to use the language of thee and thou. He or she that gets thee and thou perfectly, is a very good Quaker, they are gotten half way to the Quakers' heaven. These and such like righteousness, is the Quakers' perfection, and all the cleansing of heart they have: &c.]

Observ. O thou despiser, reproacher and beliar of the work of God in the hearts of his children. Nay, nay, there are thousands, who in God's presence can testify against thee, that they have waited for and received the inward cleansing from the filthiness of flesh and spirit, from the inward lusts and motions of sin in the mind, having felt the ax of the Lord and the two-edged sword, which cutteth up sin at the very roots. But thou art so far from having thy heart cleansed, that thou art not yet cleansed from lying lips, but bringeth forth thy false reproachful, slanderous testimony against the heritage of God in the sight of the sun.

In p. 13 he saith further of the Quakers, that [they own no other death of Christ, but what is within them, whatever they pretend by using the words of the Scripture &c.]

Observ. They sincerely and in plainness of heart, own and acknowledge the death of that body which the Father prepared for his Son, in which he did the Father's will in his suffering without the gate of Jerusalem. Therefore in this, he is a very false witness, and therein hath grossly belied the Quakers.

In p. 15. he saith, [You Quakers are the darkest pieces to interpret Scripture, of any other opinions in the world, for you will name places of Scripture, but never interpret any &c.]

Observ. It is better to bring men to that, which opens the mind to understand the Scriptures, than to give men interpretations of words or things beyond their capacity. Yet the Spirit of the Lord, in and through many called Quakers, doth often open many Scriptures in clearness and demonstration to others. (Read the book, called Gospel-Liberty or the royal Law of Love, and see if many Scriptures be not therein opened to the lowest capacity.) But the Lord hath given them the true skill and understanding, and they are not to open to and feed that in men, which the Lord hath appointed to be famished. Yet if they did not open Scriptures, the Scriptures are plain to him that hath an understanding.

Now for a close, I shall add somewhat of the testimony which is written in my heart, by the finger of God's Spirit, concerning the people called Quakers.

Indeed they have met with many reproaches, and sore oppositions many ways, since they were a people: but notwithstanding all, their bow abides in strength, and the hands of their arms have been made strong against the wicked one, with all his devices in his several kinds of instruments: and their light is still the same and their God the same, who blesseth them from day to day, even in the midst of all the revilings, slanders, persecutions and curses, which they have met with from men without, and in the midst of all the temptations, inward trials and afflictions also, which are often met with inwardly. Yea we know him to be our God and cannot but trust him, having found him to be faithful to us hitherto, and knowing his nature to be such, that he cannot but continue his loving-kindness and faithfulness, to all who are gathered by him into his holy inward, spiritual covenant of life and peace, and who dwells with him therein. And truly we are fully satisfied and at rest in him, and cannot desire another, than he who hath redeemed our souls from death, given us life, brought us out of the pit wherein was no water, into a large place, set our feet upon a rock (a rock indeed) and establisheth our goings in the path of holiness, working all our works in us and for us, by his Spirit and power. Yea, we have the witness in our hearts, even the witness which never erred nor can deceive, which testifieth to and with our spirits our sonship: so that we do not imagine ourselves sons from apprehensions upon Scriptures, but we feel ourselves sons in the true sensibleness, and know who David is, and reap and inherit the sure mercies of David daily, O blessed be our Father, O blessed for ever be the Father of life, who feeds, who nourishes, who waters, who refreshes (with the bread of life and with the pure living water) his lambs, his babes, his plants, his tender ones, of whom he is daily tender, and who are daily tender of his name and honor. And if any man preach another God, then he who creates anew in the true light, and therein puts forth his arm of salvation, death and destruction and the curse are his portion from the hand of the Lord.

Now, O people, any of you that reads this man's writings and admire them; what spirit are ye of! what is it in you that relisheth them? what do they feed in you? Not the true birth, I am sure: but that in you which must perish, and come into death and destruction, if ever your souls be saved. I speak sensibly, and from the true understanding and experience which God hath given me: yea I certainly know, that the knowledge and notions which he holds forth are not pure nor able to cleanse the heart of any that receives them.

And all people, that truly love your souls and desire the salvation thereof, O wait on God that ye may be enabled by him rightly to distinguish, between receiving notions concerning God and Christ, and feeling and receiving the power which effectually redeems from sin and death: for deceit may enter in at the one, but cannot at the other. The enemy hath all deceivableness of unrighteousness, to paint as if it were righteousness and appear in, and to enter and possess the mind by: but he is excluded the redeeming power. He that feels that which renews his heart to God, and breaks the power and strength of lusts and temptations in him, and brings him into subjection to the Truth, which from God lives in the hearts of those that receive it in the virtue, life and power of it: here his devices and deceits are at an end, and here the elect sheep feel the hand of the Father, which is stronger than all, which none can pluck out of. Here is the fold, here is the safe dwelling place, whither the Lord leadeth and where he preserveth his lambs and children, and there is not another.

Now as for him (notwithstanding all that he hath done against the Lord and against his dear people) so far am I from wishing any harm unto him, that I could wish with all my heart, that it were possible for him to come to a true sense of the true light of God's holy Spirit, that by it he might examine, wherein he hath provoked and sinned against the Lord, that the Lord should thus leave him, not only to be deceived himself, but to become an head or root of deceit to others, and so to bring the blood of many souls upon him, which will be his bitter burthen and misery in the day of the Lord upon him, when the Lord shall rebuke him for blaspheming his name, his light, his Spirit, and shall justify (in the sight of men and angels) those to be his heritage and everlastingly dear unto him, whom he hath reproached, misrepresented and cursed unto eternity: but they are gathered by God into the blessed Seed (which he knoweth not, nor in this spirit nor by this commission shall ever know) where he cannot curse, nor can his curse reach or touch them, but they therein are blessed for evermore, Amen.

A Brief Account of my Soul's Travel Towards the Holy Land and how at length it pleased the Lord to join my Heart to his pure, holy, living Truth; wherein I have witnessed the New Covenant, and Peace with the Lord therein. With a few Words concerning the way of Knowing and Receiving the Truth: which is not done by Disputes and Reasonings of the Mind about it; but in waiting aright for the Demonstration and Power of God's Spirit to open the Heart and Understanding, and by submissive Obedience to it, even in its lowest Appearances in the inward Parts.

My heart from my childhood was pointed towards the Lord, whom I feared and longed after from my tender years; wherein I felt, that I could not be satisfied with (nor indeed seek after) the things of this perishing world, which naturally pass away; but I desired true sense of, and unity with, that which abideth for ever. There was somewhat indeed then still within me (even the seed of eternity) which leavened and balanced my spirit almost continually; but I knew it not distinctly, so as to turn to it, and to give up to it, entirely and understandingly. In this temper of mind I earnestly sought after the Lord, applying myself to hear sermons, and read the best books I could meet with, but especially the Scriptures, which were very sweet and savory to me; yea, I very earnestly desired and pressed after the knowledge of the Scriptures, but was much afraid of receiving men's interpretations of them, or of fastening any interpretation upon them myself; but waited much, and prayed much, that from the Spirit of the Lord I might receive the true understanding of them, and that he would chiefly endue me with that knowledge, which I might feel sanctifying and saving. And indeed I did sensibly receive of his love, of his mercy, and of his grace, which I felt still freely to move towards me, and at seasons when I was most filled with the sense of my own unworthiness, and had least expectations of the manifestation of them. But I was exceedingly entangled about election and reprobation (having drunk in that doctrine, according as it was then held forth by the strictest of those that were termed Puritans, and as then seemed to be very manifest and positive from Rom. 9. &c), fearing lest, notwithstanding all my desires and seekings after the Lord, he might in his decree have passed me by; and I felt it would be bitter to me to bear his wrath, and be separated from his love for evermore; yet, if he had so decreed, it would be, and I should (notwithstanding these fair beginnings and hopes) fall away and perish at the last. In this great trouble and grief (which was much added to by not finding the Spirit of God so in me and with me, as I had read and believed the former Christians had it), and in mourning over and grappling with secret corruptions and temptations, I spent many years, and fell into great weakness of body; and often casting myself upon my bed, did wring my hands and weep bitterly, begging earnestly of the Lord, daily, that I might be pitied by him, and helped against my enemies, and be made conformable to the image of his Son, by his own renewing power. And indeed at last (when my nature was almost spent, and the pit of despair was even closing its mouth upon me) mercy sprang, and deliverance came, and the Lord my God owned me, and sealed his love unto me, and light sprang within me, which made not only the Scriptures, but the very outward creatures glorious in my eye, so that every thing was sweet and pleasant and lightsome round about me. But I soon felt, that this estate was too high and glorious for me, and I was not able to abide in it, it so overcame my natural spirits; wherefore, blessing the name of the Lord for his great goodness to me, I prayed unto him to take that from me which I was not able to bear, and to give me such a proportion of his light and presence, as was suitable to my present state, and might fit me for his service. Whereupon this was presently removed from me; yet a savor remained with me, wherein I had sweetness, and comfort, and refreshment for a long season. But my mind did not then know how to turn to and dwell with that which gave me the savor, nor rightly to read what God did daily write in my heart, which sufficiently manifested itself to be of him, by its living virtue and pure operation upon me; but I looked upon the Scriptures to be my rule, and so would weigh the inward appearances of God to me by what was outwardly written, and durst not receive any thing from God immediately, as it sprang from the fountain, but only in that mediate way. Herein did I limit the Holy One of Israel, and exceedingly hurt my own soul, as I afterwards felt and came to understand. Yet the Lord was tender to me, and condescended exceedingly, opening scriptures to me, freshly every day, teaching and instructing, warming and comforting my heart thereby; and truly he did help me to pray, and to believe, and to love him and his appearances in any; yea, to love all the sons of men, and all his creatures, with a true love. But that in me which knew not the appearances of the Lord in my spirit, but would limit him to words of scriptures formerly written, that proceeded yet further, and would be raising a fabric of knowledge out of the scriptures, and gathering a perfect rule (as I thought) concerning my heart, my words, my ways, my worship; and according to what I thus drank in (after this manner, from the Scriptures) I practised, and with much seriousness of spirit and prayer to God fell a helping to build up an Independent congregation, wherein the savor of life and the presence of God was fresh with me, as (I believe) there are yet some alive of that congregation can testify.

This was my state, when I was smitten, broken, and distressed by the Lord, confounded in my worship, confounded in my knowledge, stripped of all in one day (which it is hard to utter) and was matter of amazement to all that beheld me. I lay open and naked to all that would inquire of me, and strive to search out what might be the cause the Lord should deal so with me. They would at first be jealous that I had sinned and provoked him so to do; but when they had scanned things thoroughly, and I had opened my heart nakedly to them, I do not remember any one that ever retained that sense concerning me. My soul remembereth the wormwood and gall, the exceeding bitterness of that state, and is still humbled in me in the remembrance of it before the Lord. Oh, how did I wish with Job, that I might come before him, and bowingly plead with him; for indeed I had no sense of any guilt upon me, but was sick of love towards him, and as one violently rent from the bosom of his beloved! Oh, how gladly would I have met with death! For I was weary all the day long, and afraid of the night, and weary also of the night-season, and afraid of the ensuing day. I remember my grievous and bitter mournings to the Lord; how often did I say, O Lord, why hast thou forsaken me? Why hast thou broken me to pieces? I had no delight but thee, no desire after any but thee. My heart was bent wholly to serve thee, and thou hast even fitted me (as appeared to my sense) by many deep exercises and experiences for thy service; why dost thou make me thus miserable? Sometimes I would cast mine eye upon a scripture, and my heart would even melt within me; at other times I would desire to pray to my God, as I had formerly done; but I found I knew him not, and I could not tell how to pray, or in any wise to come near him, as I had formerly done. In this condition I wandered up and down from mountain to hill, from one sort to another, with a cry in my spirit, Can ye tell news of my beloved? Where doth he dwell? Where doth he appear? But their voices were still strange to me, and I would retire sad and oppressed, and bowed down in spirit, from them.

Now surely, all serious, sober, sensible people, will be ready to inquire, how I came satisfyingly to know the Lord at length; or whether I do yet certainly know him, and am yet truly satisfied?

Yes indeed, I am satisfied at my very heart. Truly my heart is united to him whom I longed after, in an everlasting covenant of pure life and peace.

Well then, how came this about? will some say.

Why thus. The Lord opened my spirit, the Lord gave me the certain and sensible feeling of the pure seed, which had been with me from the beginning; the Lord caused his holy power to fall upon me, and gave me such an inward demonstration and feeling of the seed of life, that I cried out in my spirit: This is he, this is he; there is not another, there never was another. He was always near me, though I knew him not (not so sensibly, not so distinctly, as now he was revealed in me and to me by the Father); O that I might now be joined to him, and he alone might live in me. And so in the willingness which God had wrought in me (in this day of his power to my soul), I gave up to be instructed, exercised, and led by him, in the waiting for and feeling of his holy seed, that all might be wrought out of me which could not live with the seed, but would be hindering the dwelling and reigning of the seed in me, while it remained and had power. And so I have gone through a sore travail, and fight of afflictings and temptations, of many kinds; wherein the Lord hath been merciful to me in helping me, and preserving the spark of life in me, in the midst of many things which had befallen me, whose nature tended to quench and extinguish it.

Now thus having met with the true way, and walked with the Lord therein, wherein daily certainty, yea, and full assurance of faith and of understanding is at length obtained; I cannot be silent (true love and pure life stirring in me and moving me) but am necessitated to testify of it to others; and this is it, to retire inwardly, and wait to feel somewhat of the Lord, somewhat of his Holy Spirit and power, discovering and drawing from that which is contrary to him, and into his holy nature and heavenly image. And then, as the mind is joined to this, somewhat is received, some true life, some true light, some true discerning; which the creature not exceeding (but abiding in the measure of) is safe; but it is easy erring from this, but hard abiding with it, and not going before its leadings. But he that feels life, and begins in life, doth he not begin safely? And he that waits, and fears, and goes on no further than his Captain goes before him, doth he not proceed safely? Yea, very safely, even till he cometh to be so settled and established in the virtue, demonstration, and power of truth, as nothing can prevail to shake him. Now blessed be the Lord, there are many at this day, who can truly and faithfully witness, that they have been brought by the Lord to this state. And thus have we learned of the Lord; to wit, not by the high, striving, aspiring mind, but by lying low, and being contented with a little. If but a crumb of bread (yet if bread), if but a drop of water (yet if water), we have been contented with it, and also thankful to the Lord for it; nor by thoughtfulness, and wise searching and deep considering with our own wisdom and reason have we obtained it; but in the still, meek, and humble waiting, have we found that brought into the death, which is not to know the mysteries of God's kingdom, and that which is to live, made alive and increase in life.

Therefore he that would truly know the Lord, let him take heed of his own reason and understanding. I tried this way very far; for I considered most seriously and uprightly; I prayed, I read the Scriptures, I earnestly desired to understand and find out whether that, which this people, called Quakers, testified of, was the only way and truth of God (as they seemed to me but to pretend); but for all this prejudices multiplied upon me, and strong reasonings against them, which appeared to me as unanswerable. But when the Lord revealed his seed in me, and touched my heart therewith, which administered true life and virtue to me, I presently felt them there the children of the Most High, and so grown up in his life, power, and holy dominion (as the inward eye, being opened by the Lord, sees) as drew forth from me great reverence of heart, and praises to the Lord, who had so appeared among men in these latter days. And as God draweth, in any respect, oh, give up in faithfulness to him! despise the shame, take up the cross; for indeed it is a way which is very cross to man, and which his wisdom will exceedingly be ashamed of; but that must be denied and turned from, and the secret, sensible drawings of God's Spirit waited for and given up to. Mind, people: He that will come into the new covenant, must come into the obedience of it. The light of life, which God hath hid in the heart, is the covenant; and from this covenant God doth not give knowledge to satisfy the vast, aspiring, comprehending wisdom of man; but living knowledge, to feed that which is quickened by him; which knowledge is given in the obedience, and is very sweet and precious to the state of him that knows how to feed upon it. Yea truly, this is of a very excellent, pure, precious nature, and a little of it weighs down that great vast knowledge in the comprehending part, which the man's spirit and nature so much prizeth and presseth after. And truly, friends, I witness at this day a great difference between the sweetness of comprehending the knowledge of things, as expressed in the Scriptures (this I fed much on formerly), and tasting the hidden life, the hidden Manna in the heart (which is my food now, blessed for ever be the Lord my God and Saviour). Oh that others had a true, certain, and sensible taste of the life, virtue, and goodness of the Lord, as it is revealed there! Surely, it could not but kindle the true hunger, and inflame the true thirst; which can never be satisfied but by the true bread, and by water from the living fountain. This the Lord (in the tenderness of his love, and in the riches of his grace and mercy) hath brought us to; and this we earnestly and uprightly desire and endeavor, that others may be brought to also; that they may rightly (in the true silence of the flesh, and in the pure stillness of spirit) wait for, and in the Lord's due time receive, that which answers the desire of the awakened mind and soul, and satisfies it with the true precious substance for evermore, Amen.

THE END.

A True Account of the Trial and Sufferings of Lodowick Muggleton,

One of the two last Prophets and Witnesses of the Spirit,

LEFT BY

OUR FRIEND POWELL,

WHO WITNESSED THE TRIAL AND ALL HIS SUFFERINGS,

THEREFORE

He gives a more full and particular Account of the Whole Proceedings than the Prophet has left on Record,

WHICH IS THE CAUSE OF MY PRINTING IT,

That Believers may see bow patiently our Prophet bore those Sufferings on Truths Account.

Knowing when Time is ended, he should meet his God, his King and Redeemer, with all those that truly believe Jesus Christ, that was Crucified, was the only and alone eternal God, one glorious distinct Person in the form of a Man, who now reigns in the highest Heavens, where we shall behold his glorious Face, to live with him, and praise his Holy Name for ever!

Printed for T. FEVER---1808.

By MORRIS and REEVES, 53, Red-Cross Street, Southwark.

AN ACCOUNT OF THE Prophet MUGGLETON'S Sufferings, IN THE YEAR 1676, As related by our Friend, Mr. POWELL, Who was an Eye-witness to the whole.

THE 17th of January, 1676, it was one of the dismal days that has appeared this 1350 years, to any one who hath the true light of life eternal abiding in them, and then to behold the greatest of commissionated prophets brought to the bar of justice, nay, to the bar of injustice, and there to be arraigned for being robbed, and his robbers to be his accusers; I would humbly desire of any impartial hearer of his trial to tell me, soberly, whether he in his own days, or in any record he has read, and found such inhumanity, that burglary should be committed against a man by a fraternity of robbers, and the robbers sue the robbed, and denied the benefit of the laws, which is a security for the offended and scourge to the offender, and the robbers that robbed him to be his accusers, in a plea of trespass in, the Court of Arches of Canterbury, which Lodowick Muggleton being the offended, went there to answer, by express from the Court in person; by this means the robbers got the Lord Chief Justice's warrant, and apprehended Lodowick Muggleton therewith, and brought him before Sir Thomas Davis, (then Lord Mayor of London) who committed him prisoner to Newgate, for owning the writing of a book, written against some Quakers, in the year 1663, and from thence bailed out to answer to an indictment, at the Old Bailey, for writing the said book; then Mr. Muggleton took out a sesarary to remove his trial from the Old Bailey to the King's Bench, yet, notwithstanding the Lord Chief Justice Rainsford, after he had taken Lodowick Muggleton's money for the sesarary, very unjustly and arbitrarily supercedes it, contrary to all law and justice; and the liberty of the subject commands him to take his trial at the Old Bailey, and there to answer to an indictment, as follows:

"Lodowick Muggleton, thou standest here indicted for writing a, blasphemous heretical seditious book, and to which indictment thou pleadest not guilty; what sayest thou for thyself?" Lodowick Muggleton made no answer, only desired the liberty of a counsel, which was granted; but before Lodowick Muggleton's counsel began to speak, his adversary's council opened the cause, and said, "My Lord, I am counsel for the King in this cause, and I think his crown and dignity was never so abused before" and taking one of the books by one of the clasps, said, "My Lord, here is a book contains the horridest blasphemy that ever was spoke or written before, a book that makes me tremble to hold it in my hand, I did read one side of a leaf in it, and I will assure your Lordship, it made my hair stand an end to see the horrid curses contained therein; it is composed of such horrid blasphemy, that. I would not be obliged to read it through for all the world's wealth, for the blasphemy contained is very great;" "for", said he, "it was impossible for any man to write such a horrible blasphemous book, in assuming the place of God upon him," for, said he, "it is so cunningly contrived, that it confounds all reason in man; therefore, my Lord, it is my opinion they ought to be cut off, both root and branch; with several other words to the same effect." Then

A True Account of the Trial

Lodowick Muggleton's counsel began to plead, but pleaded like a man that is either afraid to offend the judges, or like a very weak lawyer, for he pleaded no more than this:" My Lord, the book Mr. Muggleton stands indicted upon, was written before the act of grace came forth, therefore if Mr. Muggleton has offended, he hopes the act of grace will favor him." Whereupon the Lord Chief Justice Rainsford then sharply took him up, and said, That person that had the impudence to write such a blasphemous book as this was, did not want subtillity to antidate it. Whereupon one Garrat stood up, and said, "That Mr. Muggleton did own the writing of the book when he was before the Lord Mayor, in Guildhall." Then, replied the Lord Chief Justice, "that the acknowledging the book before the Lord Mayor, was a sufficient testimony against him, and a publication of the book since the act of grace." Then stood up Judge Atkins, and said, "He did not conceive that by owning the book before the Lord Mayor was a publication, since the Act; for, said he, "would you have the man to have told a lie." "My Lord," said Garratt, "it was a long time before he would confess it:" "Why", said Judge Atkins, "We have no law to make a man accuse himself; can you make it appear," said he, "that Mr. Muggleton has writ these books since the Act of Grace, or has he made sale of any since the Act of Grace, or has he offended the law:"--to which Mr. Garratt said "No." Then,' said Judge Atkins, "Gentlemen of the Jury, you see there is no proof against Mr. Muggleton, either of his writing or making sale of any of these books since the Act of Grace; therefore I do not understand how he can be denied the benefit of it, since we have no law for it." "Why", said the Lord Chief Justice, in a great passion, "If we have no law for it, I make it law," and down he sits; and it was expected, Mr. Muggleton's counsel would have pleaded, but whether the Lord Chief Justice's passion prevented him or not, I do not know, but further he pleaded not, which made the Chief Justice very much reflect on Mr. Muggleton, and, in a jeering way, said to his counsel, "Rise up, and plead for your client;" but he made no word of answer, which the adverse party made some advantage of, and the Lord Chief Justice stood up, and said, "Gentlemen of the Jury, here is a cause before you so notoriously wicked, that, I thank God, I never heard the like before; it is a cause so odious and so blasphemous, that you see his own counsel is ashamed to plead in the vindication of so notorious a villain as this is, that could foment such horrid blasphemies as these are, and publish them: Pray," said the Lord Chief Justice, "how many of these books did you find in his house;" they made answer, "they had about a porter's load." "How many may that be in number," said he; "they carried about three or four hundred:"" What," said he, all of one volume," they said "no; there was about six of the volume; as for the rest, they were what was contained in that book, but in smaller volumes." "then," said the Lord Chief Justice, "it shews his subtillity had contrived them in several potions suitable to their constitutions; they, whose stomachs were large enough to digest the whole venom might have it, and them whose stomachs were little and crazy, his cunning had contrived potions of it for their distempers. And now, Gentlemen of the Jury, although we have no proof of his selling any of these books, for it is to be believed those that bought them were of his own gang, and they will not appear against him; therefore we must by circum-stances, for what should one person do with so many books of one sort, unless it were to make sale of them; therefore, Gentlemen of the Jury, I would have you narrowly sift the witnesses before you determine, and consider it was through a pretended zeal our late king was put to death, and who knows what design this villain had both in church and government: and therefore, Gentlemen, if you do not bring him in guilty, yourselves will be sharers in his curst apostacy." The jury receiving this unheard-of charge, went out of court, and after half an hour's consultation amongst themselves, they returned; when it was demanded by the Clerk of the Peace, whether they were agreed in their verdict,---they answered, "they were;" "who shall speak for you," was then asked; they said, "the foreman;" then, said the Clerk of the Peace, "is Lodowick Muggleton guilty of writing these books for which he stands Indicted, or not guilty," the foreman said, "Guilty;" but the words came from him with so discomposed a countenance, that his Very looks shewed his conscience had accused him with unjust doing; the Lord Chief Justice having now his desired ends of the Jury, began in the most abusive, basest way, that ever a Judge did to a prisoner, Which is as follows:

"Thou impudent rogue, sirriah! thou villain, which art a rogue so great, that I want words bad enough to call you, a villainous rogue, composed of such impudence, that you see he has got a set of them, and makes them call themselves Muggletonians, after his cursed name; such a pack of villany I thought could not be invented by a rogue; yet how impudently the impostor stands; I am sorry our laws are so much unprovided that there is not a punishment severe enough to punish this rogue, according to the villainy of his crimes, but little did the contrivers of the law think that ever such blasphemy should be spread abroad in the world, and by so ill-looking a fellow as this; I would forgive the greatest rogue that should rob me of all I have, the greatest murderer in the whole world, sooner than I would forgive this villain, who is a murderer of souls." Upon the Lord Chief Justice ending his speech, Judge Atkins left the Bench, and when he came down stairs, he shook his head and said, "things are not fairly carried on here," and spoke it in the hearing of several people, as well as myself. Then Lord Chief Justice Montague stood up and said, "As for what my Lord Chief Justice said, I like it very well, for he has shewn his love and zeal to God, and his loyalty to his King; his zeal to God in endeavouring to crush this rogue, in his blasphemous pretences, who made it his business to draw away as many souls as he could after him by his damnable doctrine; I am sorry there has been occasion to publish his villainy by reading his blasphemous

A True Account of the Trial

books in open court, for fear the venom should infect some of the hearers; but I hope God will direct them otherways, and as for the Stationers Company they ought to be remembered for their diligence, in searching after such cursed delusions as this impudent villain has broached abroad to deceive the people, so likewise the Jury ought to be applauded for bringing in so just and pious a, verdict; for he had rather forgive the greatest rogue, or greatest thief or murderer than this villain, this both thief and murderer to poor souls." The Judge hereupon gave the Jury thanks for their verdict, and in a short time arose and departed the Court, leaving the Common Serjeant Jefferies to pronounce the sentence against him, when, with a disdainful countenance, looked upon the prisoner, and with words so abusively scurrilous, that it is a shame for a government to have such magistrates, as shall hereafter appear, who said, "You rogue, that stands here; you impudent rascal, sirrah! That hath such confidence to stand in presence of the Court to justify so much blasphemy, sirrah! the Court has been too favourable to such a villain as thou art, who has been guilty of the blackest deed that ever was invented by any rogue, except thyself; deeds arising from the very blackest of darkness itself, and considering all thy villany, the Court has been too favourable to the proposing a sentence,--- You are to stand three days upon the pillory, in three principal places in the City of London; and your blasphemous books to be divided into three parts, and there, with fire, to be consumed before your face; and you are to pay a little fine, but £500. It is but a little one, considering your villainy, and you must give security for your good behaviour, during your life, and such as are not of your own gang;" thus ended the pronunciation of this sentence. Now I will proceed to the fulfilling of the sentence in order; then Mr. Muggleton was carried by one of the keepers to Newgate, where he had not been above a week, but be was commanded to his first place of standing, which was at the Temple Gate, in Fleet Street; where, by the croaking frogs, he was pelted with clay, rotten eggs, and dirt in abundance, and in this place they put his head in the pillory, but Captain Richardson, the head keeper, came to them, and said, "God damn you, what makes you put the man's head in, for it is contrary to his sentence." Then he was taken out, and stood two hours; then be was taken off, and put into the cart, and so was carried to Newgate again, where he remained till his second standing, which was at the Royal Exchange, in London, where one would have thought the gravity of the City would not have suffered any violation of the law, yet he was more barbarously used by the caterpillars than he was by the croaking frogs, although several faithful believers used their utmost endeavours to hinder the throwing of things, by delivering some of them to the officers; others persuaded, and some threatened; yet, notwithstanding all this, they most shamefully used him out of the balconies, from the top of the Change; he had glass bottles thrown at him, and pieces of timber, and stones in abundance; and below there was a shopkeeper walked up to the pillory, and standing before Mr. Muggleton, hit him on the breast with an orange; which I seeing, ran at him, and, with my cane, hit him over the head, till he fell to the ground; then comes one with an unheard of confidence, and takes a brand out of the fire, and threw it at him, which, had he not sheltered, himself among the crowd, he would certainly have been laid in the fire he took the brand out of. This forwardness of mine created a deal of talk, who I was; some said I was one of his own people; others said I was the Sheriff's clerk, and that went most about with the people, and I was glad if by any means I could save him, notwithstanding he was shamefully abused; and having stood his two hours, he was taken down, and carried into a cart to Newgate, there to remain until his last standing, which was to be in West Smithfield, on a Friday, where he was no sooner come and entered the scaffold of disgrace, but the rude multitude began, in a most merciless manner, to throw stones at him almost as thick as hail, and here I am sure if some saints bad not behaved with uncommon courage, he had certainly been killed; they went to the officers, requesting their diligent care, and promising to gratify them for it, and went quite round the people to hinder, either by fair means or foul; the throwing of stones, where I, with two officers going round about, saw a fellow take up a stone, swearing a bloody oath he would beat out his brains; but that hand that took it up was so belaboured, that I believe he could hardly lift it to his head for a week; yet, notwithstanding all the care and pains, we could not bring him off safe, for he was there knocked down with a stone, and had his head broke, in a base manner, so that the blood of the last Prophet that God will ever send, is to be required of this nation; so when his two hours were completed, he was taken down, and carried in a cart to Newgate, where he had his wounds dressed. So here he ended his corporal punishment, the greatest imaginable, both in his usage and in his time of standing; for I have known several rogues, cheats, and perjured persons, stand in the pillory, whose time was but one hour, and their usage much civiller than his, who had broke no law, nor any thing of evil laid to his charge, as shall hereafter appear. He stood two hours on the pillory, with the greatest abuse imaginable, only for his conscience in Christ Jesus, and owning himself his true Prophet.

Now beloved friends, as God said to the rebellious people, so will I say to those that were Mr. Muggleton's Judges and Jury,---come let us reason together; I desire to know whether thou doest believe in an eternal creator of heaven and earth, and all things formed therein, which I am sure thou cans't not deny? If thou doth believe it, so doth Mr. Muggleton. Why, then, do thou accuse him? Doth thou believe Christ died for his elect? So doth Mr. Muggleton. Why, then, do thou persecute him? Do you believe Christ rose again for the sanctification of his elect? So doth Mr. Muggleton. Why, then, do you furnish him; O you workers of iniquity, perhaps you will say unto me, Mr. Muggleton pretends himself to be a true Prophet of God, and that there is no true minister but himself; truly if so, what a condition have you brought yourself into, for David said, "Who was a man after God's own heart, save only in the matter of Uriah's wife, touch not the Lord's annointed, nor do my Prophets harm." Now you judges, who have sat in judgment, how have you followed the commandment of our Lord Jesus Christ, who said, "He that receives a Prophet in the name of a Prophet, shall receive a Prophet's reward;" so, consequently, he that despises a Prophet despises him that sent him; so that you have pillored the Lord Jesus in your days; for, said he, "inasmuch as you have done it, to the least of my brethren, you have done it to me;" but you have done it to the greatest that has appeared this 1500 years; but you may say, "How do we know that he is a true Prophet;" "I say unto you," as the Prophet of old said, "My people are destroyed for the want of knowledge;" and you might have judged after the rule of Gamaliel, who said, "Touch him not, for if his doctrine be of himself, both him and his doctrine will perish together; but if it be of God, and you persecute him, you make yourselves fighters against God" since, therefore, no such righteous judgment has been acted by you, I will say, "Who shall deliver you from the wrath of God! O ye powers of England," and so I end his corporal punishment.

Now I shall give you an account of the chief actions that attended his personal imprisonment, also to pay the £500. Mr. Muggleton was not able, and to lie in prison among a company of rogues, he was not willing; wherefore Mr. Muggleton desired to be removed from the master's side to the press-yard, but one of the keepers told him he must not be removed; for, said he, "you are one of the best prisoners, and we give a great deal of money for our places, and at this rate we shall be losers if our best prisoners be taken from us". Wherefore Mr. Muggleton sends for a lawyer, and advised with him what to do, who asked him "whether he owed any money, and whether it was to any he could put confidence." Mr. Muggleton answered, "he did owe thirty pounds to one Mrs. Hall, upon a note under his hand, and that he knew her to be a faithful good woman by experience;" then, said the lawyer, "she must bring her writ against you, out by the Common Pleas, and charge you with it in Newgate, and then take a Habeas Corpus to remove you from Newgate to the Fleet." Mr. Muggleton did not think it convenient for Mrs. Hall to appear alone before the Judges, therefore he made choice of me, Nathaniel Powell, to aid and assist her in this weighty affair; in order thereunto, we goes and takes out a Habeas Corpus, which our lawyer gave to one of the prothonotaries of the Common Pleas, in order to have it entered; but the prothonotaries told the lawyer, that he wondered he could appear in so ill a cause; for, said he, "Mr. Muggleton is a felon, and we are not to remove felonious persons." The lawyer (surely left his reason at home) came away with this lying answer of the prothonotaries, for there was never any felony nor any other evil laid to his charge, in all his trial, but for writing a book only. When I saw how unsuccessful we were with our lawyer, I desired Mr. Muggleton to put him off, and that Mrs. Hall and I would manage the business without him; this was no sooner concluded on, but the under-keeper of Newgate came to Mr. Muggleton and told him, if he would give him ten shillings he would endeavour to get him a good chamber in the press-yard, which Mr. Muggleton was willing to do, by reason he should there be free from the trepanning visits many people made- him. Being thus retired, he considered what was next to be done; he therefore ordered Mr. Powell to go and sound the Sheriff of London, to see what he would take towards the £500; accordingly we went to Sir John Peak, and Sir Thomas Stamp, then Sheriff of London; Sir John Peak was very fair in his demands, for he said he would be contented with what his brother Sheriff did; whereupon I said to him "Suppose your brother Sheriff will omit the penal fine, which if he doth, will you be pleased to condescend to it," he said, "I will condescend to any agreement he and you doth make, and if he be willing to forgive his part, I will mine." With this civil reply of Sir John Peak's I went to Sir Thomas Stamp, but found no such kindness there; for, in the first place, be demanded the whole fine, and said it was their due, and said he did not think himself obliged to abate anything. I told him, there was no possibility to pay it, by reason of the inability of the person; he said then he must remain prisoner still;—said he cannot, by the course of nature live long, he being 68 years of age, and being confined it will be a means to shorten his days, then you will lose it all. "I do not care if I do," replied Sir Thomas, said I, "It must surely reflect upon your conscience, to have any old man die in a gaol on your account; he never did you any wrong." "I will venture that," said he, and with that tell him from me, "if he doth not leave off his public discourses, that I hear he uses in prison, I Will confine him closer." With this answer I went to Newgate, and gave Mr. Muggleton an account of what had passed, who, hearing of it, was resolved to content himself with the condition he was in some longer time. Mr. Muggleton remaining thus silent caused the Sheriffs to send to him, who sent one of the keepers of Newgate to tell him, if he would make any fair proposals, the Sheriffs would be very civil to him; whereupon Mr. Muggleton sent to them again, where it was referred to Sir Thomas Stamp, who advised me to bring him the £500. and I should see how civil he would be to me. "Sir," said I, "I hope you do not take me to be such a fool as to trust to the courtesy of a covetous Sheriff;" so I went away. After that Mrs. Hall brought a Habeas Corpus to remove him to the King s Bench, but was strangely frustrated; I called upon the tipstaff, and nobody was there to prove the Habeas Corpus, although the Lord Chief Justice Rainsford granted it, and he himself sat on the bench; yet did he suffer Jefferys to say there was no Habeas Corpus granted, and that this was like one of Muggleton's tricks; so he was remanded back to Newgate, and remained there some time after; then I went and took out another Habeas Corpus, and carried it myself to Guildhall, to the Lord Mayor, Sheriffs, and Court of Aldermen; there I was commanded to wait in

A True Account of the Trial 161

the matted gallery, and after waiting there about an hour, Mr. Tanner, the Clerk of the Peace, came to me and told me, that the Lord Mayor and Court of Aldermen had accepted the Habeas Corpus, and would be obedient to the Lord Chief Justice's order. "His order is, that you forthwith deliver his body, and I demand it." "Sir," said Mr. Tanner, "there is a great deal to be done before you can have it." "Sir," said I, "I know there is no more to be done than the return of the Habeas Corpus." "The Lord Mayor ordered me to tell you so," said he, "therefore I can-not help it." So away I went, and the next morning called on Mr. Tanner, he being at Fishmonger's Hall, who told me, I must go and search the Counters, to see if there was no detainer lodged against him; otherwise the Sheriffs cannot safely deliver him up. "Why," said I, "what hath the Sheriffs to do with him any more than what he is charged with in Newgate, or if there be any thing against him in any of the Counters, (as I am sure there is not) and if not charged upon him, in Newgate. the Sheriffs are to take no cognizance of it. I have orders from the Sheriffs to tell you so," said he; I replied, "I smell knavery in the Sheriffs," which made Mr. Tanner a little angry; but, however, away I went to the Poultry Counter, and searched there, and found nothing, and from thence to Wood-Street Counter, where the clerk said the books were carried to Guildhall, and we must go there and search; so we went to Guildhall, and when we came there, they told us we could not see till the court sat, which would not be till eleven o'clock; so there we waited, and when the court sat, they favoured us to search, (but not without our money) where we found nothing entered there; so we went down again to Mr. Tanner, and acquainted him, and desired a return of the Habeas Corpus, who told me it was superceded. "Who has done it," said I, "the Lord Chief Justice," said he. "How dared he to do that injustice," said I; "You may go ask," said he. I answered "I would," so away goes Mrs. Hall and I; but before I went to the Chief Justice, we called at Newgate, and gave Mr. Muggleton an account of what had passed, who sent us to the Lord Chief Justice to know his unjust proceedings against him; so we went and told his Lordship we were come about a person his Lordship had granted a Habeas Corpus, for, and since had denied it by a supercedure. "Who is is that?" said be; "Mr. Muggleton," said I."Mr. Muggleton," said he, "shall not be removed out of the Sheriffs' custody." "Pray, why so, my Lord;" "Why," said he, "you will not remove that for £30. that lies for £500" "My Lord," said I, "he is in for no debt but ours': "Go," said he," and pay the £500. and then you shall have your Habeas Corpus granted." "My Lord," said I, "would you have us to pay £500. to secure £30." I do believe Mrs. Hall doth act in kindness," said he, "which will be more hindrance than to act according to the justice of the law." "Why, my Lord," said he, "whether it be kindness or not kindness, is it law? If it be law, my Lord, I am a free-born subject of the king; and, as such, I claim the benefit of the law; and if it be not law, my Lord, why should you be so unjust as to put us to £35. charges to take it out". "What's that to you, sirrah!"

said he, out of my chamber; about your business, or I will send you to some other place." So away we went, and gave Mr. Muggleton an account in Newgate, who, hearing all this his injustice, said, 'He must wait some other opportunity, he being so near got out of the Sheriff of London's custody, made him afraid he would find some other way.' Whereupon they sent to him again, to treat about the fine, and be ordered me to go and treat with them; in order thereunto, I went, and did agree with them about the fine for £100. After we had agreed about the sum, I asked what time they would give for the payment: they said they expected the money now ; I said, I had not got it ready, but would give them bond and security for it; they asked me who was my security, I said Mr. Cooper in Shoe Lane, and Mr. Symonds in Cow Lane; they bid me come tomorrow, and they would, in the mean time, enquire after the securities, to know if they were substantial. So in the morning I went to meet them at the Lord Mayor's, where they told me, they did not approve of taking a security on a bond, but if Mr. Muggleton would assign over his houses, they would take them, and give him six months for the payment. I told them 'No; for when once a Sheriff had got possession of a man's estate, it was hard to get it again.' 'Pray, then,' said Sir Thomas Stamp, 'let us have our money; what interest are you willing to allow me for the six months, if I procure the money to-morrow: Sir John Peak told me, be would allow me after the rate of six per cent. I told him I would not have it so; but if he would allow me after the rate of ten per cent. I would pay it on the morrow. 'I will allow it, then,' said he. With that I went and told Mr. Muggleton what I had to do, who approved of it very well, and sent me to borrow the money; accordingly I did, and the next morning went with the money to the Lord Mayor, Sheriffs, and Court of Aldermen at Guildhall, and took two men with me for bail for his good behaviour. The Court beginning to fill, I went to Sir John Peak, to have my business dispatched, who immediately sent to Captain Richardson for the copy of the commitment, but word was brought the Captain was out of town, and they could not get at it; then he sent to Mr. Tanner, the Clerk of the Peace, and ordered him to send it; his man sent word he was not at home, and dare not send it without his order: whereupon I told Sir John Peak I did believe all that was done a mere trick, 'for how dare your servants,' said I, 'send you such petty answers, if it were not by your consent.' 'Pray,' said he, 'stay a little, and you shall see to the contrary.' So away he sends another messenger to Mr. Tanner's, and bid him tell him if he did not send away the copy of Mr. Muggleton's commitment quickly he would send him to prison; this message brought his clerk; but before he came, the Court of Aldermen broke up, and Sir John Peak told me it could not be done till the sitting of the next Court, which would not be till three weeks time. 'Sir,' said I, 'if I have not him out this day he shall lay there for ever.' 'Why,' said he, 'what would you have me to do?' 'Sir,' said I, 'invite the Lord Mayor and two or three Aldermen to a private table, to drink a bottle of wine, and it may as well be done before them as the whole Court.' 'I will do it,' said he, 'because you shall see how willing I am to serve you:' so to a private table he invites the Lord Mayor and some of the Aldermen; where they had bottles of wine and tobacco laying before them; then I and the two people who were to be bail went into the room:---'What are you?' said the Lord Mayor; I replied, 'My Lord, I am come to bail Mr. Muggleton out of Newgate.' 'Will the bail,' said he, 'swear themselves worth £300. a-piece, and all their debts paid?' 'What necessity is there for that,' said I, 'Why,' replied the Lord Mayor, 'do you think I will take less than £300. of two men for £500.?' 'I do not know what your lordship means by £500.' 'Why,' said he, 'is not his fine £500.? --- True, my Lord; but I do not put in bail for the fine; I come to pay that: I have money in Court ready for it: your Lordship may ask the Sheriff that sits there, if he be not satisfied.' 'Then' said the Lord Mayor to the bail, 'Mr. Butterill, and Mr. Clark the farrier, you shall promise that Mr. Muggleton shall appear the first day of the general sessions of gaol delivery of Newgate, on pain of £200. a-piece, to be levied on your goods and chattels.' 'No, but they shall not;' said I:' 'Why so?' said the Lord Mayor; I replied, 'because it was contrary to law:' with that one of the Aldermen stood up in a passion and said, 'Will you pretend to teach my Lord Mayor law?' I told him that was none of my business, but I would prefer my own memory equally with the Lord Mayor's, or his either, and that it was contrary to the sentence he received, and that I would have no secondary impositions laid upon him. 'Pray,' said the Lord Mayor, 'you that know so well, what is the sentence?' My Lord, his sentence was to stand upon the pillory three times, and to pay a fine of £500. and to give security for his good behaviour during life; if during life no necessity for appearance till a default be made.' 'What,' said the Lord Mayor, are you one of his gang? That is no business of your's to ask, my Lord; neither did I come here to be catchechised; 'You talk too saucy to my Lord,' said one of the Aldermen. 'Not at all, Sir,' said I, 'for I did not come here to discourse on religion, but law.' 'Who is this man?' said the Lord Mayor to Sir John Peak, who replied, 'he is Mr. Muggleton's solicitor.' 'Are you willing,' said the Lord Mayor, 'that he shall appear or no; I told him I would not go no other way than what the law directed.' Upon which Sir Robert Hanson and Sir John Peak whispered me out of the room, and kept me in talk, while the Lord Mayor, and Mr. Lightfoot, his attorney, persuaded my friends to be bound for his appearance, at the Old Bailey; when I perceived this, I was extremely troubled, but how to help it I could not tell: So having done at Guildhall, I went with the Sheriff to his house, to pay the money; before I let him have it, I told him I expected he would promise me that he should discharge Mr. Muggleton from that appearance, at the Old Bailey; he told me that could not be avoided now; but, at their appearance, he would discharge both him and his bail: I told him that would not do, for unless he would promise me he should not appear, I would carry the money back again; he hearing me say this, made me a promise to discharge him without his personal appearance. Dinner being over, and some private discourse between Sir John and I, gave me a release from the Lord Mayor, and an order signed by both the Sheriffs, to Captain Richardson, for his discharge, upon sight thereof: I told the Sheriff I did believe the Captain would not obey their order, he told me he would stay at home three hours on purpose for me, and if in that time I could not have him discharged, desired me to come and acquaint him, and he would go to Newgate himself, and lay Captain Richardson by the heels, and put Mr. Muggleton out; so giving him hearty thanks for his kindness, I took my leave, and about four o'clock in the afternoon I got to Newgate, where I went to the keeper and demanded Mr. Muggleton, the keeper was a little surprised, thinking he had made all sure for his longer confinement; so after a little pausing, he told me he would send to the Sheriffs, to know if that was their hand writing, which, if they owned, I should have him discharged; so away he sent a messenger, but we heard no more of him till seven o'clock; then I went to the keeper again, to know the reason of his long stay, be told me he did believe Mr. Muggleton could not be discharged that night; I told him unless he did discharge him, both him and his captain should sit in the stocks, in their own prison, on the morrow, and that the Sheriff had so promised me; he hearing me say so, within half an hour discharged him from the prison of hell. The sessions coming on, it was much talked of in the City of London, that Mr. Muggleton was to be brought again to the Old Bailey: I being then at Braintree, in Essex, came speedily up to London, to prevent it, and as I was going to Sir John Peak's, I met him accidentally near the Poultry, who, seeing me, made his coach stop, and took me into it, where I began to attack him with falsehood for his breach of promise; he told me he could not help it, the Lord Mayor would have it so, or take the forfeiture of his recognizance: I told him he suffered the recognizance to be forfeited, and I would sue him for the money I paid him, and besides, I told him Mr. Muggleton was gone out of town, and I could not tell when he would come back again. 'Can't you get somebody to appear for and I Will order it so, that shall do as well.' 'If that will do, I will appear for him myself,' said I: 'You will do very well,' said the Sheriff; 'But, Sir,' said I 'I have three requests to make before the Court begins--the first is, that the business may be done as private as you can; the second is, that Sir George Jefferies may not be in Court, by reason his foul tongue may raise my passion, that may give offence to the Court; and the third is, that you would get Sir Robert Hanson to sit upon the bench; for he did declare to the Lord Mayor, that Mr. Muggleton was his next-door neighbour ten years, in all which time he never knew or heard that he ever swore an oath in his life, or ever was drunk, or ever knew that he told a lye, but was always a good man, making no difference with his neighbours; the Sheriff told me he would do what lay in his power to grant my request,' so we parted for that time: the time being come I was to appear in the Old Bailey, away I went, and, going to the Sheriff, I asked him 'When would my business come on?'---He said 'now;' so coming clown from his chair, takes me into the passage, and told me, 'He had obliged me in all my requests, he had done my business very privately, and ordered Jefferies out of Court, and had got Sir Robert Hanson on the bench;' so taking a catalogue of all the prisoners' names that were to appear that day, out of his pocket, there was Lodowick Muggleton discharged, acquitted, and released, by order of the Lord Mayor; for which I gave Sir John Peak my hearty thanks, and took my leave.

Thus I have given you a true and impartial account of the whole proceedings of Mr. Muggleton's last trial and sufferings.

THE END.

Morris & Reeves, Printers, 53, Red-Cross Street, Southwark.

The Blasphemer Tryed And Cast:

Or a more full Narrative of the Tryal of

Lodowick Muggleton,

On Wednesday the 17th of this instant January, at the Sessions-House in the *Old-Bayly*. With a Relation of the Charges delivered to the Jewry, and the Sentence passed upon him for his most Impious and Horrid Blasphemies.

WHICH WAS

To stand Three Days in the Pillory in three of the most eminent places in the city, and to have his Books burnt before his Face by the Common Hangman.

And also to pay Five Hundred Pounds Fine, and to find Sureties for his good Behaviour.

Licensed *Roger L'Strange*, Jan. 22.1676.

LONDON:
Printed for J. B. in the Year 1676

The Blasphemer Tryed and Cast, &c.

The birth and Education of this Monster that the whole Christian world may expect an account of, is so obscure and low, so extreamly inconsiderable, that even his own Gang of foolish followers, upon a strict inquiry of them, can only tell you that their first acquaintance with him did arise, when first his Co-partner in Villany, *Reeve* and himself, gave themselves to be the two last witnesses; then it was that *Muggleton* leaped over the shop-board, and would conciept himself, and make sick-brained idle people believe he was a great Prophet; that the power of binding and loosing were more strongly confirmed to him then ever the Roman Bishop pretended they were to the Holy Chair, for some years last past hath the impudence of this deceiver imposed upon a Company of Rude inconstant, Debauched people, to the wonder and astonishment of good and considerate men, that Justice did not stifle such a horried Fomenter of all that was superlatively wicked in its first birth; but such are those latter days that no Heretick hath appeared upon the stage of the World, but he hath found both adherers and admirers, some professing Religion, thinking it their glory to be alwaies seeking, though that their over curious inquiry hazards the welfare of their immortal Souls; too many are the present examples of this kind, and as easy it were to give many instances how that at last the Vengeance of Heaven hath overtaken such enemies to God and Religion, and because men have not so far espoused the cause of the Almighty, as severely to punish such wretches presidents are not wanting where God himself hath made manifest by his Judgments his dislike to, by punishment upon those Sons of *Belial* that durst derogate from the power of Heaven, much more against those that would establish an opposition to it; this indeed must not be the design of this sheet to manifest, that to undertake, were to swell this sheet into a Vollumn, which is not my design, but observing a defect in the former Relation, it was thought necessary to give a more perfect account of *Mugletons* Tryal, and to inform the world that God had given us such wise and learned judges, that the greatest zeal imaginable was shewn by them, and indeed by the whole Court against the Blasphemies of the boldest wretch that ever the earth made known, who at last being overtaken by the justice of the Law, received a Tryal before many of the Oracles of Justice, whom his Majesty for their great merrits hath dignified with a Judicatory Power; on *Wednesday* the 17th. of this Instant *January,* at Justice Hall in the *Old-Baly* was this great blasphemer arraigned, and indicted by the name of *Lodowick Muggleton,* for that he had sould, uttered, and dispersed several books, contained most horried Blasphemies receited in the indictment; but too base for any man to name, and indeed too foul for any tongue to express; after his charg read; and the wittnesses heard, he was asked what he had to say for himself, who begged the favour of the honourable Court, that he might have Counsel to speak for him, and he desired Mr. *Fenner* might be the person, which was graciously granted him, who like a good man discharged his duty as a Christian, and Counsellour, he hoped the Court did not expect he should defend or once name his Blasphemies, all that he would say was, that the prisoner did confess the fact, all that he did say in defense of himself, was that the Books so sould and uttered were written before the year 1673. In which year, his Majesties Act of Grace came forth, which he hoped would bring him under that cognizans, after this had received some Consideration by the Reverend Judges, his charge was given to the Jury in words to this Effect.

Gentlemen, you have heard the hainousness of the crime this wretch stands indicted for, it is most horrible Blasphemy against the great God; such wickedness his own Council will not dare to repeat, and truly could it have been avoided, the indictment contains such horrible Blasphemies and villanies, it should not have been read, but Gentlemen, as to the matter, it is proved that he did utter, sell, and dispose several Vollums of these Blasphemous books, that great quantities were taken in his own custody, that he vented them for several prizes, the whole Vollumn for 14.s. the half for 7.s. another

The Blasphemer Tried and Cast 169

part for 3.s 6 d. and some for 18.d. a piece, so that he had prepared and fitted this poyson to all degrees; he whose stomach was strong enough, had a full cup of Poyson, and for him whose appetite was weaker the half doze should serve, and for those whose disgestion was not so good nor purses so large, he had fited and prepared a smaller proportion for them; so that as much as in him lay, he indeavoured to infect all his Majesties Subjects that could be so ignorant as to buy his impious works, now what defence doth he make, he confesses that the books were sould and dispersed after the year 1673. In the following years, 74-75-76. Yet says he, they were written before the year 1673. so I hope the Kings Act of grace reaches so far as to pardon me; now Gentlemen, what witness, what proof brings he of this, why truly here is nothing appears but his own assertion, and he tells you the Title of his most wicked Books speak that they were written before who can be proof in such a case as to what he did? what testimony can he give account of his writing his Manuscript, except his own wicked Spirit? he says it was written before, but can you believe him, do you think he will make a conscience of lying, that hath vented such unheard of Blasphemies against God, than it were hard for the Divel to out do him in his malice; as to the Titles of his hellish books, who can tell but he might give them a false date on purpose to shelter himself under the Kings Act of grace, and foretelling (The text is unclear at this point) at last that Justice would over take him, he thought to take that for his refuge, for to give books a new Title, it seems as it is easy there is nothing more ordinary. Gentlemen we are fallen into such sad times, that whatever opposeth Government, whatever pusheth at Majestacy is upheld and carried on by desperate men (The text is unclear at this point); Gentlemen, I leave it to you, I pray God direct you.

It was further insisted upon, That such was the charge against the Prisoner, and so unusual his Crimes that he did confirm that (The text is unclear at this point) the Cause of God, of Religion, and of our Dread Sovereign, which such a despicable Villan had sought to Ruin, that is was admirable that such a silly Wretch durst be so Impudent to think to make himself great, by gathering a Rabble to Intitle themselves by his Name, it was left to them, and it was not to be doubted but God would give them Direction, upon which the Jury withdrew, and found this Great Imposter *Guilty.* After Sentence past upon other Malefactors, he received judgment, in a phrase more eloquent then I dare presume to Judg myself able to rehearse, but in words much to this effect; that such a Superlative Monster of Wickedness, should dare to Belch forth such horrible Blasphemys against the great God, Creator of Heaven and Earth; that such a despiseable Fellow here should gather a party, and set himself up in defiance to his Maker, and so proceeding to his Sentence, it was as follows: "Thou art now, thou Blasphemous Wretch, to receive the moderate Sentence, of this Court, I call it so because set in the Ballance with thy Crime, it is extreamly mild, but why is it so? is it in respect to thy Person, or compassion to thee, so surely, it is because the honesty and goodness of our Ancestors was such, that they thought the Earth could never bare such a Monster as thou art, and now thy Sentence is, thou art to stand three several days in the Pillary, in three of the most eminent places of this City, where of the *Royal Exchange* is to be one, and thy Books that are already found, and which contain thy wickedness, to be devided in three equal parts, and one part of them to attend thee every time thou so standest, and because thy Proselytes shall see thy Doctrine suffer with thee, thy Books shall be burnt by the hands of the Common Hangman, thou art also judged to pay five hundred Pounds, and to find Surerys before thou art discharged from Prison, for thy good behaviour dureing Life, but they must not be of thy own party (*Muggletonian*) but men of sincere and honest conversation, and this is the moderate Sentence of this Court.

And hear it will not be amiss, that we admire at the Patience and long suffering of our good and gracsous God in permiting such a Ratsback (The text is unclear at this point) to go so long unpunished, so unwilling is that Divine being that any of his Creatures should be miserable, but wishes all to Repent, but if his Patience be abused, he hath whet his Glittering Sword, and kept his Avenging bow, so that all shall say, Righteous art thou Oh Lord, and just in all thy judgments.

FINIS

News From The Sessions House In The Old – Bayly,

Being a true Account of the Notorious Principles and Wicked Practices Of That Grand Impostor Lodowick Muggleton

Who Has The Impudence To Stile Himself One Of The Two Last Commissionated Witnesses And Prophets Of The Most High God Christ Jesus.

Collected out of his own Writings,

For which Damnable *Heresies* being bound over, he made his Appearance at the Sessions, this 14th, of *Decemb*. And gave Fresh security in order to his future Tryal

Licensed and Entered according to Order

London, Printed for B. H. 1676.

A Brief and True Account of the notorious Principles, and wicked Practices of that Grand Imposter Lodowick Muggleton, &c.

To Trace this impious Imposter from his Original, who ever takes pains but to go into *Cloak Lane* will there be informed by the Generallity of the Inhabitants, that this *Lodowick Muggleton* was at first no other than a factious Journiman-*Tailor*, whose Extravagances being too large for the competent allowance of about 1cs. p, week, began in the year 1651 to consult with one *John Reeves* (a brother both in Trade and necessity) how they might betake them to some more profitable imployment, whose larded Incomes might be more kindly indulge their Luxury: to this end they made some small inspection and progress into all forms of *Heresies* (as he has since confest to J.C. and others) but finding those Chairs already taken up, they resolv'd to be beholding to no body, but to contract such a competent measure of impudence and impiety, as should let them to stifle all the oppositions of Religion, or Conscience, and set up for themselves. And that which gave them no small incouragement hereunto was the wonderful success and almost infinite Riches, two precedent imposters *John Ronbins* and *Joh. Tauny,* had lately gained by the same damnable practice. The prosperity of these two rendred the private conditions of *Reeve and Muggleton* more unsufferable; so that the former being the more impudent and having with some curiosity perused the *Revelations* of *St. John* and found to his extreme sorrow that the Holy Ghost had never so much as dreampt of him throughout the whole Book, he resolves by the help of a feigned Enthusiasm or pretended Revelation, to force in the minds of Listening Ignorants, whose Gaping curiosity lay always open for the reception of any Novelty, a certain belief of a strange *inspiration* and *Comission* then delivered unto him whereby (for sooth) he not only pretends a Soveraignty over Mankind, but assumes a power to pass (upon the least contradiction of his wicked principles) a sentence of everlasting Condemnation, even upon the blessed Angels themselves: as is affirm'd he hath authority to do, in a book of *Muggletons,* called the *Quakers Neck broke* page 20.

To exact this necessary Credulity from his Gazing admirers, he calls one Evening of *Muggleton* to go with him to the Tavern, from whence after they had Gorged their Guts with an excess of Wine, and Victuals, they resolved forthewith to go Chew the Cud both of their discourse and Viends upon their Pillows, whereon *Reeve* had not long laid his shallow skul, but whether caus'd by fumes arising from an undigested Supper, or the important pressures of his designed greatness, I know not, but up he gets, runs to *Muggleton,* tells him as *Muggleton* does us in his nonsensical interpretation of the 11. Chap. of the *Revelations* pag. 158. *That God spake in the night unto him, and told him that he had given him more understanding in the Scriptures than all other men in the World. That he had put the two edged sword in his mouth,* and in the next words *following,* and I have *Chosen thee* Lodowick Muggleton *to be thy mouth. That I have given you power both to bless and curse, and when ever either of you shall bless or curse, it shall be in the power of a Spirit nor Angel,* No nor as Mugleton says in page 40 *in the Almighties himself to revoke from eternal Damnation.*

This fallacy being blown about by some of the graceless Adherents, the greedy Vulgarity mistake it for a Verity, and to shew their obedience, as well as Credulity, relinquish their former principles as eronious, to life themselves under the destructive Banners of his *forgeries* and impostures.

The promising superficies of this black design at first seem'd to recompence the paines of these spiritual *Engineers* with a favourable progression, but Heaven who could no longer forbear to punish their impieties, sufficiently testified its displeasure in Beckoning *Reeve* to give an account in the other World of those Damnable principles, wherewith he had tainted the minds, if not Ruin'd the Souls of divers in this; which one would have thought might have put a stop at least to the proceedings of this *Lodowick Muggleton,* who now double Gilded with Brass, pretended also to have had left him by *Reeve* a double portion, both of spirit, power, and commission; inlarging his Authority even beyond the prerogative of any deceased *Saint, Prophet,* or *Apostle,* as will by a Letter he sent *R. Fransworth*, and the said Book of his, entitled the *Quakers Neck broken*, most obviously appear. In the *Letter* page 43 he writes thus; speaking of the power he pretends God has given him to bless, curse &c. "Neither (says he) will God give this power to any after me, neither can any man come to the assurance of the favour of God now in these days but in believing that God gave this power to *John Reeve* and my self. For there is no coming to know God or see God, but by the faith in this commission of the spirit, for I having the keys of Heaven and Hell, none can get into Heaven unless the witness of this spirit doth open the Gate." *Again in his Quakers Neck-broken,* page 20. He says. "Neither doth any man know the Scriptures, neither can any man interpret them truly but my self, *and in the same page he goes on.* "God hath put the two edged sword into my mouth, that whosoever I pronounce curse, is cursed to Eternity. For I do not only say let him be accursed, but I have power to curse men or Angels to Eternity." And in Page 28. Speaking of his spiritual knowledg, how he has resolved all sorts of questions in Divinity, these are his Words.

Nay, some have gone so far as to ask who made God, and I have given answer to that also. Again in his letter to *S.H and W.S.* who in a former letter condemned him for Cursing, to which *Muggleton* answers, page 17, *As for my mouth being full of cursing, that is my commission.* Again page 18, "Full of his Cursing I confess my mouth is, and I do rejoice in it too, I know that God is well pleased in the damnation of those I have cursed, and I am wonderous well satisfied in the giving Judgment upon them according to the Tenent of my condition." In fine *Reader*, I am weary, and it makes my hair stand on end to Rake thus in the Nauseous Dunghill of his horrid *Blasphemies,* this whole *Volume* is nothing but a promiscuous composition of *Heresie, Delusion,* irreligion and *Blasphemy:* Himself a person who for this 20 years and upwards has shaken hands with *Morality, Discretion* and *Piety,* who for that inconsiderably Pels, Honor and respect, he dayly receives from the hands of his poor deluded, and without sudden conversion, I fear miserable Disciples, willingly surrenders his interest in Heaven, and as if he had too advantageous an exchange, throws the wretched Souls of his friends and acquaintance into the Bargain.

I would earnestly desire the *Reader* if he be not yet established in opinion to endeavour to seek a settlement there in, first by his prayers to almighty God to that purpose and after by the healing advice of some learned Divine, from whom he will certainly find more solid satisfaction than he can ever expect from these *Quacks* and *Empricks* in Divinity; who handle the soul, as others do their body, not so much for the patients good, as their *own* interest. Who if they can make a seasonable approach to a Death bed, & there by a pretended commission wheedle the departing Disciple into a belief that they have received the Keys of Heaven; Can turn who they will into everlasting Joys, and hurry who they please into eternal Bliss; if by the charming Rhetoricks of a Gray head, comely Visage, demure Countenance, and plausible tongue, he can but once persuade them to fall out with the World, and surrender these temporial blessings, in hopes of those spiritual ones (of which these sort of men make such large promises)there is none of them but will gladly part with, all their pretended *Keys of Heaven*, for one real one which unloks to a hundred a year upon *Earth*, or that would scruple to give a man a *note of their hands* for the securing his eternal bliss, provided the other would requite him with a considerable *Lease,* to bestow among his *sanctified children.*

Whether *Muggleton* and his Brethren have ever received any of these soul feeling blessings, I leave it to his and their consciences, and did I know it to be true I should scarcely put my self to the charges of a Tear to bemoan the cheat, for indeed, who can seriously pitty those persons who having been Educated in the wholesome principles of the Church of *England*, when he shall see them like Bastards and not Sons, forsake those Teats whereout they often have, and still might, suck such nourishing milk; when he beholds them runing after a nonsensical *Imposter*, frought up with nothing but interest and Impudence; a kid-napper of Souls, who would sell them for less money to the *Devil*, than the other do Children to *Barbados*; a fellow who if a man can find any connextion in his writings; it runs directly Diamiter to those of the Holy Scriptures, a wretch so arragant, that he dares to pretend a greater power than ever was delivered to any of the Prophets or Apostles, that denies both the real existence and absolute, and by all undoubted ubiquity of his Creator, pag. 34. pag. 23. That Nulls the Validity of several Texts of Scripture, and particularly *denies Solomon to be endued with the Spirit of God, when he writ the Book of Proverbs.* And in short, is so rediculous both in Divinity and Philosophy as to define God to be a corporeal Essence exactly in the shape of man, that his influence is confin'd within the narrow circuit of the upper Heavens only. And lastly which is enough to give any intelligible Reader a surfeit both of him and his Doctrine, he affirms his writings are in themselves more excellent, and ought to be by all men more respected and regarded than the Holy Scriptures.

The said Notorious Blasphemer being of late taken notice of by authority, has been prosecuted in the Ecclesiastical Court, and also committed to *New-Gate*, but after some days imprisonment, got bail for his Appearance at the Sessions in the *Old Bayly*, 14th *Decem.* And gave fresh security, and we doubt not but will shortly be brought to Condigne punishment according to his demerits.

FINIS

A Modest Account Of The Wicked Life Of That Grand Impostor, Lodowick Muggleton:

Wherein are related all the remarkable actions he did, and all the strange accidents that have befallen him, ever since his first coming to London, to this twenty-fifth of January, 1676.

Also, a particular of those reasons, Which first drew him to these damnable Principles:

With

Several pleasant stories concerning him, proving his commission to be but counterfeit, and himself a cheat, from divers expressions which have fallen from his own mouth.

Licensed according to order.

Quarto, containing six pages, printed at London, for B. H. in 1676.

LODOWICK MUGGLETON was born of poor, though honest parents, living at Chippenham, within fifteen miles of Bristol: his relations having but little means, and a great charge of children to maintain, they were forced to send their daughters to wait on their neighbouring gentry, and to place their sons to such trades as cost little binding them apprentices. But, amongst all the rest of those of this worshipful brood, they were blessed withal, they might have observed, even in his cunicular days, in this Lodowick Muggleton, an obstinate, dissentious, and opposive spirit; which made them desirous to settle him at some distance from them, and also to bind him to such a trade, and master, as might curb him from that freedom, which the moroseness of his coarse nature extorted from his too indulgent parents: by which means, as soon as he had made some small inspection into his Accidence, without any other accomplishment, besides a little writing and casting of accompts, he was hurried up to London, and there bound apprentice to one of the cross-legged order, but of an indifferent reputation in the place where he lived, though by trade a taylor. We will pass over the parenthesis of his youth in silence, therein being nothing but usual waggeries, which generally recommend to our expectation something remarkable, when the usual extravagancies shall be seasoned with age.

When the time of his apprenticeship grew near its expiration, so that he was admitted more liberty, than formerly was granted him, he was observed to be a great haunter of conventicles; insomuch that there could not a dissenting nonconformist diffuse his sedition in any obscure corner of the city, but this Lodowick Muggleton would have a part of it; by which means, continuing in the same idle curiosity, and taking great observation on that unknown gain, many of that canting tribe got by their deluded auditors, he proposed to himself a certain and considerable income to be got by the same means, by which he had observed many of those great pretenders gull both himself and others: for a rooked conventicler, like a bankrupt gamester, having, for some time, been cullied out of his money, learns the trick, sets up hector, and trades for himself.

Thus did Lodowick Muggleton, by sliding out of one religion into another, so dissatisfy his judgment, and run himself from the solid basis of his first principles; first degenerating, from the orthodox tenets of the Church of England, to Presbytery; from thence to Independency; thence to Anabaptism; thence to Quakerism; and, lastly, to no religion at all.

When men have, thus, once fooled themselves out of religion and a good conscience, it is no wonder, that their secular interests draw them into all sorts of impiety and profaneness, as it has done this Lodowick Muggleton; who, though, in himself, a poor, silly, despicable creature, yet had the confidence to think he had parts enough to wheedle a company of silly, credulous proselytes out of their souls and estates: and, indeed, he has had such admirable success in that wicked enterprise, that, tho' we cannot absolutely conclude, that he has cheated them of the first; yet we can prove, if occasion were, that he has defrauded them of the latter; as has been often told him, since the first day of his standing in the pillory.

It has been told already, how this impious impostor lays claim to a counterfeit commission, whereby he has infected the truths of many honest, ignorant people, with an extraordinary power, that was delivered to him by as infamous a blasphemer as himself, John Reeve; who, as he formerly rivalled Muggleton in impiety, had he been yet living, should certainly have clubbed with him in his deserved punishment.

It is about twenty-one years, since this impudent creature began his impostures; who, knowing himself as defective of reason, as of religion, made it one of the grand maxims of his policy, that his proselytes should be fully persuaded, contrary to all sense, or probability. Reason was that great beast, spoken of in the Revelation, and, consequently, not to be consulted withal, as to the examining of any fundamental point in religion; whereby he secured both himself, and his shallow disciples, from all those frequent disputations and arguments, which, otherwise, must necessarily have diverted them from adhering to his damnable, impious, and irrational tenets; which I purposely omit, as being too unsufferably profane for the modest ear of any sober, well-meaning Christian.

But we may judge a little of the theorick by the practick, I mean, of his principles by his practices, and of the soundness of his doctrine by those duties he held himself, and his followers, obliged to, in the performance of it; which, indeed, were none at all; it being his usual custom, when they met on the sabbath-day, to entertain them with a pig of their own sow; I mean, with wine, strong drink, or victuals; which either they sent in before-hand, or brought along with them; allowing them to be as licentious, as they pleased, in all things that might gratify, or indulge their senses.

A friend of mine was, one Sunday, walking in the fields; and, meeting there an old acquaintance of his, who was lately turned Muggletonian, with a young baggage in his hand, which, he did more than suspect, was light, he could not forbear expressing his admiration, to this Muggletonian himself, in these or such like terms: "I cannot but wonder to see you, my old neighbour, who have, for these many years, busied yourself in the study of religion, and was, not long since, like to have gone mad, because you knew not which opinion to stick to. I say, I cannot but wonder to see you abroad, on the sabbath-day, in this brisk posture; you are altered both in countenance, apparel, and manners, so that I almost doubt, whom I speak to." "Ah," answered the Muggletonian, "you know, friend, how I have heretofore troubled myself about religion indeed; insomuch that it had almost cost me my life, but all in vain, till about six weeks since; at which time I met with Lodowick Muggleton, who has put me into the easiest way to heaven, that ever was invented; for he gives us liberty, provided we do but believe in his commission, freely to launch into all those pleasures, which others, less knowing, call vices; and after all, will assure us of eternal salvation." Behold, reader, what a sweet religion here is like to be.

But, as Muggleton was liberal in the freedom he gave his adherents, so he was always careful to avoid the prohibitions of the law; he generally appointed his bubbles to meet in the fields, where he also permitted them to humour their sensualities with any recreation, not excepting uncleanness itself; for which profaning the sabbath he was, in Oliver Cromwell's time, committed to Newgate, where he had like to have been so dealt withal then, that Tyburn had saved the pillory this trouble now: but that perfidious usurper, conscious to himself, that Muggleton could not be a greater impostor in the church, than he was in the state, upon the consideration of fratres in malis, restored him to his liberty.

Howbeit, a little before Oliver's death, Muggleton, by continual flatteries, had got into his books, and, amongst other prophecies concerning him, had declared, that Oliver should perform more wonderful actions, than any he had yet atchieved, before he died. But, he happening to depart this life, before he had done any thing else that was remarkable, Muggleton was demanded, why his prophecy proved not true? He answered very wisely, and like himself, viz. that he was sure Oliver would have performed them, had he lived long enough.

But, since his gracious majesty's return, he has driven on a much more profitable theological cheat, having assumed the liberty not only of infusing what doctrine he pleased into the minds of his ignorant deluded followers, but writ several profane books, which, to his great advantage, he dispersed among them; poisoning their minds thereby with a hodge-podge of rotten tenets, whereby they are become uncapable of relishing the more sound, wholesome, and undoubted principles of the Church of England.

I shall conclude with one story more concerning Muggleton, and so leave him to the censure of the ingenuous reader. A timish gentleman, accoutered with sword and peruke, hearing the noise this man caused in the town, had a great desire to discourse with him, whom he found alone in his study; and, taking advantage of that occasion, he urged Muggleton so far, that, knowing not what to say, he falls to a solemn cursing of the gentleman; who was so inraged thereat, that he drew his sword, and swore he would run him through immediately, unless he recanted the sentence of damnation, which he had presumptuously cast upon him. Muggleton, perceiving, by the gentleman's looks, that he really intended what he threatened, did not only recant his curse, but pitifully intreated him whom he had cursed before; by which we may understand the invalidity both of him and his commission.

Thus, whoever considers the contents of Muggleton's whole life, will find it, in toto, nothing but a continued cheat of above twenty-one years long; which, in the catastrophe, he may behold worthily rewarded with the modest punishment of a wooden ruff, or pillory; his grey hairs gilded with dirt and rotten eggs; and, in fine, himself brought, by reason of his own horrid and irreligious actions, into the greatest scorn and contempt imaginable, by all the lovers of piety, discretion, or good manners.

The Proceedings of the Old Bailey - Court Records

First, the tryal of that grand and notorious Impostor Lodowick Muggleton, of whom to give the world a brief Account, we must acquaint you, that he was originally a Journyman-Taylor, and (some say) afterwards kept a Botchers stall; but having a strange enthusiastick head, began about the year 1651, to enter into Confederacy with one Reeves (another Brother of the Sheers) who resolve to cut out a new Scheme or Fashion of Religion; and to that purpose declare themselves, The two last Witnesses of God that ever should be upon the Earth; and that they had absolute and irrevocable power to save and damn whom they pleas'd; to which end one call'd himself the Blessing, the other the Cursing Prophet. And the said Reeves dying some years since, Muggleton pretends his Spirit was left with him, and the whole power of Witnessing, Blessing, and Cursing, devolved into his hands, which he as impiously practised upon the least affront or opposition; pronouncing persons damn'd by their particular Names, blasphemonsly adding, That God, Angels, or Men could not afterwards save them. And as all Hereticks covet to be Authors and Ring-leaders to a Sect, so by divers printed Books and Corner conferences, he easily seduced divers weak and instable people (especially of the Female-Sex) to become his Proselytes, who from him call themselves Muggletonians: So impossible it is for the wildest and most senseless, as well as most impious Notions, when broached with impudence among the Rabble, not to meet with some heads so irregular as to embrace them for serious Truths, or divine Revelations. This Muggleton's house being searched about August last, a great quantity of his books were seized, some of which, it was now proved, he owned the writing of, and that he had caus'd them to be printed; for which he was now indicted, many wicked Passages out of them being recited in the Indictment, but so horrid and blasphemous, that we think fit to spare the Christian modesty of each pious ear, by not repeating the same here, where there is no necessity for it. The Prisoner pleaded not guilty, but frustrated the general expectation, by saying nothing further either to excuse or justifie himself, but had a Counsel appear'd for him, who ingenuously declar'd himself asham'd to speak a word in favour of such a Cause; onely desired the Court to take notice, that the Books were dated before the last Act of Grace; but it being usual to Antedate or Post-date Titles of books, as best suits with the Publisher's interest, and that he had since that Act owned and published the same, that Plea was overrul'd; and the said Muggleton being found guilty by the Jury, was afterwards sentenced by the Court to stand three days in the Pillory at three the most eminent places of the City, with Papers shewing his Crime; and his Books so seized, divided into three parts, to be burnt over his head upon the Pillory: And besides, to be fined Five hundred pound, and to continue in Goal till the same be paid, and afterwards for his life, unless he procured good Bail, such as the Court should accept of, and not of his own Gang, Faction, or Sect, for his being of the good Behaviour.

Muggleton Reviv'd Or, New News Of That Grand Impostor.

BEING A NARRATIVE OF His late Behaviour since his Sentence and standing in the Pillory.

With the substance of several Discourses had with him, he still persisting in his Blasphemous Tenets, and Damning of People as formerly.

With Allowance.

LONDON: Printed for D.M. 1677.

    It was well hoped, that the Justice executed on the impious wretch in *January* last, by exposing him to publick shame, &c. might have reclaimed the bold Impostor from his blasphemous Enthusiasms, and brought him to repentance for the same; or at least that the detection of his wickedness and Animadversions of Authority, might have open'd the eyes of his seduced Followers no longer to believe in Lyes, nor suffer their understanding to be further deluded to the hazard of their Souls.

    But on the contrary, the said *Muggleton* doth incorrigibly persist in his shameless Pretensions of being one of the two Witnesses, arm'd with extraordinary Revelations, a special Commission from heaven, and Power irrevocable to Damn whom he list, and for what he pleaseth, &c. And when his detestable Pamphlets were deservedly dedicated to the Flames by the common Hangman before his face, had (as I am credibly informed by sober persons that heard him) the impudence to compare it to the burning of the Prophets Roll, *Jer. 36.22.* and Interpret that divine History as a Prophesie only of his present affairs.

    So likewise many of his silly Disciples (as if according to that of the most ingenious Satyrist,

> *The pleasure were as great*
> *in being Cheated, as to Cheat.)*

still continue their Senseless Veneration to his person and damnable Doctrines, as appears by their frequent Visits, and Presence daily made him during all this time of his Restraint: So easie it is to impose upon Enthusiastick Ingnorants, who (not considering that the Cause, not punishment, makes the Martyr: for else *Tyburn* had canoniz'd more Saints than ever *Rome* did, guided over his Correction with the title of *Persecution;* and according to their common course of profaning Scripture by misapplications to every wild Crotchet of their crazed brains, became the more hardened in their Errours.

An Ingenious person coming one day to visit this pretended last Witness, found him quaffing Ale in the Cellar, and acquainted him that by Authority derived from his feigned Commission, he lay under a Sentence of Condemnation, desiring to know if he would please to Reverse it: To which this Impostor, no less proudly than blasphemously, answered, *That if the Sentence were gone forth and pronounced, No God* (a phrase he much affects) *Angel, nor Man could Reverse it. Then,* replies the stranger, *in the Name and Power of the Lord, I do declare thee to be damn'd to all Eternity, without hearty and sincere repentance for these thy Arrogancies and Blasphemies. Where's thy Commission, where's thy Commission?* cries *Muggleton. Here it is,* replies the other, producing a Bible. To which *L. M.* shew'd no respect, but call'd him *Devil, Son of* Belial, *Seed of the Serpent,* &c. And being desired to pledge him, refused, saying, *He would not drink with the spawn of Satan;* and other ill language to that effect.

Many people coming daily to see and discourse with him, he has of late grown very reserv'd, confining himself to his Chamber, and scarce vouch-safeing to speak with any but those of his own Gang, or such as were recommended by them; a Quaker one day thundering out Judgments against him, and sentencing him as Damn'd by his magnified Light within, *Muggleton* being a true-bred Bully in Enthusiasm, resolv'd it seems to out huff and hector his Admonisher, saying, *I do hereby decare thee damn'd Body and Soul, and thy God within thee likewise:* and so proceeded in Blasphemies not to be repeated.

If any seem curiously inquisitive into his prodigious Tenets, he commonly silences them by asking, If they come to insnare him with Questions?

A Gentleman admitted into his Chamber, found him sitting Cross-leg'd on the Table very studiously perusing one of *Lilly's* old Almanacks; and after other discourse, inquiring what benefit he could reap by reading that book, he answered, There were great Mysteries contained in it, but not to be fathom'd by Carnal minds. Being thereupon ask'd if he understood Astrology, he said, He comprehended the depth of all Arts, but not as the men of this world did: for their Arts were of the Devil; but the purity of all hidden Sciences were discovered to him in their Divine Idea's and Archetypal perfection. Being questioned if he had read *Jacob Behmens* works, he said, He knew *Behmen* and his work; but he was a fool, and talkt of things that he did not understand: and that in truth there had been no books printed these 1500 years worth reading but his own, which were grounded on special Commission, and not the Spirit of Sense or Reason: (and in this last Clause I dare say all that have seen them will agree with him.)

Another time a conceited Quaker having made a long Oration one day to him, telling him of his wickedness, and that he did Judge and Condemn him in the Light, which makes manifest all the hidden works of Darkness, &c. He repli'd, *the Light you boast of is not worth a farthing, I will blow it out with the breath of my Nostrils: For you and all others Professions and forms of Religion that have been in the world these* 1500 *years, shall fall down before me, and are fallen and falling: for I have Damn'd some of every Perswasion, and all of your silly Perswasion, as might be seen in my Book called,* The Quakers Neck broken: *and therefore shall talk no more unto you; but declare that the Quakers are the seventh and last Anti angel that will sound in the world in resemblance of the church of* Laodicea; *and are the last of Antichristian forms that shall be in the world.* With much of the same insignificant Canting.

Part of a DIALOGUE between *W.P.* and *L.Muggleton,* the later being in an old threadbare black suit.

> W.P. said to him, How now Lodowick? thou lookest like a Priest.
> M. I am a Priest.
> P. After what Order?
> M. After the Order of Aaron.
> P. Where are then thy Bells?
> M. I wear them in the Mystery.
> P. If thou art a Priest after the Order of Aaron, that Dispensation and Order is now abolish'd, as the Scripture witnesseth.
> M. Thou art a Chicken, and I care not for thy Interpretation of Scripture.

The rest is so Blasphemous as not to be recited: As, *that God died and made* Elias *his Deputy in the mean time,* &c. And being severely reproved for such horrid, extravagant Discourse, replied, *I care not a T----d for thy Carnal reasoning and Bug-bear words, 'tis all of the Seed of the Serpent, the Bastards of* Cain *the Murderer, whom I declare to be the onely Devils,* &c.

Here we see enough of the Monster's Religion and Manners; let us observe a little of his Wit.

In the Epistle to his Interpretation of the *Revelations,* he says, *There is in truth no Devil but men and women; but the imagination of Reason, through ignorance, hath created such a Devil to it self, as a Spirit flying through the midst of the Air, which hath caused many men and women to lose their Wives, but indeed there is no other Devil to be Damn'd to Eternity but men and women:* And yet himself tells us, *The Devil seduced* Eve *so as to know her Carnally, and begot upon her* Cain; *whence all the wicked seed,* &c. So that by his own talk there was a Devil before. But Nonsense and Contradictions are familiar with this false Prophet.

Page 98. I would have the seed of Faith know that there is no such thing as the seed of Reason doth vainly imagine, as to think there is any such thing as a Devil and his Angels in Chains of Darkness, out of the body of man, distinct from man: for there is no Devil but man, and what is in the body of man; and this Spirit of Reason in man is the Devil, &c.

Page 73. Upon these words of the Text, *There was silence in Heaven for half an hour,*

He has this profound comment:

It might be forty hours for ought we know; but if he saith half an hour, who shall gain-say it?

Page. 38. Where 'tis said, *The four Beasts had each of them six wings, and were full of eyes, &c.*

He has these two wonderful Notes.

1. They had each six wings: the meaning is this, That each of these four beasts had six wings, that is they had six wings apiece.

2. Though it be said they were full of eyes, yet they had but two eyes apiece; that is, the eye of Faith and the eye of Reason: For the two eyes did see as much as could be seen: if they had had forty eyes they could have seen no more.

But not to trouble the Reader with a Repetition of any more of his Nonsense and Blasphemies, we leave him contriving with his Disciples how to get his Inlargement; which tis probable they might before his time have effected, had not the prudence of the Court excluded any of them to be accepted for his Bail, Which we hope no other person will be so indiscreet as to intermeddle in, nor run the hazard of engaging themselves for such a fellow's Good Behaviour during life, when the whole Course and Tenour of his life and practices are continual Violations of all Laws, Divine, Natural, and Civil.

FINIS.

Muggleton's Last Will & Testament,

(Who died Novemb.30. 1679)

Being an Absolute and Real RECANTATION of his former Notorious Blasphemous Doctrine.

Together with several Christian Instructions in order to refrain the same, shewing the Eternal Woe and Damnable Misery of all such who offer to seduce poor ignorant Souls, and the danger which infallibly accompanies such kind of False Prophets, of which he accounts himself the chief.

Published for a Caution to all ignorant and seduced People.

Mat. 23.17. He which hath sinned, let him sin no more, lest a worse thing come upon him.

London, Printed. 1679.

Courteous Reader,

I conceive this a Subject that may confuse many, reduce several, and reclaim all from the foolish, sottish, and brutish Opinion of being a Muggletonian; *you see here the lamentable and deplorable end of the Original of the Copy by which they write: If thou receives no Instruction by the same, blame thy self, and not we; for here is not only an incomparable Subject, but excellent Matter, sufficient to reduce the most brutish of Sinners. If it reclaim thee, thank the Testator; if not, thou hast just cause to fear his unhappy end: which that God may preserve us from, shall be the fervent prayer of,*

Thy most Cordial Friend,
J.B.

THE Last Will and Testament OF Lodowick Muggleton, Who died in the Marshalsea upon Sunday Novemb. 30, 1679.

And must I then go to the Tribunal of those three exemplary Judges *Eachus, Minos,* and *Radmanthus?* Is there an infallible necessity I must leave and forsake Religion for a Pillory, a Pillory for a Gaol, and a Gaol for the Rewards of my folly, which I now (though too late) perceive will be Eternal Damnation? Was his Holiness the Pope the first infuser of these Principles into me, and yet be so notoriously unkind, that though he keeps the Keys of Heaven, yet not to let me in? If these by the Wages wherewith he pays his faithful Servants, what think you can such expect who have been much more negligent in their duty, than my self has been? But although I find my self a man lost to all Eternity, yet will I give the World to understand, I have more common Honesty and Christianity in me, than to die after the Jesuitical mode, by affirming I am as *Innocent as the Child that is unborn,* of the Plots now on foot: Therefore let them know, that whatever kindness the Popes Indulgences, Pardons, and their own feigned Merits may promise them, if the words of a dying man are to be believed, they are all vain and frivolous pretences, only to delude the simple, and cheat the ignorant.

That they have daily Plotted, and do the like still, against the publick good and interest both of King and Kingdom, is not unknown to all rational men: But in respect the novelty of my cursed Principles, the strangeness of my damnable Doctrine, and the whimsical delusions of my pretended Religion, may hardly ever re-gain credit amongst the more solid people, I shall therefore conjure you, by the words of a dying man, to believe what I shall say is infallibly true, and more sincere and real than any the last words which were ever asserted by a dying Jesuit. I am now at my last Gasp, and could you but see, as I now do, the Felicity of that Eternal happiness I have through Blasphemy and Heresie slighted, and the unspeakable misery of that Eternal damnation which attends me for the same, you would certainly not only pity my condition, but give credit to my last dying words. Heaven and Hell were once offer'd to my own free choice, whereas I, like a damned Wretch as I am, have refused the former to embrace the latter; and all this, because I would rather rely upon my own Merits than my Saviours; he hath plainly told me he is the door, by which, and no other, we must enter; but I durst not believe him, but sought out inventions of my own, and thought to climb like a Thief and a Robber into that blessed Fold. And now let me tell ye all, but more particularly those whom my accursed Principles have perverted from the Truth, that this, and no other, was the main scope of my design; I had these conceptions in my head, that let me live never so much like a Reprobate all my life, and contrary to my knowledge, which I am sensible I did, yet when I came upon my death bed, if I had but so much time as to say, *Lord have mercy on my Soul, and forgive me all former miscarriages,* I never questioned my salvation. This being a thing which I suppose may be received as a general opinion by more than my self, I shall endeavor to shew them the folly of the same.

And first, were such a thing probably, as I am confident it is impossible without a Miracle from the Almighty, for nothing is impossible to God; yet how many are cut off by some sudden accident, that have not so much time allowed them to speak these words, I leave any reasonable man to judge: I could give you several examples in these Cases, for I perceive Example is more prevalent than Argument, but let this one suffice. No longer since than the 3. of

October, 1679. a Gentleman, who had been a very debauch'd liver, being viewing his Buildings in *Exeter,* sware very much at the neglect of his Workmen, when the Scaffold immediately fell, without any harm to any excepting himself, who was knock'd on the head with an Oath in his mouth, not having any the least time allowed him to call upon God for mercy. Besides, consider there is but one way to come into the world, and a thousand to go out of the same; and shall any man, except such a damned Wretch as my self, ever trust his Salvation on so small a Thread? Pray consider but onely this, If you were at a great and Princely Banquet, and had all the Varieties either Art or Nature could devise, and at the same time directly over your head should hang a Sword by a small twined Thread, pray what appetite could you have to your Victuals? Thus it hath been hither to you through my damnable perswasions; I have hitherto prompted and put you forward to such notorious evils, which I knew in my own Conscience would prove damnable to all who exercised the same; and you, poor Souls, through blind zeal, devotion, or pleasure, never refused to follow my instructions; yet never saw the Sword of Gods eternal wrath, which hung, and will hang continually over your heads, as long as you continue those wretched courses, by me tolerated and prescribed. As for the former sort of Persons who conceive it enough to cry, *Lord have mercy upon me* at the last gasp, let me tell them my self, who at this instant have more time to repent than possibly they may ever have, yet find it so hard a thing to do the same as I ought, that I fear God Almighty hath so hardened my heart, that I cannot call upon him as I would, or fear and love him either as I ought or should; and if I, poor miserable Wretch as I am, have time, yet not grace allowed me for repentance, what can such expect who die with an Oath in their mouths, as the persons above specified; or in drink, as is too frequently seen? But having a small time to live, and finding approaching death draw so near as to stare me in the face, I shall devote the remainder of my small span of time now left me to the honour of Almighty God, and preservation of the lives and souls of such of my Countrey-men and Congregation, whom I have any ways perverted by my false Doctrine, or deluded by my erroneous and Heretical opinion.

And first let me apply my self, (as briefly as my small space of Life will admit me) to such Persons who are my Teachers of false Doctrine, Heresie and Schism: Let me inform such; for such, I am confident are, (and will be to the end of the World) do not only render themselves accountable for their own sins, but likewise for the sins of all such People, who by them are seduced. But, pray Beloved, mistake not the Words of a Man, who, in a manner, hath both Feet in the Grave: Not that their answering for those they seduce, shall acquit the Persons seduced, but that they both shall joyntly suffer for their Offense, according to the respective nature of the Crimes by them committed. For on the one hand, as certainly as the Teacher of false Doctrine shall be accountable for the Souls of all Persons by him seduced, so on the other side, all such seduced Persons shall be severe Sufferers, for not trying the Scriptures, and searching out the difference between Truth and Falshood, according to their respective Abilities; for where God gives a Talent, he requires the same with Interest, and not like the sloathful Servant, that we should wrap the same up in a Napkin, and then tax him for a hard Master. I must confess, for my own particular part, had I imployed the Talent of that Knowledge God had given me, to a right life, I had not now groaned under the remarkable Judgement of the Curse of the omnipotent God. Therefore, once more, if dying Mens Words have any operation upon living Persons, let me request, and with bleeding Eyes beseech you, as ever you hope to escape those eternal Torments I expect to suffer, Never teach false Doctrine; I speak this to all Persons of new fangled Opinions in general, and likewise to all Persons in particular, who are or may be Auditors of such Seducers, That they never receive any fundamental Alteration in their Religion, until they have first tryed the same by the Touch-stone of Religion, which is God's Word: For since our Saviour hath said, *The latter days shall be full of Deceivers,* of which I must confess my self Chief, it certainly behoves every rational Man, in so grand a Concern as this is, to beware how they are cheated of their eternal Happiness. Secondly, Let no Man whatever run on in a wicked course of Life, in hopes of eternal Happiness at the hour of Death. I must confess, we have one Example, and but one Example that I know of in all the Scripture, of a Person who obtained Salvation at the hour of Death, and that was the poor penitent Thief on the Cross; which was only to keep us from Despair, rather than to prompt us to Presumption, by casting all our hopes on the last breath of Life. God Almighty under the Law requires the first-fruits of our Ground, which made *Abel's* Sacrifice more acceptable than *Cain's;* whereas under the Gospel, he requires the first fruits of our Hearts, and the service of our green Years: And had I for my own particular part, served him, then I had never come to this deplorable Condition now; and I hope this my lamentable Example will deter both Young and Old, for ever walking in my Foot-steps.

But to conclude: *Solomon* says, *A Man may sustain his infirmities, but a wounded spirit who can bear it?* Such is the wretched misery of my present deplorable Condition, that I now not only groan, but absolutely perish under this Heart-piercing Calamity. None but the *Francis Spirit,* and such a Wretch as my self, ever felt such pangs of Conscience as I now feel: Hell gapes for me; the Devils are ready to torment me to all eternity, the holy Angels laugh at me; the blessed God mocks at my Calamity; yet such is the divine Influence of his blessed Spirit, that he compels me poor damned Wretch to preach Salvation to others, who never expect Salvation my self. But since the Devils themselves have done the like, it cannot be conceived strange of me. I may, nay I can say, I put my trust in the Hands of Almighty God,

Muggleton's Last Will and Testament 189

yet cannot I believe he will save me, such is the miserable hardness of my rocky Heart, I sigh, I groan, I die, I languish, I perish, yet without any remedy. Let it once for all suffice; and I hope Almighty God will say *Amen* to my humble and hearty Soul-saving Request, That *Muggleton's* Example may preserve Thousands of Souls from Hell: For although I conceive my self justly delivered up to a reprobate Sense, yet it is the desire of my Soul, other Persons may take Example by my damnable Fall, and then all false Doctrine, as they expect Happiness either in this World, or the World to come. My Breath now fails me; I can say no more but this, The God above knows that the dying Words of the Unfortunate *Muggleton,* declare more Truth, and give more Christian Instruction, than the correct Copies of the most eminent Jesuits, and how that shames their Profession, let the World judge.

F I N I S .

A True Representation Of The Absurd And Mischievous Principles Of The Sect, Commonly Known By The Name Of Mugaletonians.

LONDON.

Printed for Ric. Chiswell, at the Rose and Crown in St. Paul's Church Yard, MDCXCIV.

The Preface.

After that I had, for the use and satisfaction of a private Friend, make some enquiry into the Principles of the contemptible Sect, known of late times by the name of Mugaletonians, *I threw the Papers aside, as thinking the time not at all well spent, that I had employ'd in reading their Books, and in the Examination of what is made up of Impiety, Nonsense, and Absurdities. But however, I was at last prevailed with to permit them to be make publick; which I did submit to, not so much for the sake of those poor deluded Souls that are won over to that pernicious Sect, that having no shadow of Reason for its support, will not submit to the tryal of it; and so are uncapable of Argument; but for the sake of others: And to give the World an instance of the power of Enthusiasm, and how far it exposes Persons to be led away by the confidence or craft of any Pretender, how ignorant or selfish soever he be.*

And of this sort were the first Ring-leaders of this Sect, John Reeve *and* Lodowick Muggleton, *in the year,* 1651. *a time of Universal Liberty; and which gave an opportunity for the worst of Men to vent the absurdist and most infamous Errors.*

The former of these, J. Reeve, by Profession a Baker, pretended that the Lord Jesus spoke to him by Voice of Words three days together; and with such a Godlike Majesty, that he saith of himself, I do not know whether I was a Mortal Man, or an Immortal God. *That the Voice told him, that he had given him Understanding in the Scripture more than all the World besides: And that he had given* L. Muggleton *to be his Mouth, and that they two were the last Commissioners to the World; and the last two Witnesses spoken of* Revelation 11th. *who exercis'd a Commission of an higher nature than those of the Prophets and Apostles; and that they knew more, and had a greater power than any of them; as they could bless or curse, save or damn, to all Eternity irrevocably. And therefore, whosoever should oppose or vilifie this their Commission and Doctrine, would be guilty of the unpardonable sin against the Holy Ghost.*

Accordingly when these two were tried, 1653. at the Old Baily, *before the Ld. Mayor* Fowke; *and ordered to lie in* Bridewell *six Months, they gave Sentence against the said Ld. Mayor, the Recorder* Steel, *and the Jury, after this manner.* In obedience to our Commission received from the Holy Spirit, &c. we pronounce you cursed and damned, Soul and Body, to all Eternity (*See Letter to Ld. Mayor, and the Remonstr.*).

Now if we come to enquire into their Doctrine, there is nothing more absurd, false, and precarious: As they tell us, God has a Body like that of a Man, of very flesh and bone; and that the Trinity, or Father, Son, and Holy Ghost, are only variety of Names: That God the Father left Heaven for a time, and became an absolute mortal Man; and died, and was buried; and that during his absence from Heaven, Elias *did there represent him; and was the Protector of God, during his Minority in the Earth; and that God was raised from the dead by a compact with* Elias, *who surrendered up all again to him.*

They say farther, that there was but one Angel that fell, and that he entred into the Womb of Eve *by her consent, and there died; and that* Cain *was the very Seed of that Serpent Angel; and so was Brother to* Abel, *only on the Mother's side. And that from him sprung all the Carnal Seed of Reprobates, who were not of the Seed of* Adam, *such as* Cain *and* Judas, *&c.*

They hold farther, that there is no Devil at all without the Body of Man; and that he is no other than Man's Spirit of unclean Reason, and cursed Imagination. Nay, sometimes they will determine as positively in matters of History and Philosophy; and tell us from the Lord, that the Epistles of the Apostles were wrote in Hebrew, Greek, and Latin: That the Sun and Stars are but little bigger than they appear to be: That the Sun's Eclipse proceeds from its nearness to the Moon; and that no one can foretell Eclipses but by Inspiration.

Marvellous Discourses! And which our Astronomers and Almanack-makers are much beholding to them for. For whilst Men of Learning in that way thought they went by a certain rule of Nature, and constant Observation, they think too meanly of themselves. These new Commissioned Men instruct them better; and tell them, they write their Ephemerides and Almanacks by Revelation, if they therein infallibly foretell Eclipses, as what Astronomer doth not?

By this, we have a taste of these new Prophets pretences; and may see that their History, Philosophy, and Divinity, are much alike, and the apparent Fruits of Ignorance, Confidence, and Imagination.

But I shall leave these to be handled in the following Treatise.

The Principlesof The Muggletonians Consider'd.

In the treating upon this Subject, there are two Questions to be taken into Consideration; *viz.* 1. Whether *John Reeve* and *Lodowick Muggleton* are sent from God? And, 2. Whether they are the *Two Witnesses* in the 11th of the *Revelation?*

Chap. I.

Whether they are sent from God?

There premise, That a man may pretend to be sent, and to have a Commission from God, when he is not sent, and has not such Commission.

So did *John Robins*, of whom *J. Reeve* and *L. Muggleton* say, that *he is the last and great Antichrist spoken of in* the Thessalonians (Remonst. p. 4. Transcend Spir Treat. p. 6,7.).

Such also were *John Tanee, Bull, Varnum, Evans*, as they confess.
So they say the Ranters and Quakers were false Christs and false Prophets (True Interpret. of Revelat. ch. 75. n. 3.5).

Therefore they plead, That *there was a necessity of the witness of the Spirit, because of late and at present so many several Antichristian Spirits are come forth* (Look. glass. Ch. 22. n. 15.).

From hence I infer, that unless *J. Reeve* and *L. Muggleton* can prove that they are sent and commissioned from God, more than those were whom they grant to be Imposters and Deceivers; we have no more reason to believe they came from God, and were sent by him, than they themselves had reason to believe that the forementioned Deceivers came from God. For do they say they were sent from God? So did the other also declare.

2. Therefore we must enquire into the Evidences and Proofs they bring of their Commission. This they grant a proper way.

So [in the Book call'd a *Looking-glass*] *If divers Men appear as Witnesses, or Prophets, immediately sent forth by a Powerful Commission from the Everlasting God, are there not certain Divine Seals to distinguish between those Embassadors which are infallible, and them that are but fallible (*Ch. 27. n. 38)*?*

In treating upon this, I shall enquire,

Q. 1. What are the Evidences they bring; and whether they are not such as other Deceivers have alike pretended to, and even exceeded them in?

Q. 2. Whether there are not as great Evidences against them, as they have against other Pretenders?

If we prove the former, we prove they have no sufficient Evidence; and they have not those *Divine Seals,* which (as they say) distinguish between those Embassadors that are infallible, and those that are fallible.

If we prove the latter, then they are no better than Deceivers.

Sect. I.

Q. 1. I shall consider what the Evidences are which they bring of their Divine Commission?

And they are these, as I find them scatter'd up and down in their Books.

1. A Voice to *J. Reeve,* three several Mornings, in the Year, 1651.
2. That their Commission is such as never was before, *viz.* wholly Spiritual.
3. That there is no contradiction, and that throughout there is no point in the Book call'd the *Looking-glass,* contradicting it self, nor one another(Look. glass. p. 60 n. 36).
4. Because it discovers all irrational Opinions concerning God, &c. (Look. glass. p. 60. n. 37.)
5. Because it allows no Man to murther another, to cut off the head Magistrate, &c. (n. 38.)
6. Because it denies all Power, Spiritual or Natural, to be capable to act without a continued Light to proceed from a spiritual Body, &c. (n. 39)
7. It's from an unerring Spirit, because they were induced to write a Volume as large as the Bible, and as pure a Language as that is, without looking in any writing whatsoever (p. 112. n. 46.).
8. That since the Apostles Worship ceased, which was in or at the end of the ten Persecutions, and above 1000 years ago, not a Man hath been commissioned till they, *J. Reeve* and *L. Muggleton,* were (Joyful News. p. 49.).

These they call *Infallible Grounds.*

These I shall examine, and try whether they are sufficient Evidences, and Infallible Proofs of a Divine Commission.

I. *Character. A Voice.* Of this *J. Reeve* saith, *The Lord Jesus by voice of words spake to me, saying, I have given thee understanding of my mind in Scriptures above all Men in the World,* &c. (See Transcendent Spir. Treatise. 1. p. 4. 5. Quakers neck. p. 67.)

This he makes a necessary and distinguishing Character of a true Commission; so he saith of others, *for want of a true Commission by voice of words from the God of Heaven and Earth, they do not declare* (Look. glass. p. 111. n. 43.), &c. *It is God's speaking plain words to the outward Ear that doth make a Man a Commissioner* (Revel. p. 49. n. 21.).

Now I shall shew this is no sufficient and distinguishing Character.

A True Representation 195

1. This is no distinguishing Character according to them; for they say others had *imaginary* and *lying Voices*. But if Voices be common, both to true and false Apostles, how can it be a proof of the truth of a Commission? and how shall we thereby distinguish the true from the false? (*Look. glass. I Epist. and p.* 112. 117. 168. *n.* 8. 169. *n.* 15. 195. *n.* 34. 197. *n.* 34.)

2. This is no sufficient and distinguishing Character, according to the Apostle, if it be alone without other Evidence, and much more is it not so, if contradictory to Scripture, *we have a more sure word of Prophesie,* &c. saith St. *Peter (*2 *Peter* 2.17, 18, 19.*).*

3. It's not sufficient in it self; not to the Persons to whom the Voice is said to come: for they may be imposed upon by Men (as Pope *Celestine* and others were) or by Evil Spirits, or by imagination, as they grant, when they call them *imaginary Voices.*

And much less is it sufficient to others that heard not the Voice, but only have it from them that say they heard it; and so are liable to be imposed upon by the Craft or Imagination of others.

So that if they will pretend to a Voice for the proof of their Commission, we expect to have some proof that they had such a Voice, and that this Voice came from God.

And especially, because they say that they Seal up Men to Eternal Life or Death irrevocably; and that whoever speaks against this Commission of theirs, hath committed the unpardonable Sin, and so is by them pronounced cursed Soul and Body to all Eternity *(Remonst. p.* 9. 11, 12. *Transcend. p.*3. 6, 8, 9, 41. *Letter to Ld. Mayor, p.* 3. *Look. glass. p.* 42. *n.* 10.).

Which being contrary to the temper of the Gospel, and what they have no written Authority for, they are oblig'd to shew such Proof for as is Infallible, or else are gross Deceivers.

II. *Character.* Their Commission is such as never was before, as it's *all Spiritual;* and as they had *more Spiritual Understanding than all the World besides;* and such as never was reveal'd before (*Transcendent. p.* 41. *Revelation p.* 158. *ch.* 77. *n.* 1. Muggleton's *Epist. to Look. glass. p.* 3.).

1. I answer the pretense to its being Spiritual is no sufficient Evidence. For they grant that amongst those that were Deceivers, there was a great pretense to Spiritual and inward Voices of Power; to Spiritual appearances in themselves; to Spiritual Light and pure Worship; to Spiritual Power and Signs, to the being Spiritual Officers and Embassadors (*Look. glass p.* 111. *n.* 43. 167. *n.* 1,2. *Transc. p.* 7.).

Which yet they themselves call Spiritual Witchcraft, and lying Wonders, and Counterfeits. And so theirs is no more true or Spiritual for their saying so, than those that they condemn (*Revel. p.* 156. *n.*

2,3. *p.* 157. *n.* 1,2, 4. 158. *n.* 3, 4, 5. *Look. glass. p.* 168. *n.* 11, 12. 171. *n.* 33.).

2. To plead that they have more Spiritual Understanding, and that they reveal what was not before, is no more an Evidence that it is true, than it may be that it is false. *John Robins* pleaded that he came from God, nay, that he was *the God and Father of the Lord Jesus Christ,* and confirmed it (as *Reeve* saith) by *great Signs and Wonders, such as the Popes could never shew, to the amazement of many deceived by him,* &c (*Transcend. p.* 7.).

And, without doubt, he would as readily declare, that he had more Spiritual Understanding than all the World besides; for the Letter of the Scripture is silent in it. And this they will grant was such Doctrine as never was before; and consequently its no sufficient Plea, nor by which they can prove their Commission to be true, more than *J. Robins* could prove that he was God the Father.

It is not then what they profess to reveal that is sufficient; but the point is, whether what they so profess is true? And that is to be proved by somewhat else, such as Scripture or Miracles.

This shews the Vanity of what they so often appeal to: As when they say, *This is a true Testimony, that he hath sent us by his Holy Spirit; because there is none upon this Earth that beareth witness unto that Man Jesus that was crucified at* Jerusalem, *to be the only God and Everlasting Father, but we only* (*Transcendent. p.* 41. *Look. glass. p.* 92. *p.* 93. *n.* 25. 99. *n.* 37.).

For so might *J. Robins* have said, there is none that beareth witness but my self, that the Trinity of Persons is *Adam, Abel,* and *Cain* (as *J. Reeve* saith he professed.)(*Transcend. p.* 7.) And so might *John Tanee* have said, there is none that beareth witness, but my self, that there is no personal God. (*Remonstr. p.* 4.)

It all rests upon their say so, but where is the proof? Where is the Scripture, where the Miracles, that they prove their Commission, and their Doctrine by? For to prove their Commission by their Doctrine, is much one as to Prove their Doctrine by their Commission. And yet this absurd way do they take. For ask them how they prove their Commission? They say, Because there is none upon Earth that beareth witness that Christ crucified was God the Father, but we. Ask them again, how they prove the truth of their Doctrine? They answer, by their Commission (*Look. glass. p.* 99. *n.* 37, 38.).

3. The matter of Fact is not true; for there have been others before them of the same Opinion; so little reason have they to claim the first discover to themselves; as I shall presently shew.

4. It's an ill sign, that this should be the first discovery, and that for above 1600 years, the whole Christian World should know nothing of it, as they themselves acknowledge.

III. *Character, or Proof of their Commission, is,* That throughout the Book, called the *Looking-glass,* there is no point contradicting it self, nor one another; which he calls *an Infallible Proof of the Truth of this Writing.*

If there was no other proof of a Point contradicting it self, than what is here asserted, that is sufficient. For he saith, That to have no point contradicting it self nor one another in a Book, is an *Infallible Proof* of the Truth of that Writing. By which Argument, every Book consistent with it self, would be necessarily true; whereas nothing more evident, than that a Book may be consistent with it self, and yet be false.

As for instance, They say that one *Bull* and *Varnum,* and others long before them, have pretended to be the two Witnesses in the 11th of the *Revelation.*

Suppose we now that those two had wrote a Book (as *L. Muggleton* has done) (*Look. glass. p.* 99. *n.* 6.) and call'd it, *a True Interpretation of the 11th of the* Revelation; would that have been a sufficient proof of the Truth of that Writing, that there was no point in it contradicting is self nor one another? I trow not; and yet no one can deny but such a Book might have been so contrived. And I durst have put it to the venture, whether, if this be true, it would not have been as much a proof of their being those Witnesses; and they might have alike Subscribed their Book, as he doth his; *viz. By* ------- Bull *and* ------- Varnum, *the two last Commissionated Witnesses.*

And as this is not an Infallible proof of the Truth of the Writing, so much less of the Divine Inspiration of it, and of their Commission: For a Book may in all points agree with it self, and contain nothing but Truth, and yet be of Humane Invention.

If a Book be inconsistent with it self, it's to be sure not of Divine Inspiration; but it may be consistent, and yet be only of Man's Composition.

And yet they fail in this point; for it will be a difficult matter to reconcile it to it self: For they say they write from an Infallible Spirit, which implies the highest certainty, and yet say, *I am perswaded in my Spirit, and I do rather believe that there was seven hundred thousand, than seven thousand* (*Look. glass. p.* 14. *n.* 29.*),* though the Revelation of John *doth express it to be but seven thousand* (*Revelat. p.* 143. *n.* 11.*).*

To *be perswaded,* and to *believe* a thing to be so, are inconsistent with Infallibility; for that admits no less than I am sure of it.

So again, *Muggleton* saith of the Angel St. *Matthew* speaks of, that *perhaps it was no more to his visible sight;* and speaking of St. *John's Revelation,* he explains it, *so it may be said.* Now these words *perhaps,* and *it may be said,* are doubtful Expressions, and not reconcileable to Infallibility (*Revelat. chap.* 60. *n.* 8.15.19.).

IV. V. VI. Suppose these Characters to be true for the matter, yet that follows not that they are of Divine Inspiration, and Infallible. 1.

Because then it would follow that all good Books and true were infallible. 2. The 5th is what others have held as well as they.

VII. If the largeness of the Book, and the not looking in any Writings, were Signs of an unerring Spirit, then the Writings of several Quakers, as *Burroughs* and *G. Fox,* &c. might pretend to it, if they may be believed, who often begin their Books with *The Word of God.* And so would those of *Jacob Behem,* who saith, he writ without Humane Assistance.

And if the Purity of the Language be a Sign of Truth and Infallibility, then I am sure that the Writings of these two are far from being either true or infallible.

This, it seems, was notorious in the former Edition of the *Looking-glass,* 1656. And therefore *L. Muggleton* doth wisely to lay it upon the *Abuse it received in the Press (Epist. prefixed to it.).*

But if *L. Muggleton* was the Corrector, and was to rectifie those abuses by his own *unerring* Spirit, it would have escaped no better than his *True Interpretation of the* 11th *of the* Revelation, which abounds with false *English* beyond number; and of which I never read a Page that wanted it.

And even, that very Book (which this is immediately spoken of, *viz. The Looking-glass.*) after his Correction of it, fails in the propriety of the Words, the Concord, the Connexion. In the Paragraph just before this bold Challenge and the Appeal he makes to the Purity of its Language [*n* 45] we find the Word *Tosticated,* a vulgar, but a much mistaken word, and is for *Intoxicated.* Where is the Concord in the Phrase, *Things of such Concernment requires.* [Epistle 1. prefixed by *Reeve. See p.* 76. *n.* 2, 4. *p.* 92. *n.* 21. *p.* 108. *n.* 3.] *And Men takes upon them.* [p 165. n. 29] *My Brethren that hath.* [p. 207. n.8] *Secrets that hath not been reveal'd.* [p. 208. n. 17.] Where is the propriety, in *Neither did he know not what Power was endued with.* [p. 127. n. 21.] *and confounded of Conscience.* [p. 96. n. 18.].

These are passages I casually met with; but if any one will have a Speciman, let him read *L. Muggleton's* Epistle annexed to that Book, and try what Purity and Elegancy is in it.

It's a sign these Persons did not understand true *English,* nor often the Sence of what they wrote, that would venture upon this, and produce the *Purity* of the Language as a Note of an *unerring Spirit,* in the compiling of it.

VIII. *Character, or Evidence is.* That since the Apostles Worship ceased, which continued about 300 years, and which was in or at the end of the ten Persecutions, not a Man hath been commissioned till they were (*Look. glass. p.* 98. *n.* 31. *Transc. p.* 6. *p.* 18.).

How many things are here taken for granted, which there is not a Syllable of Proof for?

As, 1. That there was a time when the Apostles way of Worship was to cease, and actually ceased.

2. That this time was at the end of the ten Persecutions.

3. That none was Commissionated from that time.

4. That *J. Reeve* and *L. Muggleton* are now Commissioned.

After all that has been said, where is the Evidence of these Mens Commission?
They did wisely to lay aside Scripture and Miracles: as they do.
Of Scripture, they say, *The Commission of the Spirit agreeing with, and explaining of the former Commissions of the Law and the Gospel, differing only in point of Worship (Title page to the Looking-glass.).*
And as for Signs, they are for those that are *Spiritual, Invisible Fire,* and *Burning within;* but as for *Natural Visible* Signs, they leave them to the first and second Commission, to *Moses* and Christ (*Transc. p.* 4, 5, 6, & 41. *Look. glass. p.* 158. *n.* 24. 186. *n.* 33. *Revelat. p.* 162. *n.* 4.).
But yet after all, we think we may as well say to them, as they to others; *If thou shalt imagine thy self fit to Minister, I would fain know of thee, whether thou art indued with a Ministerial Power? Doth Christ immediately pour forth the Gift of his Spirit, or cure the Sick when thou prayest over them? or doth he own thee in casting out Devils, by thy Word? or doth he own thee by raising the Dead, curing the Lame,* &c. (*Joyful News. p.* 51.)
Thus far we have considered the Evidences, which are such as are no distinguishing Characters, and what others may equal them in; and so we have no more reason to accept them as Commissionated, than they had to accept Imposters; and have as much reason to reject them, as they had to reject other Imposters. For what is there they pretend to, which Impostors have not, or might not have pretended to?
Nay, if either be accepted, they are so to be that exceed these in their Evidence, as did *J. Robbins,* who shewed many Signs, and presented his Person to some riding upon the Wings of the Wind, like unto a Flame of Fire, &c. and did plague the Bodies and Spirits of others at his pleasure, in a most dreadful manner, as they report (*Transcend. p.* 9.).
Here was a sensible Evidence; it was conspicuous, *he plagued the Bodies and Spirits of Men:* But these Men pretend only to a Voice that one of them heard, and to a Power of pronouncing Men damned to all Eternity irrevocably.

Sect. II.

Q. 2. I shall consider whether there be not as great Evidence against *J. Reeve* and *L. Muggleton,* as they had against other Pretenders; which if it be, they are as much Deceivers as the others?

1. They are Deceivers, and have no Commission, who contradict, and make void a former Commission, without sufficient Authority or Commission for it.

2. They are Deceivers, and have no Commission, who pretend to Inspiration and Infallibility, and yet have actually mistaken in what they pretend Infallibility and Inspiration for.

1. They have no Commission, who contradict and make void a former Commission, without Authority or Commission so to do.

They say in the Title to the *Looking-glass, The Commission of the Spirit agreeing with, and explaining of the two former Commissions of the Law and Gospel, differing only in point of Worship.*

1. I shall consider how they differ in Worship from the former Commission (as they call it.)

2. I shall shew, That if they differ (as they say) *only* in point of Worship, yet in so doing they do contradict, and so far make void the former Commission.

3. That they differ from the former Commission in many other things, as well as Worship; and which are of such consequence, that did they agree in Worship with the former Commission (as they grant they do not) yet those alone would be sufficient to shew that they do thereby make void the former Commission.

Which if it be made good, then what remains for them, but to shew their Commission for so doing; and if their Authority for it be not proved by as good, clear, and sufficient Evidence, as the former Commission was confirmed and established, we have good reason to think no better of them than they did of *Robbins, Tanee,* and other Imposters.

1. I shall consider how they differ in Worship form the former Commissions of *Moses* and Christ.

Of this, let us hear them.

This Commission of the Spirit doth hold forth no visible nor external outward Worship, as the other two Commissions [of Moses and the Apostles] *did;* [so *Muggleton's* Epistle to *Looking-glass.*] *that is, All visible Worship from Mens Tongues, Eyes, and Hands, was to be done away; and is now but as a Golden Calf of Mens own imaginations; and no more accepted by Christ, than the cutting off of a Dog's neck. Tis not outward Praying, Preaching, Fasting, or Thanksgiving, to be seen of Men, but it is an inward, spiritual, silent Praying and Praising,* &c. *Joyful News. p.* 40, 43.

And yet they grant this Visible Worship was the way of the Apostles, which did last till the end of the ten Persecutions; and *which was then in great force so long as that Commission stood,* as *Muggleton* acknowledges in the foresaid Epistle. So that in this point the Commission of the Apostles, and theirs, are inconsistent.

A True Representation 201

2. I shall shew, that supposing they thus differ from the second Commission (that of Christ and his Apostles) *only in Worship,* yet, in so doing, they so far make void the former Commission.

This is granted: for they say, *When God doth give a New Commission, the Old is made void, as with reference to the Visible Worship. Therefore you know, that the Apostles Commission did wholly thrust out the Visible Worship which was set up by* Moses. *So likewise it is with this Commission of the Spirit; because this Commission of the Spirit doth hold forth no visible outward Worship, as the other two Commissions did (*Muggleton's *Epist. to Look. Glass.).*

They own Christ's Commission did appoint a Visible External Worship, but this is of the Spirit (as they call it) doth not, but forbids it; and so the latter doth make void the former.

Now then, since their Commission doth as much make void the Commission of Christ, as to External Worship, as Christ's Commission did that of *Moses;* we may enquire who gave them this Commission, or how do they prove they received it from God? For certainly, they who will make void the Commission of Christ and the Apostles, ought in Reason to give as good Evidence of a Divine Authority for so doing, as our Saviour gave his; and so much the more, as Christ is above *Moses.* Our Saviour did not expect the *Jews* should give him credit to him further than he gave them Evidence; and 'tis surely then unreasonable to give credit to these persons without it. And our Saviour's Evidence would have been none, had he only that to say for himself, which these pretend to. Would it have been enough for our Saviour, when the *Jews* required a Sign, to have said, as these do, *This is the old Serpent that arraigns the glorious God at the Bar of thy Carnal Reason? (Look. glass. p.* 185. *n.* 26, &c.)

No: Though our Saviour call'd the *Jews* an *adulterous Generation,* because they continued incredulous, after the Miracles wrought among them; yet at the same time, he tells them that there was one in reserve which would convince them, or nothing would; which was his own Resurrection. *Matth.* 12.39.

It is not necessary every one sent from God should, in every case, have this Testimony of Miracles, as it was with *John Baptist, John* 10.41. But had *John* come to make void the former Commission of *Moses,* he must have produced the Evidence. And this our Saviour did, and so ought these to do; or else must be reckoned among the false Christs, and false Apostles.

3. They differ from the former Commission in many other things as well as Worship; and that of so great Consequence, that these alone would be sufficient to shew, that they thereby make void the former Commission; and so must be Deceivers, if the former Commission be in force; and it is in force, if they have no Authority to make it void; and they have no Authority, if they have not sufficient Evidence for it.

Sometimes they say, there are six Principles, *viz.* 1. The Person of God. 2. Person of Angels. 3. Person of the Devil. 4. *Adam's* Condition.

5. Joy of Heaven. 6. Eternal Death. At other times they say, there are two Foundations of all Spiritual Understanding, *viz.* The form and nature of the true God, and the form and nature of the right Devil (*Remonstr. p.* 7.).

But the things of this kind I shall refer to these Heads, *viz.* God, Angels, and Men.

1. Let us take a view of their Principles that respect God, concerning whom they hold,

   1. That God is not a Spirit, but hath a body; and is very Flesh and Bone: and so they call an *infinite Spirit an infinite nothing, a cursed, lying, and imaginary God, and a pretended Spiritual God (Transc. p.* 14. *Look. glass. c.* 18. *n.* 9, 10. *Look. glass. p.* 195. *n.* 34.*).*

   2. *That God was in the form of a Man, and like unto the first Adam from all Eternity (Transcend. ibid. Look. glass. p.* 79. *n.* 25, 31. *p.* 49. *n.* 13, 14.*).*

   3. That the words Father, Son, and Spirit, are only variety of Names, and are the same Godhead, in a three-fold Condition; and that the Man Christ Jesus is the Father, Son, and Spirit in one Person (*Look. glass. p.* 12. *n.* 11. 81. *n.* 14.); and that by Declaration of the Spirit, the addition of two Persons more proceeds only from the Serpentine Antichristian Devil in Carnal Men (*Look. glass. p.* 36. *c.* 9. *Rev. p.* 164. *n.* 4. *Look. glass. p.* 2. *n.* 10.).

   4. That God the Father uncreated himself from his Eternal and Immortal Glory, and entered into the Virgin's Womb, and became Flesh; and for a Season became an absolute Mortal Man (*Transcend. p.* 2. 11, 23, 26, 28, 29. *Letter to Ld. Mayor. p.* 23.).

   5. That the Man Christ Jesus that was Crucified, is the only God; and that the whole Godhead died, and was buried for a Moment (*Transcend. p.* 41. *Gen. Epist. p.* 5. *Look. glass. p.* 64. *n.* 27.).

   6. That *Elias* was taken up bodily into Heaven, that he might represent God the Father whilst he went his Journey into the Flesh (*Trans. p.* 31.); and so was the Protector of God for a Moment, when God became a Child (*p.* 35), and was an absolute Creature (*p.* 36); and watch'd over him all the days of his Mortality, from his Birth to his Ascension (*Revel. ch.* 60. *n.* 10.): and that fill'd him with all those great

Revelations of his former Glory, when he was the Immortal Father (*Trans. p.* 35.).

That *Elias* was the God and the Father to whom Christ said, *My God, my God* – and *Father, into thy hands* – and to whom he prayed, *Father, if it be possible,* &c. (*p.* 36. 31.)

That *Moses* (who was also Glorified, and never died, but was Translated (*Revel. ch.* 59. *n.* 3. 5.) and *Elias* did represent the Person of God the Father in Heaven; and were the Angels of whom its said, *He shall give his Angels charge over thee, lest at any time thou dash thy foot against a stone;* that is, *lest he should at any time be overcome by the Temptations of Reason, which is the Devil (Transc. p.* 31. *Revel. ch.* 60. *n.* 4.*.*).

That Christ was raised from the Dead by a *Spiritual Compact* with *Elias* (*Trans. p.* 37. (k) *p.* 38.)*;* and that he surrendred all up to Christ when he *ascended into the Right hand of all Power (p.* 38.*.*): And all this, they say, they speak by Revelation from the Holy Spirit (*p.* 35, &c. *Look. glass. p.* 96. *n.* 18.).

2. As to their Opinions concerning the Holy Angels and Devils, they say, That the Angels are Persons in form like Men (*Look. glass. p.* 9. *n.* 3.).

As to Devils, they affirm.

1. That there was but one Angel fell (*Look. glass. p.* 8. *n.* 8. *p.* 130. *n.* 4.).

2. That the Angels (cast out with him) were of his Seed and Generation, through his Union with the Entrails of *Eve* by her consent; into whose Womb he presently enter'd, where he died, and became essentially one with her: That *Cain* was the very Seed of that Reprobate Serpent Angel; and so *Cain* was Brother to *Abel* only on the Mother's side (*Quakers neck. n.*14. *Trans. p.* 21. *Look. glass. p.* 130. *n.* 5. 134. *n.* 26. 153. *n.* 15.).

3. That *Cain,* and none but he alone, is *Beelzebub* the Prince of Darkness, and the Father of all the Angels of Darkness; and so the two Seeds of *Adam* and *Cain,* though mixed together by Carnal Copulation, yet are distinct; and so *Cain* and *Judas* were not of the Seed of *Adam (Transc. p.* 21. *Look. glass. p.* 154. *n.* 22, 23, c. *p.* 156. *n.* 34, &c. *n.* 44*)*.

4. *That there is no Devil at all without the body of a Man;* so that *that Devil so frequently spoken of in the Letter of Scripture, that tempts Men to all Unrighteousness, is Man's Spirit of unclean Reason and cursed Imagination (Transc. p.* 25. *Remostr. p.* 8. *Look. glass. p.* 147. *n.* 21, 27. 148 *n.* 31.).

3. As to Men.

They say, that the Spirit of a Man is Mortal, dies, turns into Dust, and is utterly annihilated until the Resurrection. And therefore, when *Solomon* said, *The Spirit returns to God who gave it (Trans. p.* 50. 54. *Look. glass. p.* 100, 101.*);* those words proceeded not from the Spiritual Knowledge of God in him, but from his own Carnal Reason. And though he was a wise Man, his Wisdom was not Prophetical, nor was he a Pen-man of Holy Writ (*Joyful News. p.* 10, 12, 13. *Look. glass. ch.* 30. *n.* 25. *p.* 126. n. 128 *n* 30, 31. *Look. glass. p.* 5, 6, 28. 29.).

4. By Inspiration from the unerring Spirit, they positively affirm the Substances of Earth and Water were from all Elements.

I shall briefly reflect upon these.

As to God

1. He saith, God is not a Spirit, but hath a Body.

I answer,

1.) The Scripture makes a Body and a Spirit two opposite things; so that a Body is not a Spirit, nor a Spirit a Body. *Eccles.* 12.7. The Body returns to the Dust, and the Spirit to God. So a Spirit has not flesh and bones. *Luke* 24. 37, 39.

2.) The Scripture calls God a Spirit, but never a Body; which it might do, if he was a Body and not a Spirit, or if a Body as well as a Spirit.

2. They say, God is in the form of a Man.

I answer,

1.) The Scripture saith, God is invisible, *Heb.* 11.27. and as no Man hath seen him, so whom no Man can see, *I. Tim.* 6. 16.

2.) It especially takes us off from all such gross conceptions of him. *John* 5.37. *Deut.* 4.12.

3. That the words Father, Son, and Spirit are only various Names.

I answer.

A True Representation

If so, then Christ must be begotten of himself, and be in the bosom of himself. He must then send himself, and come by himself to himself; and be an Advocate with himself, and be greater than himself (*John* 1.14, 18. *John* 5.37. 14.6. *I John* 2.1. *John* 14.28.).

He must judge no Man, and yet commit and take all Judgment to himself. And after he has administred the Kingdom, he must deliver it from himself to himself (John 5.22. I Cor. 15. 24. John 5. 18.).

And to conclude this point, he must be the Father of himself.

4. God the Father became flesh.

Answer.

Quite contrary to Scripture; which saith, God sent forth his Son, made of a Woman, *Gal.* 4.4. And God sent his Son in the likeness of sinful Flesh, *Rom.* 8.3. And the Word, the only Begotten of the Father, was made Flesh, *John* 1.14. And his Son was made of the Seed of *David, Rom.* 1.3. I *John* 4.49.

But there is not one word, that the Father was made of a Woman, and was made Flesh, &c. and became a Son.

5. That the Godhead died, &c.

Just contrary to Scripture; which saith, God is immortal, I *Tim.* 1.17. and that he only hath Immortality, I *Tim.* 6.16.

6. *Elias* is all Fable.

Let any one read the Divine Prayer of our Blessed Saviour, just before his Apprehension, *John* 17. and see how it would look, if applied to *Elias.*

Did *Elias* give him Power over all flesh? &c. Was *Elias* the only true God? And would it be Eternal Life to believe in *Elias,* as the only true God? Did *Elias* give him the Work he was to do? And had he a Glory with *Elias* before the World was? Did *Elias* give him the words he was to give to his? and did the Apostles believe that he came out from *Elias,* and was sent by him? was *Elias* in him, and he in *Elias*? and were all Believers to be one in *Elias* and him? &c. O horrid Blasphemy!

I think that Chapter alone is enough to rid any of this Frenzy. So one while they say *Elias,* had charge of God for a Moment, [*Transcend. p.* 35.] and yet elsewhere, from his Birth to his Ascension: [*Revelat. p.* 130. *n.* 16.] that he was quickened by the Compact of *Elias;* [*Transcend. p.* 37.] and yet by his own Power [*General Epist. p.* 5.]

As to the Devils, they say,

1. But one Angel fell.

Just contrary to Scripture, which tells us of the *Angels* that fell, *Jude* 6. And this cannot be applied to *Cain* and his Posterity; because, according to these Mens Principles, they never fell, being Devils by Extraction and Propagation, and not by Transgression and Apostacy.

2. That the Devil entred into the Womb of *Eve,* and there died; and out of him came *Cain,* &c.

The Scripture plainly saith, that *Cain* was the Son of *Adam* as well as *Eve. Gen.* 4.1. *Adam knew his Wife, and she conceived and bare Cain.*

Reeve wisely observes, that in the Genealogy of *Adam* unto Jesus, there is no mention made of *Cain (Look. glass. p.* 158. *n.* 50.*).* This is said for want of Knowing that Jesus was descended from *Seth;* and he might as well have said there is no mention of *Abel:* For as *Abel* died without Children, so all the Posterity of *Cain* perished in the Deluge: And it was only the Posterity of *Seth* that survived and peopled the World again.

3. That *Cain,* and none but he, is *Beelzebub,* &c.

Answer.

The same Scripture that speaks of *Beelzebub,* being Prince of the Devils, speaks of him as casting them out, and so supposes *Beelzebub* then in being in his own Person; but that cannot then be applied to *Cain,* who is not in Being at all (as they hold) in his Person.

4. There is no Devil without the body of a Man, and Devils are only Mens Lusts and Imaginations.

Answer.

1. Then the Devils which the Heathens and Israelites offer'd their Sacrifices and Children to, were their own *cursed Imaginations. Levit.* 17.7. *Psal.* 106.35.

2. Then the Devil that transported Christ, and argued with him, and that hurried him into the Wilderness, set him upon a Pinacle of the Temple, must be his own imagination.

3. Then the Devils that enabled the young Man to break his Chains; [*Mark* 5.2. &c] and that tore and bruised the Child, [*Luke* 9.39.] and that go about to and fro in the Earth, [*Job* 1.7. I *Peter* 5.58.] and that contended with *Michael*; were only the Lusts of Men; that is, the Lusts of Men broke Chains, bruised and tore Persons, walk'd to and fro in the Earth, &c. which is irreconcileable.

As to Man, they say the Soul is Mortal, and turns into Dust with the body.

Answer.

The Scripture on the contrary tells us, that the Souls of Men are alive after their Departure hence.

So [*Matth.* 22.32.] Our Saviour proves from that Saying, *I am the God of Abraham, &c.* that *God is not the God of the Dead, but of the Living;* that is, God is said to be their God after they were Dead; and that he could not have been, had they not been in Being after their Decease.

This again our Saviour's argument shews, *Mat.* 10. 28. *Fear not them which kill the body, but are not able to kill the Soul;* where he not only makes the Soul and Body two distinct things, but so really such, that the one may be killed, but the other cannot. But if the Soul was mortal and turn'd into Dust, they would as well kill the Soul as the Body; and would kill the Soul, by killing the Body.

So *Luke* 16.22. The Beggar that died was carried into *Abraham's* bosom, and the Rich Man was in Hell. How! not as to their bodies surely; for they were left in this World, the Rich Man was buried. And this was before the Resurrection, for it was while their Brethren were alive, *v.* 28.

And therefore it must be as to their Souls alone, that one was with *Abraham,* and the other in Hell.

II. They are Deceivers; That plead Divine Inspiration and Infallibility, and yet have been guilty of Self-contradiction; and have actually mistaken in Principles and matter of Fact.

It has been just before shew'd, that they have grosly err'd in their Principles, which are contrary to the Word of God.

Let us then now proceed to their Self-contradictions, to Errors in matters of Fact, by which it will appear that what they say of themselves, that they are infallible, and not guilty of any mistake, is one of the number.

1. I shall consider their Self-contradictions.

In one place they say, *If any man despise this writing of theirs, he commits the unpardonable Sin against the Holy Ghost.* So the *General Epistle,* &c. And yet in another it is, *To persecute others for the sake of Christ,* is that Sin (*Look. glass. p.* 42. *n.* 11.).

At one time they tell us, that they *two were the Fore-runners of the End of the World,* and that *this was to be suddenly after they had delivered their Message (Transcendent. Spir. Treat. Remonstr. p.* 5.).

At another time it is, *Whosoever shall live to see an end of them two, shall suddenly see the Dissolution of the World (Remonst. p.* 6.).

By the first *suddenly,* they are to be understood of what was immediately to come to pass; for they say *John Robins,* the Man of Sin (as they make him) was to appear a little before the Personal Visible coming of Christ. And that the Dissolution of the World was presaged by the many Fires then happen'd in *London;* and by the Condition of the People (*Transcend. p.* 6. *Look. glass. p.* 194. 28. *Ibid. p.* 198. *n.* 15.).

Now this Message of theirs (which the end of the World was suddenly to follow) was declared 1651, as appears by their *Remonstrance,* which is above 40 years since: And *Reeve* has been dead above 30 years; for it was before *Muggleton* reprinted the Book call'd his *Looking-glass,* 1661.

But why should we wait the end of these two? for if they be the Witnesses in the *Revelation,* they are to die by the hands of Violence, and to rise again, and to ascend up into Heaven in the sight of their Enemies. And *Muggleton* may as well tell us, that it was so with *John Reeve;* as he doth that *Moses* was Translated; of whom the Scripture saith, that he died and was buried (*Revelat. c.* 59.).

But let us proceed to their palpable mistakes, and which yet they affirm to be true, as well as themselves to be infallible.

And this in the first place I take to be one, that they affirm, That they had more knowledge in the Scriptures than all the Men of the World besides; and yet every where betray the grossest ignorance in them.

1. As first of all, when they say that *Moses* was Translated, who, the Scripture saith, died and was buried, *Deut.* 34. 5. 6.

2. *Muggleton* supposes *Matthew* to have seen the Angel at our Saviour's Resurrection; and gives it as a Reason why he speaks but of one; saith he, *perhaps he was no more to his* (Matthew's) *Visible Sight* (*Revelat. ch.* 9. *n.* 8.).

3. He saith, that the Souldiers did *see the natural Vail of the Temple* rent from the bottom to the top (*Revel. Ch.* 63.5.): Whereas the Vail was in the most inward part of the Temple, and the Souldiers were at Mount *Calvary,* watching the Body of Jesus.

4. He saith, we read not of *Cain* in the Genealogy from *Adam* to Jesus: forgetting that Jesus was not descended from *Cain,* but *Seth* (*See pag.* 20.).

5. We may add to this, gross Ignorance, when he affirms, that the Apostles Epistles *were written either in Hebrew, Greek, or Latin;* and *for the most in Greek and Latin.* [*Revelat. ch.* 52. *n.* 6, 7.] Whereas those Epistles were written in Greek only.

6. He affirms, That the *Roman Catholicks were the first Professors of the Faith of Christ, and of the Apostles* (*Revelat. ch.* 53. *n.* 4.). Whereas it is notorious in Scripture, that the Jews Converted were the first Professors of it; and then the Gentiles in *Judea.*

A True Representation 209

Let us proceed to another sort of mistakes.

1. They say, *The first sort of Persons that affirm the Holy One of Israel to consist of three Persons, are* Athanasius, Socinus, *alias* John Biddle (*Look. glass. p.* 41. *n.* 2.). As if *Athanasius* and *Socinus* were of the same Opinion; where as *Athanasius* was a zealous Assertor of the Trinity; and *Socinus* and *Biddle* Oppugners of it. And as for *Socinus*, he would not allow the Holy Spirit to be a Person at all; and *Biddle* would have him only a Created Angel, and so not God.

2. They affirm that no one every taught their Principles, as that God the Father died, and that God had a Body, and was in the form of a Man, &c. Whereas there is hardly any thing new, but that there have been some as wild and fanciful as themselves in past Ages.

As, (1.) The *Anthropomorphites,* and *Audians,* and *Manichees* held, that God had a Human body.

(2.) That there was but one Person in the Deity, only called by different Names; so held the *Noetians, Colarbasians,* and *Sabellians.*

(3.) That the Father suffer'd; so the *Cataphrygians, Sabellians* (called therefore *Patropassiant*) and that the Divinity of Christ suffer'd; so the *Theopaschites.*

(4.) That the Soul died with the Body; and that there was no Resurrection of the Body; so the *Valentinians, Manichees,* &c.

(5.) That the Wicked are of the Posterity of *Cain.* So the *Valentinians* and *Sethites.*

Without raking farther into this matter, this is sufficient to shew, that they are not the first Broachers of these Doctrines.

3. They affirm, That the Reason of the Eclipse of the Moon, is through her near Conjunction with the Sun (*Look. glass. p.* 33. *n.* 50, 58.); whereas it's manifest, that it is when it's opposite to the Sun; and that the Earth is between them.

4. They affirm, That no Man can know the time of Eclipses, but by Inspiration (*Ibid. p.* 34. *n.* 59.): whereas they may be as well foretold, as the time the Sun will rise to Morrow.

5. He positively affirms from God, That the Bodies of the Sun, Moon, and Stars, are in compass not much bigger than they appear to our natural sight (*Ibid. p.* 31. *n.* 34, 35.): whereas it's evident on the contrary, that everything diminishes in its appearance to the degree of its Elevation: And consequently according to the degree of its

Elevation: And consequently those Heavenly Bodies, being vastly remote from the Earth, must be vastly greater than they appear to the Eye.

6. He affirms, That the Sun, Moon, and Stars neither borrow, nor lend light to one another (*Ibid. p.* 31, 32, 33.): Whereas we see plainly that the Moon borrows light from the Sun; and that, according as the Earth is between it and the Sun, so it's proportionably obscured.

7. He affirms positively from the Lord, That the Sun, Moon, and Stars are only in one Firmament: Whereas it's evident on the contrary, 1. That the Moon is in an Orb lower than the Sun, and both of them lower than the Stars. 2. That there are different motions, a slower and swifter in the Planets; and that those called fixed Stars only move all alike, and are in the same Firmament.

Whether these are Errors or no, let all Men judge: and if so, what becomes of their Infallibility? what of their pretence to Divine Illumination?

Chap. II.

It remains now to proceed to to the second Question, *viz.*

Q. *Whether* J. Reeve *and* L. Muggleton *are the two Witnesses spoken of in the* 11th *of the* Revelation?

This they both do avow, and *L. Muggleton* has wrote a Comment upon that Chapter, in his way, foolish and absurd enough, to try how he can work it to his purpose.

But like one that is not in himself over confident of his performance; he sometimes shrinks from it, and comes off with a *may be:* as, *We may be said to be those two Olive trees; and the two Witnesses may be said to have finished,* &c. (*Interpret. of the Revelat. c.* 79. *n.* 1. *c.* 82. *n.* 7.)

Now what more sneaking and pitiful! After they have boldly challeng'd this Character to themselves, to give it over again, and retire from it, as if they fainted under a distrust, and the fear of the inconsistencies in it. As a Specimen of which, I shall compare the Text of Scripture and his Exposition together.

Revelation, Ch. 11 Chap. 78, &c.

Text

Ver. 3. I Will give power unto my two Witnesses, and they shall prophesie one thousand two hundred and sixty days, cloathed in Sackcloth.

V. 4. They are the two Olive-trees, and the two Candlesticks standing before the God of the Earth.

V. 5. If any man will hurt them, a fire proceedeth out of their mouth, and devoureth their Enemies; and if any man will hurt them, he must in this manner be killed.

Exposition

We, J. Reeve and L. Muggleton, shall prophesie concerning the Spiritual Estate of Mankind to Eternity, and of the end of the World.

Olive trees, because of the Oyl of Joy in our Doctrine.

Candlesticks, because God hath put the Commission of his Spirit into us, which is Light.

Fire proceedeth, to pronounce blessing and cursing to Eternity.

Text

v. 6. These have power to shut heaven, that it rain not in the days of their prophesie; and have power over waters to turn them into blood, and to smite the earth with all plagues, as often as they will.

Exposition

To shut heaven; that is, the Heaven of Mens hearts.

That it rain not; that is, after the Sentence of Eternal death, it prevents the motion of the Spirit.

Turns water into blood; that is, the motions of peace and hope of Mens Souls (which are as water to drink) into wrath, and so it becomes a Spiritual Plague.

Text

V. 7. And when they shall have finished their Testimony, the Beast that ascended out of the Bottomless Pit, shall make War against them, and shall overcome them, and kill them.

Exposition

Finished their Testimony; that is, the Doctrine of Truth, which is, that Jesus Christ is God the Father, Son, and Spirit, &c.

The Beast; that is, the Spirit of Reason in the Lord Mayor, Aldermen, and Jury.

Bottomless Pit; that is the Pit of their Imagination.

Shall kill them; that is, would have killed up, if their Law would have done it.

Text

V. 8. And their dead bodies shall lie in the streets of the great City, which spiritually is called Sodom and Egypt, where also our Lord was crucified.

V. 9. And they of the People, and Kindred, and Tongues, and Nations, shall see their dead bodies three days and a half, and shall not suffer their dead bodies to be put in Graves.

For the meaning of this, he refers us to what was before, and that I find in ch. 51, 52.

Exposition

Dead Bodies; that is, the Letter of Scripture.

In the streets of the City; that is, the Hearts of Men.

The People; that is, the Jews who owned the Letter of the Law.

Gentiles; that is, those that owned the Letter of the Apostles, that is, the Roman Emperours, which overcame the Nation of the Jews, which was in the Destruction of Jerusalem, which was in the ten Persecutions.

Three days and a half; that is, 1350 years; for so long the Letter of Scripture lay dead.

Not suffer their bodies to be buried; because the Jews and Gentiles knew better what to do with the Letter than the Spirit. And so the Roman Catholicks, and those that sprung from them, have seen the dead bodies of the Scripture lie dead 1350 years.

Text

V. 10. And they that dwell on the Earth shall rejoyce over them, and make merry, and shall send Gifts one to another, because these two Prophets tormented them that dwelt on the Earth.

Exposition

They rejoiced over the Letter of the Scriptures; the Spirit and Life of them being put to Death. And now they looked upon themselves as very sure, because there were none left upon Earth that had a commission to torment them.

Text

V. 11. And after three days and a half, the Spirit of Life from God enter'd into them, and they stood upon their feet, and great fear fell upon them which saw them.

A True Representation 213

Exposition

The Spirit; that is, the Commission of the Spirit enter'd into the Letter of the Law and Gospel; and by a true Interpretation they made the dead Letter stand upon its feet, and that kills the Spirit of Reason with Death Eternal; which it never did this 300 years, till the year 1651.

Great fear; so as to convince some, and make them silent: Others were filled so with wrath, as to be damn'd to Eternity; other receiv'd it to Eternal Happiness.

Text

V. 12. And they heard a great Voice from Heaven, saying unto them, Come up hither. And they ascended up to Heaven in a Cloud, and their Enemies beheld them.

Exposition

Of this Blank. Here he seems to be at a loss.

I shall now draw all this together, and the Sum of the whole is this...

That J. Reeve and L. Muggleton are the two Witnesses, the Olive Trees, and Candlesticks spoken of in this Chapter. That these two were to prophesie 1260 days, beginning in February, 1651. And had power to save and damn irrevocably to all Eternity, &c. That upon declaring this Commission, the Beast out of the Bottomless Pit, that is, the Ld. Mayor *Fowk,* the Recorder, and Jury, out of the Pit of their Imagination, made War against these two aforesaid Witnesses, 1653. and killed them; that is, the Letter of the Scripture. And their dead Bodies, which is the Letter of the Scripture, lay dead in the streets of the hearts of Men. And the People and Kindred saw the dead Letter of the Scripture lie dead three days and a half, or 1350 years, and rejoiced at it. But at the end of the 1350 years, in which the Bodies of the Witnesses, or the Letter of the Scripture, had lay dead, the Spirit entered into them, by the Commission given to *J. Reeve* and *L. Muggleton,* 1651. and so the Bodies of the Witnesses or Letter of the Scripture, stood up again.

And it should have been added, That the Witnesses ascended up into Heaven in a Cloud, and their Enemies beheld them. But soft--- for *J. Reeve* has been long dead.

Now reconcile all this who can?

For, 1. He saith that they two are the Witnesses, and yet the Bodies of those two Witnesses are the Letter of the Scripture.

2. If the Letter of the Scripture is the Body of the Witnesses, and that lay slain 1300 years before these two say, they receiv'd their

Commission; then the Bodies of them were slain before, and 1300 years before these two Witnesses were in being.

3. He saith, The body of the Witnesses, or Letter, was slain 1300 years before; and yet makes it slain again by the Ld. Mayor. And if it was slain in his time, then the three days and a half was to begin after his time, and a new 1350 years was to follow.

4. Observe, That in the Revelation, the two Witnesses had their Commission before the Bodies were slain: But if the Bodies of the Witnesses is the Letter of Scripture, and was slain 1350 years ago; then they were slain so long before these had their Commission, which was not till 1651.

It's plain, this Shifter knows not where to fix. He would fain, like *Simon Magus,* be accounted some great One, and he and his Partner would set up for Broachers of New Doctrines, how sordid and contradictious soever; but he wants the skill to patch things cleverly together; they are at the best but tatters, and can never be brought into one intire piece. And this Exposition of his is so sorry and pitiful and attempt, that he might as well have undertaken to have proved himself and *Reeve* to be the two great Lights in the Heavens, and to as good purpose have in like manner wrote an Exposition on the first Chapter of *Genesis*.

To conclude, If confusion and self-contradiction, may pass for Exposition; if confidence and self-assuming may pass for Inspiration; if nonsence and obscurity may pass for Illumination; if cursing and damning other may pass for Charity; if Blasphemy may pass for Religion; then these two may be allowed to be what they pretend. But if these things will not pass among Mankind; then they will no more be Prophets and Witnesses from God, than they will ascend into Heaven in a Cloud, in the sight of the Enemies.

FINIS.

An Ellegy

An Ellegy On Lodowick Muggleton

Who Lies Bury'd Alive In The Colledge Of Newgate, Expecting Dayly
His Happy Resurrection.

All those that use with Watry Eyes
To Weep at Mournful Eligies;
For loss of Neighbour, or of Friend,
Or loss of Fop, that us'd to spend
His Time, and Money, e'ry day
In Tavern, and there ever pay
The Total Summ who e're is by;
For loss of such you ought to cry:
My Muse does now invite your Ear,
A Pleasant Elegy to hear:
For so I'le term it, if that you
In Elegies e're Pleasure knew:
A Prophet False, and Monster great,
Who often did Damnation threat,
To those that never would him Treat;
Lies Bury'd now Alive, not Dead,
Mistake me not; what I have said
Is very true: In *Newgate* now
He is Entom'd, and knows not how
To get away, so strong's the Stone,
Which makes him daily sigh and groan;
But all in vain, such is his fate,
He now may curse his Doom too late;
But least you should the Poem blame,
Because he was not told his Name,
He says 'tis *Muggleton,* the same
Who whilst in living liberty
Arriv'd to such Damn'd Blasphemy
That all Man kind he did out-vye;
He had such Power he did Protest,
And spoke in Earnest, not in Jest;
He many Hundred men had blest;
If all were true which he has said,
He would have made us all affraid;
If those he Curs'd, and those he Damn'd,
Could not through Faith his Doom withstand;
'Twere a hard case I must confess,
But yet again this Man could Bless
The very same he Curs'd before,
If that they had but Guinnies store;
Or Houses, or would give a Treat
With Wine, and Capons, or such Meat

For those he'd bless, and bless agen;
And to his Blessings say; *Amen.*
But if they no such comforts had,
He us'd to say their Case was bad;
And Damne 'em straight such was his power,
He'd Bless and Curse 'em in an Hour;
He said that he a Prophet was,
And did all other Power Surpass:
And with a Countenance of Brass
He said that those he Damn'd were Damn'd,
And nothing could that Fate withstand;
Nor yet Reverse his Cursed Doom,
For Blessings he had left no room;
This he did Witness to his Tomb.
The Foolish Sisters all Complain;
Crying, *Lodowick,* arise again;
Arise, arise, out of thy Tomb
Dear *Muggleton* we pray thee come:
We want thy Blessings, come away,
Our Prophet's gone, we go astray:
We here have brought a Key of Gold,
Which will release thee from thy hold,
Come forth with Courage Stout and bold.
'Twill ope the Door without all doubt,
Come *Lodowick,* thou must come out:
Methinks I hear the Boys Complain,
And wish they had him once again;
They'd fit him better then before,
For now they have got Eggs good store;
In *Smithfield* they did want supply,
When he stood their I'th Pillory;
All things consider'd by the wise,
Our *Muggleton* again must rise:
We from our Prophet cannot part,
To rise again he has an Art,
Or else he is not worth a Fart;
Now stead of Crying you may Laugh,
And Read your Prophet's Epitaph.

EPITAPH

Entomb'd I lye,
I can't deny,
Amongst Rogues, as 'tis said;
Pray do not fear,
My Voice to hear,
For indeed I am not Dead.

I shall come out,
Without all doubt,
And in my own Shape be,
But I must stay,
Until the Day,
My Golden God I see.

Printed for *E.O.* FINIS. With Allowance.

A New-Year's Gift For The Ratcliff Convert to Muggletonianism;

OR,

REMARKS On SADDINGTON'S Muggletonian ARTICLES WITH AN Antidote to expel the Venom of them. IN A LETTER to Mr. PHIL. LASCELLS.

By J. SHARPE, A.M. ---- of Stepney.

Which in the Hypochondria spent,
Because beneath it had no Vent;
And then it upwards chanc'd to fly,
And prov'd new Light and Prophecy.
Hudibras.

The SECOND EDITION.
LONDON,
Printed for R. Wilkin, at the King's Head in St. Paul's Church Yard. 1717. And Sold by Edward Baldwin and Paul Sorrel, Stationers in Ratcliff. Price 4d.

Advertisement.

This Little Tract had seen the Light some time ago, had it not been for the Negligence and ill Dealing of a certain Printer, that I deliver'd the Copy to; who detained it several Weeks, violating his Promise to me. I must declare once for all, that I have no Temporal Design in it: My pure and sole Intention is, to reclaim a Young Man from the most Blasphemous and Outragious Heresie of Muggleton. If I can do this, All Glory be to God, that made me an Instrument in so good a Work as to reduce a Straying Sheep into the Fold of Christ, the Christian Church. If I fail in my Design, my Intention was Real: I have done my Duty, and animam meam liberavi.

SIR,

Do not think it any Trouble to peruse this long Letter: I am sure, I don't think it any in writing it. My principal Design in discoursing you formerly concerning the damnable and blasphemous Heresie, into which you are lately fallen; and now in writing to you, is to recover you (if God's Grace is not departed from you, and if your Heart is not hardned, as K. Pharoah's was) to the Church (in which you was baptiz'd, I mean the Church of England, and none else) from which you have, like Lucifer, apostatiz'd: And I pray God, your Fate may not, like his, be irreversible You may remember, what I said to you; and such Things and Matters I urged, that you confess'd, that you was not Scholar enough to answer. I ask'd you, where your Religion was before Muggleton? You gave me no other Answer but this (and that was a wild one) that Religion lay hid from the time of the 10th Persecution, until Muggleton arose. Then I replied, that if that was so, then (with Reverence be it spoken) our Saviour's Words cannot be true, Lo, I am with you, even unto the End of the World: Was not that my Answer? And what said you to it? You first stuck, and then shuffl'd, and made no direct Answer. Did I not tell you, that our Blessed Lord founded his Church on the Twelve Apostles, and that he chose Seventy Disciples; That these Apostles after our Lord's Crucifixion, chose Bishops to preside in several Churches, and these chose their Successors, and they others, down to our own Time? And I do assert for a Truth, and am ready to prove it, That the whole Christian Church was govern'd by Bishops for 1500 Years; and that Mr. Calvin of Geneva was the first, (and he did it upon Necessity; the Popish Bishop being then living) that set up another Platform of Church-Government. Now then, if the constant Succession of Bishops in all the Christian Churches, down to the time of Calvin, is not a sufficient Argument to prove the Truth of Church-Government, I must confess, I know not what is. What's now become of your crude Notion of the Spirit's absconding in the latter Part of the 10th Persecution? Can you, or any one else prove, that all the Christian Bishops apostatiz'd at that time? If not (as you cannot) then the Christian Religion under the Bishops Government, continu'd thro' all Ages. 'Tis true, in Process of Time, some Corruptions crept into the Doctrines of the Church; and the Church of Rome in After-Ages, grafted Twelve Heterogeneous and Absurd Articles on the Apostles Creed. But do Corruptions destroy the Essence of a Church? That, I hope, you will not say. A Leprous Man is a Man still: Take off the Scurf, and cure the Malady, and the Man is whole. So 'tis in the Doctrine of a Church: Take away its Corruptions, prune off the Additions, remove Pope Pius's Twelve Articles, and the Church is Sound and Primitive: And this was the Method of our Governours in the Beginning of the Reformation, I say; we reformed, that is, remov'd the Corruptions added in former Times; and then our Church shin'd with its Primitive Lustre; and was, is, and I hope, ever will be, the Bulwark against Rome, Geneva, and all other Sectaries.

  I remember, I spoke somewhat of Councils: To which you replied smartly enough, that that was not a certain Rule; for in the 4th Century the Arians were the reigning Party, as Witness the Council of Ariminum, which, you said, was the greatest that ever was,

A New Years Gift for the Ratcliff Convert

To which I answer'd that you were out in History; for that the Great Lateran was far more numerous. Sir, said you then, I am not able to discourse you. I confess that Councils are not infallible; yet I say, if Councils will be determin'd by Scripture, and the Testimonies of the Primitive Fathers, the Church will be safe and secure: And this is plain in Fact from the Four First General Councils: And I dare say, that none of your Sect (out of which God be your Guide) has the Forehead to deny. Amongst other things, I ask'd you, what Reason your Sect had to throw by the Sacraments, since 'twas plain, that they were instituted for standing Ordinances in the Christian Church? As to Baptism, you replied that our Baptism was not rightly used; that you was for that Baptism of Fire and the Holy Ghost. What you meant by Fiery Baptism, you did not explain. Perhaps you are of the Opinion of the Old Hereticks that used to mark their Children with a Fiery Instrument in the Forehead By the Holy Ghost we mean what you do not: We understand by it the Assistance of that Holy Spirit, the Third Person of the ever Glorious Trinity, which you and all Muggletonians deny: For you say, that there is but One Person and One Substance, viz. God the Father; so you exclude the Son and the Holy Ghost: And you, like the Old Hereticks the Patripassians, assert (Oh Blasphemy to name) that God the Father suffered on the Cross; and like your Brother Ralph, you may ask the prophane and impudent Question, Where was the Divinity when Jesus suffered? I answer, it was where it ever was; and that 'twas the Human Nature of Christ that suffered, and not the Divine. As to other Sacrament, I ask'd the Reason of rejecting that; you replied, that you did daily eat the Body and Blood of Christ. As how, I pray? You answer'd Spiritually; and that do we, when we receive the Corporeal Elements. You referr'd me to John the 6th, concerning the Spiritual Manducation of Christ's Body, and Drinking his Blood. That's nothing to our purpose, I replied: For then Baptism and the Lord's Supper were not instituted by our Lord. For the First you find in St. Matthew, Cap. 28.19,20. Go ye and disciple (for that's the true Meaning of μαθητεύσατε all Nations, baptizing them in the Name of the Father, and of the Son, and of the Holy Ghost, (three Persons in one Essence, which you deny teaching them to observe all things that I have commanded you, and lo, I am with you, all Days (which our Translation reads always) to the End of the World. And from that time to this, Water-Baptism has been used in all Christian Churches, as may be easily made appear from this Age and upwards, to the very Apostles.

Then for the Sacrament of the Lord's Supper, we find that instituted in St. Matthew, Cap. 36. 26, 27, 28. And when they had eaten (the Paschal Supper) Jesus took the Bread, and blessing, brake it, and gave it to his Disciples, and said, Take, eat; this is my Body. And taking the Cup, and blessing it, he gave to them, saying, Drink ye all of this: for this is my Blood of the New Testament, which is poured out for many for the Remission of Sins. That you may not object, that these were pro tempore Ordinances, and to be laid side, I shall fully prove from the Words of St. Paul (I Cor. II. 23, 24, 25, 26.) For I received of the Lord (that is, after his Crucifixion) that which I delivered unto you, that the Lord Jesus, the same Night in which he was betrayed, took Break, and blessing, brake it; and he said, Take, eat; this is my Body, which is broken for you: this do for my remembrance. Likewise also he took the Cup, after Supper, saying, this Cup is the New Testament in my Blood this do, as oft as ye drink, to my remembrance. For as oft as ye eat this Bread, and drink this Cup, you shew the Death of the Lord until he come. Thus you see by St. Paul's Words, how the Lord's Supper is a standing permanent Ordinance, to be continued till Christ's Coming to Judgment. Now I would know the Reason of the daring Impudence of the Muggletonians and Quakers (put them both in a Bag, I see no difference, but that both in this point are egregiously prophane and blasphemous) I say, I would know the Reason of discarding this and the other Sacrament. From Scripture, you see, they have no Warrant; and I am sure, from History they have as little. But I believe, I can guess how it happened: The Zealous Christians in the Primitive Times receiv'd the Lord's Supper daily; then as the Fervour of Christianity abated, once a Week, and afterwards once a Month; and some time after, the Church in Rome appointed the Communion to be performed by the Priest alone; and in the Days of Glorious reformation in forty One, to the Restoration, the Saints were so far above Ordinances, that the Lord's Supper was seldom or never celebrated: The Quakers and Muggletonians in the Year 1650, finding Christianity in such a Disorder, and as it was managed by Sectaries, laid both Sacraments aside as useless, calling them Beggarly Elements, and the Cup of Devils, and set themselves up for Spiritual Men, or rather Monsters, if not Devils: And in this State do the Quakers and Muggletonians at this Day continue.

I remember, I ask'd you, how you proved Reeve and Muggleton, Prophets? You could not clear that Point; but said, they were as great Prophets as Moses and Jesus Christ. This Lascells denies, but I affirm. At which Blasphemy I stood amazed, not at your Learning, but at your Impudence. I askt you whether Muggleton had the Gifts of Tongues? You replied, No. Then, said I, he was a Cheat, a Deluder, and and Imposter; that he had no Mission from God, but was an Instrument of Satan, set up to delude the World. I told you, that the Apostles confirmed their Mission by a Series of Miracles, by raising the Dead, healing the Sick, casting out Devils, and speaking strange Tongues. All these wonderful things you may have read in the New Testament; and I with you to read them again with an humble Spirit, and with Prayers to that glorious Tri-une God to direct you, that you may be rescued out of the Snares of the wicked one. Good Men on Earth, and Angels in Heaven, will rejoyce at your Conversion; and Return to your dear Mother (I do not mean, your Mother according to the Flesh; for I am afraid that you suck'd in Quakerism at first from her, and was afterwards instructed in Muggletonianism by a Friend

A New Years Gift for the Ratcliff Convert 223

(shall I call him? No Friend, I am sure, to the Salvation of your Soul) and afterwards confirm'd by the Limehouse Prophet, the Taylor, whose Curses I expect, for which I'll return him Blessings, and Prayers to God for his Conversion; for I am told he is a hardned, and petrified, obdurate Sinner, having his Conscience sear'd, as it were, with a hot Iron;) I say, to your dear Mother, the Church of England; who with open Arms, is ready to receive all penitent Sinners; one of which I pray God you may be. Your Return to Christianity will be Joy unspeakable to your loving Father, whose Heart bleeds for you, and whose daily Prayers are for the Welfare of your Soul, which must live in a future State: And if you steer a wrong Course here, you must infallibly expect, that it will end in a Miserable Eternity, where the Worm dieth, not and the Fire is not quenched, as long as there is a God, and that will be for ever and ever. Oh Sir, pity your poor Soul, which must continue to Eternal Ages.

    I enquir'd after your Way of Worship, and ask'd if you had any Preachers amongst you? You said, there was no Occasion for them. How, said I, no Preachers or Teachers? Then I immediately replied, There can be no True Church, where there are no True Priests: A Church supposed a Priest. To this you said little or nothing. And since I had this Conversation with you, I am told, your Method of disposing your Time on Sundays, is; You meet at some House or other, (be sure, where there is good Provision) and after Dinner, the Bottle, Pipes, and minc'd Virginia are plac'd on the Table, and so your Religion vanishes in Fumo. This Account I had from a nameless Friend, who would not impose on me. And if I am not right in the Method, you would do well to give me a better Account.

    Sir, I well remember, I proposed a Quaere to you concerning the Three Hypostases in the Godhead. At the Word Hypostasis you startled, and told me that you did not understand the Greek Words. Then I propos'd it thus; Whether there are not Three Persons in One Essence? Your Answer was (I am positive) that there was but One Person in the Godhead. Which bold and blasphemous Assertion, I told you, contradicted the Holy Scriptures, and the current Testimonies of the Fathers for many Ages, and the Three Creeds, viz. the Apostles, the Nicene, and that of Athanasius. Your answer to this was, that you had nothing to do with the Fathers: And I now add, that they have nothing to do with you or Muggleton. But the Scripture, you said, was the Rule you went by. I wish you would stand by that. Then I alledged that known Text of St. John (I Epist. Cap. 5 Verse 7.) That there are Three that bear witness in Heaven, the Father, the Word, and the Holy Ghost; and these Three are, One, that is, one Being. To this you replied nothing of moment. I told you, that the Arians and Socinians went another way to work and struck it out of the Canon (for the Testimony was so flagrant, that they could not answer it) for that the Orthodox had interpolated and inserted that Text. To this I replied, that that Text was in more MSS. than it was left out of; which, I am sure, was a very good Plea against all Hereticks. Moreover, I now add, that if they admit that Text, they put another Construction on it, that the Three are One in Consent and Agreement: but this Shuffle and Put-off won't do: for that in the Greek will never bear that Sense; for that the Word is in the Neuter Gender, and signifies One thing, and Being or Essence. At this you stuck, and made no reply. And now what will you say to another Text, which I then added not; for I saw you uneasie, and willing to go. The Text is in St. John's gospel, Cap.I. Ver. I,2. In the Beginning was the Word, λόγος , and the Word was with God, and the Word was God; He was in the Beginning with God. Here's a plain Assertion of the Eternal λόγος, the Word, the Second Person of the Glorious Trinity. How does this agree with Muggleton's Scheme? I desire you to call in Assistance, and let me know what your Prophet can say to it. For to me, I confess, 'tis as plain a Proof of the Second Person of the Trinity, as can be mentioned; and I cannot see, how any Heretick can set it by, except they assert the old threadbare Objection, that St. John was a Platonist, and stole that Notion from the Works of that Divine Philosopher. For that Notion will not stand the Test: for both Targums and Philo often mention the λόγος, the Word, as a Distinct Person: And these two Texts (to mention no more, which I could easily do) are more than enough to set you right in the Christian Faith, and to bring you back into the Bosom of the Church.

I cannot call to mind any more of our Discourse at that time. At parting, I assur'd you, that I should take an Opportunity of discoursing farther; but now I shall not; and I'll give you a very good Reason for it, and that is, that you have slander'd me behind my Back, and have assured one of your Customers, that I approved of your Horrible Change (Oh, horrid and impudent Lye!) This you know, if you lay your Hand on your Heart, that 'tis a Horrible Lye, and can come from no other, than the Father of Lyes, the Devil. The Story is thus; that a certain Gentlewoman repaired to your Shop to trade with you; she told you, that she was heartily sorry that you had changed your Opinions in Religion; that she would buy of you what then was necessary; and if the Report was true, she would find out for the future some others to deal with. Then with a forg'd Invention, you replied to her, that I approved of your Opinions. The Gentlewoman is ready to make Affidavit, that you spoke these Words, I commend you, and advise you to stand to your Principles. Sir, consider there is a Future Reckoning, and at the General Audit we must all give an Account of our Words and Actions. How then durst you, in the Presence of the Great God (whom you pretend to adore, but how, I know not) assert so bold a Lye? If your Dealings with your Customers are so Dark and Knavish, as they have been with me, I know not, e're long, who will deal with you. I am sure, the Muggletonian Hereticks will never be able to support you, except you call in to your Assistance those Hereticks the Quakers. The Cheesmonger at the Cross sent for you, and afterwards reported, that you and he were of the same Opinions. I have a Voucher for it. But how can that be? For George Fox is an Enemy to Muggleton; for hear the Words of Eccles to

A New Years Gift for the Ratcliff Convert 225

Muggleton. 'Stand up, Muggleton; thou Sorcerer, (in the Quaker's Challenge, p.6. printed in 1688. And never disown'd by Fox) 'whose Mouth is full of Cursing, Lies, and Blasphemy, who calls thy last Book a Looking-Glass for George Fox (which Book was lately in my Possession) whose Name thou art not worthy to take into thy Mouth, who is a Prophet indeed, and hath been faithful in the Lord's Business, from the Beginning. It was said of Christ, that he was in the World, and that the World was made by him, and the World knew him not; so it may be said of the True Prophet (George Fox) whom John said, he was not: but thou (Loddiwick Muggleton) will feel this Prophet (George Fox) one Day, as heavy as a Millstone upon thee; and also the World knows him not, yet he is known. Sir, you may ask, why so much intemperate Heat in Solomon Eccles, in Defence of George Fox? You are but a new Convert, and so perhaps may be a Stranger to the Reason of it. Lodowick Muggleton, your mighty one, wrote a Book, called a Looking-glass for George Fox (which was lately in my Possession) and which thus begins; see Chap. I. of the Looking-glass for George Fox, the Quaker, and other Quakers; wherein they may see themselves to be right Devils; in Answer to George Fox's Book, called Something in Answer to Lodowick Muggleton's Book, which he calls, The Quaker's Neck broken; wherein is set forth the Ignorance and Blindness of the Quakers Doctrine of Christ within them; and that they cannot, nor do not know the true meaning of the Scriptures; neither have they the gift of Interpretation of Scripture. Written by Lodowick Muggleton, one of the Two last Prophets and Witnesses unto the High and Mighty God, the Man Christ Jesus in Glory. Printed in the Year 1665. The Title of the First Chapter, (Of a Catalogue of Damned Quakers) And which, as I said, thus begins: 'George Fox, I saw a Pamphlet of yours, entituled, Something in Answer to Lodowick Muggleton's Book, which he calls, the Quaker's Neck broken.

'You said well, in that you said, Something in Answer to that Book of the Quaker's Neck broken: For it is a very little Something indeed; it is so little a Something, that wise Men will hardly discern any thing in it, as a direct Answer. But how comes it to pass, that you make no mention of your own Damnation in your Answer? You know, John Reeve and my self, gave you a Sentence of Damnation a matter of 14 Years ago. When we were Prisoners in Old Bridewell (the fittest Place for them) there was you, Edward Burroughs, and Frances Howgill; you three were counted the Choice Speakers of the Quakers, that were damned by us, the Witness of the Spirit (but Lodowick, who gave you and Reeve this Power? This could not have come from the Spirit of the mild Jesus, who never exercised such Power when on Earth and who never commissioned any with such Power;) 'but since there hath fallen a many more of your Brethren under this Sentence: But you have been Fox-like; as is your Name, so is your Nature; you have lain still, and kept your Damnation to your self from the Knowledge of others, because you would not be upon Publick Record as a damned Quaker, and yet a Speaker of the Quakers.

'Also you read of your Name in that Book; you say you have answered something, but take no notice of your self, but take other Folks Parts: And if your Brethren, William Smith, Samuel Hooton, Edward Bourn, Richard Farnsworth, had not written to me, there would be no Occasion for the Fox to come out of his Hole: And now the Fox is come out, he will be catcht, and made manifest to Generations to come, who pretended to be a Means of Salvation to others, and yet he himself a Cast-away, and a Reprobate, a Son of a Devil, one that shall be recorded amongst the damned Crew to the World's End: And I am sure, your Damnation is written in the Tables of Heaven, even as the Law of Moses was written in the Tables of Stone; that is, these Men were written the Seed of the Serpent of Heaven in the Reprobate Angel his Nature, thinking your selves wiser than God, as he did. He thought, if he had been God, he could have made all those Glorious Creatures of nothing; even so be you Quakers here in Mortality: You teach your Disciples here to believe, that God made this vast Earth and Water of nothing, (and that it is true, Muggleton, as it is recorded by Moses, Gen. 1.) "Witness, that Thomas Taylor, Speaker of the Quakers, in his Letters to me, which I have given Answer to, and joyned to the Book, called The Quaker's Neck broken; and you, Fox, and others of your Speakers, doth the same: For you say, you were in Christ before the World was. Here you are quite mistaken: For you were in the Reprobate Angel his Seed and Nature, who is called a Serpent, and in this Serpent-Angel, you and others were in before the World was; and so you and others were recorded in the Table of Heaven for the Reprobate Seed, and to be damned to Eternity.

'And as I know from whence you came, even from the Serpent aforesaid, and that you were in him before the World was; so likewise you shall be recorded for damned Devils here, while the World is, as long as Time shall last: Therefore I shall set you down as followeth; you being one of the Grand Devils, you shall be first.

'George Fox, Edward Burroughs, Francis Howgill, Edward Bourn, William Smith, Samuel Hooton, Richard Farnsworth, Thomas Taylor, John Parrat, Richard Whitepan, John Harwood, Richard Hubberthon, Fox the Younger, and that great lubbardly Fellow spoken of in the Quaker's Neck broken, (a full Baker's Dozen doomed to Hell Torments, if your Sentence stands valid: But where's your Commission, Muggleton, for passing this Sentence?) 'These were generally all, or most of them Speakers of the Quakers, and exercised the Ministerial Preaching without a Commission from God; (and what did you, Muggleton?) and not only so, but they have been the greatest Fighters against a Personal God in Heaven above the Stars, of any, and have sinned against the Holy Spirit (which you deny to be the Third Person of the Glorious Trinity) that sent us (that don't appear yet, that you was sent by that Holy Spirit) 'and so have procured the Sentence of Eternal Damnation upon them; and this Record is true, and it shall be recorded in the Hearts of the Saints to the World's End.

A New Years Gift for the Ratcliff Convert 227

Now, Sir, consider what a Devil of a Prophet is your Muggleton, to assume the Province to damn whom he pleases. This Fiery Spirit cannot be of God; but must proceed from one of another Nature, viz. from the Old Serpent, Satan himself.

Now I shall shew you, that though Muggleton and George Fox jarred so about some things; yet they agreed in one thing, viz. to damn all besides their own Parties. And if you have any Spark of Grace in you to hear which, I will give you such a Shock, as to make you return from whence you were fallen. The Author of the Snake in the Grass (p. 6.) has these Words: 'Does he (Muggleton) damn all the World? so do they (the Quakers.) These two Twin-Enthusiasts, both born in the Year 1650. (for then it was Muggleton says, he got Inspiration; see p. 5. Of Muggleton's Transcendent Spiritual Treatise.) 'and have proceeded since upon the main Principle, tho' in some Particulars they have out stript one another, as if they were not Brethren. But tho' like Sampson's Foxes, they draw two Ways, their Tails are joined with Firebrands, to set the Church in a Flame.

I shall, Sir, give you a Sample of each, though I could easily multiply.

I shall begin with George Fox. (See his Book News out of the North, Pages 18, 19, 27, 31, 38.) 'Sound the Trumpet, sound an Alarm. Call up to the Battle; gather together for Destruction, draw the Sword, hew down all the Powers of the Earth, slay Baal; Baalim must be slain; all the Hirelings must be turned out of the Kingdom; and thou Beast (that is, the Civil Government) 'and thou False Prophet (that is, the Church, and all that differ from them) must into the Fire and Lake; the Lord hath spoken it; and so on. This Book of George Fox's was thus directed; To the Heads of this Nation, and all the Dominions of the Earth, Nations, Kingdoms, every where in all the World; to you Kings, Princes, Dukes, Rulers, Judges, Justices, &c. And on the Title-Page thus; News coming up out of the North, sounding towards the South, written from the Mouth of the Lord, from one who is naked, and stands naked before the Lord, cloathed with Righteousness, whose Name is not known in the World, risen up out of the North, which was prophesied of, but now it is fulfilled. Printed 1654. Re printed 1655. (See Bugg, Folio 74.) Now, Sir, is not George Fox as great a Prophet as Lodowick Muggleton? Yet the latter doom'd the former to the Pit of Hell, as you have heard already.

The next is Muggleton, who thus delivers himself (p.38. of the Transcendent Spiritual Treatise) 'All Reprobates, (that is, all those that are not of Muggleton's Opinion) 'both Rich and Poor, shall bow down unto the false Idolatrous Worship, set up by Heathen Magistrates and their false Prophets, the National Priests, who call themselves Christian Magistrates, and Christian Ministers, and are blindly called so by the People also; and yet both these People together persecute with the Sword of Steel all spiritual Christians, under the Name and Title of Blasphemers, Seducers, Heresie, Deceivers of the People, and such like; because the spiritual Christian cannot bow down unto that

Antichristian Form of Worship, set up by those Carnal Magistrates and their Carnal Ministers aforesaid; who being both Lovers of the Glory of this World, loving to be honoured as God, for that cursed heathenist Idol Worship, from their own Invention, set up to deceive themselves, and those appointed to Damnation with them. Wherefore the Dragon Magistrates, and the False Prophet the Serpent-Ministers, that commit spiritual Fornication together, and all those of their own Spirits, shall every one of them, in the Day of the Lord's Vengeance, burn in their Spirits, and Bodies together, as a Lake of Fire; those Spirits and Bodies that they shall appear with in the Resurrection, shall be the Lake of spiritual Fire and Brimstone, that by the Decree of the Lord Jesus shall burn together to all Eternity. And then Muggleton applies several Places of Scripture as fulfilled. 'And those mine Enemies that would not that I should reign over them, bring them, and slay them before me. Go ye Cursed into Everlasting Fire; Tophet is ordained of old. And (Rev. 21. 8.) But the Fearful and Unbelieving, and the Abominable, and Murderers, Whoremongers, and Sorcerers, or Astrologers, and Idolaters, and all Lyers, (that is, every one that is not a Muggletonian) shall have their Part in the Lake which burneth with Fire and Brimstone, which is the second Death. Now view this Looking-glass instead of Muggleton's; and if you are without Prejudice, you'll be of my Opinion, that Muggleton damns all the World, except his own blasphemous Sect: And that was my Business to shew you; which I hope, I have done to your intire Satisfaction.

And now, Sir, I shall present unto you the Muggletonian Articles, drawn up by John Saddington (extracted from Muggleton's Transcendent Spiritual Treatise, and some short Remarks on them, to shew their heretical and blasphemous Notions.) The Title of them is thus, viz. Articles of true Faith, depending upon the Commission of the Spirit; drawn up into 48 Heads, by John Saddington, an ancient Believer, for the Benefit of our Believers, who now are, or hereafter shall come to believe; and to confound all Despisers, that say, We (that is, the Muggletonians) know not what we believe. 1676. And transcrib'd by ---out of his Copy, 1692.

'Here I have written (says John Saddington; your Limehouse Prophet will tell you who he was, where he dwelt, and of what Trade; it's very likely a Taylor, or Shoe-maker, or of some such like Profession) 'the Articles of my Faith; wherein I do believe, and will witness to be true, with the Death of my Soul, if it be requir'd of me. Therefore let not the Words of any Canaanitish Devil, scoffing Ishamel, prophane Esau, or railing Rabshakeh, be credited, where they visibly belie the Believers of the Witnesses of the Spirit, in saying, They do own neither God nor Devil; or when they do cast any other scandalous Reproaches contrary to Truth, upon us that truly know God.

Now, Sir, I have this Favour to beg of you, if I endeavour to tell you the Truth, not to account me a Canaanitish Devil, or a scoffing Ishmael, or a prophane Esau, or a rattling Rabshakeh; But the greatest Favour I beg of you, is this, viz. That you prevent my being put under the Ban of your Prophet. This you think a sad Curse, whatever I think of it. But if I should be so unhappy, I am resolv'd to put my self under the Protection of the Great Almighty Father, Son and Holy Ghost; and he will give his Angels Charge of me, to keep me in all my Ways. Then I shall not value the Curse of any Muggletonian; For whom God curseth, is cursed; and whom he blesseth, is blessed; under whose Wings I shall be safe from all the Fiery Darts of the Wicked.

In the Name of the ever Glorious Trinity, three Persons and one God, I now proceed to lay down every Article, and give distinct (but short) Remarks on it.

ARTCLE 1.

I Do sincerely believe, that there is a God, full of spiritual Glory, above, and beyond the Stars.

REMARK.

What is this God of spiritual Glory? Is he one Essence in three Persons, Father, Son, and Holy Ghost? Not one Word of this. And why beyond the Stars? Is not God Omnipresent, every where? I am sure, I am told so in the Scripture; and those Sacred Records I believe, rather than such a Blasphemer as Saddington or Muggleton. As (Prov. 19.3.) The Eyes of the Lord are in every Place, beholding the Evil and the Good. I hope, Saddington don't think, that Evil is with God beyond the Stars. That can't be: For Old Muggleton has already plac'd them in the Lake of Fire and Brimstone. And Holy David (Ps. 139.6, 7, 8, 9) speaking of God, he says, Whither shall I go from thy Spirit, or whither shall I go from thy Presence? If I climb up into Heaven, thou art there; if I go down to Hell, thou art there also. (I hope, Saddington don't think Hell beyond the Stars) If I take the Wings of the Morning, and remain in the uttermost Parts of the Sea, even there also shall thy Hand lead me, and thy right Hand shall hold me up, &c. Now Saddington has stole his Notion of a God beyond the Stars, from Epicurus of old; who asserted, that God was confined to Heaven, and did not concern himself with the Lower World.

ARTICLE 2.

I do believe, that God is a God of Substance; and that that most Glorious, most Wise and Almighty God, that is so often spoken of in Holy Scripture, was a spiritual glorious Body in Form of a Man, from all Eternity.

REMARK

>Thus God is a Substance (if not taken in a gross material Sense) I agree: and that he is most Wise and Glorious, is true. But that he is in the Shape of a Man, is the Old Heresie of the Anthropomorphites: That is, they supposed, that God had Arms, Eyes, Feet, &c. because so represented in Scripture; which only spoke ad capsum: For the Jews were Persons of gross Intellectuals. This Heresie I have spoken of in another Place, and shall not now repeat.

ARTICLE 3.

>I do believe, that the most Wise God did create the Angels of the Dust above the Stars, with glorious Spiritual Bodies in Form like himself.

REMARK

>That God created the Angels, I agree: But what John Saddington means, of Dust above the Stars, passes my Understanding. The Place above the Stars is the Place of God's Special Residence, and will be the Place of Angels and happy Souls to all Eternity. But John's Philosophy of Dust above the Stars, is like the Ratcliff Philosopher, who takes the Sun to be no bigger than a Chedder-Cheese, and the Stars no bigger than Candles of Eight in the Pound. God created the Angels as he did the World, of Nothing. That Angels have Spiritual Bodies in Form like God himself, as you have heard already, is downright Blasphemy. 'Tis true, that Angels, by God's Order, do assume sometimes aerial Bodies, to serve the Purposes of God: For they are ministring Spirits (says St. Paul) sent forth to minister to them that shall be Heirs of Salvation.

ARTICLE 4.

>I do believe, that the Creator did with-hold the Spiritual Food of Inspiration from one of those glorious Angels which he had created; and then, for want of that Spiritual Food, which kept his Nature in Obedience to his Creator, he immediately began to imagine with himself high and lofty Thoughts against God his Creator.

REMARK.

>If this does not make God the Author of Sin, I am much mistaken: and else why should God with hold his Spiritual Food of Inspiration? This Article is a gross Description of Lucifer, and

not at all to the Purpose: For 'twas Pride, Malice, and Ambition that made a Devil, as they do a Haeretick; and that 'twas his own Fault, not God's, that from an Angel of Light, he became a Friend of Darkness.

ARTICLE 5.

I do believe, that that Angel did think himself more fit to rule over his Fellow-Creatures, than God, his Creator, was. For with Pride and Presumption that Angel became accursed in himself; and for his Rebellion did God afterwards fling him down into this World, and call him a Devil, a Serpent, a Dragon, a roaring Lion, and such like.

REMARK

There is no great matter amiss in this Article; and so I shall let it pass, having spoken to it in the Remark before.

ARTICLE 6.

I do believe, that Earth and Water were from Eternity; but without Form, until such time as the most Wise God and create them into formable Bodies.

REMARK

This is contradictory to the Mosaick Account (Gen. 1.1) where it is said, That in the Beginning God created the Heaven and the Earth. Now according to my Philosophy, Water and Earth make the Globe; and these were made by God. Moses was bred up in all the Learning of Egypt; and I hope, it may be asserted, without any Affront, that he has as much (I am sure forty times more) Philosophy as Muggleton and his accursed Crew. This Doctrine smells of Epicurus's Atoms; or else was stole from Aristotle, who asserted the Eternity of the World, and yet he asserted a First Mover. But Saddington will have Earth and Water, like the old Philosopher Thales, to be Eternal, against Sense, Reason, Scripture, and Learned Men in all Ages of the World.

ARTICLE 7.

I do believe, that God did create Adam and Eve of the Dust of this Earth, and then breathed into him the Breath of Life, which became a Living Soul in Adam; and then was Adam in the Form of God, tho' not so glorious.

REMARK

> By God, Saddington believes One Person in One Essence; which is Haeresie. That Eve was made of the Dust of the Earth, is not consonant with the Mosaick Account: Where 'tis said, Gen 2.2, 22) And the Lord God caused a deep Sleep to fall upon Adam, and he slept, and he took one of his Ribs, and closed the Flesh instead thereof; and the Rib which the Lord God had taken from Man, made he, or builded, as 'tis in the Margent, a Woman, and brought her to the Man. That Adam was the Image of God, is granted; but not in respect of a Corporal Figure of God. This is the Old Haeresie of the Anthropomorphites spoken of already.

ARTICLE 8.

> I do believe, that Adam was created so pure, that Death could not have siez'd on him, had he continu'd in his created Purity.

REMARK

> There is nothing amiss in this, only 'tis crudely express'd. Moses tells us, that they fell into Sin by eating the forbidden Fruit, which was prohibited by God. The Old Serpent betrayed them, and told them, that if they would eat, they should become Gods; and by this Cheat they brought Sin and Death upon them and their Posterity.

ARTICLE 9.

> I do believe, that as soon as Adam had sinned, then did Death enter into this World, and arrest with such a great Action of Debt, that neither Soul nor Body could escape out of his Hands: for both had sinned, and so both were carried to the Prison of the Grave.

REMARK

> That Death enter'd into the World for our first Parents Transgression, is true; and I believe, not upon the Reputation of John Saddington, but upon one greater than he, even St. Paul (Rom. 5.12) As by one Man Sin entred into the World, and Death by Sin; and so Death passed upon all Men, for that all have sinned. It rejoyces me to find the least Spark of Christian Religion among the Muggletonians: But if there be but a Gleam of Truth, 'tis soon obscur'd with Error and Haeresie; as here, when Saddington says, that both Soul and Body were carried to the Prison of the Grave. That the Soul dies, and lies in the Grave, is an Old Haeresie held by some Anabaptists as well as

Muggletonians. But 'tis a notorious Lye. (Eccles. 12.7.) Then (says Solomon, the Wisest of Men) shall the Dust return to the Earth, and the Spirit, that is, the Soul, shall return to God that gave it. And (Mat. 10.28.) Our Blessed Lord says, Fear not them that kill the Body, but are not able to kill the Soul. But rather fear him which is able to destroy both Soul and Body in Hell. Hell in this Place does not signifie the Grave, but the Place of Eternal Torment; as Dr. Hammond assures us. The Soul is immaterial and immortal, and does continue for ever, either in Eternal Joy or Eternal Misery.

ARTICLE 10.

I do believe, when God said to Adam, Increase and multiply; and when he said, Let every Seed bring forth its own Body; then did that wise Creator give Power to all Seed, both in Man and Beast, in Herbs and Trees, to bring forth their own Body, without any more additional Help from him.

REMARK

The latter Part of the Article strikes at the Providence of God: For his Conservation is a continued Creation. In him we live, move, and have our Being, says St. Paul; and 'tis by his General Providence, that every thing has a Being: and how dares this Infidel deny it, that every Herb and Tree, &c. proceed without any more additional Help from God?

ARTICLE 11.

I do believe, that God created the Sun, Moon and Stars, and placed them in the Firmament of Heaven, for Lights, and for Seasons; and appointed every one his Work and Office: And as God commanded them at the first, so still do they supply this World with all manner of Weather, viz. Heat and Cold, Rain, Snow, &c. without troubling the Creator at the least.

REMARK

Here's another Denial of God's Providence. Does this silly Reasoner think, that God does oversee the Creation, and can be so foolish as to imagine, that God cannot alter the Course of Nature? What thinks he of the Sun and Moon's standing still in Joshua's time in the Valley of Ajalon? Draughts, and Cold, and Tempests are commonly sent by God to punish a sinful People; and we pray God to deliver us from Tempest, Plague, Pestilence and Famine. To what purpose, if God does not govern and alter the Affairs of the Lower World? This Article smells strong of Atheism; and 'tis time to go out of the Stench of it.

ARTICLE 12.

I do believe, that the Souls of all Men since Adam, are generated, and come forth of the Loins of their Fathers with their Bodies; and therefore are as mortal as their Bodies, and must lie in the Earth with their Bodies till the Resurrection Day.

REMARK

That the Soul is generated, that Homo generat hominem, is an old Haeresie in Philosophy. The Soul is infused into the Body when formed. As to the latter part of this Article, I have spoken already, and shall not repeat it.

ARTICLE 13.

I do believe, that the Tree of Life, and the Tree of Knowledge of Good and Evil which Moses spake and wrote of, were no wooden Trees growing out of the Ground.

REMARK

If they were not of Wood, what were they? and that he tells in the 14th and 15th Articles, which I shall join both further.

ARTICLES 14,15.

I do believe, that the Tree of Life which Moses wrote of, was the same God that created the World.
I do believe, that the Tree of Knowledge of Good and Evil was the Serpent-Angel which God cast out of Heaven down to this Earth for his Presumption.

REMARK

This is the wildest Enthusiasm I ever heard of; and does not deserve an Answer. All Commentators are of another Opinion: and amongst all the Haeresies of the Ancients, I never met with this: For I believe (and why should I not believe as well as Saddington?) it came spank new out of the Devil's Forge, by his Servant Muggleton, or his Under-strapper Saddington. I could believe, that the Moon was made of Green Cheese, and that the Old Moons were cut into Stars, as soon as believe these two Articles: and since I cannot believe this Exposition, I'll reject it.

ARTICLE 16.

> I do believe, that the Out-cast Angel was the Serpent that tempted Eve, and that he was at the same time a spiritual Body in the Form of Adam.

REMARK

> How's that, a Serpent, and yet in a Human Form? That's strange indeed! The Mosaical History asserts it to be a Serpent, and there's no doubt but it was the Devil; the Devil cast out, says John. As if by one was expell'd Heaven: Whereas Lucifer had a great Gang with him, all of which were expell'd Heaven. (See Rev. 12.4) I cannot think that the Devil appear'd to Eve in the Shape of a Serpent that was not a tempting Form, to pervert her: But I fully agree with the Notion of some Learned Men, that the Devil assumed the Form of a Glorious Seraphim, which charmed and consequently deluded her. (See Dr. Patrick and Dr. Kidder on the Place.)

ARTICLE 17.

> I do believe, that the out-cast Angel, or Serpent-Tree of Knowledge of Good and Evil, did enter into the Womb of Eve, and Dissolve his spiritual Body into Seed; which Seed Died and Quickned again in Eve.

REMARK

> A Serpent-Tree to enter the Womb of Eve, is News indeed, and strange Divinity; and what Absurdities are too great for a Hot Enthusiastick Brain? The rest is obscene. But the Mosaical Account is rational. By our First Parents Transgression Sin entr'd into the World: Cain was the First Fruits of Sin; and David says, I was conceived in Iniquity and Sin. By their Sin Original Righteousness was deprav'd, and our Faculties impaired; and we have no occasion to repair to Muggleton and his Disciple for a Bawdy Solution.

ARTICLE 18.

> I do believe, that Eve brought forth her First born Son of the Devil, and the very Devil himself.

REMARK

> The Devil sure was in Eve, or else she could never bring him forth. The Scripture says, 'twas Cain: He was a wicked Person,

but surely not the Devil himself. We find when a Man is in the Dark, how oft he stumbles. The Cloud thickens, and Absurdity upon Absurdity arises; and I should be guilty of one, if I should stand to confute them.

ARTICLE 19.

I do believe, there is no other Devil but Man and Woman, since the Devil became Seed in the Womb of Eve, and cloathed himself with Flesh and Blood.

REMARK

Nay, if the Case be thus, as Saddington says, there's no Fear of dwelling in Eternal Flames with the Devil and his Angels. No Devil but Man and Woman, that's rare indeed, if John's Philosophy is true: But Holy Scripture says, that Satan fell from Heaven, and is now Prince of the Air, and hereafter will be doom'd with all Apostates, to live for ever in Hell-Fire. Hell and its Torments are not to be play'd with; and the Devil, tho' diminish'd to a Man and Woman, will not lose an Inch of his Authority, as I am sure you shall find to your Cost.

ARTICLE 20.

I do believe, that Cain was not the Son of Adam, tho' he was the Son of Eve.

REMARK

If this be true, I believe that Adam was the first Cuckold in the whole World. Well, 'tis strange to see some Mens Divinity. I never till now, thought Eve had been so bad a Woman, as to be guilty of the Sin of Adultery, and to make an ugly Fiend her Bed-fellow; but perhaps he lay with her in the Shape of a beautiful Tree, and so forth. After all, Scripture gives another Account (as Gen. 4.1.) Adam knew his Wife, and she conceived and bare Cain, and said, I have gotten a Man from the Lord. She took him for the Messiah, as some Commentators assert.

ARTICLE 21.

I do believe, that the Seed of the Woman is the Generation of Faithful People, which proceed from the Loyns of Seth, reckon'd as the Son of Adam, who was the Son of God.

REMARK

> I do believe, that you, John, and all the Muggletonian Crew, do believe that you are the Children of Seth, Adam and God. Credat Judeas, non ego. I am so far from believing you and the Muggletonians to be Christians, that I take you to be the greatest Haereticks that ever infested the Christian Church; and the Church that you belong to, is the Synagogue of Satan.

ARTICLE 22.

> I do believe, that the Seed of the Woman, and the Seed of the Serpent, are two distinct Generations of Men and Women in this World.

REMARK

> We differ in our Creeds. I assert with the Scripture, that the Seed of the Woman was Christ, who bruis'd the Serpent's Heel; that is, Christ should, and as he did, destroy the Devil's Kingdom.

ARTICLE 23.

> I do believe, that the Seed of the Serpent is the Generation of Unbelievers, or reprobate Men and Women, which proceed from the Loins of cursed Cain, the Son of the Devil, and the first lying and murdering Devil that ever was.

REMARK

> Hey dey! was Cain the first Devil? Does this agree with the 18th Article? Was not the Serpent before Cain? And I believe, you Muggletonians do take all that differ from you, to be the Serpent's Generation of Unbelievers. We thank you, John, for your Favour.

ARTICLE 24.

> I do believe, those Men and Women, that blaspheme against God, and despise his Messengers, are those Angels which are said to be cast out of Heaven with the Devil their Father.

REMARK

> Just now 'twas one Devil cast out of Heaven, and now many. Those that blaspheme God and his Messengers (that is, Muggletonians) are all those that write or speak against them;

and I my self, in their Opinion, am one of those Angels, cast out of Heaven with the Devil. I give you thanks.

ARTICLE 25.

I do believe, that the Difference and Opposition, which are set between the Believers and Unbelievers, concerning their Faith in God, is the Enmity which God said he would put betwixt the Serpent and the Woman, and betwixt his Seed and her Seed.

REMARK

By believers, John Saddington means Muggletonians; and by Unbelievers, all that differ from them: This is plain. There is nothing else worth noting in this Article.

ARTICLE 26.

I do believe, that Moses, David, Isaiah, Jeremiah, and several others, were true Prophets, and Penmen of Holy Writ.

REMARK

This the Holy Catholick Church all over the World believes, as well as the Muggletonians. And there needs no more Words to prove it.

ARTICLE 27.

I do believe, that God took up Moses and Elias, bodily into Heaven, and there glorified them, to represent his glorious Person whilst he went the sore Journey in the Flesh.

REMARK

That God took up Moses bodily into Heaven, is repugnant to the Mosaical Account; as Deut. 34. 5, 6. So Moses, the Servant of the Lord, died there in the Land of Moab, according to the Word of the Lord. And He, that is, God, buried Him, that is, Moses, in the Valley in the Land of Moab, over against Beth-peor; but no Man knoweth of his Sepulchre unto this Day. Now is not Joshua, an inspir'd Prophet by God, to be credited before a Crack-brain'd Enthusiastical Person. That Elias was translated into Heaven, the Scripture mentions, but not to represent God's glorious Person, whilst he went that sore Journey in the Flesh: For 'twas God, the Word, the second Person of the ever glorious Trinity, which John Saddington and all the Muggletonians deny, that assumed the Flesh, by being conceived by the Holy Ghost (which they deny) and being born of the Virgin Mary, as our Creed has it.

ARTICLE 28.

I do believe, that God gave Moses and Elias full Power to govern Heaven and Earth, for the time He, that is, God, was in the World.

REMARK

This is downright Blasphemy: For God the Father kept his Residence in the highest Heaven, and committed no such Power to Moses and Elias; and sent his Eternal Son, the Word, to assume Flesh in this World. You see here constantly in the Muggletonian Haereticks, that they mean one Person in one Essence, which is Haeresie.

ARTICLE 29.

I do believe, that Moses and Elias were those two Angels, which were to watch over Christ, when he was in Mortality, lest at any time he should dash his Foot against a Stone.

REMARK

These Muggletonians sure are deep Philosophers, and have got the Power of transmuting not only Metals, but also Prophets, into Angels: for Moses and Elias, Article 26. were Prophets: Now in this they are Angels Let not the Papists hereafter boast of Transubstantiation; these Muggletonians far exceed them. For my part I'd neither believe the one nor the other; but stand fixed and firm to the Catholick Faith. That the Angels ministred to our Blessed Lord in his great Agony, the Sacred Scripture testifies. But I no where read in that Sacred Volume, that Moses and Elias were appointed Officers to assist in his last Moments; 'tis certain they were with him in his Transfiguration on the Mount, but that's nothing to the Purpose. Now, if the Muggletonians pretend the History of the Transfiguration to be his last Agony, they'll assume again their Doctrine of Transmutation.

ARTICLE 30.

I do believe, that the most Glorious and Wise Creator did leave his Throne of Glory for a Time, and came down into this World, and enter'd into the Womb of a Virgin, and there died; or laid down his Immortality, by dissolving into Seed, and immediately quicken'd again into pure Mortality.

REMARK.

Here's a whole Heap of Blasphemy; the Particulars of which must be spoken to. God the Father did not leave the Throne of Glory; but sent his eternal Son into the World as before spoken. That God the Father enter'd into the Womb of the Virgin, is high Blasphemy: and there died, that's worse: For God cannot die. And this was the old Haeresie of the Patripassians, now reviv'd by Muggleton. That Immortality should dissolve into Seed, is what that has not a Name, to be given, 'tis so blasphemous. And was quicken'd again into pure Mortality: What's the meaning of this wretched Stuff? Oh John, Did God the Father become a Man after his Dissolution into Seed? Thou wert then in the Gall of Bitterness; and I am afraid, thou art gone, if dead, into irreversible Perdition.

ARTICLE 31.

I do believe, that the Christ Jesus which was born of the Virgin-Wife, was both the Son of God, and the Everlasting Father and Creator of all things that were created.

REMARK.

The Son of God, the Everlasting Father, as the Messiah is called, Isa. 9.6. assumed Flesh; but the Child Jesus as Flesh, was not the Son of God, and Everlasting Father (for the Divinity was united to the Human Nature) Christ is called the everlasting Father, as 'tis in our Translation; but in the Hebrew 'tis Father of the Age. The Word עד sometimes signifies a time limited, sometimes Eternity, as he is the Author of Eternal Life. So Vatablas and many others. According to the Hebrew way of speaking, he is called Father; that is, the Author of any Matter. So Forrerins and others. But Sir, I shall not trouble you with any farther Quotations. 'Tis enough to shew, that Everlasting Father in the Translation, is not God the Father, the first Person in the Glorious Trinity.

ARTICLE 32.

I do believe, that the Flesh of Christ was the Flesh of God, and that the Blood of Christ was the Blood of God.

REMARK.

If you mean, John, that the Godhead assum'd Flesh, that the Second Person of the Trinity assum'd Human Nature, and that the Blood of Christ was the Blood of God, as he was the Logos, the Word; for so 'tis called in Scripture, Acts 20.28. Church of God which he hath purchased with his own Blood; all this is true of God the Son, but not of God the Father. That the Flesh of Christ is the Flesh of God, is downright Blasphemy; but that God the Son assum'd Flesh, is true Christianity.

ARTICLE 33.

I do believe, that Christ laid down his Godhead Life for a Moment, when the Graves gave up their Dead, and the Vail of the Temple was rent in twain.

REMARK.

Christ did not lay down his Godhead Life, as 'tis oddly express'd; but the Human Nature suffered, not the Divine, as the Muggletonians blasphemously assert.

ARTICLE 34.

I do believe, that no other Blood, but the Blood of the Eternal God could wash away the Sins of the Elect.

REMARK.

The Eternal God the Father, as you mean, has no Blood: And as to God the Son, I refer you to the Remark on Article 32; not obtundere aurea, and to repeat.

ARTICLE 35.

I do believe, that Christ's Death was so effectual, that all those for whom he died, will be raised again to Eternal Life and Glory.

REMARK.

He means by the Phrase, All those for whom Christ died, only Muggletonians; and I believe, that Christ dy'd for the whole World: So the Scripture assures us: He became a Ransom for all. And if People will not embrace Christianity, 'tis their own Fault, and not his. The Terms of the New Covenant are Faith and Repentance, which are offered to all; and if all will not receive that Covenant, they must blame themselves only for their Perdition.

ARTICLE 36.

I do believe, that Christ is a quickening Spirit, and that he did quicken out of Death to Life, by his own Power.

REMARK.

That Christ is a quickening Spirit, is asserted in Scripture; and that he does it, is from the Power committed by the Father. But I am to learn what Saddington means by Christ. Does he suppose the Human Nature only, or the Divine united to it? Or does he mean by Christ, One Person in One Essence? He ought to explain himself.

ARTICLE 37.

I do believe, that the Ever blessed Soul or Spirit, which in Holy Writ is called, the Godhead, did quicken in the Body of Flesh and Bone of Christ, which was laid in the Sepulchre, and did raise it again from Death to Everlasting Life.

REMARK. The Godhead is never called in Scripture the Ever-blessed Soul: And what does John mean by Holy Writ, but the Works of Muggleton? 'Twas the Godhead that raised the Body of Christ.

ARTICLE 38.

I do believe, that the Blessed Body of Flesh and Bone of Christ, neither did, nor could see Corruption, or be left in the Grave, because it was a pure mortal Body, without Sin, Spot or Blemish before his Death.

REMARK.

This I believe too, but not upon John's Reputation; for the Scripture asserts (Ps. 16.12) Thou shalt not leave my Soul in Hell, neither shalt thou suffer thy Holy One to see Corruption.

ARTICLE 39.

I do believe, that Christ was visibly seen by the Apostles and his private Believers, after his Resurrection.

REMARK.

There's nothing amiss in this Article, if by Christ is meant that Body which was raised by his own Power, as the Scripture asserts in many Places.

ARTICLE 40.

I do believe, that Christ was visibly seen to ascend into Heaven, with the same Body in which he suffer'd Death, and rose again.

REMARK.

The Holy Scripture asserts the same, as we read in the Acts, Chap. 1.9.

ARTICLE 41.

I do believe, that the Apostles Doctrine and Declaration of Christ is true.

REMARK.

If by the Apostles John means those that were chosen by Christ our Lord, this Article is true: But if he means, as I think he does, John Reeve and Lodowick Muggleton, 'tis as false as God is true. I am forced sometimes thus to distinguish, to discover the Subtilty of these Impostors and Blasphemers.

ARTICLE 42.

I do believe, that the Spiritual Godhead, or Godhead Spirit, which was before any thing was created, and which created all Things that was created, is now in Heaven cloathed with the blessed Body of Christ Jesus Glorified.

REMARK.

What Jargon is this Spiritual Godhead, or Godhead Spirit? Godhead supposes Spiritual. I hope, he does not think of a Corporal Godhead: and Godhead Spirit is a Phrase I never met with in Scripture. That the Eternal God was before created Beings, and that he was Creator of them, the Catholick Church owns. But, John, do you remember your Sixth Article, where you believe, that Earth and Water were from Eternity; and here in this Article they were created? Eternity and Creation smells something of a Contradiction. I perceive, John, you believe Contradictions; or else your Memory, as your Faith, deceives you. That Christ in his Human Nature joyned to the Divine, is now in Heaven, the Catholick Church believes, and none but Haereticks deny it: And that he will come from Heaven to judge the Quick and the Dead at the Last Day; against which God prepare us all, that we may enter with him into Glory.

ARTICLE 43.

> I do believe, that God will raise the Bodies and Souls of all Men, out of their Graves; some to an everlasting and glorious Life, and other some, to an ever-dying painful Death, which will never end.

REMARK.

> That Souls die and lie in the Grave, hath been spoken to already, as an Old Haeresie. That there shall be a general Resurrection, the Catholick Church believes. The Prophet Daniel (12.3.) declares that many (a Hebraism taken for all, of them that sleep in the Dust of the Earth) shall awake, some to everlasting Life, and some to Shame, and everlasting Contempt; and our ever-blessed Lord assures us (Matt. 25.36.) that these shall go into everlasting Punishment, but the Righteous into Life Eternal. Where the Greek Word is the same in both Clauses.

ARTICLE 44.

> I do believe, that God did speak to John Reeve, to the Hearing of the Ear; and that he did chuse John Reeve to be the last Messenger to this unbelieving World; and that God did give him Lodowick Muggleton to be his Mouth, to declare the Mind of God to us, in this Age.

REMARK.

> The Apocalypse, John, has crazed many, both before, and after John Reeve, whom, with Lodowick, I take to be two impudent Blasphemers; and Muggleton to be a Mouth to Reeve is a prophane Allusion to Aaron and Moses.

ARTICLE 45.

> I do believe, the Doctrine and Declaration of John Reeve and Lodowick Muggleton, to be as true, as the Doctrine declar'd by Moses, the Prophets and Apostles of old.

REMARK.

> See the Insinuation of Saddington. He sets upon the Level two ignorant, simple bold Enthusiasts, no Workers of Miracles, no Speakers of Tongues; with the great Moses, and the inspir'd Prophets and Apostles: And as I believe the Prophets and Apostles to be sent by God; so I believe, that Reeve and

Muggleton were sent by the Evil Spirit, to vent their Blasphemies, and disturb the Peace of the Church of God: But they are gone to their Place to receive their Doom.

ARTICLE 46.

I do believe, there will be no Salvation at the Day of the Lord, for those that were in the Time of Moses and the other Prophets, who did not lay hold on God's Promises, made unto them by his Prophets, when they prophesied, that God would send a Son, a Saviour, or become a Child himself, to redeem his People.

REMARK.

Who made you, John, Censor Judeorum & Gentilium? God will dispose of them, as he in his infinite Wisdom thinks fit: 'Tis the best way to make sure of your own Salvation, and not to censure others, as you and Muggleton do, viz. damn the whole World, except your own miscreant Sect; of which I have told you before. A God the Father, to become a Child himself, is the old Haeresie of the Patripassians, reviv'd by Muggleton; (of which, before) and you are at it again with your censuring in the next Article.

ARTICLE 47.

I do believe, there will be no Salvation for those which were in Christ's Time, who heard of him, but could not believe him to be the Son of God, and Saviour of the World.

REMARK.

I tell you, John, you are an uncharitable Man. Who made you a Judge, to pass Sentence? Where's your Commission, given to you and Muggleton? Frantick Dreams and Delusions, and Enthusiastic Imaginations, will never pass with me for Prophets. Those that God cursed are cursed; and those Secrets belong to God. How durst proud Man, a Lump of Dust and Ashes, set himself up for a Judge; 'tis a Province too assuming, to proclaim one's self a Prophet, without a sure and certain Mission from God, which will never appear that you and Muggleton had.

ARTICLE 48.

Lastly, I believe, that there will be no Salvation for those, which are in these our Days, which have heard of the Witness of the Spirit, and have seen or heard their Writings, and yet cannot believe, that Christ is the only wise God, Father, Son and Holy Ghost, in one single Person glorified.

REMARK.

The whole Catholick Church, that does not believe that the Father, Son, and Holy Ghost, is one single Person glorified, is by Saddington and Muggleton, doom'd to the Pit of Hell. This is a bold and aspiring Presumption to damn such a Number of Men, that do not believe the Delusions of Muggleton. From whose Delusions, God deliver us all. His Curses we value not, and his Execiations with a Vengeance have fallen on his Head. You now see, Sir, what a desperate Condition you are in at present; therefore come out from among these accursed Sinners, otherwise you will partake of their Sin here, and their Condemnation hereafter. I have us'd as gentle a Method, as the Cause will bear, with you: I have not strain'd any of Saddington's Articles beyond their true Meaning and Intention; I have given very plain Remarks, and have fitted them to your Capacity; and the good Lord open your Eyes, that you may see the wondrous Things of his Law; and God grant, that you may turn from Darkness (your present Darkness of Muggletonianism) to Light, and from the Power of Satan (in which you are at present involv'd) unto God. There will be Joy on Earth, and in Heaven also by the Holy Angels, at your Conversion. Our Blessed Saviour assures us (Luke 15.7.) That Joy shall be in Heaven over one Sinner that repenteth, more than over Ninety and Nine Persons which need no Repentance. You, Sir, are the Prodigal mentioned in that Chapter, that has left your Father, the Blessed Jesus, Head of the Catholick Church; and have gone astray among those vile Haereticks the Muggletonians: Repent in time, lest otherwise you perish in your Sins: Take a noble Resolution, and desert from the Tents of those wicked Men; and say, I will arise and go to my Father, and thus bespeak him; Father, Lord Jesus, I have sinned against Heaven, and before thee, thou Eternal Son of God, whom I have blasphemed, and whose Divinity, I like a Wretch, have deny'd, and am no more worthy to be called thy Son. Read over the whole Chapter, and God grant you a true Sense and Sight of your Sins. Make your Peace with Christ, and be re-united once more to his Church, from which by Apostacy you are fallen; and Christ Jesus, upon your true and hearty Repentance, will receive you into Favour; and you'll be easie here, and happy thereafter, and that to all Eternity; which God the Father, God the Son, and God the Holy Ghost, Three Persons in One Eternal Godhead, grant you the Salvation of your Immortal Soul, for which Christ died. I have now done, when I have desired you to read this plain Letter without Prejudice and Passion; and may you be so happy, as to be convinc'd; and then shall I have what I aim'd at; and that was the Salvation of your precious and immortal Soul. Now to God the Father, Son and Holy Ghost, I commit you, and am your hearty Friend in our common Saviour, God-Man,

J SHARPE.

October 3. 1716

N.B. I am very well assur'd, that after any one has declar'd for the Haeresie of Muggleton, all Books, nay, the very Sacred Scriptures, are exploded and rejected by him; except the Works of Muggleton, which are consulted by all of that accursed Miscreant's Sect.

FINIS.

Observations On Some Articles Of The Muggletonians Creed:

VIZ.

I. That Matter existed without Beginning
II. That a Good, and also an Evil Principle did eternally exist; and that the Devil had a Carnal Knowledge of Eve.
III. That God existeth in the Form of an old Man about six Feet high.
IV. That God became an infant
V. That whilst Jesus Christ was upon Earth, there was no God in Heaven.
VI. That when Jesus Christ died, God died; and there was then no God either in Heaven or on Earth. —
VII. That Muggleton and Reeves (two Sectaries, who liv'd in the time of OLIVER CROMWELL'S Protectorship,) were two Divinely inspired Prophets; from whose Direction we can only understand the true Sense of Scripture.

Proposed more immediately - To the Consideration of the PRINICPAL of the Modern *Muggletonians.*

Beloved, believe not every Spirit, but try the Spirits, whether they be of God — for God is not the Author of Confusion, but of Peace.

LONDON: Printed for the AUTHOR; And sold by R. HETT, at the *Bible* and *Crown* in the *Poultry, 1735.* [Price Six-Pence]

A Dedicatory Preface, To The Modern Muggletonians Principal

Sir,

THE several Opportunities I have had of hearing you deliver your Sentiments respecting the *particular Profession* you make, as being a Disciple of MUGGLETON and REEVES, has induced me to consider some of the grand Articles of you *Faith,* and, in the following manner, to give you my Opinion concerning them.

As far as I know, I have father'd nothing upon you as a Principle of you *Sect*, but what you have owned as such; nor have I intended to consider all the Peculiarities of your System; but only those more general *maxims* on which the Whole of your Scheme is supported.

If I have been so unfortunate as to have represented your Principles in a somewhat different Dress to what you would have done, you must excuse me; especially when I tell you, I have made use of no other Means of collecting the several Articles herein mentioned,. But only some Pieces of Conversation I have had with you, and some others of your Fraternity.

The World perhaps may condemn me, as having ill emply'd myself, since your Notions appear so extravagant that no other *Pen* has esteem'd you worth its Notice: but as I have has no ill Design, I hope, at least, for your candid Reflections, especially when I tell you that the two Motives, which principally led me hereunto, were a sincere Love for *Truth*, or a Desire of it spread in the World; and a concern for Men, more particularly for *you,* arising from an Apprehension of your being mistaken; which if so, and this should contribute to your Conviction thereof, would as a further Consequence, prevent your diligent Endeavours to propagate those your Mistakes; and thus would not only justify, but amply reward the little Trouble I have given my self, who am,

SIR
Your Friend and Servant
The AUTHOR

Obervations On Some Articles Of The Muggletonians Creed.

THE first Thing I shall consider, is, an Opinion, which, although not peculiar to the Sect called *Muggletonians*, is nevertheless a *Maxim,* on which they lay a considerable Stress; as,

I. I have heard them assert, *that* Matter *must have existed* without Beginning; *tho at the same time as an inert, and merely passive Principle, which in some Part of Duration began to be* modell'd *and* form'd by an eternal Active Principle.

In Answer to which I would observe, that we can form no Idea at all of *Matter,* distinct from, and exclusive of *Magnitude, Impenetrability,* and *Divisibility;* but if these are essential Properties of *Matter,* then *Matter,* as a Thing, or Being, *merely passive,* could not unbeginningly exist; because, it must then have existed with such Properties as do invariably imply *Design;* For *Magnitude, Impenetrability* and *Divisibility,* are such Properties as constantly render their *Subject* capable of being altered and changed, in it's very Mode and Form: And as no Account can be given, or Reason assigned, why any one Particle of *Matter* should have existed unbeginningly in one Form, more than in another; and, as it's possessing any one *Form* must certainly be the Effect of *Design*; therefore I conclude, that *Matter* could not exist eternally i.e. without Beginning.

But again; that *Matter* could have existed unbeginningly, as an inert, unactive Principle; and afterwards, or in some subsequent Part of Duration, could begin to be passive, i.e. begin to be wrought upon, will appear absurd, if we consider, that *Duration* applied to an eternal, unbeginning Being abstractedly considered, is Nonsense, and absolutely impertinent: Beside, the Difficulty of imagining, how this eternally independent Being should *begin* to be independent, is unsurmountable. On the other Hand, as we can discern in this inert, unactive *Matter* the evident Signatures of *Design* and *Contrivance,* to answer all the Purposes for which it is made use of, we may with infinitely less Difficulty suppose it to be Kind of *Effect, or Produce* of the unbeginning active Principle, and as such, disposed of by him at Pleasure.

But again; *Matter* could not exist eternally, as an unactive, inert Principle, because no *End* can be assigned for it's so eternally existing; but it must then have existed uselessly; which cannot (I think) be supported, of an eternal, independent Principle.

It may be replied, That we can form no Idea of the eternal *active Principle*, as existing without Beginning; which is certainly true: and it must be confessed, that was he such a Being, as we could form any adequate, or full Idea of, he would lose all Manner of Claim to those *Perfections* we so properly attribute to him; and could neither be *eternal* in his Duration, nor *infinite* in his Nature, or Being. Notwithstanding this, he is so far *discoverable,* as may be of Use and Advantage to us, even in this our State of Imperfection and Tryal: Nevertheless although we can form no determinate or clear Idea of *Unbeginningness,* yet from such Arguments which may, and often have been urged *á Posteriori,* we are certain, the *first Cause* could not begin to exist; which Conclusion is undoubtedly certain.

Nor is, what some assert, at all conclusive with me, *viz.* That God could not exert his Power without a *Subject*, on which he might exert it; since the *Notion* necessarily confines Deity, and introduces the Idea of God as a dependent Being; because it supposes, *something* must necessarily exist besides himself, to render him active, or without which he could not be an active Being! There is less Absurdity to me in imagining, that the *Power of God* could give Existence, or, in other Words, produce an *Ens* or Being; and if I say from nothing, though I can form no Idea of Non-entity, yet in the Notion there is *no Opposition*; in asmuch as *Nothing* cannot oppose: Nor am I capable of reducing such an Effect of the power of God to an *Absurdity*, much less to a *Contradiction.*

But again, let it be considered, that the Production of what we call *Life* and *Motion*, seems to be an *Effect* as stupendous as the *Creation* of inert, unactive Matter, or the giving it Existence; and therefore I see no Reason why we should boggle at the Notion of infinite Power effecting the *latter*, any more than the *former*; nor does there appear to be less *Wisdom* and *Power* necessary to the Support and Preservation of the Universe, than to the making, framing, and giving it being. But to proceed;

II. *The* Muggletonians *assert, That two different* Principles *did always, or eternally exist, viz A* good, *and also an* evil Principle; *and that the Devil had a carnal Knowledge of* Eve.

I have already observed, that one Notion of the modern Muggletonians is, *that Matter existed eternally,* altho' as an inert, unactive Thing, or Being; but if so, then this *evil Principle* could not have this unactive Thing as the Subject of its Existence; because that would destroy the Notion of its being inert; and unactive; nevertheless, they seem to assert, That it existed as distinct, or really, as the *good Principle,* or God existed: I shall therefore endeavour to evince the Falsity of this Opinion, or Tenet; and would observe, that two *Opposites* could not always have existed, except possessed of equal Capacities; and even then it appears to be mathematically false, because they must then mutually destroy each other, their *Forces* or

Observations on Some Articles 253

Influences being equal, but yet diametrically opposite and repugnant to each other: But if not equal in their Forces or Influences, one must have destroy'd the *other,* that other having be *unequal* in its Force, or Resistance: But *Good* and *Evil* are direct Contraries, and according to their degree of Impetus, or Influence do oppose, *repell*, and destroy each other; therefore they could not exist eternally.

Besides, *Evil,* moral *Evil,* could not exist but in a *Subject* capable of moral *Good*, or moral *Evil,* but the *First Cause of all Things* is not capable of both, He being invariably *good*; therefore *evil* must have been originated from a Subject capable of both; which Subject must have been no other than a *Creature*: consequently, *evil* was not unoriginated.

I add, without a Power of Choice either to do well or ill, no Creature can be esteem'd a moral Agent; or, in other Words, his Conduct can have no Connection with Rewards and Punishments: consequently the *Muggletonians* talk ridiculously, when they assert, "That a Part of Mankind, are the Spawn of the Devil, or the Produce and Offspring of a carnal Knowledge the Devil had of Eve: whilst others, viz. *Themselves*, are only and truly of the Seed of the Woman;" which must import thus much, (if they have any Meaning at all,) *viz.* That the Seed of the Devil are, and can only be guided and govern'd by this *evil Principle*; and that the other, *viz.* The Seed of the Woman, can only be influenced by the *good Principle*: Upon which Hypothesis, all *moral Agency* is destoy'd; because all Mankind are hereby put into a *Necessity* of belonging to, and being govern'd by, the one Principle, or the other.

As an Instance of the incredible Infatuation of this Sect, I will relate a Piece of Conversation which passed between *two* of these *Muggletonians;* my Information was from a Person then present, who heard one say to the other, upon some Injury that he had receiv'd from him, "That he, i.e. the injurious Person, was a *damn'd Rogue*; and also wished God to *damn* him! but, says he again, I know you can't be eternally *damn'd* because a *Muggletonian!*" although he had all along insisted upon his being one of the vilest of Men! But to proceed,

I must here again ask these Gentlemen, How they can, with any Justice to their reasonable Nature, imagine that the *Serpent*, or the *Devil* in the Serpent, could lye with Mother Eve, so as to cause her to conceive and bring forth the proper Offspring of such Conception, without some distinct *Characteristics* or Marks, by which it's *Sire* might be distinguished to be the *Serpent* or *Devil*; and not Adam? Or was there no Difference in *Specie* between Adam, and the Devil? On the contrary, we assuredly know, that all mixed *Copulations* and *Engenderings* are constantly discovered by the Foetus. On the other hand, how come these Gentlemen to know that either the *Devil*, or *Serpent*, were capable of such an *act* with *Eve?*

The Muggletonians further say, That the *Tree* of which Eve eat, called the *Tree of Knowledge of Good and Evil*, was her being overcome by the glorious Appearance the Devil made in the form of an Angel of Light, --- But the text says, That after the Woman had reason'd with the Serpent about the Prohibition, that she saw the Tree was good for Food, and that it pleas'd her Eyes, &c. insomuch as being sway'd by these Motives, she took thereof and did eat, and gave also unto her Husband with her, and he did eat: No, say the Muggletonians he did *lye with Eve*, which was his eating; as her's was lying with the Serpent; therefore I infer, that the Sin of Adam was his attending to the Law of his Make, and his comporting with the Command of God, *Be fruitful and multiply!* But in v.12, of the *3d of Genesis,* Adam said, She gave me of the *Tree*, and I did eat, i.e. according to the Muggletonians, either the *Devil*, or *Eve's Body* must be the *Tree*; and then it runs thus, She gave me of the *Devil* and I did eat; or else, She gave me her *Body,* and I did eat, i.e. I lay with her. Let it be observ'd, that the *Fruit* of which both ear, was the *same,* if the History be true; and the *Action* is described as the same in both likewise, *viz.* Eating; hence it lies upon the Muggletonians to prove, that if Eve's *Transgression* in eating the *forbidden Fruit*, was her Coition with the Devil, how could Adam be guilty of violating the same prohibition? The Muggletonian's appealing to the Account of the Virgin Mary's being over shaddow'd, for Proof of the Possibility of the Devil's lying with, or transmuting himself (as they call it) into Eve, so as to cause her to conceive; is altogether romantic! Because there is a manifest Difference between the *Power of God* being suppos'd to form a *Man* in the Womb of the Virgin; and the Supposition of an *evil Spirit* or Angel impregnating a Woman; inasmuch as it is highly improbable that that Rank or order of Beings, of which the Devil is here supposed to be, were ever made capable of propagating their own Species: But upon the supposition that the Devil actually did lye with Eve, he must yet be as capable of lying with any of her Daughters, and therefore might long ere this have exterminated or debauched the holy Seed. Not is any Muggletonian assur'd that his Wife may not become such a Prostitute to the Devil, and he himself be obliged to wear his Horns! (This remark is the more a *propos,* from the account Revelation gives us, of *Numbers of Angels* who left their first Stations, and were Confederates in the Apostasy)

How shocking must this be to every virtuous Woman, to imagine that she is equally expos'd with *Eve* to lose her Virginity by the Cunning of one or other of these Devils? Except she can suppose herself more Wise and Virtuous that *Eve* was; or, that these Devils are since become more chaste, or less capable!

Observations on Some Articles 255

Besides, how can it be prov'd that the Devil, supposed to be an immortal Spirit, should communicate a Property he had not, *viz.* Death, or Mortality? Much more rational is it to suppose with some, that the forbidden *Tree* was the *Serpent's Food,* or at least was in its own nature noxious and poisonous to an humane Body; and as such, upon the eating thereof, dispos'd the vital Fluids to such undue Fermentations, which eventually must destroy their Texture and Frame. And hence may we be able to find a very rational Sense of that Text, *as in Adam all died,* or became subject to Mortality by an hereditary Conveyance of a distemper'd Constitution; *so in Christ shall all be made alive,* i.e. be raised from the Dead.

I would further observe, that the Muggletonians seem to have introduced this monstrous Notion of the Devil's begetting Cain and of Cain's being a Devil, in order to account for the *Distinction of Characters* among Men, and the true Origin of Evil.

To obviate which Difficulty, let them please to consider, the Men appear to be universally possess'd of the same Kind of Soul that Adam at first was created with; i.e. a Soul or Mind capable of *chusing* or *refusing*; nor does it appear, that our State of Tryal differs from his in any respect for the worse, except it be the *ill Examples and instructions* of Parents Guardians and others with whom we converse in our immature Age, which makes the Difference. As to *moral evil,* or *Sin,* it is certain, as this is no other than a *transgression of a Law*; so this could not be convey'd or propagated by *Generation*; and Man must be the same he ever was as to his moral Capacities; altho' the Circumstances of his bodily Frame may be alter'd; and therefore they talk wildly, who assert that the guilt of any Action of Adam in a moral Sense can be either convey'd, or imputed to me. But if the Muggletonians Sense be a truth, I being a Son of Cain have his devilish Nature convey'd to me by which I am only capable of Evil; I and may hereupon possibly condemn the Author of my Nature as being wicked, but can no way censure or condemn my self; I being only what he has made me, or suffer'd another to make me.

But I would further observe, that no *Being* whatever could be constituted and made with *evil* in his Frame, inasmuch as every Creature is the Produce of *invariable Goodness*; therefore, upon the Supposition that the Devil could propagate his own Species by Generation, such Production would only partake of his Physical Nature, but could not possibly be a Devil, i.e. an immoral, vitious Creature, till by alike acquirements with his *Sire,* he had actually made himself so. Nor do I see how it can be made appear, that any Being whatsoever, can either implant or propagate *moral Evil* in any Subject, but by the actual Consent of that Subject.

III. *Another Notion the* Muggletonians *advance is, That GOD ALMIGHTY exists in the Form of an* Old gray-hair'd Man, about six feet high; *and that this bodily Shape of God, was the Model of the humane Structure; thus understanding* Moses, *as intimating to us when he says, That God made Man* in his own Image; *that the Resemblance here intended, was the Resemblance, which the eternal Shape or Figure of Man bore to the external Appearance, or Body of God the* Supreme Being.

I remark, that such an Imagination of God, would introduce an inextricable Labyrinth of Difficulties; as first, we should be naturally led to attribute *Age*, at the same Time we can by no Means apply any Measure of Duration to him; i.e. we can't say he is older to Day, than he was a thousand Years ago; or that he was younger when he laid the *Foundations of this Earth*, than he will be at the Day of the *Restitution* of all Things. *Again,* We should hereby be led to attribute a *Change* in his *Being*; at the same Time, we cannot imagine *absolute Perfection* capable of any; and of which the Scripture expressly asserts, That with him is not so much as the *Shaddow* of Change. *Again*, We should be led hereby to affix *Limitations* to his *Being,* because any Kind of Form or Shape would imply this; but if he possess *Immensity* and *Infinity* he is indescribable, and will admit no Representation. On the contrary, it appears with great Force of Reason to me, that the supreme Being can neither have *Age,* the *Likeness of Age,* or *Shape,* or *Figure* ascribed to him, whose glorious *Nature* and *Being*, the most exalted Intelligence can neither describe, nor fully understand; but whose moral Perfections, and Designs of Government, have been explained in the clearest Manner by the Man *Christ Jesus.*

I add more positively, GOD cannot be subject to any *Form* or *Figure*; because *Form* and *Figure* are only Accidents of Beings, and are in their own Nature variable; and therefore no Being whatever can resemble GOD, i.e. in his Being, or Nature conserved abstractly, for there can be no Description of, because no Bounds unto his Being! he fill by his Presence all Things, and is filled of none! Agreeable to which, I have heard of an honest Clergyman's being in Company with the late famous Mr. *Collins,* who, in the Run of Conversation was ask'd by Mr. *Collins, with a Sneer,* "If he could tell how *big* God Almighty was? Yes, replied the honest Man, I can tell how *big*, and how *little* he is: He is so *big,* that the *Heaven of Heavens* can't contain him! And so *little*, that he can dwell in an humble and contrite Soul!"

But to return: If God existed in the Form of a Man, as I said before, he would have *Accidents* attributed to him, which cannot be applied to a Being, without Beginning of Existence in Duration, or Limitation of Existence in Space (I leave it to the Metaphysicians, to discuss the grand Question, *viz.* Whether *Space,* be not a Property of Deity, in which all Beings exist?): But *Form* and *Figure* can belong only to Beings that are mutable and limited, they themselves being so, consequently cannot belong to God. I add, that it seems very preposterous, that Man should be represented as made in the Likeness of God, because of the Resemblance of his bodily Form or Structure; inasmuch as this is allow'd by all wise Men to be the more vile and inferior Part of the Man; and not only so, but that very Part of him which was subjected by the *Curse to Mortality and Corruption.*

Besides, such an Idea of God as existing in the Form of Man, is by the Apostle condemn'd as the most gross, ignorant, and Impious, Rom. 1. 22,23. Professing themselves to be Wise, they became Fools; and changed the Glory of the *uncorruptible God*, into an Image made like to *corruptible Man*; &c. so that this appears to be the very Foundation of all that Idolatry and Wickedness which follows! But if the Muggletonians will yet defend it, they must at the same time also give us a Vindication of all the Idolatry, and Image-worship, not only of Pagans, but also of Popish Christians.

These Gentlemen surely don't consider, that should we form such Ideas as they would have us of God, we should darken those nobler, and more rational ones, entertained by a *Socrates, a Plato, an Antoninus,* and many other Heathens, who spoke and wrote of the *Supreme Being*, as the *Soul* of the Universe! The incomprehensible Mind! A spirit not to be described! And who never seem once to have thought of this superannuated, or rather childish Idea of his being an *old Man!* placed no doubt in a fine Elbow-Chair, whilst directing and governing the Affairs of the Universe.

IV. *The* Muggletonians *assert, That the supreme Being (which I apprehend is an unchangeable and impassable Being) was transmigrated into an Infant, and confin'd within the Enclosures of a Woman's Womb!*

Give me leave to say, the Notion shocks all my thinking Powers! And is truly so romantic, that there appears little need of any reply; however, if this could once be prov'd *viz.* That he could become an *Infant,* I would readily allow, that in Consequence thereof he might become an old Man too! But can a reasonable Mind *imagine,* that *Deity* could alter either its Nature, or the Circumstances or Manner of its Existence? If it can, where shall we find a sure Refuge in distress? Of old, it has been observ'd, that because *Deity* changeth not, therefore Men might rest secure in the Confidence they put in him. In fine, *Transmigration, Transmutation, or Translation* are absolutely incompatible with those Ideas we form of the infinitely supreme Being. But could he in the *Muggletonian's* sense become a Child, then the Body of God which before was in antiquated Form, might thus be renew'd, or refresh'd; by reassuming an *Infant State;* but this is so ridiculous a Subject that it is a most ungrateful Task to pursue it; therefore I leave it and proceed.

V. *The* Mugletonian's *assert, That whilst* Jesus Christ *was on Earth, there was no God in Heaven; and that we are thus to conceive of* Jesus Christ, *as being the* SUPREME GOD.

As to this article I will own, that if he was the Supreme God, then whilst he was upon Earth, there could be no god in Heaven; otherwise, there were *two* Gods: But nothing can be more express against this opinion, than the Doctrine which *Jesus* taught of himself; see all his Gospels, in almost every page of them; but more particularly, *John* v. 30. Where he says, he can of his *own self* do nothing, but as he hears, he judgeth, and his Judgment is just, because he seeks *not his own Will,* but the Will of his Father which hath sent him. *And again, verse 31.* He declares if he should refer Men to his own Testimony of himself, such Evidence would be inconclusive; then he tells them, that altho' *at his Baptism,* God bore Witness to him, yet they, not convinced by this, apply'd to *John,* to know his Opinion, whose Testimony of him was, that he was *the messiah*: Yet he did not need to rest the Evidence wholly here; for he had a greater Witness than that of *John,* or any other Man, even the *Miracles* he constantly wrought by that *Power* he *received* from his Father; for these Miracles fully prov'd that God sent him; as *Nicodemus,* one of the Jewish Rulers, had already confest, as well as others, that no Man cou'd do the Works he did, except God was with him; and it is added in *v.37,* of the 5th of *John,* That the Father himself who had *sent him,* had born witness of him. Upon the whole, if Christ was the SUPREME GOD, how could he *of his own self do nothing? As he heard he judged;* pray who did he hear? And *his Judgment was just, because he fought not his own Will, but the Will of his Father who had sent him;* here could be no Propriety of Speech, if the Father here spoken of, was himself; besides the Conclusion would be false in the 31 v. And the Argument drawn from the Testimony of his Father, would be only Delusion, referring to the 37 v. In comparison with the Context; besides, as no Being can properly be said to be a Witness of himself, so his *Testimony* cannot by any *Law* be admitted as conclusive, therefore *Jesus* refers them to *John*; to his own Works, as wrought by a *Power* he receiv'd from God; and appeals to the *verbal Testimony* which *God* his Father gave of him. I might mention his telling his Disciples that he would *ascend to his Father, and their Father; to his God, and their God;* which could not possibly have either *Truth* or *Propriety* of Speech in it, if he himself was the *Supreme God*; for he could not *ascend to himself,* or *descend from himself;* nor could there be any Being which could be call'd either his *Father,* or his *God.* But if these Mugletonian Notions of *Jesus Christ* can be defended, then I confess the *Papists* may with as much Reason expect, that their Doctrine of *Transubstantiation* may demand credit; as being, if

Observations on Some Articles 259

possible, as little offensive to those reasonable Powers with which God has endow'd us.

VI. *The* Muggletonians *say, That when Christ died, God died; and that then there was no God either in Heaven, or on Earth; but that before he died, he invested* Moses *and* Elias *with his Power, so that the World was govern'd and managed by them; nay, that by them* GOD HIMSELF *was raised from the Dead.*

Let it here be observ'd, that when they say, That God (i.e. the supreme Being) died, when Jesus Christ died; they don't consider that the Life of *Jesus Christ* was took away by the Hands of wicked Men; but no Creature can be suppos'd capable of taking away the *Life of God*; since it must give us a weak Idea of the Maker of all Things, to imagine any Being, or Number of Beings, could destroy him? Or that any *Evil* can affect or alter *unchangeable Goodness!* Or that any *Good* can be supposed to destroy its own Nature, or if self: But if God dy'd, there was an *Effect* produced by some *Cause*; when at the same time, no *cause* can be found *equal* to that *Effect*; therefore God could not die.

If after all, the *Muggletonians* should assert, That God had an *End* to Answer by dying; I should ask, what End? Had God mistaken in any part of his Conduct, the *Punishment* or *Penance* became necessary to bring him to Repentance? If not, his Creatures *doing wrong* could only affect their own Happiness; and therefore, the Creature only stood in need of an Application to *himself*, in order to his being corrected and restored. Again, as the *Justice of God* can never intend any more than a Capacity and Inclination of invariably doing Right; hence the very *Justice* of God would be impeach'd, had it demanded such a Kind of Satisfaction as its own Death. To illustrate this Matter a little by an easy Simile; "Would any human Prince be esteemed wise, should he appoint the Punishment of himself in order to correct some Rebels, and reconcile them to his Government? Or as a Means of reconciling himself to them and becoming more propitious, must he be in a Rage with himself? And pour out his Wrath upon himself? Or else, the wise Prince's Justice could not be satisfy'd; that is to say, if any of his Subjects offend, according to the Rule of Right and Equity, he must inflict Pains on himself, in order to destroy his Subjects Enmity! This Sort of Conduct indeed might appear justifyable, if the Prince had provok'd his Subjects to Rebellion by swerving from the Rules of Right himself, but otherwise, would betray *Weakness* not Wisdom in the Prince, and expose him the more to Contempt."

Nor can it be the Case with the *allwise* and *good Being*; for he could no way be injur'd by the Sin of Man; Man's Sin could only injure himself, as becoming disorder'd thereby; therefore it can never be suppos'd God should be revenged on himself! Such sort of Conduct indeed sometimes appears among the most abandon'd of his Creatures, which human Laws declare to be *Felo de Se's,* and as such punishable; but the Supposition becomes blasphemous when apply'd to God.

But further, the *Muggletonians* assert, That tho' God died, his *Power* did not die, for he invested *Moses and Elias* therewith.

This is indeed asserting that the *Power of Deity* could be alienated from *Deity,* and that Deity could be divided, separated, and disolv'd: but if God died, and not his Power; and therefore the *Power of God* must be esteemed as something distinct and foreign to himself. I am surpriz'd that Men of any *degree* of Thought, cannot see the Fallacy of the Proposition! In order to illustrate this Matter a little, give me leave to define, what is the Idea we universally form of *Power* when apply'd to God! and it is strictly a *Capacity we attribute to him as the Subject thereof, from which that Capacity cannot be separated:* for *Power* cannot exist at all without its Subject; but if the Subject be destroy'd, all Capacity of acting, &c. of which the Subject was before possess'd, or all that *Power* which could be attributed to it, must be destroyed also. I add, that the *Supreme Being* cannot communicate any Degree of Power to any of his Creatures, that can lessen or substract from his own *Capacity* or *Power.* Nor is he capable of alienating any of the real Properties of his Nature, or of becoming any other than what he always was, without the least Alteration, or Change. Besides, the *Muggletonians* themselves will often assert, That the *Essence of God* cannot be divided; but if not *divisible,* there could be no Separation, therefore *God* and his *Power* could not separated.

But let us examine how or where the *Muggletonians* say, God disposed of his *Power* before he died? Why, they tell us, That truly he put his *Power* into the Hands of *Moses and Elias*; and that they did actually govern, and manage the World, whilst God lay dead! nay, that He was defacto raised from the *Dead* by their Hands!

I cannot forbear calling this the most surprizing Stretch of Enthusiasm I ever met with, and did I not know, that a *Leader* of the *Sect* and some others are good-natur'd, and in other respects, well behav'd Men, I should have though that *Lunacy* was inseparable from the Fixedness of these *Rovings of the Imagination!*

More directly, as I have already asserted, that no *Capacity or Power* to which it is *unequal*: But the *Power* of God, (by which I would be understood to mean all along, the essential Power of God) is infinite; and therefore could not be supported by *Moses* and *Elias* did not possess or exercise any such Power. Nor can I imagine how these Gentlemen will give a Solution of the following Questions; as first,

What Quantity of this *Power* they assign to *Moses?* And how much to *Elias?* Which of these was the fittest *Subject* in which this *Capacity or Power* might best reside, and by which be exercised? Or whether an equal Part of *Power,* was bequeathed to each, each having an *equal* Degree of Skill to manage it? Or whether the *whole* belong'd to both, and that both of them became but one identical subject thereof? (If this were a Truth, it would appear that *Moses* and *Elias* differed very much from all other *Priests* that ever I heard or read of, inasmuch as when they had the *sole Power* in their hands, they did so voluntarily part with it!)

I can with some others form some consistent Notion of God's producing a being with fit Qualifications, as an Instrument by which he should make a World and then support it; and there appears nothing contradictory in this: But to suppose, that *two Creatures* should be made capable Subjects of the boundless and immense Perfections of Deity, is to suppose them *equal* to the CAUSE OF ALL THINGS! i.e. equal to that, to which they are unequal! Which is so absur'd, that it appears to me no better than a wild Flight of the Imagination.

VII. *The Muggletonians tell us, That they have received an* infallible Key *to the Bible from* Muggleton *and* Reeves, *the Founders of their* Sect: *who they assert to have been under the immediate Inspiration of God, and as such were the* two last Witnesses, *and* Prophets *spoken and prophesy'd of in Scripture.*

Before we admit this as a Truth, it will be proper for us to consider, whether the Doctrines or Opinions these Men advanced will give any room to conclude, they were Men thus extraordinarily favour'd from Heaven, or what other Evidence they have given of it: As to the Opinions they advanced, I have already taken a view of them, and imagine I have prov'd, that they are wholly inconsistent with the Suggestions of the Divine Spirit, the Spirit of *Truth* and *Order.* Neither can it be made appear, that they had any *Commission* from God as his Prophets; because, they claim'd an uncreaturly and inhumane Authority of *damning* and *saving,* whomsoever they pleased! This, if you will, I'll call a *Criterion* of their being *vile Imposters;* but not of their being *Devine Prophets!* No, the Claim is too unsufferable; the true *Apostles* never asserted such a Claim, but made rational and modest Addresses to Mankind, constantly informing them of the Connection that there is between *Virtue* and *Happiness; Vice* and *Misery:* They urged Mens attention to the *Reason and Fitness of Things,* by Motives drawn from the very Nature and Tendency thereof, and from the express Promises and Threatenings of God; hereby proving that God has confirm'd this *Fitness* by the Testimony of his Son: and St. Paul gives them a *Motive* from his own Example, asserting, that tho' he was an Apostle, yet he kept under his Body, and brought it into Subjection, lest that by any means when he had preached Christ to others, he himself should be a *Cast away;* I. Cor.ix.27. which strongly proves, that St. Paul had no such Power of *damning and saving* Men; nay, in the 2 Cor.i.24, he tells them that he had *no Dominion* over their *Faith:* and in *Gal.* vi. 4, he says, *Let every Man prove his own Work, and then shall he have rejoicing in himself alone, and not in another; for every Man shall bear his own Burden.* JESUS CHRIST himself never asserted any such *Claim,* but all the Encouragements he gave Men of Eternal Life were *conditional,* and always respected the *Fitness* of the Subject: Nay I'll add, that GOD ALMIGHTY cannot *will* any thing in the present case, respecting the final State of Men, that can be in the least contrary to his own Perfections, or the Frame and Constitution of the Creature. Therefore *Muggleton* and *Reeves,* could receive no such Power from God.

Their Pretensions to *Infallibility* must consequently stand upon a very bad Foundation: especially if we consider, that the sacred *Scriptures* can no longer be esteem'd as an universal Rule of *Faith* and *Conduct* to all who have them, if none but a small Number of these have a *Key* to the understanding of them; but if God has vouchsafed this necessary Knowledge only to one *Sett of Men,* the scriptures must be entirely *useless* to all, but those who have the Happiness of being well assur'd of the Sense of them from these *infallible Guides*; and therefore our Saviour and his Apostles should have added to their Command of searching and examining the Scriptures; that as soon as the two great Prophets *Muggleton* and *Reeves* should come, we should no longer have occasion for using our own Faculties in Searches after Divine Knowledge, but attend to them and to their Followers, by whose infallible Guidance we should have Eternal Life: Besides had this been a Truth, methinks it would have been necessary, that these special and peculiar *Favourites of Heaven,* should have had some *extraordinary* Endowments as Characteristics or Marks by which they might have been distinguished as such; but we have no authentic Account of their having had any thing like it.

On the other hand, I own that, for my part, I had rather continue my Opinion, that the Scriptures are constantly *unlock'd* and *open* to every honest Enquirer; and are yet profitable for Doctrine, for Reproof, for Correction, and for Instruction in Righteousness; and that such a sincere Enquirer may in any Age or Nation be perfected by them, and thoroughly furnished to all good Works; and that none but *unstable* or *insincere Men* can west the Scriptures to their own damage.

Again, I would observe, that a Pretence to *Infallibility,* has never served any valuable *End* either in Church, State, or civil Life: In the Church and World it has produced the most dismal Effects; wherever, and so far as it has had any Influence, it has in proportion become the Engine of all Sorts of Villanies, Cruelties, and Inhumanities! Nor can any Man be safe in any of his Properties where it gains the dominion! What havock it has every where made, the concurrent Testimonies of *History* for many Centuries full evince. In *Civil Society,* we do all abhor the Thought of being guided by an implicite Faith, or of yielding up all our reasonable Faculties, even where our *present Interests* are only concern'd; surely then in Affairs of the last Consequence, we ought certainly to view such Maxims with the utmost abhorrence! The Law of Nature, and the Revelation of Jesus, both condemn them; let us therefore guard against any and every Pretension to *Infallibility,* and treat it with the utmost Hatred and Contempt, both in our selves, and others; and instead thereof, as the holy and beloved of God, let us put on a contrary Spirit, viz. *Humility, Meekness, Charity.*

Again, the very Nature of *Religion* condemns any such exorbitant Claim in any Man, or Sett of Men; inasmuch as it requires a Conformity of Conduct to our own Principles: i.e. we are to be fully convinced of the Justness of every Principle upon which we act, otherwise the Actions we perform thereon, cannot be denominated either just, or reasonable; so that it avails nothing at all to us what is the Opinion of others, since their *Faith* can no way serve us, or stamp a value on our Conduct, any further than we see the Reasonableness of it, and by a full Conviction of Mind make it our own. Nor is it possible that any Man can form an *Article of Faith* for any other but himself, because he has no Power to command the Assent of another; he may, it is true, pronounce *Anathema's* against *another Man's* Servant, as is common with the *Muggletonians;* or he may, as the *Pope* and his Agents have done, add *coercive* Methods, to propagate what he calls the *Truth,* and think all the While he does God *good Service*: But if he reasons at all, he must see that he violates the Order of Nature, and applies the most foreign, rude, and impertinent Means to obtain the *End* he aims at! For, it is demonstrably plain, that *Judgment* and *Conscience* are the most sacred and unalienable *Properties* any Man can possess; and in the Nature of Things are absolutely incapable of becoming the *Property* of another.

To conclude, what pity is it that Men should build upon the clear, rational, and intelligible Scheme of *Christianity,* such abstruse, heterogeneous, and wild *Opinions!* With less astonishment might we have beheld such like Extravagancies among the *Religious,* or *Devotionalists* of the Romish Communion, where their *Fanaticism* arises from a recommended, and chosen *Ignorance.*

I shall finish the Whole, in the Words of the *Judicious* and *Learned* Dr. JEREMIAH HUNT.

"Since then there have been false Pretences to Revelation, it cannot but be look'd upon as highly reasonable for Men to express Caution, and to be always on their guard in Cases of this Nature. This Conduct cannot fail of being pleasing to the *first Cause*, who is the highest Reason; and it is very needful for us, unless we will lie open and exposed to the daring and delusive Pretensions of every wild Enthusiast. — That it is also reasonable, that our *Powers* should be capable of distinguishing true Revelations from groundless Pretences thereto; or else it will be to little Purpose that we express any care in the exercise of them. They may even as well drive on without any concern to direct them aright, if we are not capable of forming Measures, which, upon Examination, shall appear solid to steer them, in order to our arriving at Truth and Happiness. The bare Supposal that we want such a Capacity, is to make Man, who is the noblest Being in our System, and Reason, which is his most distinguishing Endowment, more vain, and less fitted to compass the End for which he was formed, than any Being around us; which seems to be monstrously absurd." (See his Essay for explaining Scripture Revelations, P. 7,8.)

FINIS

The Principles Of The Muggletonians Asserted,

Under the following HEADS.

I. On the Eternity of Matter
II. On the Existence of two eternal Beings, on the Angel's Fall, and the Fall of Man
III. On God's eternal Existence in the Form of a Man.
IV. That God became a Son, and manifested himself in the Flesh: and the Scripture Doctrine of the Trinity considered.
V. That Jesus Christ was God the Creator of the World.
VI. When Christ dyed God dyed: Enoch, Moses and Elias, were taken up into Heaven, and left with deputed Power there, while God was performing the Work of Redemption here on Earth.
VII. Concerning John Reeve's and Lodowick Muggleton's Commission with some Observations

LONDON:

Printed for T. Cox, at the Sign of the *Lamb*, under the *Royal Exchange*, in *Cornhill*. 1735.

(Price *One Shilling*)

ADVERTISEMENT

To *the Author of a Pamphlet, entitled, "Observations on Some Articles of the Muggletonian's Creed".*

SIR

As you have directed to me your Thoughts on some of the Principles of the *Muggletonians*, under the Title of *Observations*, in which you have been free in your Censures, I take the first Opportunity to convince you that your Objections are founded neither on Reason nor the Scriptures. I have throughout asserted those Tenets which you condemn, and endeavoured to reconcile them by Reason and the Scriptures. If I prove an Instrument of bringing one Person to the Truth, I shall think my Trouble well rewarded, and my Labour well bestowed: and whatever is the Success of this small Treatise, which I write in an Epistle to yourself it will afford me some Pleasure in the Reflection, that my only Motive to publish it was a Love of Truth. It was not merely for the Sake of answering you that I took my Pen in Hand; but I was glad of an Occasion to remove those disadvantageous Impressions which some Minds may have received of our Principles, from the Misrepresentations of others: and if what I here send you has any good Effect on yourself, it will add to the Satisfaction of

Your Friend and Servant

April, 1735.

A.B.

ARTICLE I. On The Eternity Of Matter.

YOUR first objection to the Eternity of Matter is *that we can form no Idea of Matter exclusive of Magnitude, Impenetrability, and Divisibility,* which you suppose essential Properties of Matter, therefore you say, *Matter, as a Thing or Being merely passive, could not unbeginningly exist, because it must have then existed with such Properties as do invariably imply Design,* and you add, because they *constantly render their Subject capable of being altered and changed in its very Mode and Form.* I will first observe that your Distinction of the Properties of Matter is very unpilosophical and confused: what is *impenetrable* cannot be *divided*, and what is *divisible* in Substance is *penetrable*, therefore to say Matter is *impenetrable* and *divisible*, as you do, is talking absurdly. Now to your argument. First, it does not appear to me that granting *Magnitude* and *Divisibility* to be essential properties of Matter, they are the necessary Effects of Design, no more than if we grant Matter to be eternal, Motion must be allowed to be essential to it: the Supposition of the Non-existence of Matter is absurd; because when we consider what universal Space is, we cannot frame an Idea of any Thing, that now is, ever not being in some Part of infinite Space, tho Matter has often changed its Forms and Modes of Existence. Now considering Matter as an inert unactive Being from Eternity, Motion could be no Property of it, but must be the Effect of an active Power. As Motion, and Thinking, which is an Action of the Mind were no Properties of Matter, they must be the Effect of a Being possessed of both; and Matter being void of both originally, and subject to Modification, its being eternal does not detract from the Power of an omnipotent Being.

Your next objection is, *that as no Account can be given, or Reason assigned, why any one Particle of Matter should have existed unbeginningly in one Form more than in another, and as its possessing any one Form must certainly be the Effect of Design, therefore you conclude that Matter could not exist eternally.* If the Non-existence of Matter is reduced to a Contradiction, what you say about its Form, or

Mode of Existence, is to no Purpose: here your Ideas seem confused; for does it follow, because Matter had a Form, but that a rude and indigested one, and without any active Power that such an Existence must be the Effect of Design? No; for bare Existence is no roof of Design: it is not derogatory from the Honour of God to say he cannot annihilate Space; and Space existed from all Eternity, but its eternal Existence is no Proof of Design.

You afterwards object, *that Matter could have existed unbeginningly, as an inert unactive Principle, and afterwards, or in some subsequent Part of Duration, could begin to be passive,* i.e. *begin to be wrought upon, will appear absurd, if we consider that Duration applied to an eternal unbeginning Being abstractedly considered, is Nonsense, and absolutely impertinent.* As you have used the Expressions, excuse me, if I say this Nonsense, and absolutely impertinent: who ever talked of Matter as an unactive Principle beginning to be passive, or beginning to be wrought upon? Those are Terms applicable only to the active Being: Matter did not begin to be passive, or to be wrought upon, (No-body talks such Nonsense) but God begun to work upon that which in its Nature was passive. I can justly conceive of God to have been an active Being before Creation; but I can form no Idea of his manifesting himself by Virtue of Creation, without some Subject to work upon: and tho Matter was always independent as to its bare Existence, and at the same Time passive, and in a Condition to be wrought upon as Clay in the Hands of the Potter, and tho God wrought upon it no sooner than he did, it does not follow from thence that he could not have done it before. Matter, as an inert unactive Being, independent in Respect to its Existence, void of all Signatures of Design or Contrivance, cannot appear a useless Being, because without a Subject to be wrought upon, incapable of Opposition to the self-existent thinking Being, there could have been no Manifestation of God to us: for how can the Attribute of the infinite Power be exerted, if Nothing existed from Eternity beside himself? If there was Nothing but his own Essence from Eternity, then there was Nothing for him to have Power over, or to act upon, and then he must have continued alone to all Eternity, as he had been from all Eternity. You say *there is less Absurdity to you in imagining that the Power of God could give Existence, or, in other Words, produce a Being; and if,* you *say, from Nothing, though you can form no Idea of Nonentity, yet in the Notion,* you say, *there is no Opposition, inasmuch as Nothing can oppose*: can not you see that if there is Nothing to oppose, there is likewise Nothing to be wrought upon? For Nothing is Nothing, in either Cafe: your not being *capable of reducing such an Effect to an Absurdity* is *your* Misfortune and not mine.

Your last Objection to the Eternity of Matter is, *that the Production of what we call Life and Motion seems to be an Effect as stupendous as the Creation of inert unactive Matter, or the giving it Existence; and therefore* you *see no Reason,* you say, *why we should boggle at the Notion of infinite Power effecting the latter any more than the former.* That Life and Motion are the Effect of the Power of God we grant; but that his Power was manifested without a Subject to operate upon, I deny. No Effect can be more stupendous than that of Life and Motion being produced by an active Being acting upon an unactive one; to go farther for the Manifestation of infinite Power would be to confound the Cause with the Effect, and Dishonour to God, by making him and the World essentially the same; for if you say there was a Time when all Things which have Life had a Beginning, then God must have been alone before any Thing was created to live in his Presence; or if it was not so, what you call Matter must have resided in the very Essence of God; either of which Notions is fruitful of Absurdities. This leads me another Consideration: supposing Matter not to be eternal, it can never be conceived, much less demonstrated, that God could ever create a Nature different from himself, that is, a Nature possessed of Properties different from himself; and give me Leave to say, that I think I have made it appear that God could no more create Matter than Matter him. Hitherto I have built my Demonstration on Principles of Reason; agreeable to which is the *Mosaic* Doctrine; in which we find it said that

"in the Beginning God created the Heavens and the Earth; and the Earth "was without Form and void, and Darkness was upon the Face of the Deep; "and the Spirit of God moved upon the Face of the Waters":

which Account supposes Something, tho without Form, and all in Darkness and confusion, that there was a Deep, and that there were Waters, even before Creation; and any other Notion of Creation is unscriptural, chimerical, and unintelligible. Thus have I established the Eternity of Matter, which is one of the main Foundations of the *Reevonian* System, and which is demonstrable both by the Scriptures and by Reason.

ARTICLE II. On the Existence of two eternal Beings, on the Angel's Fall, and the Fall of Man.

YOUR next Attempt to overthrow the Existence of two eternal Beings, is to put Things in a false Light, by calling them *Principles* without any Distinction in Point of Existence as Principles, and by saying that we assert them to have existed eternally as such; and from such an Existence you draw this Absurdity as a Consequence, that if *Evil* existed as a *Principle in Matter, as its Subject* from all Eternity, then, say you, it *would destroy the Notion of its being inert and unactive.* This Manner of stating the Argument is either thro Ignorance, or an ill Design arising from a Pleasure you take in finding a Contradiction in us: but you shall see how all your Endeavours are defeated, when the

Subject appears in its true Light. That two active Principles, a good and evil one, eternally existed as such is no-where asserted by us: but, on the contrary, we say that one was an unactive Principle from Eternity; and as it was not possible to be hid from the active omnipotent Being, he by making it active rendered it capable of producing Evil: therefore your Endeavours to destroy our two eternal Principles, by saying *two Opposites could not always have existed because they must then mutually destroy each other*, your Endeavours, I say, are to no Purpose, because you start a Doctrine full of Incongruities, and impose it on us, tho we assert directly the contrary. The Doctrine of two eternal Beings, one active and thinking, the other unactive and unthinking, does not destroy Priority, in Relation to Action, in the active one, and if prior in Act, he must consequently be so in all those infinite Perfections which belong to God.

I hope I have made it appear, even to mean Capacities, that the Doctrine of an eternal unactive Principle with that of an eternal active one is not inconsistent, since there can be no Opposition from an unactive Being, no Act without Life as the Spring of Action, and no Life but what proceeds from the Power of God. Matter being void of all the Properties of an active Being, is a Proof that God was the only omnifcient and omnipotent Being from Eternity: so the Existence of two eternal Prinicples, Matter passive and inactive as Clay in the Hands of the Potter, and God intelligent and active, stands unshaken notwithstanding all your false Reasoning against it.

Again you say *moral Evil could not exist but in a Subject capable of moral Good or moral Evil; which Subject must have been no other than a Creature, consequently Evil was originated*. This is another unjust Attempt to gain the Reader over to you, or it is down-right Ignorance; for where do you find the Doctrine of moral Evil being unoriginated, or that it was not in a Creature, capable of both? I am sure you find Nothing like it in our System; so that what you say has Nothing to do with us, but with your own imagination.

You farther say, *upon our Hypothesis, all moral Agency is destroyed; because all Mankind are hereby put into a Necessity of belonging to, and being governed by, the one Principle, or the other*. This is so far from containing the Truth, that the Reverse of it can be only true; for all Men act from a good or bad Principle; and moral Agency consists in Nothing more than in a Power or Liberty of chusing or refusing to do an Action supposing no external Force to hinder, or no inward Impediment by a sudden Disease: Nothing is more evident than that all Mankind are placed is such a State: that a Man's having such and such Propensities, so such or such an Action, should hinder his Choice is far from being the Truth, for such Propensities are the Cause of his Choice, tho this good or bad Principle must determine him; to suppose otherwise, would be to suppose a Man to do an Action without a Motive, which would introduce the utmost Confusion : if we consider the Definition of moral Evil, we shall find that it amounts to no more than the Disagreeableness of one Man's Actions with Respect to another, occasioned by the Passions of the human Creature; and that infinite Wisdom which contrived Things with such and such Natures, Properties and Relations, must consequently foreknow that Creatures so endued would act according to such *Natures, Properties*, and *Relations*: and this *Fore*knowledge in the Deity cannot be supposed to influence my Actions, or destroy my Liberty, it being no more than knowing that the Man who is amorous, revengeful, or ambitious, in his Temper, will listen more the those Passions than any other Man who is not possessed of them or rather by them.

The following Observation which you make is more expressive of your Wonder than of Argument: you ask *how we can imagine that the Serpent, or the Devil in the Serpent, could lye with Mother* Eve, *so as to cause her to conceive, and bring forth the proper Offspring of such Conception, without some distinct Characteristics, or Marks, by which it's Sire might be distinguished to be the Serpent or Devil, and not* Adam? You also ask in the next Page, *if* Eve's *Transgression, in eating the forbidden Fruit, was her Coition with the Devil, how could* Adam *be guilty of violating the same Prohibition?* You likewise say *there is a manifest Difference between the Power of God being supposed to form a Man in the Womb of the Virgin, and the Supposition of an evil Spirit or Angel impregnating a Woman.* You ask too, *how it can be prov'd that the Devil, supposed to be an immortal Spirit, should communicate a Property he had not, viz, Death, or Mortality? It is,* you say, *much more rational to suppose, with some, that the forbidden Tree was the Serpent's Food, or at least was in its own Nature noxious and poysonous to anhuman Body.* Hence, say you afterwards, *we may be able to find a very rational Sense of the Text, "as in Adam all died", or became subject to Mortality by an hereditary Conveyance of a distemper'd Constitution, "so in Christ shall all be made alive", i.e. be raised from the dead.* Tho the Questions which you ask, and your Observations, have more the Appearance of Wonder in them than of Reason, yet I shall answer you. I shall shew you how the Devil was capable of causing Eve to conceive, and to bring forth the proper Offspring of such a Conception: in Order to effect my Design, I must beg Leave to produce all those Testimonies, which shall occur to my Memory, out of the Writings of *John Reeve*, for the Truth of what he has advanced; and this is no more unreasonable than if, in disputing about the Validity of *Moses's* Mission with an Unbeliever, I should require the Liberty of quoting from the Writing of *Moses* those Passages which I should conceive to be sufficient Evidences for the Truth of his Mission. To proceed, what I shall first observe is, that, since almighty God hath thought fit his first and second Record on Earth should be shewed forth by Men, so also did he declare, by *John* the Divine, (*Revelations*, chap. 11.) that his third Record on Earth should be shewed forth by Men likewise, called by the Names of his two last Witnesses: and, by this third and last Testament of our Lord and Saviour *Jesus Christ*, it is declared, that, after the eternal God

The Principles of the Muggletonians Asserted 271

had created out of that Substance of Earth and Water, which was eternally in his Sight, the World and all Things therein, the Host of Angels were by an allpowerful Word called out of that dead Substance with Bodies spiritual, and Souls rational, and that one of them only, on whom he designed to manifest his infinite Wisdom, was called forth with a greater Portion of the angelick Nature than the Rest, which was all Obedience to their Creator, whilst upheld in their created Purity: it is likewise declared, that, after he had created this World also, and had placed Man upon it, whom he created with a Body natural, and Soul spiritual, he called forth the Woman also, existing, as her Husband *Adam* did, with a Body natural and Soul spiritual: all Things thus created appearing good in his Sight, the Creator give a Charge or Caution to the Man , and the Woman, that of all the Trees in the Garden, (that is, of any Thing in this World,) they might freely eat, but of the Tree of Knowledge of Good and Evil, which was soon to appear, it being not of this Creation, they are commanded not to eat, with this Interdiction, that in the Day they should eat thereof they should surely dy: Things thus prepared for that great End of manifesting himself by Virtue of Creation, (and by different Natures mixing themselves thro his Permission, that Contrarieties might appear in this World as evident Characteristics or Marks of the Seed of God, and of the Seed of the Devil,) the allwise Being though fit to leave that Angel, which he had created for his Glory, to himself, that he might act according to his Nature when not upheld in his created Purity; and when his aspiring Thoughts of dethroning his Creator were rose to the Heighth, the allwise Being thought fit to reveal it to the Rest of the Angels, telling them that he would cast him from his Presence, and at the Time he gave them to understand their eternal Election, which occasioned them to give all Honour, Praise, and Glory, to the great God of Heaven, who had preserved them to continue in his Presence, and had kept them from the outcast Condition of the other. Now the Scene of this World begins to open: the Creator, not thinking fit to punish the outcast Angel or Devil in the spiritual Condition he was in, prepares a Reception for him on this Earth, and for his lineal Descent: now *Adam* and *Eve*, tho not capable of sinning from their own Nature, yet, being left to the Temptation of another, were overcome. The Woman, being the Vehicle that was to bring forth that Serpent Devil in the Flesh, was tempted by the Appearance of so glorious a Person as the angelic Devil, who was the Tree of Knowledge of Good and Evil; and, he being in the Form of *Adam*, and a spiritual Body, she mistook him for her God, the Glory of his Person so far exceeding that of the Man; and being overcome by his subtle Language, thro the Permission of God, he conveyed himself into her pure undefiled Nature, and defiled her throughout by transmuting himself in her Womb into Flesh, Blood, and Bone, that he might in due Time be brought forth a Man-child, and be called by a Name suitable to his Nature, *Cain*, which signifies *cursed*. Thus had the Virgin Wife *Eve* conceived before she had Desire towards her

Husband; and after she had tempted her innocent Husband to cover her Folly, she conceived with *Abel*; but her first Conception being hid from her Knowledge, (I mean what was the Fruit of that Conception,) she thought her first born was from the Lord, and of *Adam's* begetting; so she said, when *Abel* was born, he also was of the Lord; and so she believed of them both till their Actions manifested their Natures; then she knew that *Abel* only was of *Adam's* begetting; and it was by revelation, after she had conceived again, that she said, *now hath God given me another Seed*, (that is different from the Seed of Cain,) *in the Room of ABEL whom CAIN slew*: and it is said of this Seed, that *then they begun to call upon the Name of the Lord*: now *Adam* being brought into a State of Morality by consenting to his Wife, thro her Possession of the Devil, no Being, but the eternal God, was capable to raise him again from the Power of that Death: and thus saith the Promise, the Seed of the woman shall break the Serpent's Head, and the Serpent shall bruise his Heel, and there shall be Enmity betwixt the Seed of the Woman and the Seed of the Serpent; and this Enmity in the Serpent is expressed by saying, he shall bruise his Heel, because it extends to the first Death only; and it is called the breaking the Head of the Seed of the Serpent, because the eternal God, who pronounced that Curse upon the Serpent Angel, or Devil, never made any after Promise to them for their Redemption; for the Promise that God made that he would become the Seed of the Woman, or manifest himself in Flesh, was never revealed to any but the Sons of God, or *Sethites*, who were the Children of *Adam*, being of his Seed; and where it is said that the Sons of *God* saw the Daughters of Men that they were fair, and took of them to be their Wives of all that they chose, the Expression means no more than that the Sons of *Adam*, who were called the Sons of *God*, intermixed in Marriage with the Daughters of *Cain*, who are called the Daughters of Men; but the God who made them knows how to separate them, notwithstanding their close Union, and to call them by Names suitable to their Natures. I shall here give you an Instance of the Scripture distinguishing betwixt the Seed of the Woman, and the Seed of the Serpent, the latter of which proceeded from *Cain* the first Devil in Flesh by Generation.

St. *Jude*, whom I shall quotes as a proper Introduction to those Parts of Scripture which follow, says, *there are certain Men crept in unawares, who were before of old ordained to this Condemnation*: Ver. 4. *These were the Angels*, which he mentions in the 6th Verse, *which kept not their first Estate, and which he hath reserved in everlasting Chains, under Darkness, unto the Judgment of the great Day*: and St. *John*, speaking of *Cain*, says *he was of the wicked one*; but no one can justly say *Adam* was that wicked one: and *Christ* tells the wicked *Jews* that they were of *their Father the Devil; who was a Liar and a Murderer from the Beginning*; which is plainly alluding to *Cain*, who was the first Devil, and cloathed with Flesh, as all his Off-springs have since been, tho called in Scripture the fallen Angles, as having fallen in him; such were they who persecuted the People of

The Principles of the Muggletonians Asserted 273

God in the Time of *Moses* and the Prophets, and in the Time of *Christ* and the Apostles; and such are they who have gone under the Names of Christians persecuting one another in several Ages, tho called *Men*: *Pharaoh* was a *Man, Sanacherib a Man, Herod* a *Man,* tho *John* calls him a *red Dragon*: and were not the *Scribes* and *Pharisees Men*, tho *Christ* calls them *Serpents*? And was not *Judas a Man* tho called a *Devil*? And was not *Nero a Man* tho *Paul* calls him a *Lion*? And, as it is said, there was War in Heaven between *Michael* and his Angels, fighting against the Dragon and his Angels, that *Michael* was the Spirit of our Lord *Jesus Christ* in all true Believers; and the *Dragon* was the Spirit of cursed *Cain* in all his Off-springs: and the Scene of this War is this Earth, tho said to have been in Heaven because the Original of both Seeds came from thence: but there was never any *actual* Rebellion there, the Date of *actual* Rebellion not beginning till the fallen Angel, called the Tree of Knowledge of Good and Evil, deceived our first Parents, and embody'd himself in the Womb of *Eve*; therefore said *John* the Divine, *Woe be to the Inhabitants of the Earth, for the* Devil (not Devils) *is come down amongst them!* So there was but one Angel that was sent down from Heaven, as appears likewise by the following Saying, *he fell down from Heaven like Lightning:* the Fulness of this fallen Angel's Spirit being in *Cain*, such of his Seed as have a great Share of his serpentine Nature predominating in them at their natural Conception become greater Devils than ordinary. *Ezekiel* justly compares *Pharaoh* to a *great Dragon*. Chap. 29. Ver. 3 hear what *Isaiah* says of the King of BABYLON, *how art thou fallen from Heaven, O! LUCIFER, Son of the Morning*? Chap. 14 ver. 12. He is here called by the Name of him from whom he came, as he had a large Portion of his Nature in him: but the King of Tyrus seems to excel them in his paternal Likeness; of whom says the Prophet EZEKIEL, *thou hast been in EDEN the Garden of God, every precious Stone was thy covering, the Sardius, the Topaz, the Diamond, the Beryl, the Onyx, and the Jasper, the Saphire, the Emerald, and the Carbuncle,* &c. chap. 28 ver. 13: and in the next Verse he continues, *thou art the anointed Cherub,* &c. *thou wast upon the holy Mountain of God, thou hast walked up and down in the Midst of the Stones of Fire:* and in the following Verse says the Prophet, *thou was perfect in thy Ways from the Day that thou was created, till Iniquity was found in thee.* It is plain that these Passages must relate to the fallen Angel in whom those who descended from him virtually existed.

    Now I hope I have performed what I proposed: I have shewed the distinguishing Characteristics which point out the *Serpent* or *Devil*, and which do not belong to *Adam*: I have likewise shewn that the Woman was tempted by the Serpent, and the *Eve* afterwards deceived *Adam*. I have also shewed that the wonderful Event of the Devil's becoming Flesh was by the same Power by which God's Incarnation was; the first was by God's Permission, that the Devil should be brought forth; and the Godhead became Flesh to fulfil the Curse pronounced against the Serpent; which was to *break his Head*.

Gen. chap. iii. Ver. 15: and the Completion of this Curse is eternal Punishment. From this we see that Mortality was so far from being a Property in him as you injudiciously term it, that it was only the Consequence of Sin, and it proceeded from him as the Effect of Sin, without which there had been no Mortality.

Before I conclude this Head, I must observe to you, that it you look into the Account of the Creation and the Fall, with an impartial Eye, you cannot avoid seeing a more consistent System, and greater Harmony, in this Interpretation of it, of God's manifesting himself by Contrarieties in Creation, than can arise from a literal Explanation of the Text, which has puzzled many learned Heads; for they have always found it difficult to account for an Apple producing an evil Seed, or how any Curse should have an Effect on a natural Serpent, who goes by Nature on its Belly; nor have they ever advanced a strenuous Reason why the Devil, then a Spiritual Being, should chuse such an ugly Shape as a Serpent to tempt a Woman in; nor can they easily tell how Sin or Evil could possibly arise out of any Part of this Creation, which God pronounced good in his Sight: therefore we must carry our Thoughts beyond this Creation for the Origin of Evil. The Text which says, *as in* ADAM *all dyed, so in* CHRIST *shall all be made alive*, can have Relation only to *Adam's* Seed; for as they only dyed in him, because of his first Transgression, they only can be made alive in *Christ*: but the Seed of the Serpent, having fallen in the Serpent, and not in *Adam*, will be made alive in the Serpent; which Life will be attended with that Worm of Conscience that never dies, and the Fire of God's Wrath that never goes out: all the great Promises therefore which God has ever made to his Church, to his People, to the Families or Nations of his true Worshipers, are evidently all along to be understood not to extend to wicked and unworthy Persons of whatever Family or Nation, or Profession of Religion, they are; for such are excluded from the Benefit of those Promises, and cut off from God's People; and worthy Persons of all Nations, from the East and from the West, from the North and from the South, shall be accepted. We are to observe that Promise was made originally not to all the Children of *Abraham*, but to *Isaac* only, and not to both the Sons of *Isaac* but to *Jacob* only; and among the Posterity of *Jacob* all were not *Israel* which were of ISRAEL: in *Elijah's Days* seven thousand only were the true *Israel*; and in the Time of *Isaiah*, tho the Number of the Children of *Israel* was as the Sand of the Sea, yet a Remnant only was to be saved: so it is all along evidently to be understood that the Children of the Promise are accounted for the Seed, and as such are true Children of *Abraham* in the spiritual and religious Sense, Saints of the most High, who shall possess the Kingdom for ever, even for ever.

ARTICLE III. On God's eternal Existence in the Form of a Man

YOUR principal Objections to God's existing in the Form of a Man are as follow: you say, *God cannot be subject to any Form or Figure, because Form and Figure are only Accidents of Beings.* —*Form and Figure can belong only to Beings that are mutable and limited, they themselves, being so, consequently cannot belong to God.* — *It seems very preposterous, that Man should be represented as made in the Likeness of God, because of the Resemblance of his bodily Form or Structure, inasmuch as this is allowed by all wise Men to be the more vile and inferior Part of Man; and not only so, but that very Part of him which was subjected by the Curse to Mortality and Corruption. Beside, such an Idea of God, as existing in the Form of a Man, is by the Apostle condemned as the most gross, ignorant, and impious, ROM.* 1.22, 23, *professing themselves to be wise, they became Fools, and changed the Glory of the incorruptible God into an Image made like to corruptible Man, &c. so that this appears to be the very Foundation of all that Idolatry and Wickedness which follows.* —*Should we form such Ideas of God*, continue you, *we should darken those nobler and more rational ones, entertained by a* SOCRATES, *a* PLATO, *an* ANTONIUS, *and many other Heathens, who spake and wrote of the supreme Being, as the Soul of the universe.*

These are your chief Arguments against God's Existence in the Form of a Man: which I shall endeavour to overthrow by Scripture and Reason. *Moses* tells us that God *created Man in his own Image, in the Image of God created be him*: for the Explanation of this Text, we must consider the Meaning of the Word *Image*, which implies Something that may be seen: so if you deny that this *Image* relates to corporeal Likeness, you are drove upon the Absurdity of having it a mental Likeness; than which no Absurdity can be greater; for can mortal Man believe his mental Parts bear any Comparison with God's? Besides how can the Word Image be applied to what is only an Object of the Understanding and not of the Eye? We can form an Idea of an Image after we have heard or seen it described, as *Moses* has done with the Image of God: we cast our Eyes on our fellow Creatures, and immediately image to our selves the Reflection of our Creator, tho not so beautifully expressed. *Moses* mentions the several Limbs of God, as his Face, Hands, and Back-parts: therefore if God had not a personal Form, how could these several Limbs be Parts of him? He likewise tells us the Effect of seeing his Face in all its spiritual and heavenly Glory; should we behold its surpassing Splendor, it would dazzle our Optics, and pierce the very Organs of Sense to such a Degree, that immediate Death would follow. He is described with the Faculties of a personal Being, in the highest Perfection: if he was ubiquitary, filling all Places with his Being, every Thing in Space must be a Part of him: besides, as he is often represented as uttering Words, whence must his Words proceed but from some Organs of Utterance? Perhaps I am answered, it is a Mystery, an impenetrable Mystery, and is only the

Object of Faith: we may with the same Reason call upon Faith in our Case: and, as Faith and Reason are both on our Side, we carry it by a Majority.

Observe what an unphilosophical Inference you make when you say that Accidents are attributed to Beings which have Form; for if God has a Form, his being necessarily existing exempts him from the Accidents to which created finite Beings are liable.

You say that God has *no Limitation of Existence in Space.* I conceive it no Dishonour to God, who is a self-existing Being, infinitely powerful, wise, and good, to circumscribed in his outward Form, since he is possessed of all the divine Attributes belonging to an infinitely perfect Being. *Christ*, who was God and Man, had Power to lay down his Life and to take it and raise it up again, yet he was in a limited Form, and that the Form of a Man, notwithstanding this extensive Power: for had not the Power existed even in his Words, beyond the Place where his Person may be supposed to stand, he could have raised neither *Lazarus* nor himself from the dead.

Where the Apostle calls them Fools for changing the Glory of the incorruptible God into an Image made like to corruptible Man, the Meaning is the same as in the Commandment, where we are forbid to fall down before, and to worship, any Image.

I shall now consider what you say just before your Quotation of the Apostle's Words, viz. *that it seems very preposterous, that Man should be represented as made in the Likeness of God, because of the Resemblance of his bodily Form or Structure, inasmuch, say you, as this is allowed by all wise Men to be the more vile, and inferior, Part of the Man, and not only so, but that very Part of him which was subjected by the curse of Mortality and Corruption.* This is of no Force; For that the Body should come under the Curse without the Soul, or be made sinful but by it, I cannot conceive: the Soul cannot be made sinful by the Body, the Body is made sinful by the Soul, *for it is the Soul that sins must dye:* if the Charge given to *Adam* was given to that Part that was capable of understanding, then the whole Man became mortal by coming under Sin, Sin being the Cause of Mortality; and Death was the Effect of that Cause, so what you say of the Body bearing no Resemblance to God, because of it being the more vile Part of Man, is of no Weight since the Soul of Man is made vile by Sin as well as the Body; your Reason therefore holds equally against both: at the Resurrection such as are saved will be all like to the Son of God, who in his outward Form was like to us, and who was the express Image of his Father's Person; the Likeness therefore of which I am speaking must allude to the outward Form, which is capable of Immortality and Glory as well as the Soul.

What you say of making God in the Form of a Man being the *Foundation of all that Idolatry and Wickedness which follow* is such Nonsense that scarcely deserves an Answer: remember that you say it is the Foundation of all that Idolatry which follows: pray what Relation to God's being likened in his Person to Man has the raising Images to the Virgin *Mary, St. Peter, St. Paul*, and to great Numbers of other Persons? In short, tho God is in the Likeness of Man, is that any Reason why an Image should be made the Object of religious Worship? Indeed I am ashamed to see any Man who pretends to write make such strange Sort of Inferences. What you say of the Opinions of *Socrates, Plato, and Antonius*, is as little to the Purpose; for if those great Heathens entertained wrong Notions of the Being of God, what signify their Sentiments any more than any other? But as what you say of them is Nothing to the Subject in Debate, you might as well have not named them; but perhaps you had a Mind to shew us that you know there were such Persons.

ARTICLE IV. That God became a Son, and manifested himself in the Flesh: and the Scripture Doctrine of the Trinity considered.

THAT God should become an Infant is a Notion, you say, that *shocks all* your *thinking Powers*. The only Shadow of an Argument which you advance against it is the Difficulty of imagining that *Deity could alter either its Nature, or the Circumstances or Manner of Existence*: but *could he become a Child*, you will *readily allow*, you say, *that he might become an old Man too*. The word *old* is Nothing to the Purpose, and might as well have been omitted: if you intended it as a Joke, I assure you it is a very aukward one: but to the Subject.

First, let us consider that our Saviour does not say *before* ABRAHAM *was, I was,* but, *before* ABRAHAM *was, I am*: by which it is plain to me that he used that Expression to shew that he was the God, whose eternal Duration is signified in that Expression, *before* ABRAHAM *was I am*: in which Sense he is said by the Apostle to the *Hebrews* to be the same yesterday, this Day, and for ever: agreeable to which is his Description of himself in the *Revelations*, I am *Alpha* and *Omega*, says he, the Beginning and the End, which is, and which was, and which is to come, the Almighty: that this is spoke of *Christ* appears in the same Chapter, where he says, I am the first and the last; and in his own Person he says, I *Jesus have sent my Angel*, &c. what can be clearer than that these Expressions are significant of Christ as the eternal God: St Paul likewise tells us, that *all Things were created by him, that are in Heaven, and that are in Earth, visible or invisible, whether they be Thrones, or Dominions, or Principalities, or Powers*: he must then be the very God, the spotless Lamb, the *Messiah, Emanuel*, or God with us, the same which *Isaiah* mentions, where he says, *all Flesh shall know that I the Lord am thy Saviour, and thy Redeemer, the mighty one of* JACOB. Chap. 49. Verse the last: to which I will add what St. Paul says to the ROMANS, *whose are the Fathers, and of whom as concerning the Flesh* CHRIST *came, who is over all God blessed for ever*. Chap. 9. Ver. 5 and says our Lord, *when ye shall lift up the Son of Man, then shall ye know that I am he;* and the Meaning of the Word *he* here is fully explained by these Words in St.

John, *he that seeth me, seeth him that sent me*: and farther, in the first Epistle of *John*, the last Chapter, and 20th Verse, *we know that the Son of God is come, and hath given us Understanding that we may know him that is true; and we are in him that's true, even in his Son* JESUS CHRIST, *this is the true God, and eternal Life*. That there is any Inconsistency in Reason that God should exist in what Mode he please, without diminishing his Purity, you will find difficult to prove: I am demonstrating, and will venture to say do demonstrate, that Christ was the very God, founding my Arguments on those Scriptures which are in Part my Rule of Faith, and the divine Authority of which you seem not to dispute. To the Texts which I have already quoted, I will add these from the first Chapter of St. John's Gospel, *in the Beginning was the Word, and the Word was with God, and the Word was God: the same was in the Beginning with God: all Things were made by him, and without him was not any Thing made that was made. Ver. 1, 2, and 3: and afterwards, he was in the World, and the World was made by him, and the World knew him not. Ver. 10 and Ver, the 14th, the Word was made Flesh, and dwelt among us, and we beheld his Glory, the Glory as of the only begotten of the Father, full of Grace and Truth*. These Expressions are so emphatical, that Nothing can be more apparent than that the *Word* which was *God was* made *Flesh*, and dwelt among us, and that was *Christ*.

You say, if he could become a Child, you will readily grant he might become a Man: I have proved *Christ* to be God, making the Scriptures my Criterion in this Argument: let us consider this Text, *the first Man was of the Earth earthly, the second was the Lord from Heaven heavenly*: to whom can the second Man allude but to *God* who was *Christ*? Surely it is no harder to conceive that the supreme Being, the Creator, should become our Redeemer, by being born of a Virgin, than that a second Person being God, existing of the same almighty Nature, should. The supreme God is a Creator and Gather in one Respect, a Son and Redeemer in another, a Sanctifier or Holy Ghost in a third: so these three glorious Titles belong to one true God: he is a Father by Creation, a Son by Redemption, a Holy Ghost by Sanctification: which Doctrine of the Trinity is further illustrated by these Texts, first, where it is said, *I will not give my Glory to another*, which, compared with what is said of CHRIST *having all Power both in Heaven and on Earth*, must make *God* and *Christ* the same; and the same was that Being who said *besides me you shall have no Saviour*.

ARTICLE V. That JESUS CHRIST was God the Creator of the World.

THO I have demonstrated this Proposition in my last Article, yet I shall here consider it under a separate Head, as you have made it a different Article in your Objections.

The Principles of the Muggletonians Asserted 279

You say, *if he was supreme God, then, whilst he was upon Earth, there could be no God in Heaven, otherwise there were two Gods.* My only Business here is to prove from Scripture the *Christ* was *God*; and, if the Authority of the Scripture is granted, you can neither expect nor desire any better Proofs.

God is called the *first and the last*, by *Isaiah*, Chap.44. Ver.6. *Christ* is called the *first and the last*. Rev. Chap.1 Ver.11. Therefore *Christ* is *God*.

Isaiah, speaking of the Coming of God himself, says, *the Voice of him that cryeth in the Wilderness, prepare ye the Way of the Lord, make strait in the Desert a high Way for our God.* Chap. 40 Ver.3. Of whom says *John* the BAPTIST, *this is he that was spoken of by the Prophet* ISAIAH, *saying, the Voice of one crying in the Wilderness, prepare ye the Way of the Lord, make his Paths strait.* Mat. Chap.3. Ver,3. Mark Chap.1. Ver.2,3. John Chap.1 Ver.23.

It is said of God, thy *Throne is established of old, thou art from everlasting*. Psalm 93. Ver.2. *Of Christ* it is said, *thy Throne, O God! Is for ever and ever.* Heb. Chap.1. Ver.8.

I am God, and there is none else. Isa. Chap.46. Ver.9. *Paul*, in the 2d Chapter to the *Colossians*, speaking of *Christ*, says, *in him dwelleth all the Fullness of the Godhead bodily.*

O! Lord, thou art exalted as Head above all. I Chron. Chap.29. Ver. 11. The same is said of *Christ* by St. *John*. Chap.3. Ver. 31.

God is said to be Judge of the World, *Gen*.18. ver. 25. *Christ* is said to be Judge of the World, 2 *Tim*. Chap.4. Ver. 1.

I will venture to affirm that the three following Texts are so strong, that there is no perverting the Sense of them to any other Meaning than that *God* almighty and *Christ* are the same. *I am the Lord thy God, the holy one of* ISRAEL, *thy Saviour; I gave* EGYPT *for thy Ransom*, ETHIOPIA *and* SEBA *for thee. — I, even I, am the Lord, and beside me there is no Saviour.* Isa. Chap. 43. Ver. 3 and 11. Here the God of *Israel* is pronounced the only Saviour; and the same is pronounced of *Christ* in the 12th Verse of the 4th Chapter of the *Acts of the Apostles*, where it is said of him, *neither is there Salvation in any other, for there is none other Name under Heaven given among Men, whereby we must be saved.*

From the Texts which I have here quoted, the same Things appear predicated of *God* and *Christ*; agreeable to which Christ often declares in the new Testament that the Father and he are one.

As our Saviour said no Man can serve two Master, so justly may it be said, that no Man can serve two Gods, or believe in two Gods: they therefore who expect Salvation thro *Christ* have all the Reason that can be to believe that the only wise God, the everlasting Father, came down from his spiritual Throne, and, in Fulness of Time, became the Seed of the Virgin, and appeared as a mortal Man, like to us, Sin excepted, that he might enter into Death, and, by Virtue of his everlasting spiritual Word, or almighty Decree, quicken and revive the same pure Spirit and Body in a far more transcendent Condition than before he dyed while he was on Earth: he likewise ascended into Heaven to be Judge both of the quick and the dead; and hereby he performed the Work of our Redemption.

ARTICLE VI. When CHRIST dyed GOD dyed: ENOCH, MOSES, and ELIAS, were taken up into Heaven, and left with deputed Power there, while God was performing the Work of Redemption here on Earth.

YOU say, *if God dyed, there was an Effect produced by some Cause, when, at the same Time, no Cause can be found equal to that Effect; therefore God could not dy.* You likewise afterwards say, that *Power cannot exist at all without its Subject; but if the Subject be destroyed, all Capacity of acting, &c. of which the Subject was before possessed, or all that Power, which could be attributed to it, must be destroyed also.* You add, *that the supreme Being cannot communicate any Degree of Power to any of his Creatures, that can lessen or subtract from his own Capacity or Power.*

I have proved before that *God* and *Christ* are the same; and the *Christ* not only laid down his Life is plain from his own Words, but that in him was the Power to take it up again; *I have Power*, says he, *to lay it down, and Power to take it up again.* CHRIST, being *God*, did assuredly know that the Power of his Word, which proceeded from him, when in Heaven and in the State of a Creator and Father, would produce so great an Effect as to raise himself from the dead, after he had gone thro the Office of a Son or Redeemer, according to his own Saying, that *Heaven and Earth should sooner pass away than his Word, till all Things were fulfilled:* so that this Word proceeded from *Jesus Christ* before he became incarnate, while he was in the State of Creator and Father, at which Time he decreed concerning what was to happen to himself when in the Condition of a Son; for the Performance of which, the Prophet says, *he swore by himself, because there was none greater than he*: the Effect therefore, which you object to, proceeded from a Cause than which there was none greater. *Enoch, Moses, and Elias*, being highly favoured by Heaven, were taken up in a different Manner from the Rest of Me, to be a typical Representation of the Godhead, while God was on Earth: God invested them with his Power; and they being of the Nature of God, and not of Angels, God knew they could not err. Had God came down in the Fullness of his Glory, this Earth could not have stood before it; he therefore invested those whom he had chosen for that great Work with it: and when he humbled himself to them, it was to his own Power; for, tho his Person was not in Heaven, his Power was there; and it was that Power which he called Father, when he said, *Father forgive them, for they know not what they do.* It is a consistent with Reason that *Enoch, Moses and Elias*, whom God took up into Heaven without seeing Corruption, should be qualified for so great a Trust, as that any other created

Beings should: and you grant that it is not inconsistent with Reason that God should produce a Being as an Instrument not only to make a World, but to support it. The Power with which *Enoch, Moses, and Elias*, were invested, being infinite, could never become finite, tho the Being possessed of it might, by Virtue of the Power itself, change itself awhile. As infinite Power cannot dy, it was by that alone that *Jesus Christ* did truly say, *he should raise himself from the dead*: because finite Power cannot exist without its Subject, you unjustly conclude that infinite cannot: Nothing can be more certain than that the glorious Person of the Deity may be resident in one Place, and his Power operating in others: by the Power of his Word speaking both Men and the Angels are made; and the World stands by his Decree alone. He left his immortal Power and Glory in the Heavens above, and brought forth himself a pure Person here on Earth: it was the everlasting Power of *Christ's* divine Word, spoken before he dyed, which raised the God from Death to Life again: if that God, who said *he had Power to lay down his Life, and Power to take it up again* , did not dy, and was bury'd in the Grave, and after the decreed Time of three Days revive again by a quickening Spirit, how can the following Parts of Scripture be Words of Truth? But, as they proceeded from the everlasting God, the God of Truth, who cannot possibly ly, they are sacred Truths: the Texts which I mean are these: *thou wilt not leave my Soul in Hell neither wilt thou suffer thine holy One to see Corruption. — he spake of the Resurrection of* CHRIST, *that his Soul was not left in Hell, neither his Flesh did see Corruption.* Acts, Chap.2. Ver.27, and 31. *To this End* CHRIST *both dyed, and rose and revived, that he might be the Lord both of the dead and the living.* Rom. Chap.14. Ver.9. *Fear not, I am the first and the last: I am he that liveth, and was dead, and , behold, I am alive for evermore, amen, and have the Keys of Hell and of Death.* Rev. Chap. 1. Ver.17, and 18. *The first and the last, which was dead, and is alive.* Rev. Chap 2. Ver. 8. As I have proved that God and Christ are the same, and the *Christ* dyed, the Inference is obvious that *God* dyed in *Christ*, if you allow those Scriptures to be true on which I found my Arguments; and as you do not appear to dispute the Truth of them, I must look on these Proofs from Scripture as valid.

What you say of the *supreme* Being not being able to *communicate any Degree of Power to any of his Creature, that can lessen his own Capacity or Power,* is Nothing to the Purpose; for we nowhere assert that the Power of God was lessened: his Power suffered no Diminution, but existed always the same.

ARTICLE VII. Concerning JOHN REEVE'S and LODOWICK MUGGLETON'S Commission, with the Words which God spoke to the former on the 3d, 4th, and 5th, of February 1651, with some Observations on them.

You object to *Reeve's* and *Muggleton's* Commission in these Words: *the Opinions they advanced are wholly inconsistent with the Suggestions of the divine Spirit, the Spirit of Truth and Order; neither can it be made appear that they had any Commission from God as his Prophets, because they claimed an uncreaturely and inhuman Authority of damning and saving whomsoever they pleased.*

  I hope what I have advanced already is of Force sufficient to obviate your former Objections: you are to consider that the Doctrines which I have asserted in the former Articles are the Doctrines of *Reeve* and *Muggleton*, and as I have proved them to be consistent with the holy Scriptures, and those Scriptures are received by us both as divine, these Doctrines of *Reeve* and *Muggleton* must be allowed to have the Stamp of Divinity on them, as they are consistent with the divine Spirit, the Spirit of Truth and Order. These Doctrines contain a Manifestation of God in his three Dispensations on Earth: and whoever will compare Scripture with scripture may clearly see that the same *Jehova* in the Time of the Law was the very same *Jesus* in the Time of the Gospel; and that which makes the seeming Difference between the Father, Son, and the Holy Ghost, as if they were three distinct Essences or Persons, is Nothing but the Appearance of the high and mighty God under a threefold Denomination to the Sons of Men. Under the Law, before his spiritual Body became Flesh, God was called *Jehova*, the high and mighty one of *Israel*, the most high God, a Man of War, the Lord of Hosts, I am that I am, &c, when he became *Jesus* in the Flesh he was called the only begotten Son of God, the *Messiah*, the Redeemer, *Immanuel*, the Lamb of God, &c. when the most glorious God had wrought our Redemption in Flesh, and was ascended on high, to his eternal personal Glory again, he was called *Holy Ghost*, because it is by the Influence of his holy Spirit that we know the Lord *Jesus Christ* as Father, Son, and Holy Ghost, were, are, and can be no other, but one undivided glorious Essence or spiritual personal Substance from all Eternity; and that same Being, as I observed in a former Article, is a Father by Creation, a Son by Redemption, and Holy Ghost by Sanctification; three Titles and one God.

  What I have hitherto said in this Article is to shew that the *Muggletonian* Doctrine is Scripture Doctrine: and I shall now offer to your Considerations some Characteristics of *Reeve* and *Muggleton* being true Prophets of God: and I will begin, as a proper Introduction, with the Words which God spake to *John Reeve*, three successive Mornings together, to the Hearing of the outward Ears: in which Words is contained the whole of his Commission.

  The Words which *John Reeve* declares were spoken to him by God three Mornings successively, *Febr.* 3d, 4th and 5th, 1651.

  "I have given thee understanding of my Mind in the Scriptures above all Men in the World: look into thine own Body, there shalt thou see the Kingdom of Heaven and the Kingdom of Hell."

The Principles of the Muggletonians Asserted 283

"I have chosen thee my last Messenger for a great Work unto this bloody unbelieving World, and have given thee *Lodowick Muggleton* to be thy Mouth."

"I have put the two-edged Sword of my Spirit into thy Mouth, that whomsoever I pronounced blessed through thy Mouth, he is blessed to Eternity, and whomsoever thou pronounce cursed through thy Mouth, he is cursed to Eternity."

"Again" says *John Reeve*, "the Lord spake unto me these Words, saying, thy Body shall be thy Hell, and thy Spirit shall be they Devil that shall torment thee to Eternity:" then, continues the Prophet *Reeve*, "for a Moment I saw this Hell within me, which caused me to say, Lord, I will go where-ever thou sendeth me, only be with me: these were the Lord's Words, says he, spoken to me the first Morning, and my Answer to my God being perfectly awake when he spake unto me, the Lord is my Witness, as I was at the writing thereof."

"The next Morning," continues the Prophet, "the Lord spake unto me, saying, go thou unto *Lodowick Muggleton*, and with him go unto *Thomas Turner*, and he shall bring you unto one *John Tanee*, and do thou deliver my Message when thou cometh there; and if *Lodowick Muggleton* deny to go with thee, then do thou from me pronounce him cursed to Eternity: these Words," says he, "the Lord spake unto me the second Morning and no more."

"The third and last Morning", continues he, "the Lord spake unto me "these Words, saying go thou unto *Lodowick Muggleton*, and then go thou unto one *John Robins*, a Prisoner in *new Bridewell*, and do thou deliver my Message to him when thou cometh there: these were the Lord's Words," says *John Reeve*, "the third and last Morning."

"The Holy Ghost," continues he, "beareth Witness in my Spirit of the Truth of that which I shall write unto you, that, the first Words which the Lord spake unto me, the Words speaking came into my Spirit and body with such an exceeding bright burning Glory of godlike majesty, that I did not know whether I was a mortal Man or an immortal God, so glorious are the Words of the immoral God, that the Tongues of Men or Angels can never express it! My Body was also changed at that Time for a Season in a most dreadful Manner to behold, of which many can bear Witness at this Time: the Lord also opened the Understanding of my fellow Witness, and made him obedient with me in the Messages of the Lord."

The first Remark which I shall now make is, that *Reeve* does not claim an *uncreaturely Authority of damning and saving*, as you say he does, and on which you found an Objection: he could pronounce neither Blessing nor Curse, but as God was pleased to do it through his Mouth.

Now to the Proofs of the Truth of this Commission. In these Words or Reeve he and *Muggleton* are said to be favoured by God with an Understanding of the Scriptures above all Men: and if their Doctrines agree with this Declaration, we have a sufficient Proof of the Truth of the Declaration; and I have demonstrated in the former

Articles, that those Doctrines of *Reeve* and *Muggleton* are Scripture Doctrines; from which I conclude that they proceed from one and the same Spirit.

Let us now come to the Discharge of their Messages to the particular Persons to whom they were sent: they went to *John Tanee*, who affirmed to them that there never was any personal God; he likewise affirmed that God could not be confined to the Womb of a Virgin; he also said that he could not be a God who suffered Death, and, afterwards, was closed in a Tomb three Days and three Nights: he denyed that *Christ* rose from the dead, and his Ascension into Heaven: he asserted that he had a Commission from God, whom he declared to be an infinite Spirit, without any bodily Parts or personal Substance; his Commission from God, he said, was to lead the Nation of the *Jews to Jerusalem*, to make them the only happy People. This *John Tance* was the Head of the *Ranters* or universal Redemptionists, who are now in the World speaking and writing against the spiritual Mystery of the immortal God cloathing himself with Flesh in the Person of a Man, the Man *Jesus*: after *Reeve* and *Muggleton* had been with him, he declined, and came to an untimely End.

The second Message on which they were sent from God was to one *John Robins* then in new Prison, to pronounce a Sentence of eternal Death upon him for his Blasphemy against God. This John Robins was the last great Antichrist or Man of Sin, that was to fulfil what is written in the 2d Chapter of the 2d Epistle to the *Thessalonians*. This *John Robins* was by many people worshipped as a God; they fell upon their Faces at his Feet, calling him their Lord and their God; and he commanded them to mention the Name of no other God but him. This is what *Reeve* and *Muggleton* were Witnesses of; but, after the Sentence delivered from the Lord *Jesus* by their Mouths against that Prince of Devils in that Age, he was constrained to disown his assumed Godhead; and his cursed Design came to a sudden Conclusion, which the Power of the Magistrates could not accomplish. After he heard the Sentence of Death pronounced against him for taking the Glory of God to himself, he spake these Words and no more, *It is finished, the Lord's Will be done.* As this Account of *John Robins* is true, the Effect which the Sentence had on him is another Indication of the Reality of their Commission.

After the Delivery of these two Messages, they were moved, by Virtue of their Commission, to make known to some of the Clergy and other Preachers that they had no Commission from God to preach to the People, which some of them confessed to be true: and they likewise assured them that, as the sacred Scriptures were uttered and written by holy Prophets, Apostles, and Evangelists, who were inspired by the holy Ghost, so none can interpret them but such as are inspired by the same Spirit.

They declare from the Lord that they two only were the last Men that ever shall speak or write by Commission from the true God to the People, whilst this World endures; and whoever shall live to see

The Principles of the Muggletonians Asserted   285

an End of this Commission shall suddenly see an End of this World and the Glory thereof; but that Day and Hour are known only to the everlasting Father who dwells in *Jesus Christ* bodily.

They farther declare the Form and Nature of God, the Form and Nature of the Devil, the Form and Nature of Angels, and what Condition *Adam* was in before his Fall, and how he happened to fall, also what the Glory of Heaven is, and what Hell is, and their Situation to Eternity.

At the Time when these two Prophets arose, there was not one in the World besides themselves who understood any of those Principles which are the Foundation of true Knowledge: but they were chosen by God to reveal those Truths to his chosen People: and I believe it will be allowed by many that if their Doctrines explain and illustrate the Scriptures, and open to us the Mysteries thereof, they carry the Marks of true Prophets with them: as they were Men, ignorant of all Languages, can it be supposed they could write a Book as large as the Bible, with Variety of Matter, and Propriety of Language, containing a rich Discovery of divine Truths, without being inspired? Their Doctrines are calculated for the Happiness of Mankind here, as well as hereafter; they prohibit the Use of the Sword of Steel, and forbid us not only to hurt, but to envy, one another.

Perhaps you will object that they have written many Things not contained in the Scriptures, and for which there is no Authority in any preceding Writings: pray what Books had Moses when he wrote of the Creation of the World? Tho *Christ* and his Apostles allude sometimes to former prophetical Writings, yet they spoke by Inspiration of the eternal Spirit only.

If after all I have said you or any other should ask for farther Proofs of *John Reeve and Lodowick Muggleton* being true Prophets, and of their writing by Inspiration, all I can say more is this, if you have the Spirit of the Scriptures no Man can deceive you.

I shall conclude with a Prayer of the Prophet *Reeve's*.

"O! Lord God of heavenly Order, and not of earthly confusion, even for the Glory of thy dreadful Namesake, deliver thy redeemed, not only from exalting the literal Scriptures above the holy Spirit which spake them, but also from disputing against the Mysteriousness of them; then no Kind of natural Witchcraft, which bears the Name of spiritual Power, shall have Dominion over them for ever; but they shall patiently wait for their Change by a peaceable Death, or being swallowed up of Life, through the Appearance of our only God and Saviour in the Air, with his mighty Angels, to reward every Man according to his Works: even so come Lord Jesus, come quickly, and make it manifest, in the Sight of Men and Angels, whether thou hast sent us as we have declared, or not."

Postscript

EXCUSE me, Sir, if I now give you a Summary of the Arguments which I have advanced in the seven foregoing Articles, in Confutation of what you have advanced against our Principles, by which I think I have asserted them by Reason and the Scriptures.

First, I have demonstrated the Eternity of Matter, by shewing the impossibility of its Nonexistence, and that it is consistent with the *Mosaic* Doctrine: I have shewed that your Arguments, if I may call them such, against the Eternity of it are unphilosophical and confused, and supported by no Texts of Scripture.

Secondly, I have proved the Existence of *two eternal Beings* by proving the Eternity of Matter, and shewed that you have set the Subject in a false Light by calling them *eternal active Principles*, which we no-where do: I have shewed from Scripture what the Fall of the Angle was, and how it was the Origin of Sin in our first Parents, and to whom the Curse at the Fall extended, and to whom the Promise of a future Blessing, and thence I have shewed who the two Seeds are.

Thirdly, I have shewed that God's being in the Form of a Man is no Abridgement of his infinite Power, or eternal Existence, and that what you have advanced in Opposition to it is weak, and your Inferences no Way conclusive; and I have proved it to be the Doctrine of the Scriptures

Fourthly, I have demonstrated *God* and *Christ* to be one, and that he became Flesh; that it is evident from frequent Texts in both the old and new Testaments I have abundantly shewed; and what you advance as philosophical Arguments against it are Nothing to the Purpose, if they were really philosophical instead of trifling; for in the Subject the Scriptures only are the Criterion to such as believe in them and Christ: and I have in this Article explained the Scripture Doctrine of the Trinity, that the three Titles are all belonging to one Essence.

Fifthly, I have farther proved that *Jesus Christ* was God the Creator of the World, by comparing several Texts of the old and new Testament together, and by shewing, in various Instances, that what is predicated of one is predicated of the other.

Sixthly, I have proved that when *Christ* dyed God dyed, and that what you have said against *Enoch, Moses, and Elias*, being taken up into Heaven, to answer the End proposed, which was to reside in Heaven while Christ was upon Earth, is no Confutation of that Doctrine.

Seventhly, and lastly, I have related the Indications of the Truth of *Reeve's* and *Muggleton's* Commission, and shewed that what you have asserted to the contrary does, no Way, destroy the Credit of it: and now excuse me, if I wish that what I have done may contribute to your embracing the Truth of what is the inward Satisfaction of your Friend and Servant.

A.B.

The END.

TRUTH and REASON defended
AGAINST
Error and Burning Envy
IN A
PUBLICK DISPUTE,

Held at the *Magpye* in the *Borough, Southwark* on the 16th and 18th Days of *Dec. 1728.*
BETWEEN
JOHN RAWLINSON, a *Muggletonian*
AND
WILLIAM HENDERSON, a *Quaker*,

In the Presence of some Hundreds of People; then taken in *Short-Hand,* and since transcrib'd by the Consent of both Parties, who have read and carefully corrected the same.

WHEREIN

The Doctrine of the *Holy Trinity* is urg'd against the Errors of the *Muggletonians,* and their *Curse* converted into a *Blessing.*

To which is added

I. A Replication to Sixteen Articles of the *Muggletonians* Arguments.
II. Some Remarks on their Principles, deduc'd from the Writings of *John Reeve* and *Lodowick Muggleton,* whom they pretend were the **Two Last Witnesses**, spoken of in the 11th Chap. Of the *Revelations.*

III. Six QUERIES propos'd to the *Muggletonians*.

Publish'd by WILLIAM HENDERSON.
LONDON

Printed for the Author, and sold for him at the Pennsylvania Coffee-house in Birchin-lane; theGeorge and Gate in Grace-church-street; Kent's Coffee-house in Chancery-lane; Little Brittis Coffee-house, the upper end of New Bond-Street near Hanover-square; the King's Head Alehouse at East lane Stairs, Rotherhithe, Powell's Coffee-house in Spittle Fields; Edward Baldin's, a Stationer, at Ratcliff-cross; Robert Clarke's a Bookseller, the Corner of Tooley street, next the Bridge-foot, South-wark; Nando's Coffee-house at Temple-Bar; the Parliament Coffee-house, in the Courts of Requests; and by John Payne at the Black Spread Eagle in Ludgate-street.

To the Lord Bishop of London.

May it graciously please thee, in thy wonted Goodness and Zeal for the Promulgation of the Gospel, and the *Protestant* Churches, (whereof CHRIST is the Head) to peruse the following Argumental Discourse, in which I have been concern'd, altho' I may not (being unqualify'd for want of proper Learning, and unacquainted with the Method of Arguments and the Force of Language) have succeeded so well as I could have wish'd in the Explanation of my Thoughts; yet have I judg'd it my Duty to defend the Christian Religion, and to detect those extravagant Notions maintain'd by a Sect of People call'd *Muggletonians*.

Dedication

Give me leave, Great Prelate, humbly to hope, that these my Endeavors, altho' in a plain illiterate Stile, may be of some Service to the Publick, and find Acceptance with thee and others of polite Learning, judicious Understanding, and Fatherly Care, in nourishing all such endeavours as any way tend to support the true Gospel Faith: Therefore have I presum'd to prefix thy venerable Name to this Publication, being fully persuaded it will both adorn the same, and help to convince the Reader, that the Verities I have defended are sacred, and that my Design is not unworthy of thy Patronage. And so shall leave this as a Testimony of my utmost Respect,

Who am Thy
Unartful Admirer,
W. HENDERSON.

The Preface.

Courteous Reader,

FOR as much as my natural Propensity is not to urge or undertake the Disputes in this public manner; knowing my own Inabilities therein, I hold it expedient to give thee a short hint how I happened to engage in this.

Being altogether a Stranger to the *Muggletonian* Principles, and never conversed with any of that Profession on Faith and Principles, until the 9th Day of *December* last in the Evening, I happened to be at my late Lodging in *Holborn;* where three Persons came and enquired for me, whom I did not know, whose Business was to tell me, that some *Quakers* and *Muggletonians* were to meet in the *Burrough Southwark,* at 6 of the Clock in the same Evening, in order to converse about some Points of Religion, on which they had met several Times before; they having heard, by a Friend of Mine, that I was willing to be at their next Meeting on that Occasion.

Whereupon I immediately went with them, it being about the Hour of the Meeting.

When come to the Place appointed, I observ'd a Company of about 16 Persons; and, having sate some Time with them, making Remarks in my Mind upon the Discourse of both Parties, I desired Leave of the Company to speak a little, in order to inform my self more fully in the Matter on which they treated: And leave was accordingly granted.

Whereupon I discoursed with one of the *Muggletonians,* for some Time; and when I had informed my self, in the Nature of the Subject, I told them, I thought it was not proper to handle such weighty and important Affairs, where Smoking and Drinking was the Diversion or Employment of the Hearers; But if any one of the *Muggletonians,* wou'd enter their Position, or Article of Faith, on which we had then discoursed, in Writing, that I would underwrite it on behalf of the *Quakers*; upon which one of the *Muggletonians* wrote the Proposition, and I underwrote it in the Negative. Then we settled Preliminaries, and agreed on Time and Place for meeting, which thou wilt find in their proper Order. So conclude,

Thy Real, And Hearty Well Wisher,

W. H.

292 Early Muggletonian Polemics

Part I.

A PUBLICK DISPUTE Between A Muggletonian and a Quaker.

Muggletonian.
Our Faith is this, **That Jesus Christ is the only God and Lord of heaven and Earth; and that, when he took his Journey in flesh, he invested Moses and Elias with Power of being Guardians of his Person, and also gave them Charge of his Kingdom till his return.**
Quaker. The Proposition is denied.
The Matter to be argued by John Rawlinson on behalf of the Affirmative, and William Henderson on behalf of the Negative; the Old and New Testaments, according to the common English Translation, are to be Matters of Proof; the said Moderators to be Judges of Time spent by either Party, that one do not infringe on the other's Time, when the Matter of his Argument requires it; that no passionate Expressions be made use of, or any Reflection on either side; and if the Disputants agree to propose any Question to said Moderators, for further Explanation, that they may give their Opinion therein, and not enter any farther on the Argument; the Disputants on both sides are agreed to dispute only in the English Tounge: To meet at the Magpye in the Burrough, at 5 of the Clock, Monday Evening, being the 16 of Decem. 1728. Sign'd by John Rawlinson, and William Henderson.
Being met at the Time and Place appointed: Rawlinson proceeded as followeth, Viz.
Muggleton. I shall begin with the first part of the Proposition, and prove Christ to be very God; and the first Text I shall quote for this, shall be Deut. ch. 32. ver. 39. See now that I, even I, am he, and there is no God with me. I kill and I make alive, I would and I heal, neither is there any that can deliver out of my hand. The next is Isa. Ch. 9. ver. 6. For unto us a child is born, unto us a son is given, and the government shall be upon his shoulder, and his name shall be called wonderful, counselor, the mighty God, the everlasting father, the prince of peace. And ch. 43 from ver. 9 to 12. Let all nations be gathered together, and let the people be assembled: who among them can declare this, and shew us former things? Let them bring forth their witnesses, that they may be justified: or let them hear and say, it is truth. Ye are my witnesses, saith the Lord, and my servant whom I have chosen: that ye may know and believe me, and understand that I am he: before me there was no God formed, neither shall there be after me. I, even I, am the Lord, and beside me there is no Saviour. And again ch. 4.5 ver. 21, 22. Tell ye, and bring them near, yea, let them take counsel together: who hath declared this from ancient time? who hath told it from that time? have not I, the Lord? And there is no God else beside me, a just god and a Saviour, and there is none beside me. Look unto me and be ye saved, all the ends of the earth: for I am God, and there is none else. I shall now leave the Old

Testament and proceed to the New; many more Proofs might be brought, but none more to the Purpose. The first I shall bring from the New Testament is Matt. ch. I. ver. 23. Behold, a Virgin shall be with child, and shall bring forth a son, and they shall call his name Emmanuel, which, being interpreted, is, God with us. You may do with the Interpretation as you please, Mr. Henderson, I shan't run over all the Texts of Scripture that might be brought for this; because I think I have brought sufficient to prove the first Part of the Proposition, **That Christ is very God**. The Text is, concerning **the Power that was invested on** Moses **and** Elias; of which I have Occasion from your Words, so that you may begin as soon as you please.

Quak. I don't think it convenient to begin, till thou has done; go on with the other Part of thy Proposition.

M. I'll then proceed; the first Text I shall bring to prove the second part of my Proposition is from Psal. 91. ver. 11. For he shall give his angels charge over thee, to keep thee in all thy ways. Ver. 12. They shall bear thee up in their hands, lest though dash thy foot against a stone. And again, Matt. ch. 4. ver. 6. And saith unto him, if thou be the son of God, cast they self down, for it is written, He shall give his angels charge concerning thee, and in their hands they shall bear thee up, lest at any time thou dash thy foot against a stone. And ver. 7. Jesus saith unto him, it is written again, thou shalt not tempt the Lord thy God. And ver. 8, 9, 10. Again, the devil taketh him up into an exceeding high mountain, and sheweth him all the kingdoms of the world, and the glory of them; and saith unto him, All these things will I give unto thee if thou wilt fall down and worship me. Then saith Jesus, Get thee behind me Satan: for it is written, Thou shalt worship the Lord thy God, and him only shalt thou serve. And ver. 11. Then the devil leaveth him, and behold the angels came and ministered unto him. Luke, ch.9. ver. 27,&c. But I tell you of a truth, there be some standing here which shall not taste of death till they see the kingdom of God. And it came to pass about an eight day after these sayings, he took Peter, and John, and James, and went up into a mountain to pray, and as he pray'd, the fashion of his countenance was altered, and his raiment was white and glistering. And behold, there talked with him two men, which were Moses and Elias. Who appeared in glory, and speak of his decease which he should accomplish at Jerusalem. But Peter, and they that were with him, were heavy with sleep: and when they were awake, they saw his glory, and the two men that stood with him. And it came to pass, as they departed from him, Peter said unto Jesus, Master it is good for us to be here; and let us make three tabernacles, one for thee, and one for Moses, and one for Elias: not knowing what he said. While he thus spake, there came a cloud and overshadowed them: and they feared as they entered into the cloud. And there came a voice out of the cloud, saying, This is my beloved Son, hear him. The first Quotations were from the Royal Prophets of old; the Inference I shall draw is this, that the saying from the Old Testament were, That God had sworn by himself to take upon him Flesh.

Q. Thou hast not quoted that Text; 'tis not in Holy Writ.

M. If I hadn't, I shall, and others, as they serve me in the Course of my Argument.

Q. Quote me what signifies as much, or to that Effect.

M. I don't come to question your God; you question my God. I am assured that the God I believe in, is not the God you believe in; and I'm sure we shan't agree there.

Q. Thou know'st our Rules are, that we should quote Text of Scripture for our Arguments; thou hast not quoted such a Text; keep to thy Test; quote what thou wilt, and keep to the Text.

M. I shall take care of you, Mr. Henderson; John ch. I. ver 14. And the word was made Flesh, and dwelt among us.

Q. That hath no Relation to God's swearing he would take Flesh upon him.

M. That I shall prove by Isaiah the Prophet.

Q. I'll drop the Argument upon that; but thou can'st not do it.

M. I'm not afraid of you, Mr. Henderson, I shall follow you step by step; I don't know the Methods you go on with, but I know my own; my general Way is, to quote the Substance of the Text.

Q. I expected thou should'st have had thy Notes of Scripture ready; its much of a Man of they Sense wou'd quote Texts, and then begin Arguments quite foreign to the Matter in them contained.

M. I hadn't gone from my Text at all, for God swore by himself, as there was none greater than he.

Q. Did he sware he would take Flesh upon him?

M. That I can prove he has done.

Q. Shew me that Text.

M. I have shewn it already in Matt. Ch. I. Ver. 23. Behold a virgin &c. And Isa. Ch. 9. Ver. 6. To us a child is born, &c.

Q. I have those Texts in view; and they don't any ways favour thy Assertion.

M. If you have it, why do you ask me for it? I'm to go with the Prophets, I never intermix a new piece of Cloth with an old Garment; my Quotations I draw from the Old Testament, that God according to his Word must become Flesh, the God that I believe in.

Q. Take thy own Way, I shan't interrupt thee, proceed.

M. I now proceed to draw an Inference from those Texts which mention that God did promise to become Flesh, and I think God did fulfill his Word, when Matthew writes of the Scripture Records, he writes of the Substance of Things, that God was incarnate in the body of Flesh, you call it the Son of God; therefore proceed and raise your Objection on mine, I shall proceed no further now.

Q. I shan't begin till thou hast done; for when I begin, I would not be interrupted till I have ended; but if thou hast done, I'll begin.

M. I have done, I insist upon Christ to be God.

Q. The first Thing I shall go upon is to prove the GOD-HEAD Omnipotent, Omnipresent and Omniscient; and to prove that God, the eternal being created the Heavens and the Earth, I shall quote Gen. ch I, ver. I. In the beginning God created the heavens and the earth. And ver. 10. God called the dry land earth, and the gathering together of the waters be called sea. And Rev. ch. 10. ver. 6. And the Angel sware by him that liveth for ever and ever, who created heaven and the things that herein are, and the earth and the things that therein are, and the sea and the things which are therein, &c. The next is from the Prophet Isa. Ch. 48. ver. 13. Mine hand also has laid the foundation of the earth, and my right hand hath spanned the heavens, &c. And ch. 42. ver. 5. Thus saith God the Lord, he that created the heavens, and stretched them out; he that spread forth the earth, and that which cometh out of it, &c. Ver. 6. I the Lord have called thee in righteousness (speaking prophetically of Jesus) and will hold thine hand, and will keep thee, and give thee for a covenant of the people, for a light of the Gentiles. This also is a Prophesy of Christ. I hope thou wilt not be angry, Friend Rawlinson, because I am now proving the GODHEAD; do I speak too fast for thee?

M. I quench not your Spirit, speak on.

Q. And in ver. 7. Proceeds further, To open the blind eyes, to bring out the prisoners from the prison, and them that sit in darkness out of the prison house. And ver. 8. I am the Lord, that is my name, and my glory will I not give to another, neither my praise to graven images. Psal. 19. Ver. I. The heavens declare the glory of God and the firmament sheweth his handywork. Ver 2. Day unto day uttereth speech, and night unto night sheweth knowledge. Ver. 3. There is no speech nor language, where their voice is not heard. Ver. 4. Their line is gone out through all the earth, and their words to the end of the world: in them hath he set a tabernacle for the sun. Ver. 5. Which is as a Bridegroom coming out of his chamber, and rejoyceth as a strong man to run a race. Ver. 6. His going forth is from the end of the heaven, and his circuit unto the ends of it, and there is nothing hid from the heat thereof. I Kings, ch. 8. Ver. 27. But will God indeed dwell on earth? Behold, the heaven, and heaven of heavens cannot contain thee. And 2 Chron. ch. 2. ver. 6 and ch. 6 ver. 18. To the same Effect by Solomon. The next I quote is from the Prophet Isa.ch. 40. ver 12. to this Effect, Who has measured the waters in the hollow of his hand? (speaking of God) and meted out heaven with a span, and comprehended the dust of the earth in a measure, and weighed the mountains in scales, and the hills in a balance? And in ver. 13. Who hath directed the Spirit of the Lord? Or, being his counselor, hath taught him? And Psal. 90. ver I. Lord, thou has been our dwelling place in all generations. Ver. 2. Before the mountains were brought forth, or ever thou hadst formed the earth and the world; even from everlasting to everlasting thou art God And Isa. Ch. 40 ver. 28. Hast thou not known, hast thou not heard that the everlasting God, the Lord, the creator of the ends of the earth, fainteth not, neither is weary? There is no searching of his understanding. Again from Heb. ch I. ver. 10, 11 12. And, Thou Lord in the beginning hast laid the foundation of the earth; and the heavens are the works of thine hands. They shall perish, but thou remainest, and they all wax old as doth a garment; and as a vesture shalt thou fold them up, and they shall be changed: but thou art the same, and they years shall not fail. Rom. Ch. II. ver. 32, 33, 34. And Colos. ch. 2 ver. 8, 9, 10. Quote the 8th and 10th to give the Substance of the Matter, and the Occasion on which my Text speaks beginning thus, according to Paul's Advice, Beware lest any man spoil you through philosophy and vain deceit, after the tradition of men, after the rudiments of the world, and not after Christ: For in him dwelleth all the fullness of the Godhead bodily. Thou won't be Angry at me now, Friend Rawlinson. The next I shall quote is from the Prophet Mal. Ch. 3. Ver. 6. For I am the Lord, I change not: I have more Quotations to offer by and by; but I will now paraphrase a little on this Text; For in him dwelleth all the fullness of the Godhead bodily. Had Christ said, that the Godhead dwelt eternally in the Body, viz. in that human Body born of the Virgin, then I should come into the Opinion of those, that say there was no God before Christ was born: But as there is no Scripture that will maintain there was a Body of Flesh, coequal in eternity with God the Father, I cannot allow it; for he that Begat is greater then he that is Begotten, and must have been before him that was Begotten.

M. There's no such Thing affirm'd.

Q. This is a Commentary deduceable from they Position.

M. I must needs break in with your Spirit there; there's no such Thing affirm'd. what is said there, you are to Dispute upon. I have proved Christ to be God; I did not say a body of Flesh from Eternity.

Q. I say God was and is from Eternity, and nothing can be Eternal but God: There be, says the Apostle Paul, I Cor. Ch. 8. Ver. 5, 6. Gods many, and Lords many: But to us there is but one God, the Father, of whom are all things, and we in him; and one Lord Jesus Christ, by whom are all things, and we by him. Now I proceed to the rest of my Proofs to the same Effect as before, Psal. 2. Ver. 8. Ask of me, and I shall give thee the heaven for thine inheritance, and the uttermost parts of the earth for thy possession. The Psalmist at this Time speak from the Holy Spirit of God, representing God the Father to his Son Jesus Christ; and the Power of the GODHEAD that was vested in Jesus was from the Father; he affirm'd it not above the Prerogative of his Father.

M. The Proof of that, Mr. Henderson.

Q. I will prove it by and by; Thou art my Son, this day have I Begotten thee. This proceeds from the same Spirit, Friend Rawlinson, Psal. 16. Ver. 10. For thou wilt not leave my soul in hell; neither wilt thou suffer thine holy one to see corruption, or to that Effect. Acts, ch. 13. ver. 35. Quoting the same Scripture, which is a corroborating of the same Text by the Apostle. Matt. Ch. 28. ver. 18. And Jesus came, and spake unto them, saying all power is given unto me in heaven and in earth. Hence it is plain, that Christ clam'd Coequality in the GOD-HEAD by Gift of the Father, not by Prerogative or Presumption; altho' he be the Son of God, yet learned he Obedience as in the Form of a Servant.

M. I did not say by Prerogative or Presumption; they are your own Words.

Q. If he took it not himself he had it given him.

M. Very well, then he is very God; I hope you don't deny it.

Q. The Father made him so, i.e., Coequal with himself.

M. You are welcome to speak as long as you please.

Q. The next Text of Scripture I add is James, ch I ver. 17. Every good gift, and every perfect gift is from above, and cometh down from the Father of lights, with whom is no variableness, neither shadow of turning. Heb. ch. 13. Ver. 8. Jesus Christ the same yesterday, and today, and for ever. Psal. 90. Ver.4. For a thousand years in thy sight are but as yesterday, when it is past, and as a watch in the night. Joh. Ch. I. ver I. In the beginning was the word, and the word was with God, and the word was God. Ver 10. He was in the world, and the world was made by him:

M. Ergo, Christ must be God.

Q. Give me leave to proceed, and make thy Remarks afterwards. The next Thing I shall go upon is, to prove that Jesus is the Son of God; Heb. ch. I. ver. 1, 2. God wo at sundry times, and in divers manners, spake in time past unto the fathers by the prophets, Hath in these last days spoken to us by his Son, whom he hath appointed heir of all things, by whom also he made the worlds. And Phil. Ch. 2. From ver. 5. To 12. Let this mind be in you, which was also in Christ Jesus: Who being in the form of God, thought it not robbery to be equal with God: But made himself of no reputation, and took upon him the form of a servant, and was made in the likeness of men: And being found in fashion as a man, he humbled himself, and became obedient unto death, even the death of the cross. Wherefore God also hath highly exalted him, and given him a name which is above every name: That at the name of Jesus every knee should bow, of things in heaven and things in earth, and things under the earth; And that every tongue should confess, that Jesus Christ is Lord, to the glory of God the Father. The next is from I John, ch. 5. Ver. 5. Who is he that overcometh the world, but he that believeth that Jesus is the Son of God? Ver. 6. This is he that came by water and blood, even Jesus Christ; not by water only, but by water and blood and it is the Spirit that beareth witness, because the Spirit is truth. Let me tough a little upon the Trinity, because the Course of my Text leads me to it; ver. 7. For there are three that bear record in heaven, the Father, the Word, and the Holy Ghost: and these three are One. This is God in Trinity.

M. Not dividing the Substance I hope.

Q. The Text distinguisheth, ver. 8. And there are three that bear witness in earth, the Spirit, and the water, and the blood: and these three agree in one. And as I allow but one Eternal God in Trinity, I shall prove it in Triunal Conjunction Unity. &c. More of this when I enter upon my General Comment.

M. Have you done?

Q. No, I haven't well begun yet; and ver. 10. He that believeth on theSon of God, hath the witness in himself, he that believeth not God, hath made him a liar, because he believeth not the record that God gave of his Son. And from ver. 11. I will shew you what this Record is, from the Words of my Text, And this is the record, that God hath given to us eternal life: and this life is in his Son. Ver. 12. He that hath the Son, hath life; and he that hath not the Son of God, that not life. The next Quotation on this Subject is from the Prophet Zech. Ch. 4. Ver. 12, to 14. When he speaks of the two Olive Branches, and the two Golden Candlesticks, which he saw in a Vision, These, faith he, are the two anointed ones, that stand before the Lord of the whole earth. And John, in Rev. ch. 11. Ver. 4. Speaks to the same Purpose, corroborating the same Text. I'll touch a little backward on the Holy Trinity, and add that God is a Spirit from the Evangelist John, ch.4 ver. 24. God is a Spirit, and they that worship him, must worship him in spirit and in truth. And to my Text of the two anointed Ones, that stood by or before the Lord of the whole Earth, to be the Water, and the Blood.

M. I desire you wou'd be as short as you can.

Q. I believe I shan't end to Night.

M. I desire you to explain the Text, concerning the Water, Blood, and Spirit.

Q. I won't break in upon other Matters, but leave that to the next Opportunity; all that I shall say to it now is from 1 John, ch. I. ver. 3. That which we have seen and heard, declare we unto you, that ye also may have fellowship with us; and truly our friendship is with the Father, and with the Son Jesus Christ. I shall say something from thy Text, because it hangs together, ver. 4. And these things we write unto you, that your joy may be full. Ver. 5. This then is the message which we have heard of him, and declare unto you, that God is light, and in him is no darkness at all. Ver. 6. If we say we have fellowship with him, and walk in darkness, we lie, and do not the truth: Ver. 7. But if we walk in the light, as he is in the light, we have fellowship with another, and the blood of Jesus Christ his Son cleanseth us from all sin. So far for the Virtues of the Blood of Christ at this time.

M. I think you might have made use of the Blood of God, as well as the Blood of Christ.

Q. I am not to make use of thy Words, but those of my Text.

M. I hope you'll explain all the Heads of your text.

Q. At another Time. He is a simple Minister, or Preacher, who goes out to explain his Text before he gives it out. I continue to prove Christ the Son of God, from John, ch. 5. Ver. 25. Verily, verily I say unto you, the hour is coming, and now is, when the dead shall hear the voice of the Son of God: and they that hear shall live.

M. I would not have you trouble your self so much, we don't deny him to be the Son of God.

Moderator, you have gone beyond your Time already.

Q. I am not to be interrupted. Ver. 26. For as the Father hath life in himself, so hath he given to the Son to have life in himself. Chap. 3. Ver. 18. He that believeth on him, is not condemned: but he that believeth not, is condemned already, because he hath not believed in the name of the only begotten Son of God. Ver. 19. And this is the condemnation, that light is come into the world, and man loved darkness rather than light, because their deeds were evil. Ver. 20. For every one that doeth evil, hateth the light, neither cometh to the light, lest his deeds should be reproved. Think on that, Friend Rawlinson.

M. What is it you desir'd me to think of? please to record that Text in particular.

Q. For everyone that doth evil, hateth the light, &c. Ver. 21. But he that doth the truth, cometh to the light, that his deeds may be made manisfest, that they are wrought in God. Again, in ver. 17, which tho' I bring after the other Text, yet 'tis the first in Order of Reading. For God sent not his Son into the world to condemn the world, but that the world through him might be saved. The next Text I bring is from Mark, Ch. 9. Ver. 2. Relating to the Transfiguration of our Lord Jesus Christ; the Words are these. And after six days, Jesus taketh with him Peter, and James, and John, and leadeth them up into a high mountain apart by themselves: and he was transfigured before them. Ver. 3. And his raiment became shining, exceeding white as snow; so as no fuller on earth can white them. Ver. 4. And there appeared unto them Elias, with Moses: and they were talking with Jesus. Ver. 5. And Peter answered and said to Jesus, Master, it is good for us to be here, and let us make three tabernacles; one for thee, one for Moses, and one for Elias. Ver. 6. For he wist not what to say, for they were sore afraid. Ver. 7. And there was a cloud that overshadowed them; and a voice came out of the cloud, saying, This is my beloved Son: hear him. The next is from John, ch. 5. ver. 37. And the Father himself which hath sent me, that born witness of me. Ye have neither heard his voice at any time, nor seen his shape. The next is from the same Author, ch. 6. Ver. 44, 45. No man can come unto me, except the Father, which hath sent me, draw him, and I will raise him up at the last day. It is written in the Prophets, And they shall be all taught of God. Every man therefore that hath heard, and hath learned of the Father, cometh unto me. The next I have to offer, is John, ch. 14. Ver. 28. Jesus saith, My Father is greater than I. I hope you will believe Christ's words? 'tis a short Text, but a very pithy one. Now if we believe that Jesus is God, we must believe that God is not capable of speaking lies. And if we believe that Jesus hath spoken Truth, we should believe the Truth of what he has said, viz. That God is greater then him; for he says, My Father is greater than I.

M. I shall take notice of all your chief Heads.

Q. don't interrupt me. My next Text is Luke, ch. 22. Ver. 42. Saying, Father if thou be willing, remove this cup from me: nevertheless, not my will, but thine be done. Here was humility in the Son of God, the Pattern of Humility. The next is from Matt. ch. 26. Ver. 39. And he went a little further and fell on his face, and prayed, saying, O my Father, if it be possible let this cup pass from me: nevertheless not as I will but as thou wilt. And ver. 53. Thinkest thou that I cannot now pray to my Father, and he shall presently give me more than twelve legions of angels? The next I have to offer is John, ch. 17. Ver. 5. And now, O Father, glorifie thou me with thine own self, with the glory which I had with thee before the word was. And ver. 3. And this is life eternal, that they might know thee the only true God, and Jesus Christ, whom thou has sent. And Luke, ch. 2. Ver 10, to 14. which was on the Occasion of the Angel that appeared to the Shepherds at the Birth of our Saviour; And the angel said unto them, fear not: for behold, I bring unto you good Tidings of great joy, which shall be to all people. For unto you is born this day, in the city of David, a Saviour, which is Christ the Lord. And suddenly there was with the angel a multitude of the heavenly host praising God, and saying, Glory to God in the highest, and on earth peace, good will towards men. And John, ch 3. Ver. 16. For God sent not his son into the world to condemn the world: but that the world through him might be saved. The next I come upon is Matt. ch. 6. Ver. 9, to 13. on the Prayer of our Lord, which he taught his Disciples in these Words, After this manner therefore pray ye: Our Father which art in heaven, hallowed by thy name, Thy kingdom come. They will be done in earth as it is in heaven: Give us this day our daily bread. And forgive us our debts, as we forgive our debtors. And lead us not into temptation, but deliver us from evil: For thine is the kingdom, and the power, and the glory, for ever. Amen. I hope thou wilt allow, Friend Rawlinson, that Christ spake Truth; for the Father was in Heaven whilst the Son was upon Earth. Our Father which are in heaven, are the Words of the Text, and signifies the present Tense: God is Omnipotent.

M. In my Opinion Christ is the Kingdom of Heaven.

Q. Thou art to expound that when I have done. I have offer'd what I think at this Time convenient, to prove Christ is the Son of God, and shall now prove him to be Son of Man.

M. We don't deny him in all his Attributes.

Q. I shan't now use many Arguments. John, ch. I. ver. 45. We have found him of whom Moses in the law, and the prophets did write, Jesus of Nazareth, the son of Joseph. And likewise, John, ch. 6. Ver. 42. to the same Effect. The next is from Mark, ch. 14. Ver. 60. And the high priest stood up in the mids, and asked Jesus, saying, Answereth thou nothing? What is it which these witnesses against thee? But he held his peace, and answered nothing. Again the high priest asked him, and said unto him, art thou the Christ, the Son of the Blessed? And Jesus said, I am: and ye shall see the Son of man sitting on the

Truth and Reason defended

right hand of power, and coming in the clouds of heaven. This proves him not only the Son of Man, but of God too.

Moderator, I'm afraid there will be no Conclusion.

Q. It is a long Night that never sees Day. Mark, ch. 6. Ver. 3. Is not this the carpenter, the son of Mary, the brother of James, and Joses, &c. Ch. 13. Ver. 32. No man, no not the angels which are in heaven, neither the Son, but the Father, knoweth the Hour of Judgment. Note this by and by; it is the Son of Man I am speaking of; Christ as he was the Son of Man, according to his Humanity: For I make a Distinction between his Humanity and Divinity.

M. I am glad to hear you say that.

Q. Thou mayst thank me for it when I have done. The next is from Luke, ch 3. Ver. 23. And Jesus, himself began to be about 30 years of age, being (as was supposed) the son of Joseph, which was the son of Heli, &c. Here St. Luke traces the Genealogy of Christ on the Mother's Side, and Matthew begins on the Father's side. Again Matt. ch. 16. Ver. 13. Whom do men say, that I, the son of man, am? I am now to conclude this Subject at this Time, these being as many Quotation as are necessary, to prove Christ the Son of God and Son of Man likewise; and that there was n him both Godhead and a Manhood; and to that Intent, I have brought my Quotations separate. He was both God and Man, The man Christ Jesus: See I Tim. Ch. 2. Ver. 5.

Moderator, Observe, that Mr. Henderson affirms him to be both God and Man.

M. I observe it.

Q. Please to hear me. Thus much for the Position, which says, **That Jesus Christ is the only God and Lord of heaven and earth.** The other Part is **And that when he took his Journey in flesh, he invested** Moses **and** Elias **with Power of being Guardians of his Person, and also gave them Charge of his kingdom 'till his return.** I have heard no Proofs from thee on that Head yet, nor any Colour of Proof.

M. I thought you had them before; What were the Angels? Hath no he given his Angels charge concerning him?

Q. As he was the Man Christ Jesus, He took not upon him the nature of angels, but the seed of Abraham: See Heb. ch.2. ver. 16.

M. Did he take the Nature of Angels too?

Q. I say it not; but he took upon him the Seed of Abraham. And when he had fasted forty days and forty nights, the Devil came to him (like a cunning Sophister) and tempted him, saying, If thou be the Son of God, command that these stones be made bread. But he answered, saying, It is written, Man shall not live by bread alone, but by every word that proceedeth out of the mouth of God. Then the devil took him up into the holy city, and set him on a pinnacle of the temple, and said unto him; If thou be the Son of God, cast thy self down: for it written, that he will give his angels charge over thee, &c.

M. And it was not so as he said, was it?

Q. I say it was so; but not in Favour of thy Position.

M. Pray what Devil was it tempted Christ?

Q. That belongs to another Discourse.

M. Can any Person come to the Knowledge of the Word of God, without God pleases to give him an Insight of it?

Q. I am not to be interrupted. I now go to the other Part of the Position, to which thou hast quoted that Text about the Angels. I shall take on me to tell thee, that I find no Text of Scripture quoted by thee for this Argument, but what will be of great use to me in mine. I can't find any Text of Scripture for Moses and Elias having the Charge, or Guardianship of Christ's Person on Earth; but I shall give some counter Proof of it, and shall take notice of the Inconsistence and Incoherence that it makes in the Nature or Essence of God; that he should reign or give up the Power of the Godhead, to Men who were created, and subject to trespass.

M. If you have a mind to challenge the Scriptures, go on.

Q. I will shew thee, that Moses and Elias were men, not only subject to Transgression and Sin, but in some Degree each did transgress and sin.

M. I grant, that in the Body of Flesh they did.

Q. I will in due Course prove, that Elias was sent down from Heaven, (before Christ came in the Flesh) i.e. the Spirit and the Power of Elias; and that a Body of Flesh was given him; and that that Body of Flesh was named John.

M. Pray be as short as you can, and make him either a God or a Piece of a God.

Q. I shall now proceed with Moses, and quote some Proofs of his Transgressions; the first Thing is as the same is recorded in Exod. Ch. 2. Ver. 12. He slew a Man, and hid him in the Sand, and some People will say, that this is a kind of Murther. 2dly, Numb., ch. 20, ver. 12. And the Lord spake unto Moses and Aaron, Because ye believed me not, to sanctifie me in the eyes of the children of Israel; therefore ye shall not bring this congregation into the land which I have given them. Ver. 10. And Moses and Aaron gathered the congregation together before the rock, and Moses said unto them, Hear now, ye rebels; must we fetch you water out of this rock? I presume, by the Words of my Text, he transgrest, in calling the people Rebels, and being angry.

M. Don't accuse Moses with a Fault, which God doth not accuse him of.

Q. Don't interrupt me. I accuse not Moses, of what God does not; for 'tis plain, that God charged him with Incredulity, from the Face of my Text, viz. Because ye believed me not, &c. Notwithstanding these transgressions committed by Moses, I believe he had his Reward, and was faithful in all his House as a Servant afterwards; and for Proof thereof, Heb. ch.3. ver. 5. Moses verily was faithful in all his house as a servant, for a testimony of those things which were to be spoken after: Ver. 6. But Christ as a Son over his own house: whose house are we, if we hold fast the confidence, and the rejoicing of the hope firm unto the end. So much for Moses. And the next for Elias, I take upon me to prove, that Elias did not do every Thing that was pleasing to God; for he was complain'd of, as my Text has it, 1 Kin, ch. 19. Ver. 14. When Elias fled from Jezebel to Horeb, God appeared unto him, and he speaks to God on this wise, saying, I have been very jealous for the Lord God of host: because the children of Israel have forsaken thy covenant, thrown down thine altars, and slain thy prophets with the sword; and I, even I, only am left, and they seek my life to take it away. Ver. 18. God answered Elias, (Elijah he is there call'd) but I take him to be the same.

M. You do well in that.

Q. God replied to him.

M. Don't charge the Prophet, with what God does not.

Q. I charge him not, it is my Text. Yet I have left me seven thousand in Israel, all the knees which have not bowed unto Baal, and every mouth which hath not kissed him. The Apostle Paul also charged the Prophet Elias in these Words, Rom. Ch. II, ver. 2. God hath not cast away his people which he foreknew. Wot ye not what the scripture saith of Elias? How he maketh intercession to God against Israel, saying, Ver. 3. Lord, they have killed thy prophets, and digged down thine altars; and I am left alone, and they seek my life. Ver. 4. But what saith the answer of God unto him? I have reserved to my self seven thousand men, who have not bowed the knee to the image of Baal. This is to shew, that St. Paul quotes the same Thing I have quoted. The next Thing that I have to remark upon Elias is, to shew that he was not a Man endued with the same Spirit that our Lord Jesus Christ was, and to shew the Difference there was between them. I find in 2 Kin. Ch. I. ver. 10, to 12. That Elias called for Fire to come down from Heaven, to consume the two Captains with their Fifties. It's very plain our Lord Jesus Christ was of another Spirit, from St. Luke, the Evangelist, ch. 9. Ver. 53. And they did not receive him, because his face was as tho' he would go to Jerusalem. Ver. 54. And when his disciples James and John saw this, they said, Lord wilt thou that we command fire to come down from heaven, and consume them, even as Elias did? Ver. 56. For the Son of man is not come to destroy mens lives, but to save them. So much for that Text; I think I have shewn very plainly a fast Disproportion between the Spirit of Elias and that of Jesus; Elias shewed what he wou'd do if he had power; Jesus, in his Lamb-like Spirit, for the good of Mankind, pursuant to the Declaration and Song of the Heavenly Host, declared, that he came not to destroy mens lives, but to save them. Elias, he destroy'd, as the Words of my Text have it. This is the Use I make of that Passage. I have another Authority to quote, but I suppose that won't be admitted, because it is not Scripture; it is in a little Book writ by one Reeve; but I shan't now quote it.

M. No, no, no.

Q. The next Thing I have to prove is the Lord's Messengers to the People, i.e. the Prophets and Priests (1st To shew in general whom they were; as in the Prophet Haggai, ch. I. ver. 13.) to be the Lord's Messengers to the People. Mal. Ch. 2. Ver. 7. For the priests lips should keep knowledge, and they should seek the law at his mouth: for he is the messenger of the Lord of host. And touching the Message of the Apostles, I John, ch. I. ver. 5. This then is the message which we have heard of him, (i.e. Jesus Christ) and declare unto you, that God is light, and in him is no darkness at all. Ver. 6. If we say we have fellowship with him, and walk in darkness, we lie, and do not the truth. Chap. 3. Ver. II. For this is the message that ye heard from the beginning, that we should love one another. The Apostle Paul's Message to the Gentiles was on this wise, Acts, ch. 26. Ver. 18. To open their eyes, and to turn them from darkness to light, and from the power of Satan unto God, that they may receive forgiveness of sins, and inheritance among all them which are sanctified, by faith that is in me, (i.e., Jesus) whom he had once persecuted; and they that preach any other doctrine are not the Lord's Messengers. The next Thing I come to is, particularly concerning the Messenger that was sent immediately before the coming of Christ in the Flesh, and that was John the Baptist; and I will prove, that he was Elias, Mal., ch. 3. Ver. I. Speaking of John the Baptist; the Words are these, Behold, I will send my messenger, and he shall prepare the way before me: that is part of the Verse. I don't give it all, because it doth not at all relate to him; the other part belongs to the Messenger of the Covenant, I'll bring that in its proper Place. The next Proof is from mark, ch. I. ver. 2. As it is written in the prophets, Behold, I send my messenger before thy face, which shall prepare thy way before thee. Luke, ch. 7. Ver. 27. This is he of whom it is written, Behold, I send my messenger before thy face, which shall prepare thy way before thee. Matt. ch. II. Ver. 10 For this is he of whom it is written, Behold I send my messenger before thy face, which shall prepare thy way before thee. Ver. II. Verily I say unto you, among them that are born of women, there hath not risen a greater than John the Baptist; notwithstanding, he that is least in the kingdom of heaven, is greater than he. Ver. 12. And from the days of John the Baptist, until now, the kingdom of heaven suffereth violence, and the violent take it by force. Ver. 13. For all the prophets and the law prophesied until John. Ver. 14. And if ye will receive it, this is Elias which was to come. John the Baptist was Elias I have now fully proved it, if you will believe Christ; 'tis his Words; and I will prove to you further, that the same John was Elias, from Mark, ch 9. Ver. 13. But I say unto you, that Elias is indeed come, and they have done unto him whatsoever they listed, as it is written of him. And from Luke, ch. I. ver. II. And there appeared unto him an angel of the Lord, standing on the right side of the altar of insence. Ver. 12. And when Zacharias saw him, he was troubled, and fear fell upon him. Ver. 13. But the angel said unto him, fear not Zacharias for thy prayer is heard; and thy wife Elizabeth shall bear thee a son, and thou shalt call his name John. Ver. 15. For he shall be great in the sight of the Lord, and shall drink neither wine nor strong drink; and he shall be filled with the Holy Ghost, even from his mothers womb. Ver. 16. And many of the children of Israel shall he turn to the Lord their God. Ver. 17. And he shall go before him in the Spirit and power of Elias, to turn the hearts of the fathers to the children, and the disobedient to the wisdom of the just, to make ready a people prepared for the Lord. I hope thou wilt allow this to corroborate my other Text. He was sent before the Lord Jesus Christ, to prepare a people for the Lord, and not left in Heaven with Charge of the Angels, or Heavenly Host. God had that Power and Prerogative in himself. The next Thing I'll prove, that Jesus Christ is the Messenger of the Covenant, to which I bring in Part of the Text I made use of, in respect of Elias, i.e. John the Baptist; because they are both contain'd in the same Text, Mal. Ch. 3. Ver. I. that part of the Text I make use of with respect to Jesus being the Messenger of the Covenant is this, And the Lord whom ye seek shall suddenly come to his temple; even the messenger of the covenant whom ye delight in, behold, he shall come, saith the Lord of hosts, &c. The next Text is to prove the same, from Isa. Ch. 42. Ver. 6. I the Lord have called thee in righteousness, and will hold thine hand, and will keep thee, and give thee for a covenant of the people, for a light of the Gentiles; Ver 7. To open the blind eyes, to bring out the prisoners from the prison, and them that sit in darkness out of the prison house. Ver 8. I am the Lord, that is my name, my glory will I not give to another, neither my praise to graven images. And from Heb. ch. 8. Ver. 2. I am about to prove, that Christ is not only the Messenger of the Covenant, but the Minister of the sanctuary, and true tabernacle which the Lord pitched, and not man.

M. It is not denied by us; so you need not prove it.

Moderator, I thought you had done, Mr. Henderson.

Q. Please not to interrupt me. I have one Quotation more, which is to prove, that Christ came not to be ministred unto, but to minister; 'tis from Matt. ch. 20, ver. 28. Even as the son of man came not to be ministred unto, but to minister, and to give his life a ransom for many. The End of my bringing this Text is, to prove, that Christ was Independent of MOSES and ELIAS for Support, either in Heaven or on Earth; they could not subsist without him, tho' he could without them.

M. You'll find the Necessity of that.

Q. If thou would'st give me leave, Friend Rawlinson, I wou'd now speak a few Words upon the Scope of the Quotations I have undertaken.

M. Have you ended your Matters?

Q. I have as to my particular Proofs at this time. I now desire Leave to comment.

M. I desire you would make an End of all your Quotations in general.

Q. I have made an end of all I have repeated; but should I collect all the Proofs that might be brought, this Room would not contain them.

M. I desire you wou'd proceed according to your own Thoughts.

Q. Don't interupt in me, and I shan't be very tedious.

M. All you have to do is, to prove a God distinct from Jesus Christ.

Q. First I have taken upon me to prove the Godhead, and that God Almighty is omnipotent, omnipresent, and omniscient; and I think I have proved that pretty fully.

M. I must break in with your Spirit there; read our Position; Christ Jesus is our only God, and therefore you must prove that to be false.

Q. Don't interupt me; the next Thing I took upon me to prove was, That Jesus Christ was the Son of God.

M. That is not denied by us.

Q. The third Thing I proved was, That he was the Son of Man.

M. Neither is that denied.

Q. I don't want thy Help. The next Thing I took upon me was, to shew some Reasons from Scripture Authority, That it was not consistent with the Essence of God, to make choice of MOSES and ELIAS, by investing them with the Guardianship of Christ's Person on Earth, or by giving them Charge of his Kingdom till his Return: I think I have prov'd that likewise. The Remarks I shall now make, are to shew some Self Contradictions on the Face of your Position: First, That Jesus Christ is the only God and Lord of Heaven and Earth. Secondly, You have laid it down as your Faith, That when he took his Journey in Flesh, he invested MOSES and ELIAS with a Power of being Guardians of his Person; and also gave them a Charge of his Kingdom till his Return. This is an Absurdity, and contrary both to the Scriptures and to Reason.

M. But it is not contrary to Faith.

Q. Don't interrupt me. What I mean by Reason is the Wisdom, not of this World, but that which is from above; which is first pure, then peacable, gentle, and easy to be intreated &c. or to that effect. And this Wisdom is the Reason that I insist upon, and it is the same that proceeds from God, the Fountain of Reason, and contradicteth not itself. Now is it reasonable for us to suppose, that MOSES and ELIAS could have the Guardianship of Christ's Person on Earth, and, at the same Time, have the Charge of his Kingdom till his Return? This is apparently contrary to Reason, and plainly esteemeth MOSES and ELIAS in a higher Station of Power than our Lord Jesus Christ: For, by this Argument of yours, there was a Necessity for a Regency, Lieutenancy, or Deputy Governours in Heaven. I say, it shews as though he had left Heaven destitute of his Presence. Now for me to believe the Truth of this Position, is really allowing MOSES and ELIAS to be greater than Jesus: For if it be possible for them to have the Charge of his Person on Earth, and his Kingdom in Heaven at the same Time, then must they have been omnipresent. And I have prov'd, that ELIAS was upon Earth, i.e. John the Baptist. You eclipse and lessen the Authority of the Omnipresence of the Almighty God, and Jesus Christ, to whom he hath committed all Power. It would seem as tho' the Omnipresence of God were abridg'd, or eclips'd by this your

Truth and Reason defended 307

Argument; and it seems by the Scope of the Position, that he was not capable of being in Heaven at the same Time he was on Earth; whereas 'tis plain, from a thousand eminent Texts of Scripture, that his divine Presence is every-where; if every where, Heaven must be some-where, and Christ was in Heaven as to his Godhead. As to his Manhood, as he was the Son of Man, the Body, which he assum'd or took on him in the Womb of the Virgin, was upon Earth. We have no Text that says it was corporeally in Heaven, till he was glorified by the Father, after his Sufferings and Resurrection. But your Position insinuates that he was not in Heaven. I say he was in Heaven.

M. Doth the Position say so?

Q. Don't interrupt me. I think, without entering into all the Quotations, your Position carries an apparent Contradiction in it; first you say, that Jesus Christ is Lord of Heaven and Earth; then you say in fact, he is not. And why? Because there was a Time, when the Lord came down from Heaven, and left behind him MOSES and ELIAS to take care of Heaven. I will produce thee a Text of Scripture to prove, that Jesus was in Heaven when on Earth, John, ch. 3. Ver. 13. And no man hath ascended up to heaven, but he that came down from heaven, even the Son of man which is IN heaven: i.e. the Godhead. I'll close up for this Time, and say what thou pleases, and let it be recorded; and when thou hast done, I'll begin again.

M. I don't design to proceed any farther to Night, because you have made so long a Harangue; but I'll answer your Arguments the next Time of Meeting.

Q. Wilt thou answer them all by word of mouth?

M. I can't tell that; but I can see your Spirit.

Q. Thou art a Spiritual Man then! Pray what is my Spirit like? Since thou can'st see Spirits, why can'st not speak without Notes?

Adjourn'd by Consent to Wednesday following, being the 18th of December, 1728; and then to meet at 5 a Clock in the Evening, at the same Place.

Part II.

Met according to Adjournment.

Muggletonian,

Mr. Henderson, I am come here to speak in some measure for the Testimony of my Faith, in the first Proposition, which is, **That Jesus Christ is Lord of heaven and Earth,** which in our last Proceeding I did in some measure prove: But you travers'd away a great deal of my Time, and I could not proceed as large as I design'd: Besides, being a Spiritual Man, I little thought you would have armed yourself with carnal Weapons, as Pen, Ink, and Paper. I shall now proceed to enlarge upon the first Article of my Faith, and prove Christ more largely in the Second Dispensation than the First; because the second is the Manifestation of Things in the Body of Flesh. I am to prove **Christ to be very God.** The second Thing I shall enter upon shall the **Power of** MOSES and ELIAS, which you seem'd in your Words to undervalue in great measure, and to revile them; as tho' God could not invest that Power on them, because they were Sinners; and not regarding that God did take away that Corruption they had in this Life, and so prepar'd them for that Office above the Stars. I shall use but few Words for the Purpose, and then shall take upon me to prove **Christ Jesus very God**. I shall only use one Text or two, if you will have Patience, concerning the Power that MOSES and ELIAS had invested on them; and shall first begin upon Mark, ch. 9. Ver. 2. And after six days, Jesus taketh with him Peter, and James, and John, and leadeth them up into an high mountain apart by themselves: and he was transfigur'd before them. Ver. 3. And his raiment became shining exceeding what as snow; so as no fuller can white them. Ver. 4. And there appeared unto them Elias, with Moses: and they were talking with Jesus. Ver. 5. And Peter answered and said to Jesus, Master, it is good for us to be here, and let us make three tabernacles; one for thee, and one for Moses, and one for Elias. Ver. 6. For he wist not what to say, for they were sore afraid. Ver. 7. And there was a cloud that overshadow'd them; and a voice came out of the cloud, saying, This is my beloved Son: hear him. I am going to speak a little concerning that which you seem to undervalue, as in respect to ELIAS, who was the preparative Way, the Fore-runner of Christ. You seem'd to assert, that it was the very ELIAS himself that came, if you mind your own Remarks: But you will find, Luke, ch. I. ver. 17. And he shall go before in the Spirit and power of Elias, to turn the hearts of the fathers to the children, and the disobedient to the wisdom of the just, to make ready a people prepared for the Lord. Mark, ch. 9. ver. II. And they asked him, saying, Why say the scribes that Elias must first come? Ver. 12. And he answered and told them, Elias verily cometh first, and restoreth all things: and how it is that he must suffer many things, and be set at nought. Ver. 13. But I say unto you, that Elias is indeed come, and they have done unto him whatsoever they listed, as it is written of him. Now the Charge I have against you is this, that from these Words you did insist, that that ELIAS, who was in the Throne of Glory, did come in a Body of Flesh, to prepare the Way of the Lord Jesus: It is denied by me. That ELIAS, after his Translation, does eternally exist, and is existent there now, and is for Duration to all Eternity. But whom the Lord there speaks justly of is John the Baptist, that he should come in the Power and Spirit of ELIAS; but the Power and Spirit of ELIAS, is not the real essential Body of ELIAS; but God did impower him with the same Spirit that ELIAS had, to prophesy, or to be a Fore-runner of Christ. You also spoke disdainfully of MOSES, if I remember it well; as that MOSES was a sinful Man, and that God cou'd not take these Men, to invest them with the Government of Heaven; But I shan't offer much upon that Head; for he that shall mark the Misdeeds of the Prophet, God will mark his Ways also: For, if, God, had not charged him with Evil, why should any Man? In so doing he finds fault with God himself. I shall now prove, that there was a Necessity that God should invest this father Power on MOSES and ELIAS, for a Royal Purpose best known unto himself: And afterwards shall prove, that Christ could not act any farther than his own Royal Will and Purpose did lead him to; for God cannot act against himself: It was his eternal Decree in Heaven to become Flesh, and when he had so eternally decreed it in himself, he sware an Oath to himself, being none greater than himself; which you seem'd to find fault with, because I made use of the Word Flesh. The Text I shall quote to prove the royal Purpose is, Psal. 89, ver. 34, 35, 36. My covenant will I not break, nor alter the thing that is gone out of my lips. Once I have sworn by my holiness, that I will not lie unto David. His seed shall endure for ever, and his throne as the sun before me.

Q. Wilt thou give me leave to speak a little upon that?

M. No, I am not to be interrupted. I wou'd not have you think, Gentlemen, that I am come here to get my self any Value or Reputation; but for God's Glory to declare my Faith, and witness it with my Blood, if Occasion calls for it. I an't a Man of Words, or of much Learning, nor perhaps do I express my self as well as some Persons may; but such as I have I give unto you, so shall make no farther Apology for my self; but shall proceed to the Purpose of the Thing, that God had declared and purposed in himself, before the Foundation of the World, that he would become Flesh; tho' he did not witness it, till such Time as his divine Will moved it; and when he moved it, it was to the Fathers of Old, and sware an Oath, that he would redeem their Condition; and no other Way was there for God to overcome that Oath, than by leaving his Throne and becoming Flesh; and to invest the Fathers with a fatherly Charge, as my Faith leads me to, in giving them a Power to govern Angels, and protect his divine Person. When God had invested MOSES and ELIAS with that Charge,

I must so far have room to speak, that it was not MOSES or ELIAS, that acted any thing of themselves, but that the Royal Decree of God acted for them. MOSES and ELIAS as creaturely Beings did not serve the Lord in any thing, in their own Centre; but in God's Centre, being invested with his Royal Word, to take care of him in the Body of Flesh. It was God that acted for himself, only they, being deem'd worthy Persons, to have the Care over him. I do not insist, that as creaturely Beings they acted any thing for God, but only as Servants trusted with a Stewardship, till such Time as he returned to his Kingdom again; then it was finish'd. It did not belong to them, but to him that was worthy to receive it again. I shall now proceed no farther on this, but shall make a Remark on the first Chapter of John, beginning at ver. 20. And he confessed, and denied not; but confessed, I am not the Christ. Ver. 21. And they asked him, What then? Art thou Elias? And he saith, I am not. Art thou that prophet? And he answered, No. Ver. 22. Then said they unto him, Who art thou? That we may give an answer to them that sent us: What sayest thou of thy self? Ver. 23. He said, I am the voice of one crying in the wilderness, Make straight the way of the Lord, as said the prophet Elaias. What End I have for taking these Texts, is to prove, that your Assertions in the last Night's Discourse must be false; because he confesses there, that he is not the ELIAS. My Quotation must be good, as you will find it upon Record hereafter against you. He says here, He is not the ELIAS: You said, He was; I insist upon that. I shall proceed now to prove Christ very God; and that the Power that was invested on MOSES and ELIAS was no otherwise durable in itself, that till such Time as Christ was Master of it again: For if he had not return'd, according to his Purpose, that Power of MOSES and ELIAS would not have stood in God's stead; and therefore I shall shew you, the Necessity there was for God to resume his Kingdom again; and the Necessity and Dependance there was on a creatural Beings for their Supply: bit if God had not return'd, MOSES and ELIAS cou'd not have supply'd them any longer. I hope, Gentlemen, you'll bear with some Things, for I don't make a Trade of the Scriptures, but I believe there are here some who make a good Penny of them: I only pin my Faith upon it, John, Ch. 14 Ver 7. If ye had known me, ye should have known my Father also: and from henceforth ye know him, and have seen him. Ver. 8. Philip saith unto him, Lord, shew us the Father, and it sufficeth us. Ver. 9. Jesus saith unto him, Have I been so long time with you, and yet hast thou not known me, Philip? He that hath seen me, hath seen the Father also; And how sayeth thou then, shew us the Father? Ver. 10. Believest thou not, that I am in the Father, and the Father in me? The words that I speak unto you, I speak not of my self; but the Father, that dwelleth in me, he doeth the works. Ver. 11. Believe me that I am in the Father, and the Father in me, or else believe me for the very works sake. Ver. 12. Verily, verily, I say unto you, He that believeth on me, the works that I do, he shall do also, and greater works than these he shall do; because I go unto my

Truth and Reason defended 311

Father. Ver. 13. And whatsoever ye shall ask the Father in my name, that will I do, that the Father may be glorified in the Son. Ver. 14. If ye shall ask anything in my name, I will do it. Ver. 15. If ye love me, keep my commandments. And I will pray the Father, and he shall give you another Comforter, that he may abide with you for ever. Ver. 17. Even the Spirit of truth, whom the word cannot receive; because it seeth him not, neither knoweth him; but ye know him for he dwelleth with you, and shall be in you. The occasion of my bringing these Texts is to prove, that Christ, being in the Condition of Mediatorship, had a Necessity to pray to that fatherly Power invested on MOSES and ELIAS; it not being properly their's, but only a Charge which God invested upon them;; and therefore he uses the Words, to pray to a Father seemingly. Upon which account, Philip alone desires him to shew the Father; for they thought of consequence there must be another Father, distinct from his Person, and therefore desir'd of the Lord, that he would manifest him to them plainly. And when he began to speak some Things strangely, they said, Lord, dost thou now speak in parables? And were unsatisfied. For this Purpose, the Lord did manifest himself to them as far as he could, granting that he might, if it had been his royal Will, have told them all Things. I don't deny, that the Lord did know their Hearts and Intentions, but he satisfied them as far as was necessary: The time shall come, says he, when I will shew you plainly of the Father. Now there was a Necessity for the Lord's Return to his own Kingdom, that he might plainly shew them who the Father was. [I shan't touch on the Condition of the second Dispensation, because it does not belong to me at present; but I am to touch upon the Foundation of all the Principles, that is, Jesus Christ to be very God. I shan't mention Christ to be the Son of God and Man; but, grant it to be Truth, it was Life eternal, to know Christ to be the Son of God in the second Dispensation: But I am to prove, Christ to be God in an higher Dispensation, and shall prove him the very Emmanuel-God.] But to proceed, I say there was a Necessity for the Lord to return to his own Kingdom again, that he might enable them and endow them with Power from on High, to understand these Things, of which he spake in the Body of Flesh here below. And when Christ ascended, 'tis said in one of the Apostles, that there were above 500 Disciples who saw him ascend locally, bodily, with the very same Body that he suffer'd in; And when he ascended he led captivity captive, and gave gifts to men. I must go back a little way, for some Words that he behind, to advance me to the Purpose of my Argument, and that is, 'Til I go, the Comforter cannot come: it is expedient that I go away. When Christ ascended to his Throne of Glory, and resumed that Throne from whence he came, several Texts of Scripture assure us, that he led Captivity captive; and all Power in Heaven and Earth was given to him, which he had before the Worlds were, Ephes. ch. 4, ver. 9, 10. Now that he ascended, what is it but that he also descended first into the lower parts of the earth? He that ascended, is the same also that ascended up far above all heavens, that he might fill all things. Isaiah, ch. 44. Ver. 6. Thus saith the Lord, the king of Israel, and his redeemer the Lord of hosts, I am the first, and I am the last, and besides me there is no God.

Q. I fear tho'lt tire our Patience, Friend Rawlinson.

M. Let us do all things in Decency and Order. You have the same priviledge of proving your Faith, as I have mine. I won't tire your Patience; I proceed as fast as I can. When Christ ascended up on high, and led Captivity captive, those Disciples that followed in his Mortality, waited for the Income of his glorious Spirit when ascended into Immortality, far above all Angels and Men. This I am quoting to you, a Quaker, call'd so by Name; tho' I don't despise the Name of a Quaker, more than some may that of a Muggletonian: I bear the Testimony of one in my Soul, (not in Characters of Words) because they have declared Christ to me to be very God; and to that Testimony will I seal my Faith, and my Life, if Occasion calls for it. But to proceed, when Christ ascended, and led Captivity captive, those that were Followers in the Resurrection, must be Followers of him in their Conversion: For when ye are converted, saith Christ, strengthen your brethren. They were convinc'd before they were call'd Disciples.

Q. I beg leave to interrupt thee there; Conversion and Convincement is not our Subject: Keep to thy Articles.

M. I'm coming to my Article.

Q. Thou art to prove, that Jesus Christ is the only God and Lord of Heaven and Earth; (that's the first Part.) The next is, and when he took his Journey in Flesh, he invested MOSES and ELIAS with a Power of being Guardians of his Person, and gave them the Charge of his Kingdom till his Return; that's the Point thou art to prove.

M. I am at his Return now, and am shewing, that when Christ ascended in the Sight of his Disciples, they being Followers of him, did often talk of his Sayings, how that the Comforter cou'd not come until he was return'd to his Kingdom again; and that then he won't send them the Comforter. The other Sayings must have been void till that Comforter came. And Christ charged them to tarry at Jerusalem, till they were endued with Power from on High. All that I say is, that there was a Necessity that God should send down the Comforter, and when this Comforter was sent down, and they had received Power from on High, they went forth, and did administer Christ crucified. Now I shan't touch on this any farther, then that they did bear Testimony of his Sufferings. The next Thing I shall proceed upon is, the infinite Godhead of Christ, which I shall prove, by quoting some Texts of Scripture; Col. ch. 2. Ver. 9. For in him dwelleth all the fulness of the Godhead bodily. I Tim. ch. 3. Ver. 16. And without controversy, great is the mystery of godliness; God was manifest in the flesh, justified in the Spirit, seen of angels, preached unto the Gentiles, believed on in the world, received up into Glory. I John, ch. 5 ver. 20. This is the true God and eternal life. John, ch. I. ver. 14. And we behold his glory, the glory as of the only begotten of the Father, full of grace and truth. Psal. 2. ver. 7. Thou art my Son, this day have I begotten thee, The next is Col. ch. I. ver. 15. He is the image of the invisible God. Ver. 17. He is before all things, and all things subsist by him. Rom. ch. I. ver. 3. Concerning his Son Jesus Christ our Lord, which was made of the seed of David according to the flesh. I quote this only, because when I wanted to make Use of the word Flesh, concerning God's taking upon him our Nature, you seem'd to demand a Proof of it. I am also to prove the Necessity there was, that God shou'd not have taken on him the Nature of Angels, but the Seed of Abraham; Heb. ch. 2. Ver. 16. For verily he took not upon him the nature of angels; but he took on him the seed of Abraham. All I have to speak to this Purpose is, that when Christ did ascend, and give Gifts, to Men, that they might go forth in their Ministry, and declare Christ the Son of God, he was pleased to say to them. When go, I will shew you of the Father: And, as I said before, when he resum'd that Glory, which he had before the World was, he then did in Time make himself manifest to the Disciples and Apostles; but they must first suffer Death, for the Testimony of the Lord Jesus Christ, before God could manifest himself in that Order which he speaks of; for it was only to John: For when the Disciples were there (he being the beloved Disciple of the Lord) and feeling he loved that Disciple more than any of the rest, they said, Lord, what must become of that man? And Jesus said unto him, If I will that he tarry till I come, what is that to thee, John, ch. 21. Ver. 22. And the Rumour of the Word abroad, and the Commonality, doth not know whether that John is Living or Dead yet, but that I shan't insist upon, because I believe many here know he is Dead. There's another Text I want, viz. When the Saints were to shew forth the Lord's Death, by the Bread that was broken; and that Sign was no longer to remain, or else our Scripture is not perfect: But, not to tire the Company, I will mention a Text of Scripture, which manifests, that Paul saw there was a Necessity in his Day, to reprove the Saints for bringing in those Persons that might spy out their Liberty.

Q. The Saints Liberty is not our Subject, my Friend, I can't help interrupting thee there.

M. Don't quench my Spirit, I did not quench thine.

Q. I'll take no Notice of any Thing thou sayst, that's foreign to the Subject.

Moderator. This is spending Time, Gentlemen, to no Purpose.

Q. It is contrary to our Articles, to depart from the Subject.

M. I am at my Subject; I'm only going to speak of the second Dispensation, and if you take away that Dispensation of mine, you are welcome. I must also prove my third Dispensation, else I can't prove Christ to be God. You must have a Commission, else you are none of God's Servants. My Business is here to prove Christ Jesus to be the Lord of Heaven and Earth, and I will make what Use of the Scriptures I please: I Cor. Ch. 11. ver. 26. For as often as ye eat this bread, and drink this cup, ye do shew the Lord's death till he come. Ver. 27. Wherefore whosoever shall eat this bread, and drink this cup of the Lord unworthily, shall be guilty of the body and blood of the Lord.

Now I shall speak to that Purpose, and another, and then conclude, and then give you the Liberty of speaking. There was a Necessity for the second Dispensation to end, else the third could not begin; there was a Necessity for the Saints to shew forth the Lord's Death till he came. He made a Promise to John and the rest, that he wou'd shew them who the Father was; that they were to shew forth his Death till he came. Now if the Lord had not fulfill'd his Promise, he would have been worse than his Word; but they did shew forth the Lord's Death. I shall now proceed to that Text, I spake of before; but it was no Ways my Business then to mention it, because I had nothing to do with that Dispensation; for I was then on a Higher. The Apostles found Fault with the Saints, for admitting any into their Communion, because they went out and spake slanderously of them; wherefore the Apostle Paul had a Charge, of admitting no such into their Communion; Whoever shall eat this bread or drink this cup of the Lord unworthily, shall be guilty of the body and blood of the Lord. And the Apostle did well in that, because none could break Bread or drink Wine, but those that saw his Sufferings. The Argument I shall mention next is the Necessity of Christ's appearing again to John; because Christ had given a Royal Promise, to shew them plainly of the Father; and till he did come, they were to break Bread and drink Wine; and John was persecuted for his Faith, tho' he had not the Effect of it; but that I don't know whether I can prove by Scripture: But John was pleased to say, he was bannish'd into the Isle of Patmos for the Lord; and in the Lord's Day, he heard a Sound of might Waters; but I will read the Words themselves, and shew the Necessity there was, that John was not to pay Adoration to the Angel that came and spake to him; for he fell down at First, and would have worshiped him. Rev. ch. I. ver. I. The Revelation of Jesus Christ, which God gave unto him, to shew unto his servants things which must shortly come to pass; and he sent and signified it by his angel unto his servant John. Ver. 8. I am Alpha and Omega, the beginning and the ending, saith the Lord, which is and which was, and which is to come, the Almighty. Ver. 9. I John, who also am your brother, and companion in tribulation, and in the kingdom and patience of Jesus Christ, was in the isle called Patmos, for the word of God, and for the testimony of Jesus Christ. Ver. 10. I was in the Spirit on the Lord's day, and heard behind me a great voice, as of a trumpet, Ver. 11. Saying, I am Alpha and Omega, the first and the last: and what thou seest, write in a book, &c. Ver. 17. And when I saw him, I fell at his feet as dead: and he laid his right hand upon me, saying unto me, fear not; I am the first and the last: Ver. 18. I am he that liveth, and was dead; and behold, I am alive for evermore, Amen; and have the keys of hell and death. As to the Necessity there was, that John should not pay Adoration to the Angel, were are told in the last Chap. of Rev. ver. 8. And I John saw these things, and heard them. And when I had heard and seen, I feel down to worship before the feet of the angel, which shewed me these things. Ver. 9. Then said he unto me, See thou do it not: for I am thy fellow servant, and of thy brethren the prophets, and of them which keep the sayings of this book: worship God. Mr. Henderson, I shall draw an Inference or two from Jesus Christ's appearing to John, in the Isle of Patmos, according to his Word; for when he there appeared, he shewed him plainly what the Father was, as he says there, I am the beginning and the end, the first and the last, that was dead am alive, and behold, I live forevermore; and of my kingdom there is no end.

Q. I don't think thou can'st do better than end there.

M. I shall have done presently. The two last Verses of the Epistle of Jude, Now unto him that is able to keep us from falling, and to present us faultless, before the presence of his glory, with exceeding joy. To the only Wise God our Saviour, be glory, and majesty, dominion and power, both now and for ever. Amen.

Moderator. Give me leave to speak a few Words Mr. Henderson.

Q. No, No; If he hath done; 'tis my turn to speak.

M. I'll only draw up in a few Words.

Q. No, no; I wou'd be glad, if you would all sit down; I believe there may be some here, that were not here the last Night we met; and as the End of this Communication is for Edification, which is my full Intention, it is not amiss that they should understand the Preliminaries; and for that End I shall read the Position of my Friend's Faith, as I have it under his own Hand, and likewise read my Answer to it. **Our Faith** (says he) **is this, that Jesus Christ is the only God and Lord of Heaven and Earth, And that when he took his Journey in flesh, he invested** MOSES **and** ELIAS **with Power of being Guardians of his Person, and also gave them Charge of his kingdom till his return.** (That is the Position.) The Answer which I under wrote was this. The Proposition is deny'd.

M. But if you observe, there was an Article of yours not made use of.

Q. That's out of the Question now.

M. It was granted, I should have it, if demanded; but however, proceed, I won't baulk your Spirit.

Q. If we are both spiritual, we are the better met: We enter'd at that Time into Preliminaries, which I shan't spend Time in repeating; but we were to meet last Monday in the Evening, between 5 and 6 of the Clock; when we came here, as my Friend was the Affirmative, it was his Business to prove his Position. He enter'd upon his Proofs, and quoted several Scriptures from the Old and New Testaments, all which I have noted, many of them I had before remark'd. I had then the Opportunity of speaking to the Negative, and took upon me to shew negative Proofs. The First Thing I took upon me to prove, was the Godhead, the Omnipotency, the Omnipresence, and Omniscience of the Almighty God. Upon that Paragraph, I made use of such of my Friend's Texts, as were properly adapted thereunto: I proceeded, and gave a great many Texts of Scripture, which are noted. The Second Part, I took upon me to prove, was, that Jesus Christ was the Son of God; and such of those Quotations, that my Friend offer'd as Proofs on his Part (which were applicable to the same) I made use of as Counter-proofs. In the Third Place I likewise prov'd, that Jesus was the Son of Man; but I have other Texts to add: St. Mark in his Gospel, ch. I. ver. I. begins thus, The beginning of the gospel of Jesus Christ, the Son of God. I have observed, that St. Matthew, in the 1st Chapter of his Gospel, traces the Genealogy of our Saviour from Abraham down to Joseph, the Husband of Mary, the Mother of our Lord, in the Lineage of his Humanity; and St. Luke, from Joseph, the Husband of Mary, back to God. What I have farther to add, as to his being the Son of Man, is from Luke, ch. 12. V. 10. Whosoever shall speak a word against the Son of man, it shall be forgiven him; but unto him that blasphemeth against the Holy Ghost, it shall not be forgiven. Upon this I shall take leave to ask my Friend two or three Questions; I have refused to answer no Questions put to me. Quer. I. Who is the Son of Man?

M. You are to proceed according to our Articles: Christ is the Son of Man.

Q. Who is the Holy Ghost?

M. The Word proceeded from the Father.

Q. Are they both equal?

M. No.

Q. Well, is there any Affinity between Christ and the Word proceeding from the Father? Are they two separate Beings, or are they once and the same?

M. They are One in Union.

Q. But my Text tells me, That whosoever shall speak a word against the Son of man, it shall be forgiven: but whosoever blasphemeth against the Holy Ghost, it shall not be forgiven him. Now the Text tells you plainly, if you'll believe it in the literal Sense, as was our Agreement, that there is a certain Difference between that which shall be, and that which shall not be; for he that speaks against the Son of Man, &c. The text doth not say, that the Son of Man is Christ in his Godhead; but the Text is plain, that the Holy Ghost is from the Father; and it's as plain, that the Holy Ghost is his Godhead. Now the Son of Man was not the Godhead, else my Text is false, but the Power of the Godhead dwelt in him; For all power in heaven and on earth was given to him, according to Mat., ch. 28. Ver. 18. He had the Godhead dwelling in that Body; for the Power of the omnipotent God is every-where, the Heaven of Heavens cannot contain him; the Body of Flesh could not contain him; the Godhead dwelt in him, but not eternally in the Body of Flesh. So my Remark is plain, that there is a Distinction between the Godhead and the Manhood of Christ. The next Question I shall ask is, Where was God when his Spirit descended from Heaven upon Christ, in the Shape of a Dove? An Account of which we have in Mat. ch. 3. ver. 16.

No Answer was given.

Q. Proceeds. 'Tis Plain, that he was in Heaven, because nothing could come down, but what was from above: For to suppose, that he was not above, is denying his Omnipresence. The Fourth thing I prov'd the other Night was, God in Trinity, shewing the two Anointed Ones, standing by or before the Lord of the whole Earth, who they were. The Fifth Thing I went upon was, to prove two Offences in MOSES: And the Sixth was, the like in ELIAS. The Seventh was to shew, the Lord's Messengers to the People, which were the Prophets and the Priests, whose Lips were to keep Knowledge, &c. The Eighth Thing I went upon was, the Lord's messenger, John the Baptist, i.e. ELIAS, who came in the Spirit and Power of ELIAS. I shall touch a little more upon it, when I come upon thy Notes. The Ninth was the Apostle's Message, that God is Light and Love. The Tenth, that Jesus is the Messenger of the Covenant, the Minister of the Sanctuary, and the true Tabernacle, which God has pitched, and not Man. These are the ten general Heads, which I have prov'd pretty fully.

M. I hope you'll be so kind as to let me ask you a Question; What is meant by that Tabernacle?

Q. Thou art not to ask Questions now; thou hadst Time to do it in before: There are twelve Hours in a Day, wherein Men may work.

M. Well, work on, and see if you can destroy the Divinity of Christ.

Q. The several Texts I offer'd shew'd plainly, that the Father, Son, and Holy Ghost were before the World was made, Man or any thing else that was made; and that corporeal Flesh and Blood, or any created mortal Being is not eternal, but the Father, Son, and Holy Ghost are eternal: Yet not three Gods, but one eternal God. These were the general Heads on the first Part of the Position; and as to those on the second Part, shewing, that MOSES and ELIAS had not the Guardianship of Christ's Person on Earth, nor the Charge of his Kingdom till his Return, I made it plainly appear, not only by Scripture and Reason, but on the Face of your own Position. Moreover, there was nothing advanc'd by thee to prove the Affirmative, or any thing like it; but quite the reverse. God is a jealous God, (my Friend) visiting the Iniquities of the fathers upon the children, to the third and fourth generation of them that hate him, &c.

I shew'd thee likewise, that it was highly repugnant to the Godhead, to the Wisdom of him who is the Fountain of all Wisdom, to appoint Men to be Regents of the Kingdom of Heaven, or to be put in Trust with it: For, as I observ'd before, of God the Father, his Son Jesus Christ, and the Holy Ghost, being the three (that one of my Quotations makes mention of) which bear Record in Heaven, it is repugnant to the Nature of the Holy Ghost, the Godhead in Trinity, to give away his Glory, or to give his Praise to any created Being. That MOSES and ELIAS were Men, I shall prove more largely now, than I did the other Night; and I think I am able to prove it from the Quotation thou mad'st use of, relating to the Transfiguration of Christ, Luke, ch. 9. ver. 27. I shall repeat the Words, and make my Remarks afterwards. But I tell you of a truth, there be some standing here which shall not taste of death, till they see the kingdom of God. Ver. 28. And it came to pass about eight days after these sayings, he took Peter, and John, and James, and went into a mountain to pray. Ver. 29. And as he prayed, the fashion of his countenance was alter'd, and his raiment was white and glistering. Ver. 30. And behold there talked with him two MEN, which were Moses and Elias. So far I have proved them Men, and not God, or Gods.

M. Who said they were? We don't own them as God.

Q. I have not asserted or insinuated, that thou said'st they were so, any further than the Consequence of thy Position makes them so. For it's plain, from Reason, that if they had the Charge of Heaven, and the Guardianship of Christ's Person on Earth, at the same Time, they must not only be Deputy Gods, but even omnipresent Gods; for, by thy Position, it appears, that they were both in Heaven and on Earth at the same Time; and, by the Scope of thy Argument, thou insinuatest, that Christ was only on Earth, and not in Heaven. But I will go on with my Text, Ver. 31. Who appeared in glory, and spake of his decease, which he should accomplish at Jerusalem. Ver. 32 But Peter, and they that were with him, were heavy with sleep: and when they were awake, they saw his glory, and the two men that stood with him. So far I took upon me to prove, from the Text tho quoted'st the other Night, MOSES and ELIAS were Men; and therefore repugnant to the Godhead, that Men shou'd have the Charge of Heaven, and be present on Earth at the same Time. To me it appears a kind of Heresy, and not only a Heresy simple, but really a Blasphemy against the Son of God. That Word will admit of a double Entendre, of his Humanity and Divinity, of his Humanity at least; 'tis a speaking against the Son of Man. But to proceed, Ver. 33. And it came to pass, as they departed from him, Peter said unto Jesus, Master, it is good for us to be here: and let us make three tabernacles, one for thee, and one for Moses, and one for Elias: not knowing what he said. Ver. 34. While he thus spake, there came a cloud and overshadowed them: and they feared as they entered into the cloud. Ver. 35. And there came a voice out of the cloud, saying, This is my beloved Son, hear him. Ver. 36. And when the voice was past, Jesus was found alone. These Quotations I have brought to shew that MOSES and ELIAS were Men, appeared in the Shape of Men, were Men before they laid down their earthly Tabernacles, and entered into Glory; and that they appeared again on Earth, in the Form of Men, in the overshadowing Power of the Holy Ghost, from Heaven. Now I would ask a Question on this, Pray who had the Guardianship of Heaven, when MOSES and ELIAS were upon Earth?

M. Enoch.

Q. If Enoch, thou has confronted thy Position; for that says, That MOSES and ELIAS had the Charge of it till Christ's Return. Enoch is not there mentioned: I only insist on these two, viz. MOSES and ELIAS, according to thy Position. I have yet a few Things to add, with respect to Jesus being the Son of God; Matt. ch. 3. Ver. 16. And Jesus, when he was baptized, went up straitway out of the water: and lo, the heavens were opened unto him, and he saw the Spirit of God

Truth and Reason defended 319

descending like a dove, and lighting upon him. Ver. 17. And lo, a voice from heaven, saying, Tis is my beloved Son, in whom I am well pleased. Now I would ask a short Question upon this, Where was God, when his Spirit descended upon his Son? Having no Answer to this before, I move it again.

M. Doth that belong to the Position? Is it in the Articles?

Q. I appeal to the Company, if it be not a pertinent Question, which I desire an Answer to.

M. You demand, Where was God, when his Spirit descended upon his Son? Why the whole Essence of God did exist in the Body of Jesus, and it was no more than a vertnal Power, that had Power to send down that Person, in the Form of a Dove.

Q. This is branding the Holy Evangelist with Untruth, and giving God the Lye. 'Tis plain from common Reason, and on the Face of a familiar Argument, that nothing can descend, but what cometh down from above. Did the whole Essence of God dwell in the Body of Christ, as thou say'st, where was the Body of Christ, when the Holy Ghost came upon him?

M. Upon Earth.

Q. How could the Holy Ghost come down from Heaven, if neither Father, Son, or Holy Ghost were there? Take heed, my Friend, don't play Tricks with God Almighty; he won't be pleas'd with Trifles, as Children are with Glass windows on their Bread and Butter. Thou arraign'st God with Inconsistency and self Contradictions, was the Position true; but I say thy Argument is Untruth; it is Heresy, and evil Speaking of God, of his Son, and of the Holy Ghost, that gave forth the Scriptures. I'll proceed again, I have got an Answer, such as it is. I have another Question to ask, with respect to the Godhead, of the Nature of the Omnipotency of God; Is God omnipotent eternally, or no?

M. God is omnipotent and eternal; it is not deny'd by me, nor are any of his Attributes.

Q. Is Jesus omnipotent and eternal?

M. How do you mean?

Q. I mean as I speak, and speak as I mean: I ask'd thee before, If God was omnipotent eternally? And now I ask, If Jesus is the same?

M. He is omnipotent and eternal, as in respect to his Godhead.

Q. Now thou art come into my Measures. Was the Son of Man, as he was a corporeal Body, like unto us in all Things? (Sin excepted.)

M. Yes.

Q. Then if he was like unto us, (Sin excepted) he was corporeally Flesh and Blood: And thou hast own'd, that God is omnipotent, and affirm'd, that Jesus Christ is the same. Now I will turn to the Position, and compare it with what thou hast said, and see if it will allow of two Eternities; viz. **Our faith is this, that Jesus Christ is the only God and Lord of heaven and earth.** Now in thy Answer, thou deniest the Matter of thy Position: but I will go on again.

M. Go on as long as you please, I shall Answer no more of your Questions.

Q. If thou wilt Answer no more, knock under, and give up the Cause.

M. Destroy the Foundation of my Faith, if you can.

Q. I ask thee whether the Holy Ghost is God?

M. In Power so.

Q. Is there any God without Power? Was MOSES vested with God's Power?

M. Destroy what I have asserted, if you can.

Q. Answer me that Question.

M. I did not come here to be catechised.

Q. Were MOSES and ELIAS vested with God's Power?

M. With God's Power.

Q. Then by what Power did our Lord Jesus Christ work Miracles upon Earth?

M. By that Power which was invested on MOSES and ELIAS, which not being their Power, but Go's, they were ordered at such a Time, that the Lord in Heaven had appointed before all Things. He had fixed his eternal Decrees in Heaven himself, and ordered every Thing, how MOSES, and ELIAS, and ENOCH should Act, and appointed a Time when they should send down that Power.

Q. Here now he has own'd, that MOSES and ELIAS had the Power of God in Heaven. Then again, to shew a Colour of Jesus's having some Power, I find, by the Scope of his Argument, that he had that Power from Heaven by Courtesy. I must confess, if they had that Power, Christ had it not; and the Question I put was, By what Power did Christ work miracles? And he has in effect said, that Christ had that Power; and again, that he had it not, but left it with MOSES and ELIAS.

M. I never said so; for in him are hid all the Treasures of Wisdom and Knowledge. And how shou'd you say, he had no Power.

Q. Was John the Baptist vested with the Power of ELIAS?

M. You read the Words, don't you? I shan't deny them: He came forth in the Power and Spirit of ELIAS.

Q. Is God Light?

M. Yes.

Q. Is the Light God?

M. 'Tis a vertual Quality proceeding from God.

Q. Then there must be more Attributes to the Godhead than thou assertest; but I'll come to the Attributes by and by. I'll ask another Question; they Position says, that Jesus Christ is the only God and Lord of Heaven and Earth: Now, who was God before Jesus Christ was born?

M. Jehovah.

Q. Who was Jehovah?

M. The very God.

Q. Did he take Flesh before he was born?

M. No otherwise than by Decree; for he had decreed before the Foundation of the World, to become Flesh; but he had not that Body of Flesh existing in Heaven above the Stars.

Q. Was Christ born before he was conceived?

M. According to the Promise, he might be so.

Q. Was he conceived without a Womb?

M. No, no.

Q. Who prepared the Womb for him, if we had no God before Christ was born?

M. I own a God before he assum'd Flesh; And therefore why did you ask me for a God, when I own him the same God in Flesh as before?

Q. When I spake of the Trinity the other Night, I quoted a Text, from I John, ch. 5. Ver. 8 and then I told you, I had not time to expound the Nature of the Three that bear witness on Earth. As to the Three that bear record in Heaven, the Father, the Word, and Holy Ghost, the Apostle says These Three are One. And the Three that bear witness on Earth, the Spirit, Water, and Blood, agree in One; not that any One of the Three is singly God, either of the first Three or the second Three. The first Witness of the Three on Earth, is the Lord of the whole Earth, by whom the other two Witnesses stand, and that is the Spirit of God; and the Water, and the Blood agree in One with the Spirit of God. I told you I wou'd speak a little farther on the Quality and Operation of the Spirit of God, the Water, and the Blood; Joh. ch. ver. 24. God is a Spirit; and therefore the Spirit is God; and the Water and Blood, agreeing with the Spirit, must be spiritual. Jesus, in Chap. 16. Ver. 7 tells his Disciples, saying, It is expedient for you that I go away: for if I go not away, the Comforter will not come unto you; but if I depart, I will send him unto you. Ver. 8. And when he is come, he will reprove the world of sin, and of righteousness, and of judgment; Ver. 9. Of sin, because they believe not on me; Ver. 10 Of righteousness, because I go to my Father; Ver. 11, Of judgement, because the prince of this world is judged. Now the Blood of Christ, agreeing with the Water of Regeneration, is properly applicable and essential to Salvation; as these two co-operate together, the Water is for washing, and the Blood for sprinkling, &c. If we walk in the light, says the Apostle, as he is in the light, then we have fellowship one with another, and the blood of Jesus Christ his Son cleanseth us from all sin, I John. Ch. I. ver. 7. Where I to quote no more Texts of Scripture, this is sufficient to shew, that the Blood of Sprinkling is Spiritual; and there is a spiritual Co-operation with the Water, Blood and Spirit: The Water is that which regenerateth; our Lord speaks of it, under the Title of living Water, in the 4th of John, ver. 10 to the Samaritan Women at the Well, If thou knewest the gift of God, and who it is that saith to thee, Give me to drink; thou wouldst have asked of him, and he would have given thee living water. But, to metaphorize or figure the Water, Spirit and Blood; Christ as he is one with the Father and Holy Ghost, they are equally God eternal in Power: Christ is a Spirit, and he had the Spirit with him in the fleshly Body. And when he was crucified, and pierced in the Side with a Sword or Spear, there came forth Water and Blood; these are the two Witnesses that stand by the Lord of the whole Earth. These agree with the Spirit, these are the Witnesses ordain'd of God. Jesus himself, the Ordinance and the Standard, which is plainly set forth in the Transfiguration of Christ; and the Disappearing of MOSES and ELIAS shew plainly, that the Dispensation of the Law and the Prophets (as I take it, but I submit my Judgment to Men of better Sense) passed way, which was a Schoolmaster to lead us to Christ, to the New Covenant: The Old was fulfill'd in Christ. And the passing away of MOSES and ELIAS, our Lord Jesus Christ remaining alone, shews plainly, that he is the standing Ordinance of God for ever; he is the Only minister of the sanctuary, and the true tabernacle, which God has pitched, and not man: And it is to him, that Every knee must bow, and every tongue confess; for there is No name given under heaven, whereby men can be saved, but by the name of Jesus. The Work and Operation of the Holy Spirit is represented by Water, to wash away the Sins of the People; Wash ye, saith the Prophet Isaiah, ch. I. ver. 16 make you clean; put away the evil of your doings, &c. And come let us reason together, if your Sins were as Scarlet, I will make 'em as white as Wool: if as Crimson, I will make them as Snow. Now this is the Water, this is the Fountain of divine Life, that was open'd by Vertue of the Death and Sufferings of Christ, and represented by the Piercing of his Side, and by the Water and Blood gushing out of the Wound. The Blood is the Blood of sprinkling, that sprinkleth the Conscience from dead Works, &c. It is the Blood of the immaculate Lamb of God, that takes away the Sins of the World, that was shed, not spilt or wasted, but shed upon the Cross, for the Sins of the World. And, to shew his Mercy and Love to Mankind, he has declar'd That he came not to call the righteous, but the sinners to repentance. Now this plainly shews the Unity of the Godhead, the Co-operation of the Spirit of God working by the Water of Life, by the Blood of Sprinkling; the Blood of Jesus Christ his Son, that cleanseth from all Sin, them that believe in him. I shall now look a little back upon the Notes of some of my Friend's Arguments. The first Thing he propos'd was, to prove Christ in the second Dispensation; and told us plainly, he would do it.

M. To be the Son of God.

Q. He offer'd a few Quotations, many of which I made Use of in the Course of my Proofs and Arguments. Then he comes on to the 12th Article, and told us plainly, that he should not touch on the Condition of the second Dispensation; first, that was the Point he should go upon, then told us, he would not. The second Thing he went upon was, to prove Christ the very God; but he hath offer'd no Quotations to prove Christ the very God, but what I have offer'd to prove him the Son of God, &c. And I will shew plainly, that he hath many other Attributes; John, ch. I. ver. I. it's there said, Christ was in the Beginning; i.e., In the beginning was the word, &c. But that corporeal Body, born of the Virgin, was not in the Beginning. The Evangelist

Matthew traces the Genealogy of Christ, as to his Humanity, from Abraham to Joseph, the Husband of Mary, the Mother of our Lord; St. Luke traces it back from Mary, the Mother of Jesus, to God, viz. which was the Son of God. As to the attributes to the Almighty, it wou'd be an endless Story, for me to repeat 'em all, but I will give you a few of em; he is call'd God; he call'd himself, I am that I AM, when he spake to MOSES out of the Bush. He is call'd the Lord, Jehovah, the Father Almighty, the everlasting Father, Wonderful, Counsellor; but I don't find in the Text from Isaiah, that the Prophet call'd him the eternal Father, when he speaks of him in the Prophecy and Vision; To us a child is born, to us a Son is given, and his name shall be called Wonderful, Counsellor, everlasting Father; (I am now speaking of Christ in the same Sense, that I take the Prophet Isaiah to have done.) he spake here of the Son that should be born of a Virgin: He is here, as to his Humanity call'd the everlasting Father. And from another Text, Thou wilt not leave my soul in hell, nor suffer thine holy one to see corruption, it's plain, that the holy Body saw not Corruption, but was rais'd again in Glory and Power: He was glorified with the Father, with the same Glory that he had with him, before the World began.

M. What Father was that who glorified him?

Q. The eternal Father: I don't say, the everlasting Father; for it's one Thing to be eternal, to have no Beginning; and another Thing to be everlasting, to have no End. As to his Godhead, I affirm he is coeternal with the Father; but as to his Humanity, which was the Body that should be born of a Virgin, the Prophet doth not give him any other Title, than the everlasting, Father, the Prince of peace, &c. Now I say, he is call'd again Emmanuel, which signifies, God with us; that shews that he is omnipresent, that he is God in Heaven and on Earth, else we give the Holy Ghost the Lye. He is call'd again a Stem, that should spring from a Branch, as to his Humanity. He is call'd the Word of God: Our God is a consuming fire, saith the Apostle. He is call'd the Sword; he is call'd the Hammer; he is call'd Truth, &c.

M. That is God out of Christ; take Notice of that.

Q. I will now speak a little of his Attribute, as he is the Word of God, with which John the Evangelist begins his Gospel, and tells us, he was from Eternity, (as to his Godhead.) I find no Gospel Authorities which say, that the Body, which was born of the Virgin, was from Eternity. Were it so, it would shew an Inconsistency in the Text; And when he said, Come let us make man, who spake it he to? This shews there was a God in Trinity; therefore 'tis not reasonable to account that Body eternal, which was begotten. The Evangelist John tells you plainly, chap. I. ver. I. In the beginning was the word, and the word was with God, and the word was God, &c. Here John did not treat of his human Race, but of his Godhead; (he leaves that to the Credit of the other Evangelists, especially St. Luke) Ver. 6. There was a man sent from God, whose name was John. Ver. 7. The same came for a witness, to bear witness of the light, that all men thro' him might believe. Ver. 8. He was not that light, but was sent to bear witness of that light. Ver. 9. That was the true light, which lighteth every man that cometh into the world. Ver. 10. He was in the world, and the world was made by him, and the world knew him not. Now the World, such Part of it as Jesus in the Body was conversant with, they knew him personally; and had John meant of his Person, it would have been contradictory to the other Evangelists: But as to his Godhead, the World knew him not. Ver. II. He came unto his own, (And who were his own, but the Jews, the Seed of Abraham, according to the Flesh?) and his own received him not. They believed not in him, but cryed out to Pilate, Crucifie him! Crucifie him! &c.

M. To what End is all this Preaching?

Q. I find my Friend is so much in love with the Flesh, that whilst I was quoting the Evangelists on Christ's Humanity, he was very quiet, and seemingly well pleased; but now, when I come to touch on the Spirit, he seems angry. I admire that my Friend, who profess'd himself a spiritual Man, and cou'd see into my Spirit, the other Night, shou'd now grow uneasy, when I am treating of spiritual Things.

M. I know you can't measure your own Spirit; Pray how long is it you design to speak?

Q. Till I have done. Well, since the Matter of the Gospel is so tedious, I will begin upon Questions again.

M. I'll have no Questions; Do you think I'm come to be catechisied?

Q. Thou say'st, thou'rt a Muggletonian, art thou also a Reevonian? Dost thou profess the Faith of John Reeve?

M. Yes.

Q. Very well then, I have a Question or two to ask thee. There's a Book intitled, A Transcendent Spiritual Treatise, wrote by Reeve. Wherein he lays down, for Truth **That Immortality died, and that mortality died** See. pag. 24 of the said Book; And in the 34th page of the same, he says, **That the Body or Person of God was all spiritual, and not subject to Mortality.** Now here's a Contradiction in plain Terms, and not a Mistake in the Press; the Subject in both Pages, wherein the same is mentioned, favour thy Assertions. I can quote Authorities from the Fathers, where these Principles of yours are mentioned as old Heretics; and if you would give me Time, I would quote William Penn's Works, who answered this Book of Reeve, by a small Book intitled, The New Witnesses proved Old Hereticks; published in the Year 1672. Wherein he lays open those old rusty Heresies, and damnable Blasphemies; and in page 12, 18, and 31. He quotes several Historians, viz. Theodorus of Heresies, Socrates, St. Augustin, Eusebius, &c. Reeve and Muggleton say they are the Two Last Witnesses spoken of in the Revelations; which I deny, and will proceed to shew the Two Last Witnesses, viz. Jesus Christ, the standing Ordinance of God, he is the Minister of the Sanctuary, &c. He will never give way to another; and his Witnesses are the Water and the Blood, agreeing with the Spirit, and co-operating together for the Salvation of Men. Reeve and Muggleton were Impostors, and not Ministers of God, but Emissaries of Satan: And I think these Men, that take part with them, ought to lay their Hands on their Mouths, and their Mouths in the Dust. We have it from the Antiquities aforesaid, that these Heresies were invented and maintain'd some time in the Years 200, 350, and 403 after Christ.

M. What is it you call Heresies? Did I come with railing Accusations against your Principles.

Q. Thou railest carnally, when thou refusedst to let me go on in the Spirit with the Divinity of Christ.

M. Prove your Assertions as you go; prove what Heresies Reeve hath wrought.

Q. Thou toldst me, thou wert a Spiritual Man; I'm sorry thou shouldst be in the Number of those Galatians St. Paul rebuked, saying, O foolish Galatians! Who hath bewitched, you, &c.

M. Am I bewitched, to believe Christ to be very God? What do you call bewitching?

Q. Disobedience to the Spirit of Truth, thinking to be made perfect in the Flesh. When I come to tell thee of thine own Principles, thou canst not bear it; I'll either go on with the Subject I was upon, or continue upon this of Reeve, which thou pleases.

M. Tell me what Reeve has wrought.

Q. Reeve has wrought Heresies and Blasphemy.

M. I look upon John Reeve and Lodowick Muggleton's Writings to be as true as the Scriptures.

Q. I say Reeve and Muggleton were Impostors, and not the Two Last Witnesses: It is by faith we are saved, and not by works of righteousness which we have done, (not by the blasphemous Heresies of Reeve and Muggleton) but by the washing of regeneration. If you please I'll turn Limner for 2 or 3 Minutes and picture the Devil to you; and that by dipping my Brush in the Paint of your old rusty Heresies, and damnable Blasphemies.

M. I believe you have no occasion to picture him; I fancy you are the only Resemblance of him: So you have no occasion to shew him; for in you we see him plainly.

Q. Your Heresies, Blasphemies, Self-contradictions and Confusions are Evil-Doings, and he that doth Evil, is the Picture of the Devil. I have three Things before me, take thy Choice, whether I shall proceed with the History of John, upon the Divinity of Christ; with Reeve and Muggleton; or with the Picture of the Devil.

M. Proceed with what you accuse Reeve and Muggleton.

Q. I have proved his Heresy and Blasphemy, in the Pages I quoted, viz. 24 and 34, of the Transcendent Spiritual Treatise.

Muggletonians, aside.] Pin him down, don't let him go on thus.

Rawlinson, aside.] Let me alone; if I can't manage him, the Devil shall.

Q. I will proceed then with the Heresies of Reeve, and give you either a Spoonful, a Pint, a Choppin, i.e. a Quart, or a Gallon of it: For though the Sea be a great Ocean, you may taste in a Spoonful the Nature of the whole. (Pray Neighbour Rawlinson desire thy Friends to be quiet, and not breed a Mutiny.) In the 24th Page Reeve affirms, **That Immortality died, and Mortality died:** And in the 34th he affirms **That the Body or Person of God was all spiritual or heavenly, and not subject to mortality.** I offer this as a Self-Contradiction. I'd repeat the Substance of Reeve in pag. 24 and 34. If thou'lt have me turn to the Book, and read 'em, I'll do it.

M. I won't answer for the printing of the Words, but for the Meaning I will.

Q. The Words are these in pag. 24, **Thus Immortality died, and quickened in Mortality; and thus pure Mortality died and quickened in Immortality and Glory again,** &c. Page 34, **The Body or Person of God was all spiritual or heavenly, not subject to Mortality.** Now I say it is Blasphemy to assert, that **Immortality died:** Can there be any thing a more plain Self Contradiction than this?

M. Immortality, before it became Flesh, is God himself; and when the eternal Majesty left his Throne of Glory, and incarnated himself in the Womb of the Virgin, _____

Q. Did the Godhead leave the Throne?

M. Yes.

Q. Then thou deniest his Omnipresence: For if he was not in Heaven, he was not every-where.

M. May I say, that the whole essential Godhead left the Throne of immortal Glory, entered into the Womb of the Virgin, and dissolv'd himself into Flesh, Blood and Bone.

Q. The whole Godhead?

M. The whole Godhead.

Q. Oh Blasphemy against the eternal God!

M. I think in the Colossians it is written, that in Christ dwelt all the fullness of the Godhead bodily; and yet you now seem to question, whether it did take Flesh or no, and call it Blasphemy: And for that very Saying, **I pronounce you, in the name of the Lord Jesus Christ, damned to all Eternity, Body, Soul and Sprit, before Men and Angels.**

Q. Neighbour Rawlinson, hast thou any Thing more to say?

M. No; for I look upon thee to be a Reprobate, before ever thou wert born or conceived in thy Mother's Womb, thee and thy Seed for ever.

Q. The Curse is heavy in Words, but light in Power; I don't account my self above Six-pence worse for it. Were I to meet my Friend in the Street, take him to the Host-house, and spend Six-pence on him, I doubt not but he would soon turn his Curse into a Blessing. I suppose he speaks ironically; and, to give it a more familiar Term, he perhaps acts the Boatman, rows one Way and looks another. However, I shall make the best Use I can of it; to speak my Mind freely, by the Rules of his Curse, I shall conclude my self in a much fairer Way of being saved, than he. Whereas he **saith I was a reprobate before ever I was born;** if so I must be in the Number of Sinners, and I suppose he accounts himself an elected and righteous Person: Hence may I hope for Salvation from Sin by Jesus Christ, who came Not to call the righteous, but sinners to repentance, Matth. ch. 9. ver. 13. And if I repent, and do the Will of God, though my Sins be as Scarlet, he will make them as snow; and though they be red like Crimson, they shall be as Wool; if willing and obedient, I shall eat the good of the Land, (in a twofold Sense) and be received into everlasting Life, in the great Day of Judgment. And if Salvation be not attainable (as certainly it is not) by any other Name or Power, than of Jesus Christ of Nazareth, by whose Stripes we are healed; and by his Death for Sin, we die unto Sin, by Faith in him, and Repentance for Sin, without which no Man can be saved. And God hath concluded all under Sin, or in Unbelief, that he might have Mercy on all, Rom ch. II. V. 32. Hence my Friend Rawlinson can have no just Pretence to Salvation, allowing him to be a righteous or elect Man, before he was born; the Whole need no physician, but they that are sick: And if my Friend Rawlinson be one of God's Elect, he should be born of God; and he that is born of God, sinneth not, but is God's Elect, and in this the Election stands, and the wicket One toucheth him not, neither is he soon angry, or stirr'd up to Wrath, Envy, Hatred, Cursing, &c. I observ'd my Friend, in the Course of his Argument, declar'd, that he would shed his Blood for the Testimony of Reeve and Muggleton's Principles. I must confess that Love must be strong, which induceth a Man to die for his Friend; and the most pertinent Case in the Scriptures, at this Time in my Remberance, is in Paul to the Romans, ch. 5. V. 7, 8, For scarcely for a righteous man will die yet peradventure for a good man some wou'd even dare to die. But God commendeth his love towards us, in that while we were yet sinners, Christ died for us. Hence it's clearly manifested, that my Friend's presumptuous Curse, is a most wicked daring Blasphemy: To affirm or speak likes against God, the Scriptures, and the Holy Ghost, this is speaking Evil against the Holy Ghost; and our Lord Jesus Christ hath declar'd That whosoever speaketh against the Holy Ghost, it shall never be forgiven him neither in this world, nor in the world to come, Mat. ch. 23. v. 32.

Friend Rawlinson, since thou wilt not stand thy ground, and hear what I have to say, by way of Replication to thy long Argument, on the several Remarks or Notes which I have taken, I shall be oblig'd to reply to them in Writing, and commit them to the Press, with the whole Discourse, as it's taken by (I believe) an impartial Hand: And I desire thou wilt now declare, whether thou art willing the same shall be publish'd.

M. With all my Heart.

****

Forasmuch as John Rawlinson (Disputant on Behalf of the Muggletonians) absolutely refused to bear with Patience what I had to say, in Answer to the several Remarks, which I then made on the Course of his Arguments, and that I promis'd to reply in Print, I therefore hold it my Duty to proceed therein; and have, as followeth, made such Remarks as I think are in any way proper or expedient, without in'arging beyond the Bounds of Moderation, &c.

I. Muggletonian, Undertook to prove Christ more largely in the second Dispensation, than the first, &c.

Quaker. The large Proofs to me appear'd no Proofs, whatever they might be to him. And as to that incultivated and disrespectful Expression concerning Christ (viz. more largely) is an Insinuation of Variableness and Uncertainty in the Power of our Lord Jesus Christ, who as to his Godhead is the same yesterday, to day, and for evermore, with whom there is no Shadow of Turning. I would gladly know what my Friend means by the First, Second and Third Dispensations? Till then, I cannot replay properly thereto.

2. M. He saith, he will enter upon the Power of MOSES and ELIAS, and alledgeth the Quaker slighted them, &c. Quotes Mark ix. The Transfiguration of Christ.

Q. Although he promised to enter upon the Power of MOSES and ELIAS, he shewed no Colour of Proof. The Passage he quotes of Christ's Transfiguration is an eminent Proof against him; and, in the Course of My Counter proofs, I made use of the same Passage, to prove that MOSES and ELIAS were Men, and talk'd with Jesus in the Mountain: See my Commentation on that Passage.

3. M. Alleg'd, that I seem'd to assert, that John the Baptist was the very ELIAS himself; and quotes Luke I. 17. and Mark ix II. And lays a Charge against me, for proving ELIAS to be come.

Q. It's a false Allegation; and the Text he quotes to confront me is the same I made use of, in proving that ELIAS, i.e. John the Baptist, was indeed come by Spirit and Power in the Body of John. And as to his high Charge against me, of insisting that ELIAS, who was in a Throne of Glory, was come in a Body of Flesh; for Answer I refer to the Quotations I offer'd; and the Commentation I made thereon was consonant with the Scriptures in the Words of the Holy Text, That ELIAS WAS INDEED COME, &c. And therefore I argued, that it was contrary to the Scriptures and to Reason to insinuate; that the Guardianship of Christ's Person, and the Charge of his Kingdom were committed to MOSES and ELIAS.

4. M. Asserts, That ELIAS, after his Translation, does eternally exist, and is existent there now, and is for Duration to all Eternity, &c.

Q. How easy is it for the meanest Capacity, to comprehend the notorious Blasphemy of such his Assertion, and the apparent Contradiction that it contains; even against his own Position and Article of Faith, sign'd with his own Hand-writing, viz. **That Jesus Christ is the only God and Lord of heaven and Earth:** And now he affirms, that he is not; by saying, that ELIAS, after his Translation, does eternally exist, and is existent there now, and is for Duration to all Eternity. By this Assertion there must be two Eternities, else Jesus Christ is not eternal in Godhead. It is a contradicting Blasphemy, to say, ELIAS, after his Translation, externally existed; if he was translated, then was he not eternal; and if he were eternal, he could not be translated. Was it reasonable to believe a Possibility of Conception, and bringing forth a natural Son of Satan, in human Shape, begotten on the Body Mystery Babylon, the great Mother of Harlots, and Abominations of the Earth, I would readily conclude, the first Inventor of those damnable Tenets to be such an one.

5. M. Saith, that he who marks the Misdeeds of MOSES, finds fault with God; and alledgeth, that God did not find fault with him.

Q. By this he insinuates, that MOSES is God, or equal with God: but, contrary to his Allegation, God did find fault with MOSES, Num. xx. 12. Saying, Because ye believed me not, to sanctify me in the eyes of the children of Israel; therefore ye shall not bring this congregation into the land which I have given them. 'Tis plain from hence, that God charg'd MOSES with Incredulity, and inflected a Punishment for the same.

6. M. Saith, There was a Necessity, that God should invest fatherly Power on MOSES an ELIAS.

Q. I wish my Friend Rawlinson would give his Proofs to this Assertion; till then, it is not worth while to waste Ink and Paper about it.

7. M. Says, it was God's eternal Decree in Heaven to become Flesh, and swore an Oath to himself on the same; and, for Proof of the said Oath, he quotes Psal. lxxxix. 34, 35, 36.   God   swore   by   his holiness, that he would not lie to his servant David, &c.

Q. I want a Proof for this Decree in Heaven, and of the Oath he swore to himself; the Test quoted is no Proof, except he means, that David is God; and if so, then it's not one, two or three Gods will serve his Turn; but such a Plurality of Gods, as he himself cannot certainly give an Account of: For when I proved MOSES and ELIAS on Earth with Christ, then he called up Enoch.

8. M. Quotes John I. 21. John Baptist confessed he was not ELIAS.

Q. There was good Reason, for John's Confessing he was not ELIAS; first, in regard to the Persons who put the Question to him were Priests and Levites, Messengers sent by the Jesus, a People of ceremonial Rites, and carnal Reasoning; and no doubt but John was truly sensible, that they inquired not after the Spirit and Power of ELIAS, but after his natural human Body, they being Men of dark Understandings; (as appeared soon after in the Crucifixion of our Lord Jesus Christ.) Yet I confess they were not so devilish, neither did they commit such high Crimes, Misdemeanours, treasonable Conspiraces, Usurpations and Assassinations against the eternal Father, his Son Jesus Christ and the Holy Ghost, the Almighty God, and King of Kings, as my Friend Rawlinson, John Reeve, Lodowick Muggleton, and their Adherents. The former only perpetrated the Murder of the corporeal Body of his Humanity, which they effected by false Witnesses; and although they brought many such, yet found they none, till at last came two false Witnesses, and said, This Fellow said, &c. Matt. xxvi. 60, 61. And by the Testimony of those two false Witnesses Jesus was condemned. But as to the latter, viz, the Reevonians and Muggletonians, they have contrived and formed a more hellish and damnable Plot against the Godhead as it is in triunal Union. They have most presumptuously attempted to dethrone the King of Kings, Lord of Lords, the eternal Father, the everlasting Father, the Son of God, and Holy Ghost; and to place MOSES, ELIAS and ENOCH in and upon the Throne of Heaven; and, bloody Jews like, have sought out for many false Witnesses, yet found they none, till Reeve and Muggleton appeared, who strain'd at nothing, neither Straws nor Camels, Hills or Mountains, Sea or Land, Priest and People, Judge and Bailiff, Lords and Commons, King and Subject, to bring about their hellish Plot; and have strenuously insinuated, that the immortal God and Jesus Christ his Son were dead; and have issued out their infernal Proclamation, that MOSES and ELIAS were vested or invested with the Throne of Glory; and that Reeve and Muggleton were the Two Last Witnesses. I suppose they mean, that as MOSES and ELIAS are their Kings, they have a Right to be their prime or first Ministers of State. I cannot help nothing that they seem to be very powerful Ministers, and what if I say, dangerous ones; and may in a little Time conspire against MOSES and ELIAS; and in my Opinion they have made some Progress that way already, to wit, in assuming the ment of the Subjects at their own Wills and Pleasures; as appears by their Writings, intitled Transcendent Spiritual Treatise, pag. 3. In these Words; Whosoever despiseth these Writings, whether he be a King or a Beggar, by calling it Blasphemy, or Heresy, or 'Delusion, or a Lye, or Speaking Evil of it in any kind whatsoever, in so doing they have committed that unpardonable Sin against the Holy Ghost, or Spirit that sent us.' Wherefore, in Obedience to our Commission from the Lord Jesus Christ, whom they have despised and not us, we pronounce them Cursed, both Soul and Body, from the Presence of the Lord Jesus, elect Men and Angels, to all Eternity, John Reeve and Lodowick Muggleton, the Lord's Two Last True Witnesses and Prophets, spoken of in the Eleventh of the Revelations, a little before the coming of him that sent us, who is Judge of both Quick and Dead. And in pag. 4. Claim a Power from God by the two edged Sword of his Spirit in Reeve's Mouth, to Bless and Curse; and that whosoever he shall pronounce Blessed is so to Eternity, and whosoever he shall pronounce Cursed is so to Eternity.

Consider, gentle Reader, in the Course of human Conduct, when a Prince is set upon a Throne by the Testimony of two false Witnesses, and those are made not only the two chief Ministers of his State, but have Power to act and transact, to set up and to cast down, to plant and to pluck up, to bless and to curse, to make rich and to make

Truth and Reason defended 331

poor, to make happy and to make miserable, whom they please and when they please, what they please and as they please; and all by Authority of their Prince's royal Signet, Seal and Power; insomuch that the Prince himself cannot reverse their Decrees: What a tottering Condition must such a Prince be in! how unsafe are his Kingdom and Subjects! How unsecure is his royal Person! And since such Prince was set on the Throne by those two perjur'd Witnesses, may they not be as soon moved to dethrone him for their own Promotion, as they were to enthrone him for his Honour? He that swears falsly on one Side of the Question, will not stop to do in on t'other, when the gilded Bait of his Interest and Promotion, or of his humourish Fantasy takes with him. Riches, Glory and Power are tempting baits.

9. M. Takes upon him to shew in Christ, a Necessity and Dependance there was on creaturely Beings for their Supply, &c.

Q. To this he gave no Demonstration, though he made a long and blasphemous Speech upon it.

10. M. Quotes John xiv. From ver. 7, to 17. To prove, that there was no Father, but what existed in Jesus, as he was a Body of Flesh; and that there was no Father in Heaven, nor any governing Power but MOSES and ELIAS.

Q. The Scriptures, he quotes, are so plain and clear against his heretical Notions, that I need not expostulate or paraphrase on them; and particularly Ver. 16. In these Words, And I will pray the Father, and he shall give you another Comforter, that he may abide with you for ever: From hence it's as plain as the Sun at Noonday, that there is a Father, a Son and Holy Ghost, i. e. Spirit; and in that he saith, he shall send another Comforter, it is easy understood, that the Father would not send him, i. e. his Son in the fleshly Body again, but the Holy Spirit proceeding from the Father and the Son, to be and abide with all who receive, obey and believe in God the Father, and in his Son Christ Jesus, through the Power and Operation of the Holy Ghost, the Comforter, the Spirit of Truth, which leadeth into all Truth every one that loves the Appearance of it, in self Denial and the Cross of Christ, without which none can be Heirs of the Crown of Glory that is laid up for all them that love the Appearance of the Comforter.

11. M. Saith, Christ uses the Word to pray to a Father seemingly.

Q. In this he chargeth Christ with Insincerity, Hypocrisy and Vanity; And shall we give Credit to such vile, base and hellish Aspersions, falsely cast upon the Lord of the whole Earth, the inestimable Fountain of all Sincerity, Truth and Humility? God forbid

12. M. Takes upon him to prove Christ in a higher Dispensation than the Second.

Q. He hath not explain'd, what he means by a higher Dispensation; so I shall say no more to that, but note that Jesus Christ, as to his Godhead, and Coeternity with the Father and Holy Ghost, was, and is, and shall be the same that ever he was in all Dispensations, eternally blessed and happy in triunal Deity, without the Help, Courage or

Friendship of any creately Being; nay, MOSES, ELIAS, ENOCH, NOAH, DANIEL, and JOB are not capable to administer to him.

13. M. Quotes Colos. ii. 9. For in him dwelt all the fullness of the Godhead bodily, &c.

Q. The text is allow'd, but it's no Proof to thy Position, but very strong against it; in that he saith bodily, sheweth he was both God and Man, Even the Man Christ Jesus: But the Text doth not say, nor in any way insinuate, that the Fullness of the Godhead dwelt eternally in that Body; and the Reason is plain, because the corporeal Body of Christ was begotten, conceived and born of a Woman, therefore could not be eternal, altho' it be everlasting.

14. M. Christ in time did make himself manifest to the Disciples and Apostles, but they must first suffer Death.

Q. This is a mystical Manifestation, that in time it should be made, and yet they must be out of Time before it could be done. I tell thee plainly, my Friend, tho art under a strong Delusion, whilst thou stept into thy Bed of carnal Security, an Enemy hath sown Tares, the Seeds of Heresy and Blasphemy, in the Ground or Field of thy Heart or Mind. Remember the Case of ELYMAS the Sorcerer, who withstood Paul and Barnabas; he fought to turn away the Duty from the Faith; Paul set his eyes on Elymas and said, O full of all subtilty and all mischief, thou child of the devil; thou enemy of all righteousness, wilt tho not cease to pervert the right ways of the Lord? Acts xiii, 8, 9, 10. Remember likewise, that the Messenger of the Covenant, in the great Power of God, the eternal Father, by the Holy Ghost, will come near to Judgment, and will be a swift Witness against the Sorcerers, i.e. false Witnesses, Mal iii. 5. Beware of Subornation; I love thee for thy Soul's sake, and I pity thy deplorable Condition, O thou poor, deluded, suborn'd and bewitch'd Soul! Seek the Lord whilst he may be found, call upon him whilst he is near, forsake thy wicked Ways, and all thy vain Thoughts, turn unto the Lord, and he will have mercy upon thee, and to our God and he will abundantly pardon, Isaiah lv. 7. Let a mature and solid Consideration seize thy Mind, consider what Spirit it is that leads into Error, Confusion and Inconsistency. There is but Time and Eternity, and if the Apostles were not to have the Manifestation of Christ by his Spirit, until they suffered Death, then must they not have it in Time: But what was that Pouring forth of the Holy Ghost, which appear'd like Cloven Tongues of Fire to the Apostles, filled them, and caused them to speak with other Tongues, and as the Spirit gave them Utterance? Acts II. And by what Power did the Apostles work Miracles? Was it not the fulfilling of the Prophecy of the Prophet Joel, which was, That in the latter days he would pour forth of his Spirit upon all flesh, and your sons and your daughters shall prophesy, &c. Joel II. 28. And did not the Latter Days, i.e. the Gospel Dispensation, commence with Christ suffered on the Cross, and said, Now it is finished, to wit, the Law in the Ceremonies thereof? And was not the Pouring forth of the Holy Ghost, in that irresistible, powerful and plentiful Manner as aforesaid, a powerful and uncontroulable Testimony and Witness, of the Commencement of the Gospel Dispensation, and of the Fulfilling of Christ's Promise to his Disciples, of coming again in Spirit to them? I hope, when thou considerest this, thou wilt not dare to resist the Truth of it. Had not God poured forth of his Spirit upon his Disciples, and fill'd their Hearts with his Power and Wisdom, they could neither have wrought Miracles, nor have preached his Resurrection in the Power of the Gospel. Away with those wild Bedlam Notions! and receive the Truth in the Love of it.

15. M. Going to speak of the second Dispensation.

Q. In the Article he first began with, he took upon him to prove Christ in the second Dispensation. Again, in the twelfth Article, he says, he will not touch on the Conditions of the Second Dispensation. Again farther, in this Article, he saith, he is only going to speak of the second Dispensation: And all this while, he said not one Word relating thereunto in proper Order. This I note to shew the Reader, how difficult it was for me to compose or form Arguments to turn the Fox out of all his dark Holes. However, I have laid open some hidden and iniquitous Mysteries to the View of my Reader, as plain as my Judgment, Reason, Memory and Time would allow.

16. M. Saith, John was persecuted for his Faith, tho' he had not the effect of it.

Q. How could he fear God in a true Sense, preach the Gospel in the Spirit and Power of it, and suffer for the Testimony thereof, and for his Faith, if he had not the Effect of it? But it was the Effect of his Faith that gave him Power and Courage to suffer for it, and to work the Work of God; for Faith is the Work of God, and leads to do his Will: But Faith without Works is dead; and for thee to insinuate, that John had not the Effect of his Faith, is a notorious Untruth, a Reflection upon the great Power and Justice of God; and not only so, but it is inconsistent in Terms, and false in Fact. The Sanctification of his Soul, Redemption from his Sins, were the Effect of his Faith; but as to the exceeding Fullness of the Glory and Felicity that was prepared for him, in the World to come, i.e. Eternity, he had not the full Fruition of it, whilst he remained in the earthly Tabernacle; yet no doubt he had a sufficient Measure of Comfort and Power, to encourage him in well doing, and enable him to resist the Devil and all his works. To suppose it other-wise would be to accuse God of being a hard master, and an austere man, gathering where he did not sow, and reaping where he did not sow, &c.

****

Some Remarks on the Muggletonian Principles, from a Book published by John Reeve and Lodowick Muggleton,

In the Year 1653, and reprinted in 1729, intituled, A Remonstrance from the Eternal God, declaring several spiritual Transactions unto the Parliament and Commonwealth of England, unto His Excellency the Lord General Cromwel, the Council of State, the Council of War, &c. And from a final Book, intituled, Transcendent Spiritual Treatise, wrote by John Reeve; and the Divine Looking Glass by Lodowick Muggleton.

As touching the Commission of John Reeve, and Lodowick Muggleton, I think it's not amiss to make some few Remarks upon the many Inconsistencies, and Self-Contradictions in them contained, from the aforesaid Books.

In Transcendent Spiritual Treatise, p. 4, 5. the said Reeve, speaking in his own Person, saith, That on the 3d, 4th and 5th Days of February, 1651, three Mornings successively, much about one Hour, the Lord Jesus, the only wise God, &c. by Voice of Words, spake unto me, John Reeve, saying, I have given thee to understand my Mind in the Scriptures above all Men in the World. The next Words the Lord spake unto me were these, saying, Look into thy own Body, there thou shalt see the Kingdom of Heaven, and the Kingdom of Hell: The Lord spake these Words to me twice together. Again, The Lord spake unto me these Words, saying, I have chosen thee my Last Messenger, for a great Work unto this bloody unbelieving World, &c. And farther saith, He was as perfectly awake, when the Lord spake unto him, as he was at the writing thereof. So much for the first Morning.

Again saith he, The next Morning the Lord spake unto me saying, go thou to Lodowick Muggleton, and with him go unto Thomas Turner, and he shall bring you to one John Tane, and do thou deliver my Message, when thou comest there; and if Lodowick Muggleton deny to go with thee, then do thou from me pronounce him Cursed to Eternity, &c. So much for the second Morning.

The third and last Morning, saith he, The Lord spake unto me these Words, saying, Go thou unto Lodowick Muggleton, and take such a Woman along with thee, and then go unto one John Robinson, a Prisoner in New Bridewel, and do thou deliver my Message unto him when thou comest there. These were the Lord's Words the 3d and last Morning, and all the Words in the Commission of the Lord spoken unto me, &c.

And he saith also, He did not well know whether he was a mortal Man, or an immortal God &c.

In the aforesaid Remonstrances to the Parliament, Pag. 3., the said Reeve and Muggleton join in Commission in these Words, viz. By

Virtue of a Commission, which we received by Voice of Word from Heaven, &c.

In Transcendent Spiritual Treatise, Reeve declares as aforesaid, that this Commission was given to him only, and that God had chosen him his Last Witness, and had given him to understand his Mind in the Scriptures, above all Men in the Word, consequently above Muggleton; although he allows Muggleton to be equal with him in Commission, as aforesaid. How inconsistent is this with it self, I leave to the Judicious. If the first Mission of Reeve was true, the second in Company with Muggleton must be false: And if the second be true, the first must be false: Ergo, they are both false, carrying an apparent Contradiction. God forbid either should be true! Again, in the said Remonstrance to the Parliament, the said Reeve and Muggleton say, in the 3d page, That they were first directed to go to one John Tane, to convince him of Error, &c.

In Transcendent Spiritual Treatise, Reeve saith, He was first to go to Lodowick Muggleton, and with him to go to Thomas Turner; and if Muggleton denied, to go with him, to pronounce him cursed, &c. This he saith was the 2d Morning: And on the third Morning, he saith, He was to go to Muggleton, and take such a Woman along with him, and then go to John Robinson, &c. Who can tell whom such a Woman was? And if they offer for a Reason, of Muggleton's Co-equality in Commission with Reeve, that of his being sent to him; then, by the same Rule, such a Woman must have equal Share with them in the said Commission. Again, Who can have any Grounds to imagine, that Muggleton had any Share in the said Commission, when Reeve was to curse him, if he denied to go with him: But perhaps Muggleton join'd Reeve, for fear of the Curse. And why was not such a Woman to be cursed also, if she disobey'd, as Muggleton was to be? And if Reeve, Muggleton, and such a Woman were to go first to John Robinson, as in the 3d and last Morning's Commission to Reeve as aforesaid in T.S.T. How can Reeve, and Muggleton's Message in Conjunction be true, that they were first to go to John Tane as aforesaid, where was such a Woman then?

If the Kingdom of Heaven and the Kingdom of Hell were both in John Reeve, as he saith, 'tis no Wonder he could not stand long to any one Notion, or steer his Course free of Confusion and self Contradiction, as Our Lord Jesus Christ observes, Mark, iii. 25. And if a house be divided against it self, that house cannot stand.

Reeve farther blasphemeth, saying, He knew not whether he was a mortal Man, or an immortal God, and not only so, but contradicts his own Words thereby; where a little before he saith, he was as perfectly awake when the Lord spake to him, as he was at the Writing of it, &c.

Remonstrances, pag. 6. Reeve and Muggleton say in these Words, viz. We Two only are the Last Men, that ever shall speak or write by Commission, from the true God, unto the Powers and People whilst this World endureth, therefore whosoever lives to see an End of us, shall suddenly see the Desolution of this vain World, and all the Glory thereof, &c. And farther say, That they two are the two spiritual Witnesses, prophesied of in the 11th of John in the Revelations. And that the only true God, the Man Jesus, hath by his Spirit revealed unto them more Spiritual Understanding, of that glorious Mystery concerning himself, than ever was, is, or shall be revealed unto Man, until Time shall be swallowed up of Eternity, &c.

If Reeve and Muggleton, as they say, be the two Last Men, that ever shall speak or write by Commission from the true God, &c. Then are the Speeches, Writings and Curses of John Rawlinson ineffectual; not only against Henderson, the Quaker, but against all others. And for him to pretend he would shed his Blood for the Cause and Principles of Reeve and Muggleton, and at the same Time act contrary to their written Precepts, is plainly declaring himself to be an Impostor and Deceiver, in pretending to Curse all who oppose them.

Divine Looking Glass, Chap. I. p. 3. Muggleton saith, Notwithstanding every divine Vertue in the Creator's Person be infinite, yet I affirm, that there was never any kind of Reason in him. And he farther affirms, That what Men call pure Reason, &c. is a dark tormenting fiery Devil of burning Envy. And in p. 4. he calls Reason that proud angelical Serpent-Devil; and challengeth the whole Scriptures for one Saying that signifieth God's divine Nature to be pure Reason, or by pure Reason we know the true God or any thing that is Spiritual, &c.

The Absurdity of these Quotations is so manifest, that I think I need not croud Scripture-Proofs by way of Consultation: But I shall only produce one more manifest Self-Contradiction out of the same Book, Chap. 3. pag. 7. Moreover, I positively affirm, saith he, from the same Light, that all the Angels, in the heavenly Throne aforesaid, are Persons in Form like Men, and not body-less Spirits, as the learned have long declared; and the Nature of their Angelical Spirits are pure Reason. Tis a strange Thing that Angels should be all pure reason, if God be void of it!

A few Queries to Rawlinson and his misled Adherents, part of which I find mentioned in the New Witnesses prov'd Old Hereticks, &c. written by William Penn, and published in the Year 1672; to which I never found or heard of any Answer.

1. If John Reeve and Lodowick Muggleton were the Two Witnesses mentioned in the Revelations, how comes it that they bear not the same Testimony?

2. Why have they not prophesied 1260 Days, i.e. Years, and have been slain together for three Days and a half in Spiritual Sodom and Egypt, and where our Lord was crucified, and then have risen from the Dead together?

3. Have not they been dead a great many Years, and yet this Word is not desolved; although they prophesied the Desolution thereof

should suddenly be seen, by those who should live to see an End of them?

4. When did they shut up the Heavens, that it rained not, turn Water into Blood, and smite the Earth with Plagues?

5. Whether these Men in their Commissions and Doctrines, are most like unto the Last Witnesses of the Lord Jesus Christ, or those ungodly proud Boasters, wandering Stars, Clouds without Rain, raging Waves, exalted above all that is called God, and Perverters of the Truth.

6. How prove they this Assertion of Muggleton's, in the 2d Chap. p. 5. and 6. of Divine Looking Glass, That the Substance of Earth and Water were from all Eternity uncreated, &c.

FINIS

A Conference Betwixt A Muggletonian And A Baptist, On These Propositions:

I. There was no GOD in Heaven when Christ Jesus was on this Earth.
II. God became as a Creature, Sin excepted.
III. God dyed.

LONDON: Printed for T. Cooper, at the Globe in Paternoster-Row, 1739.

Introduction.

The following Pages are a Defense of certain Propositions, contain'd in the Writings of *John Reeve,* which were taken out by a *Baptist,* and asserted to be false, and contrary to the Scriptures; who likewise affirm'd that there was not a Man in the World who could defend them; which was the Occasion of what follow; which was utter'd before some Hundreds of People, who met to hear the Conference. I thought it better to commit my Defenses of the Proportions into the Method in which they now are than to write them as they spoke Extempore, even if I could have remember'd them exactly: However, I have vary'd but little, added but little, and left little out. They who were present may recollect that the Answer that was then made to what I advanc'd consisted of some Quotations from Scripture, which were intended to prove, That there was a God in Heaven distinct from *Christ:* To which I reply'd, that I acknowledged those Texts to be true, and that they relate to *Christ* in the state of the Father; and I then proceeded to shew the Truth of my Assertion by producing those Passages from the Scriptures, which make *Christ* and the Father one: I likewise observed that the Scriptures are not reconcileable upon any other Hypothesis but that of *Christ Jesus* being the very God: I also said that God witnessed to the Truth of himself being both God and *Christ,* when he condescended to talk to his Creatures; which Expression occasion'd a little Laugh, and this Question was ask'd upon I, Did ever any one hear before of God's talking to his Creatures? Which Ignorance in them arose from their not knowing that *Christ* was that *Word* which was made *Flesh,* and, as the Scripture says, *that*

Word was God: And when *Jesus,* after his Resurrection, appear'd to the Eleven on a Mountain in *Galilee,* he said, *All Power is given unto me in Heaven and in Earth,* Matt. Chap. xxviii. Ver.18.

I think the Preservation of these Texts in the Mind necessary for Believers that they may not be suddenly drawn to think, with the World, that there is any Absurdity in the three following Propositions.

First, *There was no God in Heaven when* Christ Jesus *was on this Earth.*

Secondly, *God became as a Creature, Sin excepted.*

Thirdly, *God dyed.*

These Truths of God's Existence are in his sacred Records, and are not to be known but by his Spirit; and where that is not they will be as Stumbling-blocks. As the Knowledge of God's Existence in Heaven, and while on Earth, is contain'd in the Knowledge of these Propositions, (which is of the highest Importance to Mankind, it being no less than eternal Life, as the Scripture assures us, *to know the true God,*) I hope it will be a Motive sufficient to product an impartial Enquiry.

PROPOSITION the 1st.
There was no God in Heaven when Christ Jesus *was on this Earth.*

PROPOSITION the 2d.
God became as a Creature, Sin excepted.

PROPOSITION the 3d.
God dyed.

The Inferences which are drawn from these Propositions, by the Objector, are *first,* That we deny the Father. *2dly,* That if God was a Creature he was finite, so consequently not God. *3dly,* That if God dyed, then there was no God in Heaven or on Earth.

As the Ideas which the Objectors annex to these Propositions arise from a false Foundation, if I remove the Causes of those Ideas; then the Propositions will hold good, and those false Ideas, and the Inferences drawn from them, will fall to the Ground.

I will previously observe to that Part of the World call'd Religionists, that they jointly acknowledge the Existence of one God, whatever Demonstrations they go by, but the Mode of his Existence is the principal Subject of Dispute among them, and which, I believe, will continue as such to the End of the World: That the World by Wisdom knows not God can not be understood of his Existence only, but of the

Mode of his Existence; and as the Knowledge of his Mode of Existence is the Effect of Revelation, it is evident that it can not be attain'd but thro God's Assistance; and that Knowledge is contain'd in a Demonstration of the following Propositions:

1st. *There was no God in Heaven when* Christ Jesus *was on Earth.*
2d. *God became as a Creature, Sin excepted.*
3d. *God dyed.*

On these Propositions arises the Demonstration of the Manner in which God was a *Father,* in which a *Son,* and in which the *Holy Ghost.* If I can shew how God is a *Father,* how a *Son,* and how the *Holy Ghost,* without dividing the Essence or confounding the Terms, I shall gain my Point, and the Argument will be at an End. The first Proposition in Natural Religion is, That there is one God; so the Unity of God is a Part of both Natural and Reveal'd Religion rightly understood. All Men, who have undertaken the Proof of the Existence of one God, have proceeded on Observations made on sensible Objects; and tho' they unanimously agree that the Essence and Mode of his Existence, are abstracted from all sensible Ideas, yet they as unanimously agree that the Knowledge of his Existence, and of his Attributes, is to be acquir'd by the Judgment of Sense. This is all that is necessary to be offer'd from the Province of Reason; for if Reason proceeds any farther than the Knowledge of the Existence of God, he wades out of his Depth. Now we have arrived thus far by the Use of our Rational Faculties, we must have Recourse for farther Discoveries to Revelation; for Reason is here at his Journey's End. As the Existence of one God is the Foundation of all Natural Religion, the Divine Being was pleased to make the Knowledge of the Mode of his Existence the Foundation of all Spiritual Religion.

Here we enter into the Province of Faith: What I have already offer'd shews how unanimous the wiser Part of Men are in the Acknowledgment of God's Existence and his Unity: And great is the Absundity which arises from a Supposition of two or more such self-existent intelligent Agents.

I now proceed to shew that God was Creator and Father, Son and Redeemer, but in different Respects.

Moses, having discover'd by Revelation from God that the Almighty was a Being in the Form or Image of Man, according to these Words, *In the image of God made he Man,* he goes on in his inspired Strain, delivering his Message to *Pharoah,* and saying to him *I am* hath sent me. Here it is plain there is one Father, not two Fathers: And *Isaiah* tells us the Love which this Father bore to his People in these express Words, Ye are my Witnesses, saith the Lord, and my Servants whom I have chosen, that ye may know and believe me, and understand that I am he: Before me there was no God form'd, neither shall there be after me. I, even I, am the Lord; and beside me there is no Saviour, Chap. lxiv. Ver. 10,11. From these Words it is plain that, to effect their

Redemption, there was a Necessity for him to become a Son; for by becoming a Son he became their Redeemer: And when all the Prophecies which are contain'd in the Old Testament became fulfilled in him, when he was born of a Virgin, by that great Change he was a Son and a Redeemer; and tho' he was the very God, yet in the Condition that he was in, they would not have respect to him as a Creator and a Father, but, suitable to that State, they regarded him only as Son and Redeemer: For God as Father has respect to himself as in the State of a Creator; and God as a Son has respect to himself as a Redeemer; and God as Holy Ghost has respect to himself as a Sanctifyer: And if we do not keep these different respects in our Minds distinctly, we shall not only confound the Terms, but be liable to divide the Essence.

I think what I have already offer'd is a sufficient Proof of the Title of *Father* having Relation to *Christ Jesus* when he was in the State of *Creator,* and of the Title of *Son* having Relation to him as a *Redeemer,* and of the Title of *Holy Ghost* having Relation to him as a *Sanctifyer:* So here is a Trinity which creates no confused Ideas, but presents to us a clear Idea of one personal God, who is a *Father* and *Creator,* a *Son* and *Redeemer, Holy Ghost* and *Sanctifyer:* which are three glorious Titles centring in the Divine Person of our Lord *Jesus Christ* in his threefold Appearances or Manifestations of himself according to Scripture-Records; which fully prove that the Holy One of *Israel,* the God of *Abraham, Isaac,* and *Jacob,* is one identical Person, and not two or three, as most *Christians* ignorantly imagine. All, since the Time of *Moses* and the Prophets, who believed in their Declarations, did expect the great *Jehovah* to fulfil his own Prophecies in his own Person, in becoming a Creature or a Son by taking on him the Seed of the Woman, that he thereby might bruise the Serpent's Head, as he had promised in this saying, *I will put Enmity between the Seed of the Woman and the Seed of the Serpent;* and, that we may not be ignorant of what is meant by the Seed of the Woman, the Creator declar'd that he would not take on him the Nature of Angels, but the Seed of *Abraham:* So was he call'd a Man of Sorrows, a Son, a Saviour, the everlasting Father, the mighty God, *Immanuel,* which is, God with us: This is the Language of the Prophets, as of *Isaiah* and others.

Whoever hath the knowledge of the Mind of God, contain'd in the written Records, will undoubtedly perceive what is meant by that Saying in Scripture, *Great is the Mystery of God, manifesting himself in Flesh:* And it will ever remain a Mystery to the Natural Man, who cannot conceive how the Creator of all Forms should condescend to leave his glorious Throne, that he might become a Creature himself, and subject himself to his own Divine Power, with which he had invested *Moses* and *Elias,* to fulfill the Prophecies, and that Saying, *I will give my Angels Charge concerning thee;* which Charge was given by him while he was in the State of a Father, and had Relation to himself when he should come into the State of a Son: and when he said he thought *it no Robbery to make himself equal with God,* he said it because he had humbled himself to his own Power, or Decree, which he made when in the State of a Creator or Father. As this Knowledge of the Divine Being (which he has been pleased to manifest of himself, and which is the Knowledge of the Mode of his Existence) is wholly out of the Reach of the Natural Man, and belongs only to the Man of God, or the Seed of Faith, who are the spiritual Men capable to be made wise to Salvation, and they only, they consequently are capable above other Men to see the perfect Harmony of the Doctrine of the Holy One of *Israel* being *Father* by *Creator, Son* by *Redemption,* and *Holy Ghost* by *Santification:* Herein only are the Scriptures reconcileable, without confounding the Terms or dividing the Essence. This is the Manifestation of the Mode of Existence of One God under three Titles; which is suitable to his Appearance under his different Dispensations, according to that Scripture which saith *There are three that bear Record in Heaven, the Father, the Word, and the Spirit, and these three are One: And there are three that bear Record on Earth, the Water, Blood, and Spirit, and these three agree in one.* Moses' Commission was the Commission of Water, and he bore Record of God to *Abraham* that he was the Creator and Father: The Commission of the Apostles was the Commission of Blood, and they bore Witness of that *Word,* (which was the Creator and Father) when it became Flesh, being a Son and Redeemer: *John Reeves's* Commission was the Commission of the Spirit, and bore Record or Witness of the Lord *Jesus Christ* being that *Holy Ghost* or *Spirit:* So as *Father, Word,* and *Spirit,* are three Titles, there are three Commissions which bear Testimony thereof: The first, bore Testimony of God before he became Flesh that he was the *Father,* the second, bore Testimony after he became Flesh that he was the *Word* or *Son,* and the third, bore Testimony that, after he had risen and ascended into Heaven, he was the *Holy Ghost* or *Spirit,* of whom it is said, *I am ALPHA and OMEGA the first and the last; I am he that was dead, and am now alive for evermore.* This is the Trinity in Unity, that is, a Trinity of Names or Titles worthy the Divine Being, as being a *Creator* and *Father* in one respect, a *Son* and *Redeemer* in another respect, a *Holy Ghost* and *Sanctifyer* in a third respect; which neither confound the Terms nor divide the Essence; for which Reason there is nothing in the Doctrine to shake our Faith.

By this Time, I suppose, the Mode of God's threefold Existence appears from what I have said, agreeable to Revealed Religion, and not inconsistent with Reason: Since therefore I have removed the Stumbling-blocks which lay in the Way, I may venture to say that the three Propositions which I undertook to defend are obvious to an impartial Enquirer. When we say, *God* died, we do not say he died as a *Creator* or a *Father,* but as a *Son:* 2dly, When we say *God* became a *Creature,* we mean no more than that God in becoming a *Son* became like us, Sin excepted: 3dly, When we say there was no God in Heaven when *Jesus Christ* was on this Earth, we do not mean that the Power of God was not there, but that his Person was not: So the Inferences which are drawn against us that, by these Propositions, we deny the Father, that we make him finite, and thereby deny his being God, and that by making him die we destroy his very Existence, these Inferences, I say, all vanish; and what I have said opens a Way to the easy apprehending the Consistency of a Trinity in Unity; which is discover'd by the threefold Manifestation of the great God of Heaven, which neither confounds the Terms nor divides the Essence.

Now let me ask which Hypothesis seems most consistent with the Unity of God, that which neither confounds the Terms, nor divides the Essence, or that which makes a second *Person* in the Trinity co-equal and co-eternal with God? No one surely can think it more absurd that the eternal God should become a Son and redeem us, than that a second Person, who they say is God, should do it.

I think I have said all that is necessary for the Support of my Argument: And I am inclin'd to believe that what I have advanced will stand like a Rock not to be shaken, it being impossible to prove a Trinity in Unity on any other Hypothesis: No other Doctrine of a Trinity can be consistent with the Unity of God, or with the Scriptures; and no other can be advanced without confounding the Terms, and dividing the Essence.

The END.

The Amorous Humours and Audacious Adventures of One Wh*******D.

By A Muggletonian.

Jew, Turk, *and* Christian, *differ but in* CREED;
In Ways of wickedness they're all agreed:
None upwards clear the Road; they part, and cavil:
And all jog on, unerring to the Devil. Landsd.

LONDON: Printed for the AUTHOR, and sold by M. WATSON next the *King's Arms Tavern, Chancery-Lane:* at the Corner of *Cock-Court,* facing the *Old-Bailey, Ludgate-Hill,* and at the Pamphlet Shops of *London* and *Westminster.* [Price 6*d*.]

The Amorous Humours and Audacious Adventures of One Wh*****D.

Have You not seen, with dauntless Pride,
The QUACK ascend with haughty Stride!
His *Moor-field* Stage, to gull the Throng
Of Health and Wealth, with artful Tongue?
His Packets vend, by pois'nous Breath,
To give You Ease, -- or certain Death.

So *Wh******d*, in another Sense,
Is QUACK to Souls, for ready *Pence*:
Fills all the Rabble with Surprise,
But Meteor-like deludes their Eyes,
And leads the gazing Wretch astray,
Out of the sure and ready Way;
To a Religion false and foul,
Which drains the purse --- deceives the Soul.

Ye Follow'rs of this *Witling's* Noise,
Be cautious, when you hear his Voice;
Observe his Words, they'r loose as Sand;

And like his Doctrine ----- *contraband*
Whose fell Deceit is so apparent ----
To get your Gold, --- Know, Gold's his Errant.

Let Reason aid and guide your Senses -----
He's lov'd, 'tis true, -- by whom? – *by Wenches:*
Or, think they'd give fine Cloaths away,
Or, leave off drinking *Hyson* Tea;
Or, break their fine enamell'd China

(note- A young Lady, whom W------d persuaded to break her rich China, for that her keeping such gaudy Vessels, took off her Thoughts from *Him* and Ch-----st.)

For Love of one that's lov'd by many:
Or, wear Straw Hat, and Ruffet Gown,
If that his PARTS ----- were not well known?
His PARTS so large ----- inflam'd my Lady,
That ever since, she's had the *Hey-dey*
In her Blood, from Head *all over* -----
Down to the bubbling Spring of Lover!
Now feeling talks to female Friends,
And W------d's Doctrine recommends;
That he's the Man ----- Of *vastest Sense!* -----
And, *That he acts by th' Influence*
Of Moon and Stars: ----- *Interprets Latin* -----
That we shou'd wear no Silk or Sattin;
Give all our Riches to the Poor:
So follow him ----- *and sin no more.* -----
Thus, he depriv'd the Croud of Sense,
And Pick'd, as fast as Hops, Fool's Pence;
To build, at *Georgia*, Orphan-Houses,
And lie in *London* with Cits Spouses;
Because, forsooth, he's better *hung* ------
With florid Speeches, ----- *Velvet Tongue,*
Than all your common, simple *Laymen,*
Who, to his godly Cant, cry ----- *Amen*

See him erect, upon a Common,
Casting his Eyes of *Heav'n,* ----- and *Women!*

Filling the croud with panic Fear,
With first a *Smile*, and then a *Leer*!
Keep trifling with the Name of JESUS!
With Views to grow as rich as *Croesus*:
His Words are wild and incoherent,
Yet, he asserts, he's GOD'S Vicegerent!
But Reason tells me by the Bye,-------
No Priest has Privilege to lye:

Tho' he of Heav'n makes a Trade
And dresses Saints in Masquerade:
The glorious Place to scandalise,
Serves *Nonsense* up for *Sacrifice*!
Just so of old the cunning Priest
Th'Offal burnt and kept the rest.

In *Wh-------d* this is verify'd;
He loves *Tit-bits*, ------or, he's bely'd:
His *common* Sisters recommends
T' indiff'rent Christians ---or, his Friends:
For well he knows his Friend *Jack W-----*,
In *probing* Consciences is less sly:
And if my Memory tells me right,
At a LOVE-FEAST one pious Night!
A youthful Creature's lily Breast,
Did much invade th' Imposters Rest;
Which, as she sigh'd, did fall and rise, -----
So, caught my Neighbour *W-------d's* Eyes:

The urchin God in Ambush lay,
And smil'd as *W------d* seem'd to pray:
As on her Breast he sat astride.
He smok'd the Doctor's half-blind Side;
And tho' one Eye was much distorted,
The Doctor with the other courted:
Now *Lust* his GRACE divine assails,
And o'er the Spirit, *Flesh* prevails:
With fierce Desires his Passions flush,
And *Exposition* now grows hush!
By Love inspir'd, the letch'rous Priest

Longs for the TIT-BIT of the Feast.
He felt, --- Oh Heav'ns! sad Shame to tell, ---
A Flame as hot -----as hot as H---ll! ------

This is your Priest for Abstinence! ---
This is the Priest from Providence! ---
Who'll shew us Heaven's *Milky Way*,
And keep our Thoughts from going astray!
With Sawciness assumes to teach;
And shew us Heaven --- out of Reach:
Our Wives and Daughters too defiles,
Each Day our Reason he beguiles!
If through such Hands Religion comes,
I'll haunt no more the sacred Domes,
To hear thee, second-handed, tell
The Joys of Heav'n and Pains of Hell!
No; --- I'll follow *Muggleton*
And *Reeve*, --- as all my Life I've done;
Before I'd follow such a Priest ---
Whose Life has been a *Publick Jest!*

Offspring of *Lust!* Sly Debauchee!
Old Father *Girard* lives in Thee:
Thy Brother *W-----ly's* full as bad;
And 'twixt you both the Girls run mad.
An Instance we've before our Eyes,
Of one, a Stranger unto Vice;
A pure and spotless Virgin *Sister*,
'Till you and *W------ly, Finely kist her*,
Then took her under your *Tuition*;
So now she's in a fine Condition!

(note- A certain Girl, who was not only seduced from the true Religion, but vilely abus'd by the Imposter and his Friend, and being with Child, was prevail'd upon by 'em, to take Medicines and cause Abortion)

Your Love for her, poor Girl, was such,
You made her rightous *over-much*!
And 'cause her Soul shou'd not be lost,

Inspir'd her with the ------ ------
So when for *God of Lust* she burns,
 You both inflame her ------ by Turns:
Both Nature and your God abuse,
With vilest Arts that Man can use!

Vile Letchers, of the tip-top Sort!
Who warmly pray, but *hotter sport*:
Well vers'd in Arts of *Quietism*,
You shew your Heav'n through a Prism.
Salvation is the Bait you use,
Weak *Innocence* the *Prey* you'd noose:
Damnation is your only Driver,
And Satan is your sole Contriver.
With *Whine* and *Cant*, and such like Tools,
A Knave may trap ten thousand *Fools*.

Like Doctor *Rock*, thou'rt impudent;
But what is worse, --- more confident!
For, in the last Page of thy *Journal*,
When you've gone thro' your Vice diurnal,
You'd fain assume ALMIGHTY POWER!
Be *steeld with Shame*! --- For *Shame* giver o'er.

Be honest Priniples your Guide,
And lay the knavish Cloak aside;
Nor vily lead teh weak astray,
To make 'en quit the trodden Way,
And, erring, follow thy *new Modes*,
Through thick and thin, in dirty Roads.

Thou false, unlearned Hypocrite,
Whose *Journal's* like thy *Doctrine,* --- light:
Who tak'st JEHOVAH'S Name in vain;
And Sacrific'st his Son again!
Thy Voice tho' loud, thy Mind's so low,
It never can to Heaven go.
Your *Heav'n's* on *Earth,* --- well may you love it:
For 'tis our *Wives,* and *Wealth* you covet.
"When King and People seek Extremes,

"Conscience, Religion are their Themes:
"And when a Change the State invades,
"The Pulpit forces, or pursuades:
"If others give the Fuel Fire,
"The Breath of Priests the Flames inspire.

Thou *holy Cheat*, thou Son of Night;
Offspring of the dullest Light; ---
Desist, and hide thy brazen Face;
Nor prate of *New-Birth*, or of *Grace*:
Thy *Doctrine* preach to Brutes in Stable,
Where thou wer't bred, and where thou'st able,
For Horses have both Eyes and Ears;
Go preach to them --- they too've Fears:
And if great *Pythag's* not bely'd,
The Souls of Men in Brutes reside:
According to the Life they've led,
The Soul has momentary fled
Into a Bear, a Snake, or Fly,
There to remain till that does die;
Or any Thing that's animated,
Which the *first Cause* at first created:
Thine, for thy future Ease, shall pass
Into the sluggish *Sand Cart Ass*.

Thou foul abominable *Seducer,*
Thou diabolical *Accuser,*
Thou Fiend of pestilential *Evil,*
Thou hypocritical sly *Devil;*
Thou *Knave of Knaves*, thou *Holy Cheat*,
Elate with Pride, and fell Deceit:
Witness the Merchant's Wife at *Bristol*,
Who lent thee Pounds and many a *Pistol*,
And follow'd thee o'er Hill and Dale,
T'allay the *Itch* rais'd in her *Tail*:
This was her Way to be *New-born*,
And make her Husband wear the *Horn*?
Yet you must be reputed Just,
Because thou art brim-full of *Lust;*
Nor had this ever been found out,

The Amorous Humours

But that a *Butcher* was in doubt,
About the Payment of a *Bill,*
Who, in your *Cunning* had some Skill;
He paus'd and thought, then paus'd again,
From Time to Time he rack'd his *Brain,*
How such a One, who always was,
A Man who paid him present *Cash,*
Shou'd be so backward in his Payment,
Which made him lack both *Food* and *Raiment.*
One Day poor *Kill-calf* chanc'd to meet,
This worthy Merchant in the Street,
His *Hat* pull'd off, and shrugg'd his *Shoulder,*
Both Smil'd and Hemm'd to make him Bolder,
God bless you Sir, I'm mighty Poor,
You ne'er had such a *Bill* before:
A Bill! The Merchant quick replies;
Yes, Sir, the needy Butcher cries,
A *Bill*, which shou'd it not be paid,
Must shut up *Shop*, and knock off *Trade:*
Forever since these *Preaching Fellows,*
Who Merit nothing but the *Gallows,*
Have hither been, all *Trading*'s dead,
And all the People seeming *Mad;*
Your Wife I've seen in *briny Tears,*
But durst not speak on't for my Ears,
The squint-ey'd *Parson* too I've spy'd,
Thro' Parlour Window, *Kiss your Bride?*
The Neighbours say, he came from LONDON,
To save the Souls of *People undone*:
But he's a cunning crafty Elf,
At saving Souls, to serve Himself?
The Merchant hearing what he said,
Well, well, says he, --- *and shook his Head!*
Went Home, and looks upon his Half,
As Cow does on a bastard Calf;
But keeping Temper, cries *my Dear,*
Was Mr *W-------d* lately hear?
Yes, yes, my Dear, and he does say;
I ought to Fast as well as Pray:
That what I lend is to the Lord,

He said so of his own Accord!
Now don't you think that he's inspir'd,
And by the Holy Spirit fir'd,
Such noble Thoughts he does express,
He must be Saint, or little less.

The Husband, Passion still subduing,
Gave Honey-words, as he'd been Wooing:
Say he, My Dear, *Do what you can*
To serve so good and just a Man:
Did ever Mr W------d kiss ye?
Come, Speak the Truth, I'd fain confess ye:
Did you Money ever lend him?
Or ever any Presents send him?
Still keeping Temper within Bounds,
She, sighing, said, ---*Yes*---Fifty Pounds;
Which in Three Days will be restor'd:
'Twas lent to him,--- not to the Lord.

Cou'd not I see this great Divine?
Replies the Man, in Fear of's Coin,
Invite him, pray, with us to dine;
And get some 'Sparagus and Chicken;
Perhaps he loves such Sort of Picking:
But, for the Rest of all my Life,
I'll hate Religion --- *and my* Wife.

No sooner said, away she went,
Brim-full of Joy, and sweet Content;
Until she reach'd the *Doctor's* Sight,
And spoke to him thus, in seeming Fright,
Dear Sir, I tremble ev'ry Joint!
I hope in God I've got my Point:
Hy Husband Sir's been pleas'd to say,
He wants to dine with you To-Day;
He longs to see you: --- So do I ---
It may be, Sir, for --- Charity.
For God's Sake do not fail at One:
Your most obedient --- I must run.

The Amorous Humours

As *Priests* pursue their Interest,
Without Reserve, --- With *damn'd* or *blest;*
'Tis equal whose they get, the *Ready,*
From Rich or Great, or Poor or Needy:
So *W------d* follows Lust and Ease,
Deludes the Whole, himself to please.

The Clock had scarcely struck, before
The *Imposior* knocked at the Door,
Who was most courteously receiv'd,
(*Saint-like* he spoke, tho' scarce believ'd;)
He talk'd of *New-birth,* then said *Grace*
Look'd round, and formal took his Place:
He eat and drank and talk'd of *Love,*
And othe Things divine above,
'Till he had satisfy'd his Nature,
Then return'd Thanks to his *Creator.*
The Cloth at length is took away,
The *Doctor* pleads he cannot stay;
The Merchant said, he should, in Jest! ---
Order'd a Bottle of the best;
`Ask'd him Questions somewhat odd,
`About his Thoughts of *Christ* and *God;*
`Desiring mildly of his *Spouse,*
`To quit the Room, or leave the House?
`For he'd a Scruple in his Breast,
`Which Scruple solv'd he should have rest.´
As *good Wives* always will obey,
She dropt a Court'sey, went away.

The busy *'Doctor* ask'd the doubt,
But, in a Manner round about;---
`Why, --- *Doctor* --- since you are so free,
`With my weak Wife as well as me; ---
`The Question that I ask profound, ---
`Did not you borrow fifty Pound?
`Of my poor easy, simple Wife,
`To save her Soul, and tease her Life'?
Yes, cries the *Doctor,* full of Fear;
The *Money* --- that --- I had of her, ---

Was for the *Service of the Lord*,
To her again 'twill be restor'd.
'But when? --- Good *Doctor*, I must know ---
'Before from hence I let you go:
'Refund the *Cash*! --- Or, I'm a *Sinner*,
'I'll make you now refund your *Dinner*.'
In Charity it is bestow'd,
To Poverty, I have avow'd;
You'll have it trebly to you paid,
At th'Wicket of th' *Elysian* Shade?
'Thou Son of *Dagan* talk no more, ---
'I'll stick you up agains the Door;
'This Moment give to me your Note,
'Or else, by *G---d*, I'll cut your Throat;
'And draw it justly, on Demand,
'Then sign it with thy pious Hand;
'That I may have it paid To-morrow,
'Or else, this Sword shall end your Sorrow.'
He durst not trifle any longer,
With one he found to be the Stronger;
But draws the *Note*, which *Note* was paid,
Or, he at *Bristol* had been flea'd.

This is the Priest, without Design,
Who'll kiss your Wife, and lie with mine,
Who makes *Ch--- J---* Pimp to Vice,
On *God* the Father, father Lies:
This is a hopeful *Dog* indeed!
To pins one's *Faith* upon his *Creed*;
Who calls on *God* to lend his *Aid*,
And makes chief *Handle* for his *Trade*:
Who frightens simple, honest Men,
With being damn'd --- and born again;
And that the beaten Path now trod,
Is not the Way to meet with *God*!
And that the *Holy Ghost* attends him;
And *Christ* from's Enemies defends him:
Makes use of all this *Prophanation*,
Only to trick and cheat the *Nation*.
Is there no *Law* extant to catch,

This vile, designing, studpid Wretch;
Who makes the *Subject* sell his *Land*,
And boldly says, 'tis *God's* Command?
Can nothing shew his Doctine flagrant;
Yet have an Act against the *Vagrant?*
Who makes poor *Coblers* quit their Stalls,
And leave behind their *Ends and Awls*;
And on the *Parish* leave their Wives,
To follow --- where the *Devil* drives:
Who has no Licence yet to preach;
Nor Sense, save Impudence, to teach:
Who gathers all the *Shirtless Train*,
To hear him pray, and then blasphame?
The mongrel Work of Heaven he gets,
T'applaud his Acts and counterfeits:
In's *false Religion* Error shines,
And *true Religion* undermines?
For let him start Absurdities,
Tho' they're the grosest, basest Lies;
Some serious *Fools* will him approve,
By often hearing, blindly love:
His time's consum'd in *gibble gabble*,
To the unthinking head-strong *Rabble*.
Such medling *Priests* who vex the World,
Shou'd all be in Coufusion hurl'd;
For those that sow such Discontent,
Should live in *Hell*, and there repent.
But let him go where-e're he will,
He helps the Scripture to fulfil;
For he's false Prophet, base Diviner,
A canting, footy, fawning Whiner;
An inconsistent, mongrel Preacher,
A fly, inveigling, secret Letcher!
Who has debauch'd more Maids and Widows,
Than there are *Piss-a-beds* in Meadows;
And strolls about from Place to Place
To find who has the prettiest Face.

Should I but give a Catalogue
Of Tricks perform'd by this same Rogue,

His sly Intrigues, his hidden Vice,
My Readers would believe 'em Lies:
But I'll not any thing assert
That's founded merely on Report,
These Facts I state, I know 'em true,
So take 'em in a curs'ry View:

This Villain, whose deceitful Tongue
Has drawn to's Lust a greater Throng
Of Women than the letch'rous *Turk*,
Can yet --- for Gain --- do Porter's Work.
Near the *Wheat-sheaf*, nigh the *Ditch-side*,
He did seduce a Porter's Bride;
Who now for W-----d's mighty zealous,
Speaks of his *Parts* --- at ev'ry Ale-house;
That's Doctrine's found, nay, strong and nervous
Would pierce a thing almost imper'ous:
That she'd five Guineas to him given,
To put her in the Road to Heaven: ---
But 'twas her Husband she'd befriend,
And, from pure Love, would thither send.

Two maiden Sisters, near th' *Old Jury*
He did debauch --- both now in *Drury*
A widow Lady --- now half mad,
He kiss'd her out of what she had.

A Goldsmith's Wife, who liv'd in *Cheap*
A fort'night in the Country kept

Fourteen i'th Parish of *St. Bride*,
In their Turns, have all comply'd.

I have not heard of one at Court
That to his Love-Feasts did resort;
The Reason's plain --- there every Lady
Has other Drudges always ready.

But ner the *'Change*, there's many one,
Who all the Night have been from home

At *W-----d's* luscious *Feast of Love*,
Whose ev'ry Action they approve,
Stand by him, with their Spouses Fortunes,
And give him *ALL* within the Curtains.

Near *Lombard-street*, there is but two
That ever had with him to do.

In *Holborn* five or six there liv'd
Who follow'd --- only to be f----d;

Snow-hill and *Newgate-street* there's seven
He shew'd, by turns, the way to Heav'n.

In *Fleet Street* and near *Temple-bar*,
He'd three on Night to his own Share;
And each confess'd --- she'd been done over ---
Most vigorously --- by their black Lover.

In *Fetter-lane* and *Dewgate-hill*
Nineteen submitted to his Will
Some now convuls'd with the *New Birth*,
Which, in good time, will be *brought forth*;
Some sisters big with hold Child,
And Numbers made half mad and wild:
And I am sure, in six Months more
You'll find about a single score
Of Sisters, who now tightly lace,
Produce a holy Babe of Grace.
This is as true, as now I live,
So help me *Muggleton* and *Reeve*.

FINIS.

www.ingramcontent.com/pod-product-compliance
Lightning Source LLC
Chambersburg PA
CBHW061424300426
44114CB00014B/1532